Power, Place, and State-Society Relations in Korea

Power, Place, and State-Society Relations in Korea

Neo-Confucian and Geomantic Reconstruction of Developmental State and Democratization

Jongwoo Han

LEXINGTON BOOKS
Lanham • Boulder • New York • Toronto • Plymouth, UK

Published by Lexington Books
A wholly owned subsidiary of Rowman & Littlefield
4501 Forbes Boulevard, Suite 200, Lanham, Maryland 20706
www.rowman.com

10 Thornbury Road, Plymouth PL6 7PP, United Kingdom

British Library Cataloguing in Publication Information Available

Library of Congress Cataloging-in-Publication Data Available

ISBN 978-0-7391-7554-5 (cloth : alk. paper) -- ISBN 978-0-7391-7555-2 (electronic)

∞™ The paper used in this publication meets the minimum requirements of American National Standard for Information Sciences—Permanence of Paper for Printed Library Materials, ANSI/NISO Z39.48-1992.

Printed in the United States of America

Contents

List of Tables, Diagrams, Maps, and Figures

TABLES

MAPS

FIGURES

IMAGES

Acknowledgements

A big question that has long lingered in my mind is what made state power integral and infrastructural in Korean political history. Subsequent questions that emerged from this puzzle have focused on the issue of how to reach an answer without relying on either of the two main theories of late development: modernization theory and dependency theory. This angle of inquiry also grew naturally out of my own reflections on the failure of so many different theories that originated from foreign settings and were tested among Korean scholars. This compelled me to look into the simultaneous phenomena of the Miracle of Han River, the fall of the military dictatorship, and the birth of the most vibrant and democratic civil society in Asia. A sense of pride in my own history also inspired me to work on this book project, examining the changes and continuities in power dynamics and state-society relations over the course of Korea's history.

It has proven valuable to adopt a fresh approach that embraces two of the most dominant ideologies in Korean political culture—Confucianism and geomancy—as sources of evidence for the main argument of this book. Many Korean scholars on these two fundamental beliefs have been extremely helpful to my study, and rather than mentioning them each individually, I want to thank them as a whole.

The first version of the book manuscript that failed to be published about a decade ago only examined the role of the developmental state in Korea's unprecedentedly rapid economic development; however, as my study on this topic has deepened, I have gained confidence that both the economic and political aspects of the Korean experience could be understood through coherently integrated scheme.

Throughout this process, I have owed a great deal to the personal and academic mentorship of Professor Chung-in Moon, whose numerous works on this topic are quoted throughout this volume. More importantly, Professor Moon's sharp critiques and insightful suggestions to improve and complement my reasoning and methods played a critical role in the completion of this book, my most important academic output to date. I can't thank him enough. One more person I want to recognize here is my editor, Eric Berlin, who became my friend in the final stages of finishing up this book. We ran together at my favorite location near Syracuse, Green Lakes State Park, while discussing the main topics of this book so that he could then strengthen the presentation of my ideas and help to articulate their subtler implications.

I would like to recognize various institutions and presses for their generous permissions to use many valuable maps, images, and photos as well as texts: Seoul Museum of History (especially their maps and images for the cover of this book), Hyangto Seoul, Keonchook, Jisik-sanup Publishing, Institute of Seoul Studies, Seoul Development Institute, Kyujanggak Institute of Korean Studies, Woongjin, COSMODREAM, and Stanford University Press (excepts used in Appendix 1 from The City in Late Imperial China by G. William Shinner, ed.). I also want to thank Soon-Ki Lee for her help in Making the appendics (2-7).

When I was struggling with everyday life as a graduate student in Syracuse University, my uncles Simon Sung-do Cho and Sungdon Cho consistently encouraged me to persist. Over the six years of my Ph.D. studies, their support was utterly indispensable.

My dear companion and wife, Kyunghee Lee, has blessed me with two daughters, Hyemin and Jeongyoon, who have always been with me, and I have cherished all of the time we've spent together in Syracuse from their births to their teenage days. My mother, Sung-ja Cho, may be blind to some of my weaknesses and perhaps some of my strengths as well, but I am certain that I never would have become that which I am now without the gift of her love. Finally, I would like to dedicate this book to my father, Yong-kyu Han, who unfortunately was hurried off to the dwelling place that Jesus had prepared for him. I had hoped for us to spend more time together after my study in Syracuse University, but we never got that chance. With this book, it is my hope that I have done something good, small though it be, for my father.

Jongwoo Han
May 2013

Chapter One

Introduction

THE KOREAN PHENOMENON: SIMULTANEOUS ECONOMIC DEVELOPMENT AND DEMOCRATIZATION

From the end of the Korean War in 1953 through the mid-1990s, the Republic of Korea received various kinds of aid (e.g., military and economic) in such abundance that the nation's economic development can hardly be discussed without mentioning how funds flooded in from the United States, the United Nations, and other international organizations. While it is true that many newly independent countries and former colonies have received economic aid in a diversity of forms ever since the United States emerged as a hegemon of the free democratic and capitalist pole in the Cold War, the case of Korea remains unique—the ROK is the only country to date that has been able to rise out of its ashes and transform from an aid-recipient country into one that offers development assistance to other countries in the Organization for Economic Cooperation and Development (OECD).

As noted by *The Korea Times* (2010, August 4) and other US news and media coverage of this dramatic transformation, Korea has featured prominently in the rhetoric of President Barack Obama's major speeches on economic development and has been frequently cited as a prime example of success alongside other major allies. Clearly, the Obama administration has a deep interest and trust in Korea as a role model for economic success and education. Both the tone and sheer abundance of these references reflect this regard: 36 of Obama's 342 public speeches since taking office in January 2009 have made explicit reference to Korea as of summer 2012, while mentioning other allies, such as Japan and France, only 17 times.

What remains absent from such references to Korea's economic success, though, is that its democratization transpired at the same time, culminating in the 1987 People's Resistance Movement against the twenty six-year-old military dictatorship and represented today by an extensive series of civic, electoral, and political instances of activism utilizing networked information technologies (NITs), such as the Internet, mobile phone technology, and various online social media. In the last decade, examples of such vibrant activism abound: the success of the Web-based negative election campaign—the Defeat Movement—against corrupt politicians in the 2000 General Election, the digital election campaign in the 2002 Presidential Elections, the Internet-led impeachment movement against President Lee Myung-bak's decision to reinstate the import of American beef in 2008, and the decisive role played by Twitter in the April 27 and October 26 re-elections in 2011 (Han, 2007, 2009, 2012). What stands out about the case of Korea is that its development contradicted the formula widely accepted in the West of economic development preceding that of democracy; Korea achieved the status of a democracy, with one of the most dynamic and resilient civil societies, from 1960 to 1987—the same period as the development of its economy.

Korea's unprecedentedly swift economic development (i.e., in less than a half-century) and successful transition to substantive democracy have been considered as an alternative model for the development of Third World countries. After making a solid recovery from the 1997 financial crisis that hit hard in the East and Southeast regions of Asia, Korea's new strain of state-led capitalism has been considered to be more potent than the free market system and has been emulated by developing countries as a sustainable model for catching up in economic development and democratization. This book explores the factors that permitted the unique phenomenon of Korea's simultaneous achievement of flourishing democratization and unprecedentedly rapid and sustainable economic growth.

Although these two topics have been discussed to a limited extent in the existing literature, they have never been analyzed as concurrent phenomena. To fill that gap in the research and explain these interrelated occurrences by means of an integral paradigm, one would need to trace the historical origins of state-society relations and the way in which those relations were shaped by interactions with global forces. With regards to Korea's economic development, modernization theory has long been the dominant paradigm for explaining how traditional and economically poor countries become modernized, while dependency theory has been widely adopted by objectors to the modernization school worldwide and by forces opposing the military dictatorship in Korea (Lim, 1982; Choi, 1989). Although both theories addressed some aspects of Korea's development, such as the growing GDP and the disparity between the haves and have-nots, modernization theory failed to account for democratization during the economic development period, while dependency theories failed to explain the success and increasing independence of the Korean economy. With regards to political changes, most analyses on the rise and maintenance of authoritarian regimes focus on two main perspectives: one justifies the need for an authoritarian regime in economically catching-up states by highlighting the advances in industrialization that were thereby made possible (e.g., Huntington's *Authoritarian Politics in Modern Society*), while the other explains the emergence of an authoritarian political system from a Latin American perspective (e.g., Collier's *The New Authoritarianism in Latin America*, Linz's *Totalitarian and Authoritarian Regimes*, and O'Donnell's *Bureaucratic Authoritarianism*). Rather than focusing on the concurrent nature of Korea's processes of economic success and democratization, which were assumed to be incapable of occurring at the same time, these studies focused on economic success and political backwardness.

Interestingly, most literature on the developmental state of East Asia in general, and Korea in particular, tends to overlook a long list of important points: the historical origins of state centrality and hegemony in the East Asian developmental state, the nature of non-Western and non-liberal state-society relations, local-global interaction and its impact on state hegemony and heteronomical forces in society, consequential changes in state hegemony over time, the emergence of democracy, and the need for a holistic perspective to explain Korea's simultaneous economic and political development. In so doing, late development theorists have inadvertently legitimated despotic and authoritarian rule, military dictatorship, and its attendant "economically efficient" bureaucracy in developing economies. Thus, existing studies provide only a partial understanding of the source of state hegemony in East Asia's "developmental state" and of the militant opposition forces that arose during the concurrent economic development and democratization.

For example, modernization theory generally posits that a linear relationship of causation exists between economic growth and democracy; however, this main argument has been critically refuted by the post-modernization school (Lipset, 1994; Chilcote, 1981; Appelbaum & Henderson, 1992; Berger & Hsiao, 1988; Berger, 1988; Castells, 1992; Choi, 1989; Corbridge, 1986; Cumings, 1987; Deyo, 1987; Dietz, 1992; Evans, 1987; Grabowski, 1994; Gulati, 1992; Haggard & Moon, 1983; Han & Ling, 1998; Harris, 1992; Han, 1995; Im, 1987; Kohli, 1994; Kim, 1988; Koo, 1991; Leeson & Minogue, 1988; Luedde-Neurath, 1988; Moon, 1988; Perkins, 1994; Wade, 1988; Westphal, 1978; White & Wade, 1988); solid evidence of a clear relationship between these two variables, in either direction, has yet to be provided.

Due to the lack of comprehensive and indigenous theoretical approaches to studying the state-society relations of Korea, most literature on Korea's developmental state falls short of accounting for "why" it emerged where it did and not elsewhere: most literature merely ends up reifying authoritarian or despotic regimes and their power to intervene in the economy.

Scholars generally agree that essential elements in the success of a developmental state include the state's role of implementing industrial and redistributive policies, its developmental structure (i.e., a stable, centralized government with cohesive bureaucracy and effective coercive institutions), and the commitment and technical capacity of state leadership (Kohli, 1994; Luedde-Neurath, 1988; Koo, 1991; Haggard & Moon, 1983). This book argues that, in addition to these features, the most fundamental aspect of a successful developmental state is the legitimacy of its efforts and authority to intervene in society and the economy; however, since most literature focuses on the contemporary period, military dictatorship has been singled out as both a positive factor for rapid economic development and a negative element for both democratization and the expansion of civil society in Korea. Contrary to this view, however, this book finds that the original seeds of such state centrality in Korea mostly took root during the Confucian era of the Joseon Dynasty (1392-1910). The Confucian doctrine that political considerations should always take precedence over economic principles and that state should rule over civil society—and not vice versa—was strongly infused into Korea's traditional relations between state (government) and economy as well as the mind-set of the masses during this period. In fact, it continues to pervade Korean political culture today.

The problem with existing literature on the developmental state and democratization in Korea is that no attempts have been made to explain the origins of this elevation of the political over the economic or how the democratization process could have evolved from the limited but co-opted heteronomical forces that were deeply embedded in the Confucian mind-set. Neither Confucian doctrine nor indigenous schools of thought, such as geomancy (*pungsu jiri sasang* in Korean or *feng shui* in Chinese),[1] have been examined as original and legitimate sources of Korea's state-society relations to which the Korean phenomenon of simultaneous economic and political development can be attributed. Geomancy has been largely overlooked as a source of theoretical explanations because it has often been treated as a superstitious belief system of the Orient. In addition, no serious attempts have been made to seek the factors that led to the formation of a limited but militant form of dissenting voice in Korea, i.e., the heteronomical[2] forces. Such an attempt would need to explore how Korean civil society developed from its own Confucian hierarchical political system, expanded in the era of the Japanese colonial period (1910-1945), and established a strong civil society from the 1960s to '90s. In our delineation of state-society relations, it is essential to understand how the ideologies of Confucianism, which permeated Korean society since the era of the Three Kingdoms (57 BC-AD 668), Neo-Confucianism (since the 14th century), and geomantic political culture have served as a bedrock of moral, cultural, economic, and political values grounding and legitimizing both state power and heteronomical forces of dissent.

To appreciate the original sources of Confucian heteronomical force in traditional Korea, one must look to two major Joseon institutions:[3] the *Seongkyunkwan* (National Confucian Academy) and the *Sarim* (Neo-Confucian literati and their private schools) in the provinces. The Seongkyunkwan, which was the highest educational institution, served as the keeper of the Confucian shrine and a center of recruitment for high-level government officials. The students of the Seongkyunkwan, where the tablet of Confucius was enshrined, were given exclusive rights to administer the ritual ceremonies that upheld Confucius as the ultimate source of power and Confucianism as the highest governing ideology.

Since Confucianism was of foreign origin (i.e., from China), the National Confucian Academy can be considered as an extraterritoriality within the power structure in regards to the royal authority and meritorious subjects; compared to other government organizations, the Academy was largely independent of government and military intervention and thus maintained autonomous governing rights on internal affairs as a heteronomical force within the Confucian hegemonic state. As students of the highest educational institution, they were granted the right to make official appeals against the King and government whenever they felt that the actions of their officials were not sufficiently in accordance with or violated Confucian ideals. Reid (1923: 188) says "Dealing with political questions and the science of good government, Confucianism naturally alludes to revolution and teaches us when it is right, and still more how it may be avoided." Confucian students' right to raise their voice of dissent, at moments when they thought that either the king or government policy did not adhere sufficiently to the Confucian notions of virtue or righteousness, was a self-correcting function intended to avoid major political rebellions within the power structure. Despite the paucity of these students and their inherent nature as members of an educational institution (as opposed to an official political power group), the foreign-oriented extraterritoriality represented the heteronomy (dissenting voices) of a checks-and-balances institution holding in check the hegemony and hierarchy of the royal family and Confucian bureaucracy, especially Dynastic Foundation Merit Subjects.[4]

The other significant heteronomical force in 16th-century Joseon society was the Sarim, comprised of local Neo-Confucian literati who had formed various schools of Confucian thought and who emphasized reform as a means of overcoming the negative outcomes of excessive government centralization policies. The Sarim originally emerged as a social dissident force in the 15th century and quickly became an alternative source of power in the highly centralized Confucian state of the Joseon Dynasty. The fact that the National Confucian Academy recruited students from the offspring of local Sarim members meant that the Academy was strongly influenced by the political views of the Sarim leaders, starting in the mid-Joseon Dynasty. Even though strong factions formed among the Sarim due to a divergence in their scholarly and worldly views about the application of Confucian principles and their pursuits of political interests, the presence of a powerful Confucian literati shows traces of the existence of civil society in Korea's traditional socio-political system. As this book will demonstrate, these two sources of heteronomical forces—the Seongkyunkwan and the Sarim—eventually contributed to the expansion of resistance against Japanese colonial oppression, with help from the Joseon governing classes (i.e., hegemonic and hierarchical power elites), and served as the basis for the establishment of democratic forces during economic modernization in 20th-century South Korea.

While many studies have been conducted on the impact of Confucianism upon contemporary political culture in Korea and other Asian countries, this book contends that the views of such studies lean toward journalistic or psychological determinism—reductionist tendencies that prevent readers from fully appreciating the comprehensive nature of Confucianism and geomancy as well as the deep influence of these ideologies on state-society relations in Korea. In this regard, the typical assumption that so-called Asian values are hostile to democracy and political rights deserves critical scrutiny.

Accordingly, it is important to decode the principles of Confucianism and geomancy as reflected in Korea's political culture in general and state-society relations in particular—specifically in the choice of the location of the capital city, the design of the city's layout, and the monumentality of political, economic, educational, and cultural institutions as fundamental sources and traces of state-society relations in premodern Korea. The adoption of Neo-Confucianism as articulated by Chu Hsi (1130-1200) as the official governing ideology of the state during the Joseon Dynasty resulted in the establishment of a highly centralized state hegemony and hierarchy (bureaucracy) and the precedence of politics over economy and society. Also, the ideology of geomancy (*pungsu jiri sasang*)[5]—that is, the art of adjusting the features of the cultural landscape to the cosmic breath (*gi*) by creating topological configurations similar to the layout of an ideal astronomical chart so as to maximize good fortune and minimize bad fortune—played an integral role in the creation of strong state legitimacy in Korea's political history. Geomantic principles that were applied in the choice and design of the capital city clearly served as a central element in establishing the hegemonic state (Lee, 1984: 165), co-opting the heteronomical forces through a central Confucian power system that enabled such forces of dissent to function as a built-in loyal opposition of extraterritoriality. This book's analysis of heteronomical elements as reflected in the design of the capital city and its layout as well as their political features and functions will shed light on the seeds and growth of strong civil society, thereby elucidating the means by which militant civic organizations emerged and became influential in contemporary Korean politics.

The trajectory of state-society relations that had spanned nearly a half-millennium of Joseon rule took a sharp turn when Japan annexed and then colonized Korea in 1910. How exactly did Japanese colonial rule (Kyeongseong period, 1910-1945) affect Korean state-society relations from the archetype of its Confucian origins? First, Japanese imperial militarism reversed the Confucian practice of elevating civil society over the military as well as that of looking down upon and limiting all activities that were commercial or industrial in nature. The biggest transformation from Confucian state-society relations, however, arose in response to Japanese rule with the massive expansion of heteronomical social forces—originating from the built-in loyal opposition that had been established during the Confucian era—in a series of militant demonstrations led by students and intellectuals against colonial Japan. It was this upsurge of dissenting social forces in the Korean political arena that would change the configuration of domestic political power in the modern era (i.e., Seoul era) and eventually achieve democratization in the 1980s. The expanded heteronomical forces continued to resist the military dictatorship in the Seoul era and ultimately drove President Park Chung-hee to seek ways to legitimize the authoritarian nature of his regime in the eyes of the people by emphasizing his economic development plan and providing financial prosperity for the middle class. The Park regime inherited many of the legacies of the Hanyang and Kyeongseong eras, including (1) state centrality, (2) political intervention in the economy, (3) centralized bureaucratic control, and (4) the heteronomical opposition forces. While the developmental state played a strategic role in taming domestic and international market forces and harnessing them to serve the national economic interest (Wade, 1988, 1990a, 1990b), a belligerent civil society ultimately overthrew military rule at the end of a successful developmental period in 1987.

While scholars interested in understanding Korea's unprecedented growth during the 1960s and '70s generally agree that the most important factor was strong state leadership, current analyses tend to focus disproportionately on authoritarianism, thereby overemphasizing the contribution of Park's military dictatorship during that period. Such interpretations tend to imply that Korean economic success is tainted, somehow undemocratic, and thus inferior. In researching the sources of Korea's economic growth, investigators tend to limit their inquiry to the state itself, overlooking more likely explanations of the state's successful promotion of economic development. The Korean state's legitimacy to intervene in the economy stems not solely from its exercise of arbitrary military power but also from the operation of rule-governed processes, constructed over three distinct eras of Korean history, in relations between state and economy.

As briefly mentioned above, the ROK exemplifies the mutually reinforcing successes of rapid economic development and democratization. Economically, the ROK has risen from the smoldering ashes of post-Korean Conflict (1950-1953) to become a member of the world's most advanced economies. Politically, the ROK transformed itself from a Confucianism-oriented authoritarian regime of military dictatorship into a "Third Wave" democracy with a resilient democratic civil society. Furthermore, the developmental models of Korea's rapid economic growth and democratization have been tested in terms of their sustainability. The Korean economy began its late development in the early 1960s, became the world's 12th largest economy by the time of Asian financial crisis in the late 1990s, and now advances its pre-IMF crisis status, having recovered from financial bankruptcy with emergency bailout funding from the International Monetary Fund (IMF). Currently, the Korean economy is reported to be the most resilient and fast-recovering economy among OECD countries in the midst of global economic crisis.

The beginning of democracy in Korea was officially marked by the student-led "June Resistance" of June 10, 1987—the largest anti-government demonstration in South Korean history—toppling the military dictatorship that had lasted since Park's coup in 1961. In the several weeks preceding the June democracy declaration by Rho in 1987, four to five million Koreans became involved in the democratic movement against the military regime (Pak, 1998: 60; Armstrong, 2002: 1). Since then, Korean democracy has witnessed a return of civil superiority over military forces and the peaceful turnover of power among major stakeholders; in fact, peaceful transfer of power has been institutionalized, from traditional right-wing conservative to the left-wing liberal labor parties (Hahm, 2004).

In order to more fully comprehend the role of such a developmental state and the emergence of democratic opposition forces, we must examine state-society relations in a non-Western and non-liberal context, reconstructing the ROK's historical origins and the changes it has undergone as a result of local-global interactions. Han and Ling (1998)[6] in their study of Korea's "Authoritarianism in the Hypermasculinized State" attempted to explain how the old Confucian political culture of Korea's developmental state contributed to the developmental state in Korea's economic development period and how Western scholarship tends to orientalize the phenomenon of the rapid economic development and the role of the developmental states in Asia by explaining state-society relations in the context of a gendered relationship between masculinity (state) and femininity (society) articulated and embedded in Korea's long history under Confucianism. Han and Ling (1998: 57) expound upon the prevalent dichotomous scheme of juxtaposing Western and Oriental culture:

> Liberals decree that democratization means, in essence, a conversion to Western masculinist capitalism; that is, the West should lead the rest. Critical theorists may denounce Western masculinist capitalism as yet another kind of hegemony, but they still assign to it a structural/ideological supremacy that is denied to non-Western traditions like Confucianism; that is, the West acts alone. It absorbs, if not obliterates, pre-capitalist forms of production, consumption, and hegemony. Indeed, Gills (1993: 200) outrightly dismisses the two-millennia-old Chinese world order as irrelevant, non-existent or, at best, "misplaced" when compared with the contemporary world hegemony of Western masculinist capitalism. . . . Normatively, they see capitalism as revolutionary, individualist, rational, and universal. Epistemologically, it is active, articulate, standard-bearing, and super-real. Confucianism, by contrast, is seen as just the opposite. Normatively, it is conservative, collectivist, affective, and ethnocentric. Epistemologically, it is passive, mute, flexible, or nonexistent. At most, Confucianism may be granted a certain cleverness in coping with the West, but it remains reactionary in comparison to the West's exciting, generative powers.

For this reason, this book begins with the classical period of the capital city, Hanyang (1392-1910), as the period when state hegemony and the legitimacy of the state's authority to intervene in the economy were established and the seeds of heteronomical forces were sowed. Next, Japan's occupation of the city, which they renamed Kyeongseong (1910-1945), will be examined as a period reflecting both major changes and continuities in the relations between the state and the economy. Together, the Hanyang and Kyeongseong eras formed a foundation that facilitated the emergence of the developmental state in Korea, bequeathing their traditions of strong state intervention in the economy and an upsurge of heteronomical forces. Seoul (1945-present), as a symbolic center and physical place, still embodies these legacies today.

Through an analysis of extant literature on Korea's economic development and democratization, chapters 1 and 2 will debate the theoretical dimensions of how Korea's simultaneous achievement of these goals can be understood from the perspective of state-society relations theory. In chapter 2, the current understanding of East Asia's "developmental state" will be critically examined with a focus on three main approaches—neoclassical, institutional, and late developmentalist. Methodologically, this chapter also explains how the capital city in Korea can be read as text and how Onuf's constructivist theory on the three rules of hegemony, hierarchy, and heteronomy can be used to articulate state-society relations as reflected in Hanyang.

THE COLD WAR AND AMERICAN AID

After nearly a half-millennium of rule under the Joseon Dynasty and thirty five years of Japanese colonial control, the liberated country of Korea in 1945 was one of the poorest in the world. To make matters worse, the three-year war between North and South Korea, backed by China and the United States, respectively, destroyed roughly 42-43 percent of the production facilities in South Korea that had been inherited from Japanese colonial industrialization (SaKong & Koh, 2010: 125). Aid from the United Nations and United States played a critical role in the reconstruction of the Korean economy, which had been devastated by the Korean War. "During 1945-1950, a total of $585M in aid was provided by the United States (Government and Relief in Occupied Areas and the Economic Cooperation Administration) and the United Nations (Civil Relief in Korea and the UN Korean Reconstruction Agency)" (SaKong & Koh, 2010: 126). President Park Chung-hee, the architect of Korea's economic miracle, also described the desperate situation of ROK as follows: "From September 1945 to 1959, the US government provided the Republic of Korea with direct military aid of $1.3 billion" (Park [2], 1969: 44). Overall, US agricultural surpluses under the US Public Law 480, known as the "Food for Peace Act," passed in 1954 under the Eisenhower administration, accounted for roughly 30 percent of all US aid to the ROK (Park [2], 1969: 45).[7] From such dire economic straits, the ROK has gone on to accomplish a rapid and sustained economic development unprecedented in 20th-century history with per capita income skyrocketing from $1,342 in 1960 to $19,227 in 2008. Despite national bankruptcy in 1997, the South Korean economy ranked 12th in terms of GDP, based on purchasing power parity (PPP).

In the face of the communist threat that was perceived to exist in Southeast Asia, Europe, and the Middle East, US aid aimed to reinforce countries in these regions against communist expansionism. From 1944 to 1946, US aid was mostly economically oriented to provide relief and rehabilitation, and from 1946 to 1951 it focused on longer-term reconstruction; however, with the outbreak of the Korean War, the basic features of American aid to these countries suddenly shifted as military purposes became a more dominant aspect of the American program.

> While the percentage of US aid allotted to military assistance was 24% in FY-51 and 38% in FY-52, the FY-53 allocation, the first under the Military Security Act of 1952, channeled over two-thirds of all foreign aid to military assistance. The intensification of the Cold War triggered by the outbreak of hostilities on the Korean peninsula thus made it almost impossible for Korea to become the beneficiary of a program along the lines of the Marshall Plan." (Callow, 1995: 17)

Despite the unparalleled scale of the aid, fiscal assistance from the United States was mostly utilized for military fortification of Korea to prepare against another military disaster.

In 1961, when Army General Park Chung-hee seized power through a military coup, he emphasized the need for a long-term economic plan to maximize the allocation of national resources and, starting in 1962, implemented a series of the Five-Year Economic Development Plans (Park [1], 1969: 281) with the intention of establishing a domestic economic development platform that would take full advantage of large-scale aid from America as well as the US market and technology transfer in the context of Cold War international politics. In his view, solutions to South Korea's economic woes could not even be imagined without American aid; thus, the quickest solution absolutely depended on American cooperation (Park [2], 1969: 42-43).

In implementing a kind of planned economic development, however, President Park was well aware of the dangerous possibility that a planned economy might stifle competition in the market. Accordingly, his catchphrase was to encourage "full-scale competition and necessary planning at a minimum" (Park [1], 1969: 284). This planned economic development was also partially motivated by political reasoning: President Park and his aides were well aware that economic success would play a crucial role in legitimizing his military coup (Park, 1969).

Does Foreign Aid Buy Growth and Promote Democracy?

On August 8, 1953, the *Chosun Ilbo* featured an editorial on the Eisenhower administration's decision to provide $200M in post-Korean War reconstruction funds. While the editorial suggested how this aid should be spent, a small news article on the same page recounted the arrival of President Eisenhower's special envoy, Dr. Henry Tasca, who had hinted that the $200M was just the start of American aid to help Korea recover from the devastation of the Korean War. The headline announced a series of meetings between President Rhee and Secretary of State Dulles, which aimed to lay out the two most important elements in US-Korea relations: the ROK-US Mutual Defense Agreement and the US economic aid program for the reconstruction of Korea.[8]

The Korean War had done far more damage to the peninsula than World War II had done to the Europeans and Americans. Recognizing the magnitude of the problem, Eisenhower sought to mount a broad response. Having promised aid to Syngman Rhee during negotiations over the armistice, Eisenhower acted swiftly to fulfill this promise. On July 27, 1953, two days after the armistice was signed, he asked Congress to spend $200M on reconstruction in Korea, with funds coming from defense reductions attributable to the cessation of hostilities (i.e., a "peace dividend"). On July 31, Eisenhower went further in a memo to the Secretaries of State and Defense (i.e., Dulles and Wilson, respectively), saying that the Eighth Army under General Maxwell Taylor now had a golden opportunity to rebuild South Korea. He saw it as:

> . . . something almost unique in history. It is the opportunity of an army in a foreign land to contribute directly and effectively to the repairing of the damages of war; to rebuild and revive a nation, to give to itself the satisfaction of constructive and challenging work, dedicated to the preservation and enhancement rather than to the destruction of human values. (Callow, 1995: 16)

At the time, the most popular method of US aid was military arms and personnel; during the 1980s, for example, the top recipients of US aid in Africa were Somalia, Zaire, Egypt, Liberia, and Sudan. In fact, "the United States was the world's largest monetary provider of foreign aid to the Third World" (Blackadar & Kreckel, 2005: 8). As America's first major aid programs, these were politically oriented to serve the national strategic interests of the United States and were developed as "a tool for containing the spread of communism; in order to win leaders to its side" (Blackadar & Kreckel, 2005: 8).

As briefly mentioned above, between 1946 and 1960, the United States provided Korea with economic and military aid in excess of $4.2B, with all but $45M of this in the form of grants. Significantly, Korea's economy did not take off until after this period. Indeed, the record suggests that the effectiveness of the aid provided was compromised both by US policies and by those of Syngman Rhee, Korea's leader from 1945 until his overthrow at the hands of South Korean students in 1960. Nonetheless, it would be a serious mistake to conclude from the Korean example that the United States is unable to help build a prosperous, democratic nation. Despite mistakes and difficulties, US efforts in Korea created the preconditions that made Korea's economic miracle possible (SaKong & Koh, 2010; Callow, 1995: 2). In fact, the Korean case is one of the most successful cases of American aid programs since the end of World War II.[9]

That said, it would also be unreasonable to argue that US aid always brings economic growth and promotes democracy in aid-recipient countries. Burnside and Dollar's (2000) epoch-making article "Aid, Policies, and Growth" argued that aid has positive correlations with the economic growth of developing countries that have good fiscal, monetary, and trade policies but little effect on those that have poor policies. This report positively influenced the United States and other international aid organizations as a strong suggestion to increase aid to developing countries; however, there exists an opposing argument—i.e., that economic aid from advanced Western countries to a group of newly independent countries (NICs) after World War II does not seem effective toward the goal of forming a long-term and self-sufficient economy and mature democracy. Regarding this situation, Easterly (2003: 30) explains, "Clearly, the empirical links from aid to economic growth are far more fragile than the drumbeat of media and development agency reference to the Burnside and Dollar (2000) paper suggested . . . the result that aid boosts growth in good policy environments is fragile to defining growth, aid and policy over a sufficiently short period."

Generally speaking, foreign economic aid can positively affect democratization in recipient countries in several ways: by improving the technological infrastructure of electoral processes, by assisting the functions of legislature and judiciaries against administrative power, by promoting civil society, by supporting education, and by bolstering per capita income. Some argue that economic aid, instead, undermines the accountability processes essential for sound democratic institutions or creates corruption and bribery. To assess which of these views is best supported by the data, the World Bank analyst Stephen Knack (2004) conducted a multivariate analysis of the impact of aid on democratization in a large sample of recipient nations over the period from 1975 to 2000 and found no evidence of a causal connection. Thus, the causal relationship between foreign aid and the processes of economic growth and democratization in aid-recipient countries has not yet been generalized; however, the above-mentioned studies have at least resulted in an emphasis on variables other than foreign aid that might have more influence on the course of economic and political development among aid-recipient countries.

The Dialectical Nature of Korea's Economic Development and State-Society Relations

Under Japan, South Korea produced about 63 percent of the peninsula's agricultural output and only 24 percent of its heavy industrial goods. Most of the electrical generating plants were located in the north, as was the peninsula's only chemical fertilizer plant. The South's loss of power and fertilizer hurt both industrial and food production badly. The influx of nearly 1.5 million refugees from China, Manchuria, Japan, and North Korea from August 1945 to August 1946 not only exacerbated the food shortage but also gave rise to a housing shortage and severe labor surplus. Even before US authorities considered disengagement from Korea, they were forced to manage the threat of starvation and other economic problems. In May 1946, the United States began an Emergency Economic Program; by 1948, the United States had provided to Korea $25M in loans and another $409.3 M in relief funds. UN relief programs had also provided an additional $1M worth of food, medicine, and clothing (Callow, 1995: 8). American aid and UN relief programs were critical in the establishment of post-colonial basic industrial structure in Korea. However, the breakout of the Korean War in 1950 mostly destroyed it.

Since the Korean government's decision to seek a bailout from the IMF in 1997 to avert a financial fiasco, a record-breaking amount of dollars—$90B—has infused an ailing Korean economy. As the most successful case of state-guided capitalism, Korea is regarded as a new model of economic development for other developing countries—"a new strain of capitalism more potent than the free-market system." From this, a series of related questions arises. Why would such a nation suffer from an unprecedented financial crisis? Where can we find the cause of such economic failure? Even more seriously, is Korea's economic success sustainable or not? One answer can be found in the dialectical nature of the process of South Korea's economic success and the current financial crisis.

The Seeds of Financial Fiasco: Dialectical in Nature

According to Lee Kyung-shik, the Head of Bank of Korea, it was the collapse of several conglomerates (*chaebols*), such as Hanbo and Kia, and the unsoundness of several financial institutions that left the domestic stock and foreign exchange markets in shambles. In turn, the abrupt decline of stock prices precipitated the depreciation of the South Korean *won*. Fears of additional depreciation then caused foreign investors to dump their stocks, creating a vicious spiral. It is dialectical in that the chaebol, the institution that had played the most significant role in the miracle of Han River (Korea's successful economic development), became a major cause of the current economic failure. Behind the surprising capabilities of the chaebol, of course, was the unlimited support of the developmental state of Korea imposing high standards for performance. The regime took slush money, which in turn became one of the causes of the current financial disaster.

Developmental State

It is worth examining more closely the role of these two key institutions, the state and business, as well as the reciprocal relationship that formed between them in the process of Korea's experience of economic development. As Alice Amsden's "*Asia's Next Giant*" (1989) aptly points out, the government worked as an entrepreneur deciding what, when, and how much to produce. It targeted national strategic industries based on the comprehensive evaluation of efficient bureaucracy and secured financial resources for the major players, the chaebols, through the nationalization of banks. The Heavy and Chemical Industrial (HCI) policy during the period of 1973-1980 serves as a good example of this. Also, the government intentionally distorted relative prices to maximize economies of scale and nurtured conglomerates through huge investments in infrastructure. The state's power and legitimacy to intervene in the economy stemmed from rule-governed interrelations between state and society, which have been embedded in the political culture for over 600 years of Korean history. In exchange for the government's comprehensive service to big business, the chaebols furnished an enormous amount of political funds, and these collusive relations have repeated in a vicious cycle as well.

Financial Institutions

It goes without saying that, in such relations, the government ordered banks to make loans to uncreditworthy companies and industries. For years, the government had treated the banks as tools of state industrial policy. Consequently, bad loans accumulated and backfired. At Korea's nine largest institutions, bad loans comprised 94-376 percent of the banks' capital in 1997; technically speaking, most of these banks were already insolvent. Convinced by government's guarantee of an anytime rescue policy, bankers were pressured for groundless bad lending customs and failed to examine the financial risks they were undertaking. The two most representative cases can be found in the merger of Korea First Bank and Seoul Bank. At the end of September 1997, the accumulated bad loans came to 4.5 trillion *won* (about $4.3B) or 16.7 percent of total credit at Korea First (3.4 trillion *won*) or 15.1 percent of total credit at Seoul Bank.

There is another problem in the bad lending judgment of banks—namely, the snowballing accumulation of nonperforming loans. According to a report of the Seoul branch of US-based Morgan Stanley, nonperforming loans at Korean banks and merchant banks were estimated at a total of 48 trillion *won* ($45B), or 12 percent of Korea's nominal GDP as of October 31, 2012. Thirty of the nation's merchant banks had a total of 3.8 trillion *won* (about $3.6B) in nonperforming loans at the end of October 1997 on an outstanding basis, more than triple the total of 1.2 trillion *won* that was recorded at the end of 1996.

Chaebols

Extensive diversification and central coordination are the two main characteristics of the Korean version of big conglomerates, the chaebols. Strong government support of chaebols made high aggregate concentration possible as well as the realization of economies of scope. The chaebols' unrelenting desire to expand their business lines, which is idiomatically described in Korean as an octopus extending its arms, facilitated intra-group transfer of both money and personnel, despite the astronomical amount of bank loans with various favorable conditions. These conglomerates were able to establish such intersubsidiary relations due to their characteristic structure of family ownership and high degree of coordination. The IMF and the Korean government share the view that chaebols' intersubsidiary payment guarantee and internal trading served as the two major pillars that supported the conglomerate system and, at the same time, became the main factors leading to the recent financial turmoil. Other officials also indicated that this management structure brought about the chaebols' excessive and highly leveraged diversification, thus making conglomerates much more vulnerable to the poor performance of individual units, especially in the economic slowdown. The failure of such interdynamics of big business can be best illustrated by the collapse of South Korea's twelfth-largest conglomerate, Halla Group, in what was seen as the first of a series of major bankruptcies expected under the strict economic supervision of the IMF.

Halla Group, best known for its shipbuilding and auto parts manufacturing, declared bankruptcy after defaulting on $220M in maturing debts. It was the first chaebol to collapse under the strict conditions that the IMF attached to its record-breaking $60B bailout package to help South Korea's floundering economy. Halla could obtain no more funds because banks refused to provide new loans and began calling in the loans they had already provided. The conglomerate owed $6.4B, or 20 times the total value of its equity.[10]

The Inevitable Path of the Korean Economy: Dialectical in Nature

In summary, the financial difficulties in 1997 in Korea was a dialectical result of the outgrowth of the very social and political features that have long been regarded as Korea's greatest strengths. The reciprocal relationship between the state and big business, which functioned well in the early stages of Korea's development, has turned out to be untenable in Korea's mature economy.

Some may attribute the shortage of foreign exchange to the extravagant consumer spending patterns involved in celebrating Korea's recent economic boom—"champagne opened too early," so to speak. According to the customs administration, the total imports for luxury items reached $4.92B during the period from January 1995 to October 1997, accounting for approximately 5 percent of the current IMF bailout and approximately 4.2 percent of Korea's gross foreign debt.[11]

Despite chronic problems in Korea's economy, there are several reasons to maintain an optimistic outlook for Korea's economic future. First, the causes of the financial crisis originate not in the activities of the Korean economy as a whole but in the cyclical nature of inefficient collusive relations between state and business. If this financial disturbance were the result of the sluggish performance of the economy in general, it would take much more serious long-term measures to recover from stagnation. If that were the case, the economy would likely be unable to recover the glory of its past and instead degrade itself to the status of a third-class nation.

The financial collapse in Korea, however, seems different from those of other countries that sought bailouts from the IMF. Economic growth in East Asia is still higher, and inflation far lower, than in Latin America as the banking crisis there built up. Korea's GDP grew 6.3 percent year-to-year in the third quarter of 1997. Major economic indicators show that the national economy achieved a modest growth in the third quarter, due mainly to a surge in exports and a slowdown in imports. Merchandise exports alone expanded by a whopping 31.3 percent, up from 25.9 percent in the second quarter and 14.8 percent in the first, according to Central Bank. Overseas shipments were led by HCI items, such as semiconductors, industrial chemicals, and primary metal products.

The national humiliation that was caused by squandering the foreign exchange reserve actually provides a rare opportunity to rectify the vicious cycle of collusive cooperation between state and big business. Without such a humiliating shock, it would have been unimaginable for Koreans to break from such a historically embedded practice of collusive reciprocity between the state and economy (i.e., chaebols and banks). The best guide for such economic reform can be found in Latin America's banking crisis of 1994-1995.

This optimistic prediction of the stabilization of the financial crisis is further supported by the resilience of heteronomical forces in Korea. Current literature on East Asian development tends to overemphasize either the role of the military state or the free market principle as the determining factor in the phenomenon of rapid economic development in East Asian newly industrialized countries (NICs). Despotic rule based on military power and economically efficient bureaucracy is not the only explanation for the ROK's rapid development in the 1960s and '70s—militant dissenting voices actually compelled the politically illegitimate and fragile Park regime to become a regime of fanatical economic development. In the midst of the nation's economic hardships, this resilient citizens' movement, which played the most important role in the democratization of the late 1980s, was again driving national leaders and political structure to reform. Citizens' campaigns to collect or deposit dollars have been gaining momentum in South Korea with the hopes of alleviating the nation's foreign exchange crisis, which has damaged the booming economy.

VARIABLES OF DEMOCRACY: SEYMOUR MARTIN LIPSET

Max Weber famously argued that modern democratization can only occur as a result of capitalist industrialization, meaning that economic development must precede democratization. Han and Ling (1998: 56) criticize the prevalence of the Western understanding of non-Western Asian political culture in political culture scholarship:

> Pye's (1985) analysis of Asian power and culture serves as a classic example. Contrary to Weber (1951), Pye concedes that elements of Confucianism may promote capitalist economic development. Furthermore, he acknowledges that different Confucian societies may vary in their interpretations and applications of Confucianism. Nevertheless, Pye echoes Weber in asserting an "Oriental despotism" for all Asian, especially Confucian, societies. "They share," he writes (1985: vii), "the common denominator of idealizing benevolent, paternalistic leadership and of legitimizing dependency." Throughout, Pye contrasts Confucian authoritarianism with the norms of Western liberal capitalism. Where the West prizes "autonomy" and "individual identity," Asians desire "personal security" in the form of a childlike dependency. Where the West defines power as "participation," Asians view power as the epitome of non-decision-making. Where the West seeks choice, Asians desire just the opposite. Accordingly, Pye concludes that Asians will always lag behind on the democratization track because, at heart, they yearn for order and security as proffered by the twin compact of authoritarianism and dependency.

This has become the outlook of modernization theory as prescribed by the United States for newly independent countries after World War II. Many variables have been suggested as prerequisites for democracy, the most representative of which include level of income, education, religion, and political culture. The American political sociologist Seymour Martin Lipset (1960), in his *Political Man: The Social Bases of Politics*, also emphasized the importance of economic development as a variable affecting the course of democratization. Since then, Lipset's view has been reduced by many scholars to that of an economic determinist in the study of the democratization process, especially in regards to late-development countries; however, Lipset made clear in his widely recognized 1993 address to the American Sociological Association that the economic variable "may be necessary but not sufficient" (Lipset, 1994: 3), adding that it was "merely associational, not necessarily causal" (1994: 16). Instead, he argued that cultural factors seem more important than economic ones (1994: 5). Contrary to Weber and Huntington, Lipset agrees with Tu's perspective that "democracy in Confucian societies is not only possible but also practical" (1993: 7).

No generalization is possible, Lipset concludes; moreover, generalization is not desirable since the democratization process is multivariate due to the nature of the causal nexus (1994: 17). Rather, Lipset agrees with Karl's observation that "Rather than engage in a futile search for new preconditions, it is important to clarify how the mode of regime transition (itself conditioned by the breakdown of authoritarian rule) sets the context within which strategic interactions can take place because these interactions, in turn, help to determine whether political democracy will emerge and survive" (Karl, 1990: 19). While Karl's argument is based upon his contemporary research of the economic situations and democratic status of Latin American countries, his point regarding the specific context within which political interactions occur and the mode by which regime transition is established serves as a guideline for the three main foci of this book: namely, tracing how the prototype of Korea's state-society relations were established during the Hanyang (Joseon) era; how the three rules of hegemony, hierarchy, and heteronomy were affected by interactions with Japanese colonial rule during the Kyeongseong era (1910-1945); and how such changes resulted in the developmental state and democratization in the Seoul era (1960s-'80s).

In Lipset's paradigm for the elements that affect the course of democratization, the variable of education receives great emphasis. Proposing four main indices for economic development—wealth (e.g., per capita income), industrialization, urbanization, and education—Lipset (1960: 31) finds that education plays a much more important role in democratization than income or employment (Lipset, 1960: 40). Rapid industrialization produces a basic political problem: working-class movements are a necessary outcome (Lipset, 1960: 54). In the Korean case of democratization, the rapid industrialization led by President Park Chung-hee's Five-Year Economic Development Plan was well received by the general populace; however, university students aggressively protested the Park regime's repressive policy toward working-class and dissenting voices. Not only did these students engage in street demonstrations, they also led the unionization of factory and industrial workers; many were arrested and incarcerated for covertly entering factories as laborers to incite unrest and lead unionization.

These university students, inheriting the tradition of the dissenting voice—which had been exclusively given first to students of the National Confucian Academy during the Joseon Dynasty and then to university students in the national resistance movement of the Kyeongseong era—became critical of government in the June 10 Resistance in 1987. Lipset's emphasis on education in the democratization process is highly relevant to the case of Korea, especially due to the tradition of student demonstrations being recognized by governing elites and the general populace as a barometer of the legitimacy of political regimes, dating back to the Joseon Dynasty.

Grand theories such as modernization theory and dependency theory, in their explanations and prescriptions for economic and political development, overlook the particular historical and cultural contexts of individual countries. They tend to assess the political development in a country according to a dichotomous judgment that the country either possesses or lacks a certain ideology, such as Protestantism; in doing so, such theories tend to miss the point that successful democratization can reflect the "varying strengths of minority political groups" in a country (Lipset, 1994: 5), such as the historical legitimacy of university students in the Korean context. Confucianism has been largely dismissed by grand theories as being merely a source of national characteristics, as in the controversial argument between Singapore's Prime Minister Lee Kwan-yu and US President Bill Clinton on Asian values and the American work ethic. Accordingly, Confucianism has received insufficient attention as a source of theoretical explanations for the rapid economic development and political democratization of modern Korea.

If a substantial goal of democracy is ultimately for power to reside in the hands of the masses, for example, then any path toward that goal must be recognized as a way of achieving democracy; that is, the Western path must not be the only valid way. Korea's unique phenomenon of industrialization and persistent opposition to the controlling regime mobilized the whole nation toward economic development in the early 1960s and achieved unprecedented economic development and democratization by the end of the 1980s as explained below; accordingly, the case of Korea requires approaches that are much more historically specific than any grand theory can provide, especially if these two phenomena are to be explained together. Rarely has an approach attempted to explain these two simultaneous achievements within one explanatory framework; yet, it seems likely that it was the aggressive opposition movements against the Park and Chun regimes from the 1960s to 1987 that actually motivated these regimes to implement effective industrialization policies as a way to strengthen their political legitimacy. At the same time, rapid industrialization certainly produced a multitude of socioeconomic problems, which provoked stark opposition from modern Korea's heteronomical forces. Modernization theory is incapable of clearly depicting such concurrent phenomena because it dictates which should come first based on the Western experience. To make matters worse, such a prescription that democratization must be preceded by economic development often ends up justifying the argument that democracy can and should be delayed until a more opportune moment.

The solution, according to Lipset, is to find the main actors in each case and articulate the particular contexts for specific outcomes because "it is inevitable that any given variable or policy will be associated with contradictory outcomes" (Lipset, 1994: 17). He specifies such contexts as dependent "on whether the initial electoral and other political institutions are appropriate to the ethnic and cleavage structure of the given country, on the current state of the economy, as well, of course, on the abilities and tactics of the major actors" (1994: 17).

In conclusion, Lipset (1994: 17) confirms that "we cannot generalize by a formula" regarding the relationship between economic development, or any other variable, and democratization. This book begins with the premise that the state monopoly capitalist dictatorship, its stark opposition from a new student-led civil society, and the simultaneous achievement of economical development and democratization can best be understood from the indigenous perspective. Based on this belief, this book attempts to explain the formation and changes of state-society relations over the course of the three main eras of Korean history, utilizing as evidence the spatial arrangements, architectural monumentality, and visible traces of the state's centrality and society's acceptance of such state authority and influence as articulated and reflected in the layout of the capital city. Focusing on Lipset's point that successful democratization can come from dynamic interactions among the "varying strengths of minority political groups" in a country, the next section will suggest how Korea's democratization can be understood in the context of Neo-Confucian political tradition, which has been embedded in Korean political history for more than a thousand years.

Heteronomy: Loyal Opposition or Semi-Loyal Dissenting Voice

What leads people to believe in the legitimacy of a democratic regime? According to Linz and Stepan (1978: 18), explaining this is "almost as difficult as explaining why people believe in particular religious dogma." Forms of political socialization, such as educational systems, mass media, and high culture, play a decisive role in the ability of long-established democratic regimes to enforce their legitimacy in the minds of the population (Linz & Stepan, 1978: 18). They (1978: 18) even refer to a mystic element, "a feeling [zeitgeist] shared across the national boundaries, that a particular type of political system is the most desirable or the most questionable." This book raises the same question: What made the state in Korea so central, and from what origins does such strong centrality of state originate in the case of Korea? At the same time, how did such a strong state-oriented political culture result in democratization? This book argues that two factors—namely, the Confucian notion of state-society relations and the deeply ingrained influence of geomancy—enabled the state to co-opt the consensus and gain legitimacy in the minds of Koreans during the Joseon Dynasty; yet, these two factors have long been neglected in the explanation of this phenomenon.

What makes the Korean case more interesting is that the heteronomical dissenting voice was built within such state hegemony; however, when Joseon hegemonic and heteronomical forces faced the common enemy of Japanese colonial control, they generated a form of resistance nationalism that laid the foundation for strong civil society. Later, during Korea's modernization period, these same forces challenged the Park regime. This book sees the heteronomical forces that were built into the hegemony of the Joseon Dynasty as a form of loyal opposition, a concept developed by Linz and Stepan in their discussion of modern democratic regimes. This loyal opposition transformed into disloyal opposition during the period of Japanese colonial control, the Kyeongseong era; however, since Linz and Stepan's notion of loyal, semi-loyal, and disloyal opposition was based on modern democratic regimes, a mechanical application of these notions to the explanations of state centrality and democratic forces in Korea may create an issue of relevancy; nonetheless, this conceptualization of opposition helps illustrate how voices of dissent actually contributed toward the consolidation of a central state in Korea as well as the subsequent expansion of civil society.

Through their conceptualization of categories of opposition, Linz and Stepan (1978) sought to articulate power dynamics among groups in the two-party system of established democracies and how these dynamics have contributed to democratic stability. The categories of loyal and disloyal opposition occur in the context of a two-party format that is subject to "maximal ideological distance and centrifugal competition" (Linz and Stepan: 24). When these two confront each other, however, semi-loyal parties take full advantage of the situation. The source of major political changes in the regime's focus is fomented by the action of one or more disloyal opposition forces that question the existence of the regime and aim to change the regime's power base. Linz and Stepan argue that between the disloyal and loyal opposition parties, a form of semi-loyal opposition that is usually based on a tacit middle class can play a decisive role in the transfer of legitimacy. Despite the fact that these two concepts describe the contemporary political system of established democratic regimes, the concepts of loyal and semi-loyal opposition are useful in capturing how the dissenting voices that had been built into the limited hegemony of the Hanyang era subsequently facilitated the consolidation of the centrality of state and later the expansion of civil society during the Kyeongseong era and the democratization of modern Seoul. The concept of loyal opposition will be applied in chapter 3 to the heteronomical institutions of Seongkyoonkwan and the Sarim, which became, this book argues, the origins of civil society in the Joseon era. These concepts also offer insightful ways to analyze the transformation from the hegemony of the Joseon era to that of the Japanese Kyeongseong period and finally modern Seoul with the success of the developmental state and substantial democratization in Korea.

PURPOSE, SCOPE, AND METHODOLOGY

Does it make sense to claim that Confucianism and geomancy must be incorporated into any study on the origins of Korea's developmental state and democratization in the 20th century? How does this book explain that the influence of geomancy was not limited to just the geographical and architectural principles involved in the choice of Hanyang as the capital city or the building codes utilized for major Confucian political institutions but rather played a significant role in the formation of the concept of power in Korean political history? What is the basis of this book's argument that Confucianism and geomancy must both be theoretically considered in the study of hegemonic state tradition in Korea? Foucault's notion of "ubiquitous power" seems to serve as a conceptual tool for understanding how these aboriginal ideological, philosophical, and cultural elements played critical roles in the formation of state-society relations in Korea and have sustained their influences throughout the modern phase of the developmental state and power reconfigurations in Korea's democratization process.

Foucault's Notion of Ubiquitous Power: Confucianism and Geomancy

According to Foucault, power has always stemmed from preexisting forms of power relations in society. Rejecting the claim that power is constructed by the wills of individuals or a collective, he states that "power is constructed and functions on the basis of particular powers, myriad issues, myriad effects of power. It is this complex domain that must be studied" (Gordon, 1972: 188). Finally, Foucault says, "The idea that the State must, at the source or point of confluence of power, be invoked to account for all the apparatuses in which power is organized, does not seem to me very fruitful for history, or one might rather say that its fruitfulness has been exhausted" (Gordon, 1972: 188).

Foucault's insight into the power of state is quite relevant to the role of the developmental state in Korea's speedy industrialization. In studying the developmental discourse that occurred during Korea's rapid economic development, it would seem shortsighted to account for the role of the capitalist developmental state (CDS) by invoking Park Chung-hee's charismatic dictatorship or the physical force of the military regime as the source or point of confluence of power. Such specific relations of domination between men and women, parents and children, rulers and ruled, and old and young are immanent in any society, and Korea is no exception. In fact, the Confucian legacy in Korean society exemplifies "the concrete, changing soil" (Gordon, 1972: 187) in which the CDS in Korea was grounded, the conditions which make it possible for the CDS to mobilize the whole society into an intense developmental mode.

Confucius viewed human relationships as being intrinsically hierarchical in terms of how each individual should behave. Han and Ling (1998: 62-63) explain how state and society were interpreted hierarchically in classical Confucian literature:

> The Analects instruct the state to "act as if you were watching over an infant" (Grazia, 1973: 205). The Ritual Records (12 BC) note that "the happy and gracious sovereign is the father and mother of the people" (Book 26: 1); even Laozi (6 BC), the Taoist advocate of "doing nothing" (wu wei), advocates that the state regard the people as "a child" (Thomas, 1968: 42, 163). In the Book of Documents (12 BC), the role of parent and state is imbued with universal, almost divine, authority: "Heaven and earth are parents of all creatures. Sincerity and wisdom become the sovereign; for he is the parent of the people" (Thomas, 1968: 163, 283). Similarly, Mencius (c. 372-289 BC) teaches that "no benevolent man ever abandons his parents, and no dutiful man ever puts his prince last" (Book I of Mengzi quoted in Grazia, 1973: 131).

In Chinese classical literature, parents and the ruling elites have a status linked to that of Heaven, while the members of the public are regarded as children. In this set of relations, the patriarchal power relationship within the family automatically extends to the public domain.

To describe the various types of relations that exist, Confucius set forth generalized models that he called the "Five Codes of Conduct." These codes advocated certain behaviors as most appropriate in relations between benevolent king and loyal subject, loving parent and filial child, exemplary teacher and respectful student, protective senior and loyal junior, and virtuous husband and obedient wife. Confucius saw these codes as a way to address the disastrous and chaotic state of war that existed during the periods of the Warring States

(475-221 BC) and to restore the peace, order, and prosperity of the first three kingdoms—the golden age that had prospered before the Chou Dynasty. In addition, Confucian governance upholds the *Samganghaengsildo* ("Principles of Behavior for the Three Bonds") of superior-subordinate relations: ruler to subject, father to son, and husband to wife. Also, the *Naehun*, codified by Queen *Han Soheonwanghu* in 1475, has served as a moral and practical manual for women ever since the Joseon Dynasty and continuing into contemporary Korean society as well. These Confucian codes of human relationships can be taken as a form of social knowledge or a belief system in which power relations, including gendered ones, among the members of community are represented.

In this perspective, the gendered power relationships between men and women and husband and wife during the Joseon Dynasty extended to state-society relations, where the state was seen as masculine and society as feminine. This historically specific Confucian belief system of gendered domination made Korea's developmental state play the role known as developmental. Here, it is important to note that such a gendered power relationship is the "concrete changing soil in which the sovereign's power is grounded, the conditions which make it possible for [sovereign power] to function," as Foucault (Gordon, 1972: 188) points out. These power relations that exist on the micro level of society extend to the macro level of state-society relations as well. Without grounding the governing system in such a concrete ideological and historical context, one can only achieve a limited understanding of the role of Korea's developmental state because the conditions that enabled it to function are not fully considered. In presenting authoritarianism as a one-way imposition by state onto society, one sheds little light on the historical, cultural, and/or institutional contexts of authoritarianism in Korea. Consequently, little can be learned of how state authoritarianism is perpetuated or why it remains embedded in Korean society.

Foucault emphasizes the concept of power not as a set of institutions and political apparatuses but as a multiplicity of relations of force immanent in the basic social structure in the form of power and knowledge. As Foucault observes (Gordon, 1972: 187-188):

> Between every point of a social body, between a man and a woman, between the members of a family, between a master and his pupils, between everyone who knows and everyone who does not, there exist relations of power which are not purely and simply a projection of the sovereign's great power over the individual; they are rather the concrete, changing soil in which the sovereign's power is grounded, the conditions which make it possible for it to function. . . . For the State to function in the way that it does, there must be, between male and female or adult and child, quite specific relations of domination which have their own configuration and relative autonomy.

To Foucault (Gordon, 1972: 189), every relation of force implies relations of power, and every power relation makes "a reference, as its effect but also as its condition of possibility, to a political field of which it forms a part." Foucault added, "To say that 'everything is political' is to affirm this ubiquity of relations of force and their immanence in a political field; but this is to give oneself the task, which as yet has scarcely even been out-lined, of disentangling this indefinite knot" (Gordon, 1972: 189). As an example of disentangling those endless loops in power relations, Foucault (Gordon, 1972: 188-189) stated:

> I have in mind studies like that of Jacques Donzelot on the family (he shows how the absolutely specific forms of power exerted within the family have, as a result of the development and expansion of the school system, been penetrated by more general mechanisms of State power, but also how State and familial forms of power have each retained their specificity and have only been able to interlock so long as the specific ways in which they each operate have been respected).

In Foucault's insightful observation on how power relations are formed and constantly re-produced among myriad social, political, and cultural institutions ranging from the sovereign state to lower-level institutions such as family and school, this book finds rationale for incorporating Confucian political doctrine and geomancy into its study of Korea's integral state and its relations with society. Even though Foucault did not specifically mention this point, the Confucian codes of conduct (i.e., between king and subject, parent and child, teacher and student, husband and wife, and senior and junior) fit perfectly into his notion of the complex domain of the myriad issues and effects of power. Also, the geomantic impacts on politics and the everyday lives of the masses in ancient Korea match with Foucault's notion of ubiquitous power immanent in every level of social and political realms.

The complex domain of myriad issues and effects that shaped power relations in Korean history can be found in Buddhism, Confucianism, geomancy, astrobiology, and varieties of superstitious belief systems—all of which penetrated into the minds of the masses. Buddhism and Confucianism served as both state religion and governing ideology, each in its turn. Of great relevance to this book is Foucault's argument that every set of power relations in a society functions as conditions that make the state function in the way that it does. An important point of this observation is that the masses and ruling elites share the same forms of ideology or religion as a symbol of state power.

In conclusion, Confucian parental governance exemplifies Foucault's "concept of power as a multiplicity of relations of force immanent in basic social structure in Power/Knowledge" (Gordon, 1972: 188). Korea's developmental state has inherited this Confucian set of relations, including those between parent and child and between king and subject. Confucian parental governance serves as a perfect example of what Foucault brilliantly understood: that there must be specific relations of domination between male and female or adult and child (Gordon, 1972: 188). Foucault's theoretical observation becomes clear in the notion of Confucian parental governance regarding "how State and familial forms of power have each retained their specificity and have only been able to interlock so long as the specific ways in which they each operate have been respected" (Gordon, 1972: 189). Understood from this perspective, it is quite logical to revisit the Confucian prototype of state-society relations established in the Hanyang era as a step toward understanding the origin and characteristics of the CDS.

The Will of Heaven and Dynastic Change in Confucianism and Geomancy

There is another important reason why this book reflects on the role of Confucianism in Korea's democratization process. Some extend this Confucianization of modernization to democratization. Advocates of an "Asian-style" democracy cite the Mandate of Heaven as an arbiter of good governance, claiming that the people have a right to rebel if the state violates their trust, as clearly expressed in Mencius' notion of *Yeokseong hyeokmyeong*. Advocates also refer to classical texts like the *Minben Zhengchi*, which teaches officials to respect the will of the people "as heaven itself." Indeed, as Kim (1994: 191) suggests, Confucianism offers the potential for developing democracy "even beyond the level of the West."

A theoretical basis for dynastic regime change or political revolution—called *Yeokseong hyeokmyeong* (i.e., revolution of changing the current regime's surname)—was provided by Confucianism when the founder of Yi Seong-gye withdrew from Wihwa Island in 1388 and overthrew King Kongyang in 1392. As Haboush (1988: 11) observes, it was believed that the virtue of General Yi led Heaven to confer the mandate upon his house as expressed in the founder's coronation edict of 1392. Han (2010: 30) explains Yi Seong-gye's overthrow of the Goryeo Dynasty as follows: "Boasting that it had gained the support of the public and heavens, the new government justified this change of dynasty under the notion first advanced by Mencius of revolutionary dynastic change as decreed by the Heavens." Here, the important point is that Joseon society's widely accepted belief in Mencius' notion of *Yeokseong hyeokmyeong* enabled General Yi to convince the masses that his revolt was mandated by Heaven. The Confucian idea of justifying the regime change was based on Mencius' claims about the will of the public being ratified by that of Heaven. Confucianism functioned as the "changing soil" (Gordon, 1972: 187) in which power elites, including General Yi, the Neo-Confucian literati, and the public were all grounded; such were the conditions that made the overthrow of the Goryeo Dynasty seem justified and righteous. Han (2010, 30) points out the uniqueness of the Joseon Dynasty's founding, "in that it was achieved with only a minimal use of military power, and the new rulers were able to cement the legitimacy of their rule by courting public support through such means as the reform of the existing system while also obtaining the approval of the Privy Council." To borrow Foucault's terms, the Confucian political belief system's widespread and successful penetration into the public worked as "the basis of particular powers, myriad issues, myriad effects of [previous forms of] power" (Gordon, 1972: 188). One of the main goals of this book is to unearth and disentangle the complex power domains on which Korean state-society relations were founded and explain how these relations operated from the perspective of its indigenous ideologies and history.

To a large extent, these two ideologies are politically oriented: Confucianism supports a highly centralized and meritorious bureaucracy, while geomancy predicts the rise and fall of political regimes (see chapters 2 and 3). Also, we will examine how Confucian gendered power relations between male and female first extended into the relations between state and society and then were utilized by the hypermasculinized developmental state to mobilize the society (economy) for rapid industrialization. Second, while these two ideologies contribute toward the newly emerging political power, they also justify regime change for granted. As briefly mentioned above, both Confucius and Mencius recognized the rights of the public to change the regime in power when that regime did not govern according to the Will of Heaven. Reid (1923) aptly observes the viewpoints of Confucius and Mencius on this:

> Confucius himself appears to have regarded with favor rebellious movements in the hope of bringing a sage to the throne. Mencius is certainly very outspoken in this respect. He justifies the dethroning and even the murder of a bad ruler. No wonder, then, that rebellions have occurred on a large scale, over fifty times in about 2,000 years, and local rebellions are almost yearly events. . . . Confucianism is to blame for it. (188)

How then did people in ancient Korea ascertain the Will of Heaven? This is where geomantic and astrological belief systems connect with Confucianism. Both the rulers and the ruled looked up to heaven for signs regarding what actions to take. The teachings of Confucius clearly described what to seek: "He who exercises government by means of virtue is like the Pole star, which keeps its place, while all the other stars revolve around it" (Reid, 1923: 189).

As the focal point, the Pole star represented to the people the unchanging nature of all things virtuous and righteous. Reid (1923: 189) indicates that the term for "revolution," *koming*, was first used in the *Book of Changes*, where Confucius said "*Tang* and *Wu* in their revolutions were following Heaven and ratifying the wishes of the people."[12] It was Heaven that instructed the people on occasions for revolution and functioned as an ultimate source of ratification for such actions. Mencius regarded revolution as inevitable and as a right that is merely the carrying out of a natural law (Reid, 1923: 199).

Mencius advanced his radically democratic political theory by drawing the Will of Heaven from the voice of the people. He added the democratic idea that sovereign rule stems from the people, identifying the Will of Heaven with the people's voice: "To follow Heaven is to be preserved; to act contrary to Heaven is to perish" (Reid, 1923: 200). Confucianism regarded each person as born with a social and political status and thus supported the maintenance of such hierarchical relationships among members of the political community as an essential way to recover the social order that had completely collapsed due to constant wars. Accordingly, Confucianism stood for the status quo; however, Mencius' justification and support of revolutionary dynastic changes, at the same time, gives Confucianism room to adapt to the changing political dynamics so that it may overcome its own rigidity as a governing ideology and justify political transformation. The existence, development, and expansion of heteronomical forces within and outside the Confucian governing structure during the three eras of Korean history in general, as well as the democratization process in modern Korea in particular, could be understood through Confucianism's unique flexibility of recognizing the masses' right to revolt against unrighteous rulers.

Contrary to the Confucian doctrine on political revolution as an exceptional case, geomancy predicts that a political regime will fall when the virtue of its capital city has been depleted. In this sense, geomancy was like a tool utilized to measure the duration of a political regime and weigh the work of kings just as, in the Book of Daniel (chapter 5:1-28), God numbered and weighed the kingdom of Belshazzar and brought it to an end. After Belshazzar's astrologers failed to decipher the mysterious words "*Mene, mene, tekel, parsin*" on the palace wall, Daniel was asked to interpret these words and explained them as meaning that God had "numbered" the kingdom of Belshazzar and brought it to an end, that the king had been weighed and found wanting, and that his kingdom was divided and given to the Medes and Persians. Widely believed by both elites and the masses, geomancy taught that people's individual lives and the destiny of the kingdom were predetermined by their choice of a place for housing, business, and political institutions. In this perspective, geomancy is deterministic of the duration of a dynasty. Due to such flexibility to embrace the possibility of a regime change, which affords the public the right to revolt against a regime, these two major traditional political ideologies may have provided reasons for wider acceptance by the ruled and successful penetration into the society. The next section will examine the influence of geomantic and astrobiological principles in the construction of ancient cities and upon political power of state.

Cities in Asian and Western Societies

The most essential feature of cities in Western civilization has always been their economic function: manufacturing, trade, liberal professions, and transport (Paulsson, 1959: 15). Thus, the center in Western cities has typically been designated for the leading tradesmen or commercial areas, while commoners inhabit the periphery. As Paulsson explains, "In the competition for the good location, it is the total assets and the economic resources that are decisive" (1959: 18). Thus, location is the primary factor in the creation of space for trade and services (Paulsson, 1959: 16).

Such emphasis on economic functions is represented clearly in the ten criteria of the Western urbanism proposed by V. Gordon Childe: 1) concentration of relatively large numbers of people in a restricted area; 2) craft specialization; 3) the redistributive mode of economic integration; 4) monumental public architecture symbolizing the "concentration of the social surplus"; 5) developed social stratification; 6) the use of writing; 7) the emergence of exact and predictive sciences; 8) naturalistic art; 9) foreign trade, which, by definition, had to be conducted over reasonably long distances; and 10) group membership based on residence rather than kinship (Wheatley, 1971: 373). Of these ten criteria, six are economic or related functions.

Some classical authors and thinkers have indicated that non-economic factors such as political or legal institutions are necessary elements of cities as well. Max Weber, for example, claimed that economic function alone does not make an agglomeration into a town in the Western sense of the word. To support this point, he mentions the case of a legal and political constitution that makes an autonomous community (Paulsson, 1959: 29). Going back to classical thinkers, in Plato's *Republic*, Socrates listed the persons most indispensable to a city. These included a weaver, farmer, shoemaker, and builder—all makers of goods. Interestingly, though, he also added several professions that serve as complements—a smith, cattle-tender, wholesale merchant, and retail tradesman. Together, these constitute "the first town." Aristotle also mentioned that it is "not sufficient for a town to have only the classes that provide the necessities of life. The town is not established for the sake of economic life only but also 'for the sake of the good.' Therefore, one must have citizens who administer justice, judge what is just and manage other public matters" (Paulsson, 1959, 34). In a way that embodies this social order, Paulsson points out, the monumentality of political institutions and structures in the Roman Empire articulate a dominating senate and a submissive people. Despite such recognition of the importance of political and administrative institutions in Western cities, the most salient feature in the archetype of Western cities was economic functionality.

Ancient Asian cities, however, differ quite significantly in terms of their essential features. The ideal-type cities that Wheatley identified in India and China reveal the importance of abstract forms of images of the universe. Wheatley (1971: 450-451) observes:

> But in my reading of the evidence the *ideal-type*[13] cities of India and China are affinal expressions of shared conceptions of the ordering of space, of a common '*astrobiological*' mode of thought. Each was established only after an array of *geomantic considerations* had been satisfied. Each was constructed as an *axis mundi* incorporating a powerful impulse to centripetality. Each was laid out as a *terrestrial image of the cosmos*, in a schema which involved cardinal orientation and axiality and, as a corollary, strong architectural emphasis on the main gates. On the capitals in both traditions, at whatever level of the political and administrative hierarchy they occurred, developed the maintenance of the prosperity of their respective territories, and, as such, they became paradigms for all other cities.

Compared to Western city layouts that emphasize economic functions and professions, ancient Asian cities emphasize religious or mystical characteristics. In both cases, images of the celestial body were strongly reflected in the choice and designs of cities:

> Weber's concept of European urban origins failed to consider the role of the ceremonial center, the axis of the kingdom, where alone the ruler could seek counsel and intercession from the ancestors who had served the state in the past and who now watched over its future, where alone he could preside over the universal harmony that, under a virtuous monarch, manifested itself in the spontaneous co-operation of animate and inanimate nature, and where alone, at the pivot of the universe, he could ensure the continuance of the cosmic process. (Wheatley, 1971: 178-179)

Constructivism and Extracting State Centrality from Korea's Capital City

Based on the understanding that the centrality of state power stems from the political, moral, and religious hegemony of Confucianism in Korea, in order to better understand the complex phenomena of state autonomy and power, one must gain insight into the complex processes whereby rules and relationships have been constructed and reconstructed among social agents and government institutions. This agenda has been tackled by constructivism (van Fraasen, 1981; Goodman, 1984; Gergen, 1986; Onuf, 1989; Kratochiwil, 1989; Wendt, 1992).

Philosophically, constructivism dates back to Kant's formulation of the concept of that which is "constitutive," which refers to the logically necessary relations among givens. Later, other philosophers' concepts contributed to the formation of the constructivist paradigm: Wittgenstein's language game, Peter Winch's "rule-governed" nature of social phenomenon, Alfred Schutz's intersubjectivity, and Gidden's structuration theory linking agent and structure. Social constructivism aims to reconstruct the meaning of social phenomena by analyzing their generative rules in dominant and embedded cultures; and "reality," which is taken to be objective knowledge and truth, is understood as being "the result of perspective" and "of the social processes accepted as normal in a specific context" (Schwandt, 1994: 125).

Bruner (1986: 95) argues that "there is no unique 'real world' that preexists and is independent of human mental activity and human symbolic language." By the same logic, as Foucault indicates, no power can be constructed independent of prior power relations. Power relations are ubiquitous and, as such, exist in every part of society in the form of language, social norms, symbols, actions, and political institutions, to name a few. The major role of constructivists has basically been to elucidate "the process of meaning construction and clarify[ing] what and how meanings are embodied" in the language, social actions, and social institutions (Schwandt, 1994: 118). Gergen and Gergen (1991: 78) aptly explain that an account of the world "take[s] place within shared systems of intelligibility—usually a spoken or written language. These accounts are not viewed as the external expression of the speaker's internal processes, such as cognition or intention, but as an expression of relationships among persons."

Onuf's framework provides an empirical basis for tracing the types of rule that characterize relationships between state and society as well as changes in these rules over time. Onuf argues that there are two general properties pertaining to political society: "rules" and "rule." Rules govern human conduct and give it social meaning; however, rule results when asymmetric social relations—as defined and constrained by social rules—create an unequal distribution of advantages. As mentioned briefly, Onuf (1989: 206-218) categorizes rule into three distinctive yet integrally related types: hegemony, hierarchy, and heteronomy.

This conceptualization of rules and rule serves as a way to examine the centrality of state hegemony in Korea as represented by Hanyang, the capital city of the Joseon Dynasty (1392-1910). Representing the height of the dynasty's prosperity and Confucian ideology, Hanyang provides an excellent precapitalist, pre-Western point of departure for documenting how state hegemony has been constructed in its relationship with society.

It is the task of this book to gather up the several strands of the developmental state's characteristics: state hegemony over economy, the government's capability to manage, the legitimacy of state intervention in the economy, and the people's consent to such controls. To accomplish this, we must retrace the process by which the developmental state was launched; and to this end, this book will take a social constructivist approach. Onuf (1989, 1996: 3) espouses a constructivist understanding of "the world," which is composed of "agents, rules, and social arrangement, each continuously changing in relation to each other," and initiates a constructivist approach in the realm of social science. According to Onuf (1996: 2),

> Social relations make people social beings. People as social beings make a whole world, and not just a world of meaning, out of their social relations. The co-constitution of people and society is a continuous process. General, prescriptive statements, hereafter called rules, are always implicated in this process. Rules make people active participants, or agents, in society, and they form agents' relations into the stable arrangements, or institutions, that give society a recognizable pattern, or structure. Any change in a society's rules redefines agents, institutions and their relations to each other; any such change also changes the rules, including those rules agents use to effectuate or inhibit changes in society.

In this view, constructivists posit that rules characterize every society, international society included. Thus, social constructivism aims to reconstruct the meaning of social phenomena by analyzing their generative rules. More specifically, constructivism seeks to understand "the world" by providing "a systematic account of the ways in which rules make agents and institutions what they are in relation to each other, and of the corresponding ways in which these relations constitute the conditions of rule to be found in all societies" (Onuf, 1996: 3).

The developmental phenomenon in modern Korea, this book argues, came about as a result of the social construction of rules and relationships between state and society, formed by a historical narrative regarding the construction of social institutions such as state-society relations and, later, through interactions with global forces. As Schwandt (1994: 118) explains, "particular actors, in particular places, at particular times, fashion meaning out of events and phenomena through prolonged, complex processes of social interpretation involving history, language, and action." In this way, the developmental process that occurred in modern Korea involved dynamics among various actors. Koreans under the military regime in the mid-20th century were mobilized for rapid industrialization, but that was only made possible by the fact that it was occurring within the context of the Confucian prototype of state-society relations, state legitimacy to intervene in the economy, and the changes made during the Kyeongseong era.

The developmental phenomenon in modern Korea was a result of the social construction formed by the historical narrative of the Korean people, their construction of social institutions (state-society relations), and their interaction with global forces. An understanding of "the collective generation of meaning as shaped by conventions of language, and other social processes" (Schwandt, 1994: 127) provides a broader perspective for explaining the dynamics of class relations in the process of Korea's economic development.

Koo (1991), for example, explains how the middle class influenced the process of democratization and class formation in modern Korea (493). He conceptualizes the intellectuals as a special class that contributed to democratization even though they were part of the larger middle class, and emphasizes the role of the middle class in this process more than that of the minor militant intellectual forces. Partially acknowledging the role of the intellectuals in democratization, he characterizes their progressive orientation as a result of "distinctive culture—the culture of critical discourse of their alternative position" (Koo, 1991: 499). However, merely mentioning this "distinctive culture" fails to account for the details of its contents. Onuf's constructivist framework of three different rules and rule shows how historically embodied rules impacted the dynamics of class relations, especially among heteronomical forces in Korean society. In contrast to Koo's argument, this book highlights the role of militant heteronomical opposition forces in the economic development and the workings of the developmental state.

According to Akiwowo (1988: 158), "indigenisation is an empirical, culture-bound but emancipatory approach to the subject matter. Indigenisation also is the view that the study, analysis and explanation of the phenomenon called *society* must take into account, as much as possible, several elements which either make up society, or which account, in full, for social realities." In Cumings' explanation of regional political economy, there is no place for the subject or the principle of state legitimacy to intervene in the economy. Constructivism helps researchers to find those socially dominant principles of political precedence over economy and legitimate intervention in the economy in Korean political culture. Thereby, constructivism successfully links the objective external context given to Korean people (i.e., regional geopolitical dynamics) with the subject (i.e., Korean people or social institutions).

In sum, two main points stand out. Firstly, the phenomenon of the developmental state is the result of social construction; "that is, particular actors, in particular places, at particular times, fashion meaning out of events and phenomena through prolonged, complex processes of social interpretation involving history, language, and action" (Schwandt, 1994: 118). Such a reconstructive process provides an overarching principle that explains the dynamics of class relations involved in the developmental process rather than performing ahistorical analyses of class relations. Secondly, constructivism directs researchers to culture-bound, context-specific realms, thereby drawing attention to the agents and their principle of interpretation.

Based on this philosophical understanding of constructivism, this book claims that the most important rules that led to the success of the developmental state were the establishment of state hegemony (politics) over society (economy) and the legitimacy of state intervention in the economy. Where should one look in order to reconstruct those rules? Clearly, Korea's capital city can be considered a manifestation of state-society relations in Korea. The city's layout and design reflect the relations between state and economy as well as the relative positions of social forces. Also, since the capital city transformed from the Joseon Dynasty (1392-1910) through the Japanese colonial period (1910-1945) and up to modern Seoul (1945-present), continuities and changes in the relations of state and society can be traced very closely through their physical manifestations. An exploration of alternative realms of research, such as city layout and legibility as well as building structure, can serve as a rich resource in the project of reconstruction. In fact, in elucidating the process of constructing meaning in the diverse world of lived reality and political culture, such realms correspond to the philosophical orientation of constructivism in that the city has resulted from the co-constitution of agents and society. There are both textual and structural sources of evidence for reconstructing the rules of state-society relations. While textual sources provide a broad variety of information, structural sources reveal which ideas society is committed to and concretely show the positions of those ideas in relation to each other. In this sense, the city itself is a touchstone for discerning the dominant rules of state-society relations.

A constructivist approach helps to establish an operational framework for examining the underlying rules that account for the sustained centrality of state power in Korean economic and political life. Thus, identifying the explicit and implicit system rules that existed during major historical epochs helps clarify the underlying logic of events and the order of their occurrence.

From history, theorists have generated some paradigms applicable to the case of the Korean capital. Onuf's description of political society in terms of two general properties (i.e., rules and rule) is based on Wolin's (1980) definition of "political society" as containing "definite social arrangements, certain widely shared understandings regarding the location and use of political power, [and] certain expectations about how authority ought to treat members of society" (183-184). Onuf's framework provides an empirical basis for tracing changes over time in terms of what constitutes rule and rules in a given society.

Methodology

Social constructivism seeks the meaning of social and political phenomena by analyzing their generative rules since such rules characterize every society, including international organizations and institutions. To trace changes in society over time, this book adopts Nicholas Onuf's (1989) analytical framework, which categorizes three distinct yet integrally related types of rule of a political community: hegemony, hierarchy, and heteronomy. Onuf's formulation of these concepts provides useful tools for drawing distinctions among (1) the centrality of state hegemony and the legitimacy of the state's intervention into the economy, (2) an economically interventionist hierarchical bureaucracy, and (3) militant heteronomical social forces.

To articulate how state power in Korea is mutually (re)constructed and (re)produced by both state and society over time, and to present a more comprehensive understanding of state hegemony, this book focuses on state hegemony as symbolized by Korea's capital city, hierarchy as a source of centralized bureaucracy, and heteronomy as an origin of Korea's dissenting voices, opposition forces, and civil society. Specifically, three representations of Korea's capital city will be examined to extract the state-society relations relevant to the main features of the developmental state and democratization in Korea: (1) Hanyang (1392-1910), the period when the origins of state hegemony and the state's legitimacy to intervene in the economy were established with a limited and co-opted dissenting voice of heteronomy; (2) Kyeongseong (1910-1945), a period reflecting major changes and continuities in the relations between state and society (economy); and (3) Seoul (1960-current), the symbolic center and physical place that still contains traces of the legacies of the developmental state. Together, the Hanyang and Kyeongseong eras became the foundation for Korea's developmental state and democracy, bequeathing a tradition of strong state intervention in the economy and the seeds of expandable, loyal opposition forces. In extracting the rules embodied in the center of politics of two major political eras, one must understand how power interacts with place and vice versa. Political geographers have focused on ancient cities as places of power symbols and how power relationships have been constantly reproduced in the process of building capital cities.

In his book *Pivot of the Four Quarters* (1971), Wheatley emphasized four basic modes of symbolism that are essential to the ideal city type: the imitation of a celestial archetype as a replica of the universe, parallelism between the macrocosmos and the microcosmos necessitating the practice of ritual ceremonies to maintain harmony between the world of gods and that of men, symbolism of the center as expressed by some form of *axis mundi*, and the techniques of orientation necessary to define sacred territory within the continuum of profane space. These four basic modes of symbolism in the ideal city type can be interpreted as humans' efforts to realize a cosmic archetype on earth and within their social and political systems. Human understanding of the cosmos was reflected in the Chinese Taoist philosophy of the Yin-Yang and Five Elements Theory. Geomancy (*feng shui* or *pungsu jiri sasang*) was a specific method for finding a celestial archetype on earth. Groups of the governing elite in the ancient cities of Asia set up their national capitals and sacred places for the government in such ideal spaces. An additional factor was Confucianism, a political ideology and method for realizing an ideal society on earth through strong state leadership and Confucian meritocracy.

While textual sources report what has been said, graphic and concrete sources testify to what has been built, just as fossils reveal pictures of ecosystems long gone. While the former can be inaccurate in that speeches and texts aim to persuade, the latter directly reflects the dominant paradigms of an era. In that sense, the latter better serves researchers in their efforts to secure evidence on state-society relations. Accordingly, urban geographical analysis has been applied to all three eras of this book's exploration into the origins of the developmental state and heteronomical social and political forces. Since the city's monumentality serves as a record of the changes and continuities imprinted upon it by each period of society, researchers can avoid reductionist tendencies in analyzing the phenomenon of political culture and institutions by locating evidence of state-society power relations in artifacts that represent the major ideology of each era. This book lays out hard evidence regarding state hegemony and its position relative to civil society based on the geomantic topological configurations reflected in the choice of capital city, city layout, and Confucian architectural monumentality. As concrete evidence, maps related to each period in the capital's history are also analyzed extensively. In addition, a qualitative analysis of those elements and changes over the eras of the capital's history will reveal the state-society power relations from hegemonic, hierarchical, and heteronomical perspectives.

This book's thesis provides a unique alternative to current paradigms for explaining the unprecedented economic growth and simultaneous democratization in Korea—the neoclassical (neoliberal) and late developmentalist paradigms, which attribute such growth to society (market) or the state, respectively. Specifically, this book counters the oversimplification of attributing such economic growth either to military dictatorship or an authoritarian state. Furthermore, it puts Confucianism in adequate perspective by showing how Confucianism functioned as a main source of state hegemony and legitimacy, how it regulated economic activities, and how it has been modified since the Joseon Dynasty to eventually form the modern developmental state in Korea. As a result, this book liberates us from the reductionist view on Confucianism, especially in explaining the authoritarian political culture of Korea, and from the journalistic perspective of treating Confucianism as merely a source of national characteristics, such as diligence, obedience, and aspiration for higher education.

The meaningful contribution of this book lies in its transcending the false dilemma faced by developing economies—i.e., to convert to Western liberalism or be incarcerated by authoritarianism. By reconstructing the social rules that function differently from Western state-society relations, this book crafts an indigenous model based on neither Western liberalism nor authoritarianism. Its non-dichotomous perspective, grounded in the local reality, provides an adaptable and flexible framework that reflects the continuities and changes in state-society relations over the course of Korea's history.

Reconstruction of State-Society Relations: Hanyang, Kyeongseong, and Seoul

To understand the fundamental causes underlying the state's integral power and legitimacy to intervene in the economy as well as the establishment of democracy led by heteronomical forces that originated from the authoritarian Confucian political system, it is necessary to disentangle the relations of power advocated by both Confucianism and geomancy. The scholarly approach of constructivism is used to reconstruct the rules and norms embedded in social and political institutions that made them function as they do. Taking a constructivist approach, this book reconstructs an indigenous model of state-society power relations in Korea in order to thereby provide a general explanation for Korea's concurrent economic and political development in the late 1980s. By so doing, this book analyzes the Confucian principles of politics and economy and the geomantic notion of place and power that has been embedded in Korea's capital city for three distinctive eras. Since Korea's capital city has remained in the same spot for just under a thousand years, it serves as a physical manifestation and microcosm of state-society relations, reflecting the major political and economic ideologies and dominant political culture of each era. In reconstructing state-society relations, this book re-articulates three distinctive yet integrally related principles of polities—hegemony and hierarchy as the dual origins of state centrality, and heteronomy as the origin of the previously small but recently expanded strong civil society—by reading those three principles as reflected in the city layouts, architectural designs, and monumentality of the Confucian capital Hanyang. Next, this book retraces how the prototype of state-society relations was modified and adapted through the Kyeongseong and Seoul eras in order to provide a theoretical paradigm capable of explaining the simultaneous phenomena of rapid economic and political development in the 20th century.

Immanuel Kant's term "heteronomy" connotes the background condition against which episodes of hegemony and hierarchy are set. The "rule of heteronomy" provides a place for elements in society that are not in keeping with the rules of the dominant group. Heteronomy is subordination or subjection to the law of another—political subjection of a community or state, i.e., the opposite of "autonomy" (Onuf, 1989). My interpretation of Kant's "heteronomy" in the context of power dynamics in the Joseon political system bears more resemblance to being "heterogeneous" to the hegemonic royal family and hierarchical Confucian bureaucracy. Geomancy contributed to the rise and demise of political forces, emphasizing the changes of political power configurations, while Neo-Confucianism reified the power of Confucian literati (Wheatley, 1971; Eliade, 1954, 1957; Lee, 1984; Han, 2010). This book goes on to retrace how this prototype of state-society relations was modified and adapted through the Kyeongseong and Seoul eras in order to provide a theoretical paradigm capable of explaining the simultaneous phenomenon of rapid economic and political development in the 20th century.

It is essential to understand how Confucianism, which has been deeply ingrained in Korean society since the era of the Three Kingdoms (57-668), together with geomantic political has laid a foundation of moral, cultural, economic, and political values that legitimize state power. The reductionist tendencies of current literature hinder scholars from fully appreciating the comprehensive nature of Confucianism and geomancy as well as their impact on state-society relations throughout Korean history.

In turn, Japanese colonial rule changed Korean state-society relations from the archetype of its Confucian origins. First, Japanese imperial militarism reversed the Confucian practice of giving precedence to civil over military authority as well as the tradition of scorning commercial and industrial activities. The biggest transformation from Confucian state-society relations, though, was the massive expansion of heteronomical social forces from the loyal opposition that had been built into the Confucian state hegemony (represented by university students, religious leaders, and intellectuals) into a much broader heteronomical force of opposition against Japanese colonial rule. This upsurge of dissenting social forces in the Korean political arena ultimately changed the domestic political power configuration in the modern era (Seoul era) and facilitated the accomplishment of democratization in the 1980s. And since the Park regime inherited from the Hanyang and Kyeongseong eras the legacies of state centrality, political intervention in the economy, centralized bureaucratic control, and militant opposition, a paradigm of continually re-articulated state-society relations may be the best way to gain insight into the causes of Korea's simultaneous economic and political development from an indigenous perspective. These processes were indeed concurrent, for while the developmental state played a strategic role in taming domestic and international market forces and harnessing them to a national economic interest, a belligerent civil society was working to overthrow military rule, which it finally accomplished by the end of a successful period of economic development.

Hegemony, Hierarchy, and Heteronomy

The central rules that led to the success of the developmental state are the establishment of the state's political and moral hegemony over the economy and the legitimacy of state intervention in the economy. Chapters 3, 4, and 5 utilize Onuf's model of rules and rule to examine state hegemony in Korea and reconstruct/rearticulate the principles of the developmental state embedded in Korea's capital city throughout its modern history: (1) Hanyang during the Joseon Dynasty, (2) Kyeongseong during Japanese colonial rule (1910-1945), and (3) Seoul during the Park regime (1961-1979). Since Hanyang represents the height of Joseon Dynasty prosperity and Confucian ideology, it provides an excellent precapitalist, pre-Western starting point for documenting how state hegemony changed over time. Kyeongseong and Seoul represent two modernizing and internationalizing phases in modern Korean history, the former under Japanese colonial domination and the latter under US hegemonic leadership after World War II. Kyeongseong, in particular, warrants attention, given the Japanese colonial authority's aim to reshape Korea's capital city in 1922. Their plan had two main goals: (1) to weaken the state by relocating or destroying its main government buildings and political and national symbols, and (2) to adjust the city layout so as to reflect changes in the economy. Seoul in the 1960s and '70s, by contrast, reflects the city's most intensive industrialization and internationalization, which occurred under US geopolitical and economic influence. A comparison of these three capital cities will shed light on the questions raised by the literature review in regards to the following: (1) the historical origins of Korean state hegemony,

(2) the nature of its state-society relations, (3) the impact of local-global interactions during internationalization and industrialization, and (4) transformations in state hegemony over time. More specifically, this book will examine the following rules in detail.

To delineate "hegemony," we will focus on the ideology that designed Korea's capital city in each of its three representations. For Hanyang, we will examine archival materials on its ruling ideology, administrative law regarding economic activities, and locations of government and public buildings (e.g., government offices, housing, schools) obtained from the National Central Library. For Kyeongseong, we will examine Japanese colonial documents, such as white papers on the New City Plan, also obtained from the National Central Library. Lastly, for Seoul, we will rely on urban planning records from the Korea Research Institute of Human Settlements in the 1960s and '70s.

To delineate "hierarchy," we will examine primarily the organization and management reflected in the city designs and layouts: for Hanyang, the *yangban* bureaucracy and literati; for Kyeongseong, the Japanese colonial administration, military, police, entrepreneurs, and diplomatic mission; and for Seoul, the state bureaucracy, military, police, entrepreneurs (chaebols), politicians, multinational companies (MNCs), and the diplomatic mission.

To delineate "heteronomy," we will examine how each regime of hegemony and hierarchy dealt with dissidence: for Hanyang, Confucian student protests and the location of the Confucian National University; for Kyeongseong, independence movements and student demonstrations; and for Seoul, student-labor-religious protests.

Table 1.1 summarizes this comparison across the three capital cities and their relations to Onuf's identification of hegemony, hierarchy, and heteronomy.

This book argues that state hegemony in Korea stems from an interaction between state and society. While conventional theorists tend to emphasize only its coercive aspects, they neglect its integral underside—i.e., society's consent—thereby failing to understand the intrinsic nature of a state and its relation to society. Without this more comprehensive perspective, we fail to appreciate how sometimes society tolerates or, more profoundly, produces state violence. In Western liberalism, state-society relations are portrayed as mutually exclusive, dichotomous, and confrontational. Therefore, there is no conceptual room for understanding society's role in state violence; however, with a Gramscian reformulation of the developmental state, we see how state and society together produce hegemony. This recognition of society's tremendous role in state hegemony bears significant implications for Korea's democratization in the next century.

Table 1.1 Hegemony, Hierarchy, and Heteronomy of Korea's Capital Cities: Hanyang, Kyeongseong, and Seoul

	HEGEMONY (Ideology)	**HIERARCHY** (Organization)	**HETERONOMY** (Dissident Movement)
Hanyang (15th century)	Confucianism & geomancy	Bureaucracy yangban literati	National Confucian Academy (Seongkyunkwan) students & Neo-Confucian literati (Sarim)
Kyeongseong (1920-'30s)	Japanese imperial authority, military superiority over civil bureaucracy, introduction of capitalistic economy (reverse of Confucian value of agriculture)	Colonial government (continuation of hierarchical bureaucracy), comprador, military, police, entrepreneurs, diplomatic mission	Western liberal political ideas and educational institutions, expansion of heteronomical forces, National Independence Movement led by students
Seoul (1960s-'70s)	Military dictatorship and state monopoly capitalism	Continued bureaucracy, military, entrepreneurs	Students, labor union, Church

	Goryeo	Hanyang (Joseon) Archetype	Kyeongseong (Japanese colony)	Seoul (ROK)
Ideology	Buddhism (ideological and materialistic hegemony of old aristocracy) & Confucianism (reforming ancient Goryeo regime) & geomancy	Confucianism (governing vs. opposition Sarim) & geomancy	Japanese militarism & capitalism	State capitalism under US Cold-War hegemony & democracy
Political System	Feudalism	Centralized Confucian governance	Industrial capitalism	
Archetype of Joseon (Power dynamics among three powers)		Hegemony	External (Japanese colonial militarism) vs. Internal (hegemony & hierarchy join heteronomy to form national resistance)	State-led capitalism, developmental state
		Hierarchy (bureaucracy)		
		Heteronomy (Seongkyunkwan, Sarim, heterogeneous)		Demonstration against military dictatorship

In articulating state-society relations, this book employs a social constructivist approach to discover the meaning of social and political phenomena by analyzing their generative rules since such rules characterize every society, including international society. To trace changes in the rule of Korea's political community over time, this book adopts Nicholas Onuf's analytical framework of hegemony, hierarchy, and heteronomy—three distinctive yet integrally related types—useful tools for decoding (1) the centrality of state hegemony and the legitimacy of state intervention in the economy, (2) an economically interventionist hierarchical bureaucracy, and (3) militant heteronomical social forces.

To articulate how state power in Korea is mutually (re)constructed and (re)produced over time by both state and society, and to present a fuller understanding of state hegemony there, this book focuses on Korea's capital as the symbolic center and embodiment of its state hegemony, hierarchy, and heteronomy. Specifically, this book compares three representations of Korea's capital city as summarized in Figure 1.1 below: (1) Hanyang (1392-1910), the period that saw the establishment of state hegemony and the legitimacy of state intervention in the economy and society with a limited and co-opted dissenting voice of heteronomy; (2) Kyeongseong (1910-1945), a period reflecting major changes and continuities in relations between state

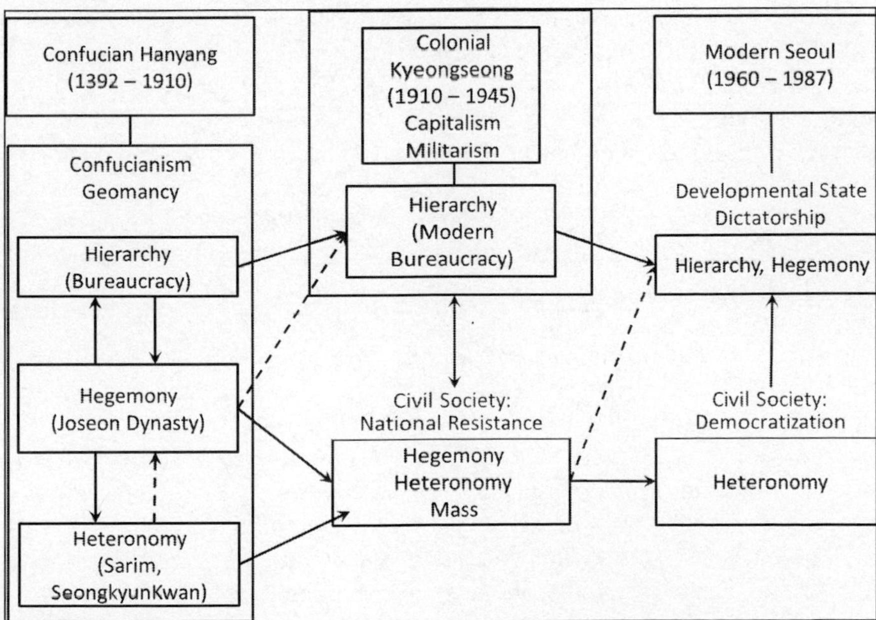

Figure 1.1 Hanyang, Kyeongseong, and Seoul, created by author Han, Jangwoo.

and society (economy); and (3) Seoul, (1960-1980s) the symbolic center and physical place that contained those legacies of the developmental state. Taken together, the Hanyang and Kyeongseong eras became the foundation for Korea's developmental state and democracy, bequeathing a tradition of strong state intervention in the economy and the seeds of strong civil society.

In *Pivot of the Four Quarters*, Wheatley (1971) points out four basic modes of symbolism that are essential in the ideal city type: a function of the imitation of a celestial archetype as a replica of the universe; parallelism between the macro- and the microcosmos necessitating the practice of ritual ceremonies to maintain harmony between the world of gods and that of men; symbolism of the center expressed by some form of *axis mundi*; and the techniques of orientation necessary to define sacred territory within the continuum of profane space. These four modes of symbolism in the ideal city type can be interpreted as humanity's efforts to realize a cosmic archetype on the earth and in its social and political system. Human understanding of the cosmos was reflected in the Chinese philosophy of Taoistic yin-yang and Five Elements Theory as well as the folk belief of geomancy (*feng shui*), which was used specifically for finding celestial archetypes on earth. Governing elite groups in ancient cities of Asia built capital cities and sacred places for government in those ideal spaces in order to strengthen their legitimacy to govern and the basis for their power. Added to this was Confucianism, a political ideology and method for realizing an ideal society on earth through strong state leadership and Confucian meritocracy.

This book sets forth hard evidence regarding the state hegemony and its position relative to civil society drawn from the geomantic topological configurations reflected in the choice of capital city as well as the Confucian architectural monumentality and city layout. As concrete evidence for each manifestation, maps related to each period in the capital's history are analyzed extensively. In addition, a qualitative analysis of those elements and changes over the three eras of the capital city's history will reveal state-society power relations from hegemonic, hierarchical, and heteronomical perspectives.

The debate over the original type of state-society relations that existed in traditional Korea can be viewed from the perspective of the evolution of democracy in Korea. Following the literal definition of "democracy" as "power in the hands of the masses" (*demos* + *kratia* = masses + power), the democratization process can be understood as a shift of power from being concentrated among the few in the center to the many on the periphery. Another way to describe this phenomenon is through Onuf's three types of rule that form a political community: the hegemony of the kings and the oligarchy in the center, as well as the hierarchy that the hegemonic forces create, are checked and balanced at first; however, they are eventually overpowered by the heteronomical forces of the masses. It would not be unreasonable to argue that democratization can be equated with the expansion of heteronomical forces in a society, which can be generalized as empowered dissenting voices.

Habermas (1991) explains this process as the formation and expansion of the public sphere in Western history. The expansion of the power in the hands of newly emerging bourgeoisie in 18th-century Europe was conceptualized as the emergence of the public sphere, which "may be conceived above all as the sphere of private people come together as a public; they soon claimed the public sphere regulated from above against the public authorities themselves, to engage them in a debate over the general rules governing relations in the basically privatized but publicly relevant sphere of commodity exchange and social labor" (Habermas, 1991: 27). In Western society, the emergence of the public sphere signaled the formation of heteronomical forces based on the bourgeoisie's material interests, such as commodity exchange and social labor. It is quite a contrast to note that the heteronomical forces in traditional Korea arose in a form that had been built into the Confucian hegemony and hierarchy and was based on purely political, rather than material, interests.

NOTES

1. The terms *geomancy*, *pungsu jiri* sasang in Korean, and *feng shui* in Chinese are used interchangeably in this book since they all represent the same idea – i.e., that topological configurations reflecting the sacred and profane aspects of the celestial body of Heaven have both direct and indirect influences on human lives and the sociopolitical affairs of greater organizations, such as states. In this book, *geomancy* is used in the general context and the latter two terms in specific contexts where the countries of the origin need to be discerned.

2. The term "heteronomy" was coined by Immanuel Kant to connote a force that is different or autonomous from hegemonic and hierarchical forces in a political community. It is used in this book to refer to "opposition forces" or "voices of dissent" against central power or anti-democratic forces, such as military dictatorship. It is discussed more fully in the section titled "Purpose, Scope, and Methodology."

3. There was a government institution called *Daegan*. It was the term used to describe government posts in the Office of the Inspector-General (*Saheonboo*) and the Office of the Censor-General (*Saganwon*). Thus, *Daegan* was a part of the Confucian government, which does not seem to fit the definition of "heteronomy"; however, these agencies served as a check-and-balance within the government against established, meritorious, high-level bureaucrats.

4. In Joseon's early years, these Neo-Confucian power elites who helped Yi Seong-gye to overthrow the Goryeo Dynasty and establish a governing structure according to Neo-Confucian political ideology wielded political power from their base

in the joint deliberative organ called the "Privy Council." They were called *Gaegukgoingsin*, meaning the subjects who were critical in the foundation of the Joseon Dynasty, such as Jeong Do-jeon and Cho Jun.

5. *Sasang* here means an idea or an ideology.

6. Han, J. and Ling, L. H. M. 1998. Authoritarianism in the Hypermasculinized State: Hybridity, Patriarchy, and Capitalism in Korea. *International Studies Quarterly*, 42: 53-78.

7. The total amount of military and economic assistance fell from $622.1M in 1958 to $463.3M in 1959, and generally continued to diminish. Korea was further affected by a worldwide reduction of 20 percent in American aid for FY-58 (Callow, 1995: 19). From 1953 to 1960, South Korea benefited from over $2B in foreign aid, most of which came from the United States. US aid accounted for more than one-third of the government's budget, nearly 85 percent of Korea's imports and almost 75 percent of fixed capital formation. The aid prevented the economy from collapsing, but growth was very slow and uneven with per capita income only rising from $67 in 1953 to perhaps $83 by 1961. Some of the assistance undoubtedly demonstrated the validity of the law of unintended consequences. For example, food assistance under US PL-480, while probably essential to survival–at least initially, given the land reform problems–was not simply an altruistic program but allowed the US government to dispose of US agricultural surpluses. Thus, the import of US grain in 1957 contributed to a serious drop in the price for a bumper crop of rice, a drop that hurt Korean farmers and damaged the prospects for rational agricultural development (Callow, 1995: 20). With the United States providing about 77 percent of Korea's military budget via military assistance–$527.8M from 1953 to 1957, $331.3M in 1958, $190.5M in 1959 and $190.2M, as well as an additional $133M in Title I common defense grants from 1953 to 1959–South Korea itself did not bear the full weight of its defense burden, but its sacrifices were considerable (Callow, 1995: 15).

8. Callow (1995: 17-18) confirms the *Joseon Daily* news report, saying, "Even though US priorities centered on security, the Eisenhower administration provided a great deal of non-military assistance to Korea. The $200 million in post-armistice reconstruction aid was accompanied by an additional 10 million pounds of food. In 1953, the new administration sent Henry Tasca to Korea to investigate Korea's economic situation. Subsequently, the National Security Council established the position of Economic Coordinator 'to coordinate all US and UN aid programs, including those of the United Nations Korea Reconstruction Agency and of the Korea Civil Assistance Command,' with a view to preventing Rhee from disrupting the Armistice" (Callow, 1995: 17-18).

9. Chalmers Johnson considers such an American policy as a basic means to contain Soviet expansionism during the Cold War era and to maintain American imperialistic ambition in the post-Cold War era. For details, refer to Chalmers Johnson's *Blowback: The Costs and Consequences of American Empire* (2004 ed., Holt Paperbacks) and *The Sorrows of Empire: Militarism, Secrecy, and the End of the Republic* (2004 ed., Metropolitan Books).

10. Also to blame for the group's problems was the reckless signing of overseas investment projects by Honorary Chairman Chong In-young, who committed the

conglomerate to over twenty projects a year, an overly ambitious amount impossible to fulfill. In fact, less than 10 percent of the projects actually got off the ground. Chong was apparently relying on his elder brother, Chong Joo-young, owner of the Hyundai group, to bail out the company in the event of cash flow problems, a rescue that Hyundai was ultimately unable or unwilling to perform.

11. The top ten luxury items accounting for this amount are, in descending order, automobiles, tobacco, cosmetics, footwear, alcohol, furniture, golf clubs, furs, ski sets, and chandeliers.

12. Confucius said that "Tang was the founder of the Shang Dynasty and overthrew the degenerate king of the Hsia Dynasty; and King Wu overthrew the Shang Dynasty and established the Dynasty of Chou, which lasted nearly 1,000 years through the times of Confucius and Mencius" (Reid, 1923: 189). The criteria was whether each dynasty was virtuous: "Three dynasties, Hsia, Shang and Chou, gained imperial rule through benevolence; and they lost it through lack of benevolence. It is in this way that nations decay or flourish, are preserved or perish" (Reid, 1923: 199).

13. Italicized by author.

Chapter Two

Indigenous Model for State Hegemony: Neo-Confucianism, Power, and Place

Most of the existing literature on Korea's developmental state and democratization process has paid scant attention to the indigenous sources of Neo-Confucianism and geomancy. Accordingly, this chapter revisits the developmental structure of the Joseon Dynasty and the way in which it was made possible by geomancy and Neo-Confucian political doctrines and principles, such as state centrality (hegemony), centralized and effective bureaucracy (hierarchy), and a co-opted dissenting voice (heteronomy) that served as a seed of civil power and a mechanism to check and balance the dominant state. This chapter will also review what has been said on the role of the developmental state in general and Korea's developmental state in particular. Next, this chapter will examine the failure of grand theories to explain the phenomena of economic and political development. As an alternative explanation, an indigenous approach will be explored with a special focus on place and power.

CONTENDING MODELS OF KOREAN POLITICAL ECONOMY OF DEVELOPMENT AND STATE-SOCIETY RELATIONS

As we begin our investigation, it may be best to examine conventional definitions of the "developmental state." White and Wade (1988:1) define "developmental states" as "states that have played a strategic role in taming domestic and international market forces and harnessing them to a national economic interest." This definition singles out the developmental state's interventionist economic policy as an important factor. The most significant factor in the success of the developmental state, this book proposes, is how such interventionist economic policy is legitimized in society so that the state can intensively and extensively intervene in its economic sectors.[1] In other words, the key to the state's success is the means by which it gains consent for its interventionist role.

For several reasons, among East Asian NICs, a clear representative case of a successful state interventionist economic policy is the Korean experience of rapid economic development. Even among successful East Asian economies such as Japan, Taiwan, Singapore, and Hong Kong, Korea has maintained the strongest tradition of Confucian political ideology upholding state authority, thereby accentuating the need for government intervention in the economy. Korea was the last of the East Asian NICs, with the exception of China, to open its doors to the Western political and economic system. In addition, an empirical study of the economic policies of the so-called Four Tigers in East Asia (i.e., South Korea, Taiwan, Singapore, and Hong Kong) locates the most extensive and intensive government policy of economic intervention in the Japanese and Korean experiences of economic development (MacIntyre, 1994; Haggard & Cheng, 1987, 1987a; Haggard, 1986, 1990; Haggard & Moon, 1983, 1989, 1990). Similarly, World Bank research reports (1993) conclude that Japan and Korea, among the Four Tigers, have maintained the most rigorous interventionist industrial policies. MacIntyre (1994: 4) also considers Korea as one of the strongest states in that it is insulated from the pressure of established interests. In the category of export-push strategy, Korea ranked as the least dependent on foreign markets among the Four Tigers,[2] which seems to imply the least foreign influence and highest degree of domestically oriented economic system, and which leaves the most room for state intervention in the economy. Lastly, Korea has maintained the most repressive form of state control over society due to its having the most militant heteronomical forces in East Asia.

By focusing on Korea's capital city as the symbolic center of its state hegemony, one can trace how state power in Korea has been mutually reconstructed and reproduced over time by both state and society, and present a more comprehensive understanding of state hegemony in a non-Western, non-liberal context. To the Korean people, the capital city represents the Korean state. Interestingly, the Korean term *kukka* translates to mean both "state" and "house" as well as "family and "lineage," signifying both the place where the King lives and the place where all functions of the state are concentrated. Specifically, three representations of Korea's capital city in its modern history—(1) Hanyang during the precapitalist, Confucian rule of the Joseon Dynasty (1392-1910), (2) Kyeongseong during Japanese colonial occupation (1910-1945), and (3) Seoul during Korea's American-dominated developmental period (1960s-1970s)—offer valuable historical insight into the underlying rules that account for the sustained centrality of the state. Moreover, comparisons from its founding in 1392 to the present day will provide a sound empirical basis for demonstrating how power relations in state and society transform over time.

In this perspective, current analyses on the East Asian developmental state suffer from a static, ahistorical, and post-hoc state-rationalist perspective. A more insightful perspective must include the political culture and political geography, which addresses the relations between space and power. To account for the Korean developmental state, it is necessary to explore its hegemonic origins, its Confucian foundations in state-society relations, its interactions with global forces, and its changes over time.

Schools of Thought

Currently, in regards to East Asia's rapid economic growth, three schools of thought prevail—neoclassical, institutionalist, and late developmentalist. The first of these, the neoclassical approach, claims that the region's unprecedented economic growth reflects the benefits of free market economics; that is, the spirit of enterprise promotes growth and establishes the foundation for developmental "take-off" (cf., Rostow, 1960; Chen, 1979; Balassa, 1981, 1988; Little, 1982; Kuznets, 1982; Galenson, 1985; Friedman, 1988). Neoclassical economists generally attribute East Asian developmental success to five closely related policies: (1) limited government intervention in the economy, (2) a low level of price distortion in the economy, (3) an export promotion strategy (Jones & Sakong, 1980; Mason et al., 1980), (4) a stable macroeconomic environment and reliable legal framework, and (5) high-quality human capital.[3]

Institutionalists, however, highlight the role of an autonomous state with an efficient bureaucracy as a necessary and sufficient condition for hyper-economic growth in East Asia (cf., Haggard & Moon, 1983; Johnson, 1987; Deyo, 1987; Luedde-Neurath, 1988; White & Wade, 1988; Amsden, 1989, 1990; Evans, 1989; Wade, 1990a, 1990b; Zhao & Hall, 1994). They locate a set of institutional and political requirements for effective state intervention in the form of strategic industrial policies. Evans (1989) examines how these complex sociopolitical relations function in the case of Brazil, and concludes that the relative effectiveness of Third World states as agents of industrial transformation reflects differences such as class composition, state-society relations, and external relations with the capitalist world economy. The most effective states are characterized by an "embedded autonomy" (Evans, 1989) as when a well-developed, internal bureaucratic organization joins with close public-private connections.

Lastly, late development theorists focus on economic development within a specific sociohistorical context, i.e., that of the late-developing, "catch-up" state (cf., Hirschman, 1945; Prebisch, 1950; Singer, 1950; Nurkse, 1953; Myrdal, 1957; Rosenstein-Rodan, 1957; Tinbergen, 1958; Seers, 1969; Chenery, 1975; Colclough, 1991). "Late development" refers to the gap between industrialized and non-industrialized economies as measured by differences in national resources, economic output, the size of the country, and its relations to the international economy. According to Gershenkron (1962), a late-developing state actively intervenes in the economy when the developmental gap becomes too great for any private institution to bear the cost. The state may do so by, say, supplying capital for nascent industries. Moreover, late development or economic backwardness triggers state action because domestic elites feel humiliated by, or perceive a threat from, external forces (Clark & Lemco, 1988: 2).

There are several problems with these analyses of Asia's rapid economic development, especially in the case of Korea. By attributing economic development to non-democratic political power, development theorists tend to view Asian experiences of economic development as an exception to the path followed by early starters, i.e., Western developed countries where economic development has been strongly associated with democratic political power. Asian development processes are exceptional to the Eurocentric universal development model of politics and the economy, which rests upon the fundamental assumption that new states can follow a path of development essentially the same as that pursued by current advanced states. This neglects the overall context in which development occurs (Taylor, 1985: 5-6). Furthermore, in this perspective, NICs are regarded as undemocratic and inferior. Such a perspective places East Asians in an oversimplified and false dilemma: either convert to Western liberalism or remain incarcerated by authoritarianism.

Such a pursuit of Western universalism may be considered patronizing as it bears "a tendency to explain the problems of Third World societies in terms of their lack of the characteristics of Western societies" (Ake, 1979). In this sense, it is simply inadequate to label Korea today as authoritarian without understanding the roots of its state authority. The prescription of Western liberalism does not necessarily apply in non-dichotomous environments that regard state and society as inseparable. Indeed, democratization is currently in progress in Korea, albeit not in a form identical to that of Western democratization. As state-society relations in Confucian political culture differ strongly from those in the West, any attempt to convert to Western liberalism is most likely unsuitable and bound to fail.

Based on the assumption that relations between state and economy are dichotomous and confrontational, Western liberalism upholds the virtue of the least intervention of political power in the economy; however, in Confucian political culture, where the rule of politics takes a position of precedence over the economy and the state-society relations are not dichotomous but rather are closely interwoven, political intervention is a given and expected. Such precedence is a non-Western and non-liberal notion clearly exemplified by Asian countries such as China, Taiwan, Hong Kong, Singapore, Japan, and Korea—all strongly influenced by Confucianism. In these countries, the masses expect the state or politics to lead and intervene in the economy for the good of all. In fact, state or government take hold of every means possible to influence private enterprise, as do military regimes or authoritarian government in other countries. What is unusual is that the masses and society take for granted such government intervention in the economy. In liberal thought, however, there is a neutral area within which individuals and private enterprises are free to pursue their own plans for development and their own advantages as natural rights. Or, the ideology of *laissez-faire* upholds the typical power relations between state and society (economy) in the Western tradition: the minimalist state and free market principle, which has been contrary to the East Asian Confucian tradition. Clearly, this liberal dichotomous tradition of *laissez-faire* is absent from the schools of thought on Korea's late development.

State-Society Relations

These three perspectives each rely upon different notions of state-society interaction under developmental conditions. Neoclassical theorists present the most restrictive vision of state involvement in the economy, i.e., state intervention causes, rather than redressing market failures. Along these lines, Porter (1990b) contends that the proper role of government is to serve as a catalyst by encouraging companies to advance to higher levels of competitive performance. In Korea's rapid ascent in the world economy, for example, Porter highlights the importance of the role played by the government's substantial investments in education and infrastructure, its aggressive export promotion policies, and its cultivation of a national consensus on the importance of international competitive success. Even then, as noted by White (1984) and White and Wade (1988), neoclassical theorists assert that once liberalizing reforms are enacted, market mechanisms eventually replace state investments in the economy. Little (1970, 1982), for instance, finds that Taiwan's state actively developed heavy and chemical goods industries in the early 1970s but, during the long boom period from 1963 to 1973, played no important steering role.

The beneficial role of the state in economic development, however, is not denied by neoclassical theorists. Jones and Sakong (1980), for example, acknowledge that the selective promotion of certain industries and specific products in East Asia's NICS helped to reduce the economy's vulnerability to foreign suppliers and generate a higher value-added, more elastic income as well as a more closely interlinked set of productive activities. By helping to provide relatively stable market conditions for selected domestic sectors, the state ensured that investment in key sectors would be undertaken on a sufficiently large magnitude to capture economies of scale within the national unit.

Nevertheless, neoclassical theorists maintain that the state must be "restricted largely, if not entirely, to protecting individual rights, persons and property, and enforcing voluntarily negotiated private contracts" (Buchanan, Tollison & Tullock, 1980: 9). In its minimal neoclassical form, the state remains exogenous—a "black box" (Evans, 1989: 563) whose internal functioning is not a proper subject for economic analysis (Bauer & Yamey, 1957).

Institutionalists, however, suggest just the opposite—namely, that "appropriate" state intervention enhances market performance. According to institutionalists, bureaucratic maneuvering of public-private cooperation constitutes a central characteristic of the developmental state. Chalmers Johnson (1982), who pioneered the concept of the capitalist developmental state (CDS), identifies these state-driven arrangements as common to all of the high-growth economies in East Asia. The term "administrative guidance" refers to the pursuit of growth and international competitiveness as well as the underlying guarantees of private property and market principles by an elite economic bureaucracy such as the Economic Planning Board (EPB) in Korea and the Ministry of International Trade and Investments (MITI) in Japan. In addition to there being cooperative relations between public and private sectors, Deyo (1987a, b) emphasizes the coexistence of unusual degrees of bureaucratic autonomy. In the developmental state, this is manifested, according to Deyo (1987a, b), in government-business relations such as the extraordinary dependence of business conglomerates (i.e., the chaebols in Korea and the *keiretsu* of postwar Japan) on the state for their survival.

Wade (1990) proposes a "governed market theory" of East Asian industrialization, wherein the state promotes and directs high levels of investment in certain key industries that would not have occurred in the absence of government action. Then, there arises the important question of how the state is able to implement an unfair and selective industrial policy risking opposition from those sectors not supported by government. Relatedly, all the dominant classes of East Asia's hyper-growth economies were either destroyed, disorganized, or totally subordinated to the state, with the partial exception of Hong Kong (Grabowski, 1994; Schwartz, 1994: 273). To describe this phenomenon, Grabowski speaks of the rise of a "hard state" in East Asia as opposed to that of the "soft state" found elsewhere in the developing world.[4]

Amsden (1989, 1990) describes Korea as a prototypically guided market economy wherein the priorities of state-guided industrialization constrain its market rationale. According to her, the Korean government strategically harnesses domestic and international forces to benefit national economic interests. The state also heavily subsidizes and directs a select group of conglomerates (chaebols) to prepare them for international competition. Thus, a central feature of Korea's industrial policy is a high degree of state-driven selectivity, motivated by long-term rationality that is ensured by a stable and predictable environment. The central insight to emerge from Amsden's study is that Korea's government not only subsidizes industries to stimulate growth but also sets stringent performance criteria in exchange for these subsidies, thereby manifesting the state's dual strategy of support and discipline. Indeed, Luedde-Neurath (1988) claims that the extent of Korea's liberalization is exaggerated—it was a liberalization process managed by and under state control.

The third school of thought, that of the late developmentalists, suggests that state action is a relational and reactive policy; i.e., the more backward the economy, the more interventionist the state. Indeed, the late-development notion of "development" relies upon a notion of the state as the prime mover of socioeconomic progress. It draws upon a historical argument that successful "late development" (e.g., Russia, Germany, Japan) takes a form very different from that of early industrializers such as France, the United Kingdom, and the United States (Gerschenkron, 1962; Landes, 1969). Late development is less "spontaneous" and more the subject of "teleological determination" (White, 1984: 1-2) with the state playing the role of historical animator. For Gerschenkron, therefore, the ideology of "developmentalism" is inseparable from the interventionist state. In this sense, late-development theory explicitly recognizes the social basis of state action. Gourevitch (1986: 238) writes that state autonomy relies upon political support or at least compliance or enthusiasm from societal actors. When that support disappears, so does state strength.[5] Nevertheless, late developmentalists presume that once late-developing states finally "catch-up," they no longer need active states and convert instead to the condition of early developers, i.e., to unfettered market economics.

Regarding the factors that contributed to economic development in Korea, late developmentalists attribute the Korean economic success, including that of East Asia's Four Tigers, to "industrialization through learning"

(Amsden, 1989: 3-23), "belligerent developmental state" (Macintyre, 1994; Haggard, 1986, 1990; Haggard & Moon, 1983), or "state as an effective institution" (Greenspan, 2007; Fukuyama, 2000; Johnson, 1982, 1989; Moon, 1988). Some development theorists inadvertently legitimate despotic rule, military intervention, and its attendant "economically efficient" bureaucracy in these high-producing Asian economies (HPAEs) by using descriptions such as "catch-up" fascism in prewar Japan (Landes, 1965), the "interventionist state" (Johnson, 1982; Amsden, 1989: 8; Woo-Cumings, 1991), "bureaucratic authoritarianism" in Korea (Im, 1987), "soft authoritarianism" in Singapore (Denny, 1994; Jones, 1994), "estatisme" in Taiwan (Gold, 1986; Amsden, 1985, 1979), and "neo-authoritarianism" in China (Petracca & Xiong, 1990).

Han and Ling (1998: 56) argue that central to the CDS is a "catch-up" ideology. Meiji Japan rallied its first industrialization effort in the late 1860s to avoid being colonized by foreign invaders. Then, a second round of industrialization was undertaken by postwar Japan to placate unrest at home as well as geopolitical concerns abroad. "Similarly, Singapore mobilized economic development by drawing on anti-colonialist sentiments against Britain as well as anti-Chinese prejudice from the Malaysian federation. Likewise, South Korea, Taiwan, and Hong Kong motivated their rapid growth under the banner of anti-communism" (Han & Ling, 1998: 56).

Han and Ling (1998) also find that the developmental states in East Asia have applied macroeconomic management through such measures as favorable licenses, loan incentives, tax exemptions, and financial subsidies to regulate economic growth (Gold, 1986; Johnson, 1987); however, it commands greater political and cultural authority in national decision-making than its European counterpart. Identified as "plan-rational" (Appelbaum & Henderson, 1992), the CDS oversees a "governed market" (Wade, 1990). For example, it restricts foreign investments to specific industries such as electronics or to geographical locations such as export-processing zones (Haggard & Cheng, 1987). The CDS also counters foreign competition through nontariff barriers at home. For overseas markets, the CDS accomplishes this by providing structural assistance, such as government-business "liaisons" to conduct market research, purchase resources, negotiate deals (especially with other national governments), and/or reduce transactions costs (e.g., establishing flight routes with national airlines to access new markets) (Han & Ling, 1998).

Han and Ling (1998: 56) aptly summarize the achievements of the CDS in East Asia:

> Each CDS, accordingly, nurtures a depoliticized, techno-rational, bourgeois elite. The CDS offers a social contract of sorts: political exclusion in exchange

> for economic accumulation. An education-intensive program reinforces this highly competitive, economically oriented but politically docile managerial class (Dore, 1965; Rohlen, 1983). Some contend that this social contract no longer holds since many advocates of democratization in the CDS come from this class of social and economic elites; yet, others question how democratically inclined this class can be, given its vested interests in the state. (Brown & Jones, 1995; Kim, 1993)

The key factor in the late developmentalists' analyses of Korea's miraculous economic development from the 1960s through the '80s is the role of state: the developmental state. The main feature of the developmental state is its autonomous power to intervene, to pick a winner and loser, and to legitimize those apparently non-economic decisions that are made in the process of industrialization. Internationally, the developmental state is capable of strategically managing the demands and changes that come from the global economy by consolidating and mobilizing various domestic actors to seize opportunities in global competition. More simply put, the developmental state is that which can distort market mechanisms when needed in order to catch up with early starters.

Critique of the Literature

While the first two prevailing schools of thought—neoclassical and late developmentalist—have enjoyed success in the Western context, they possess intrinsic limitations when applied to other contexts, especially non-Western ones. Similarly, the institutional approach has a limitation of its own in that it focuses on describing the institutional end product without explaining the fundamental processes by which those institutions emerge. The neoclassical approach is criticized because industrial policy and state intervention in financial markets are not easily reconciled within the neoclassical framework. At the same time, institutionalists have successfully addressed the extent and scope of government intervention to promote economic development; however, it has been proven that some government policies have had negative or little apparent impact on industrial structure; clearly, the Korean government's policy of promoting heavy and chemical industries has backfired. A critical flaw of the late developmentalist view is evident in the fact that Korea's government continues to intervene, in a different way, in the economy even after economic development has been accomplished.

One problem with the mainstream developmental approach is its presumptions about state-society relations: that it implicitly adheres to the neoclassical notion of the state as predatory and cynical in nature (Grabowski, 1994: 414).

It also views the state as an instrument of individual and collective interest maximization. For example, Marxist, liberal, and functionalist traditions of state theory reify the power of state to preexisting structures of civil society. Each sees the state predominantly as a place, an arena, in which the struggles of classes, interest groups, and individuals are expressed and institutionalized. Though such theories disagree on many issues, they all deny significant autonomous power to the state (Mann, 1986: 185). Thus, neoclassicists portray government "intervention" in product and factor markets as the source of "policy-induced distortions" that are "excessive," "misguided," and "irrational" (Leeson & Nixson, 1988: 64). As White and Wade (1988: 26) aptly note, though, we should be alert to the "ideological roots of the language of intervention" as a linguistic expression of an economic liberalism that polarizes state from market and is of limited utility in grasping the roots and dynamics of East Asian development.

Development theorists, whether neoclassical, institutionalist, or late developmentalist, typically begin their analyses at the time of economic internationalization[6] in these countries. Rarely do they examine the meaning and significance of the transition of state power. Furthermore, when such analyses are undertaken (cf., Ohkawa & Rosovsky, 1973; Hirschmeier & Yui, 1981), they tend to focus on the structural and/or sociopolitical aspects of transitions in state power without concomitant attention to its impact on state hegemony and how it may have transformed over time.

This preoccupation with the institutional setting for economic development risks overlooking the dynamic nature of state-economy relations and their importance in regards to policy choices and economic performance. Herein lies a critical misapplication of Western notions of state-economy relations to East Asia. According to Granovetter (1985: 481), "much of the utilitarian tradition, including classical and neoclassical economics, assumes rational, self-interested behavior affected minimally by social relations (thereby producing) an atomized, undersocialized conception of human action." Neoclassical arguments—which also underlie late developmentalist and institutionalist approaches—disallow any impact of social structure and social relations on production, distribution, or competition. For example, neoclassicists believe that the ideal minimal state should remain outside the economic arena. Thus, the social construction of power in state and economy is precluded from consideration. In development theory, consequently, neoclassical theorists tend to direct their concern toward a simplified model based on "economistic" logic.

Another misleading point in terms of the state-economy relations of developmental states is the view that such rapid economic development is due to the presence of strong state. Clark and Lemco (1988) object to the idea that strong states promote development; examples in world history, especially in post-WWII Latin America, Africa, and Asia, demonstrate that such a proposition is not always true. In all of these regions, there were military dictatorships with exclusive use of power that did not produce economic success. Thus, it would be overly simplistic, Clark and Lemco (1998) explain, to correlate the economic development with a strong state since state intervention in developing nations presents both opportunities and risks. "There is equal danger in assuming that development is solely a function of the magic of the marketplace, the immutable international hierarchy, or the omnipotent state" (Clark & Lemco, 1988: 5). Thus, they argue, analysis of the role of the strong state in promoting development must extend beyond the simplistic equation of strong states = development. State autonomy and strength, both external and internal, are complex and ambiguous concepts that evolve from a complex interaction among internal and external factors. Furthermore, state-economy relations can change radically as part of development processes.

Not only the state's power but also the people's acceptance of that power and their social consent to the legitimacy of state hegemony contributes toward state-society cooperation. Amsden (1990) and Moon (1995) agree on the importance of understanding the sources of the state's ability to discipline the private sector in the Korean political economy. Both scholars locate the explanation of the state's legitimacy to intervene in the economy in either contemporary government policies or material forces applied by the state. Amsden (1990: 18) holds that developmental differences among late industrializers are best explained in terms of the discipline imposed on big business; however, she dismisses the social consent to state hegemony as social indoctrination. In discussing what factors facilitate state domination over the private sector without being supported by civil society, Moon (1995: 2-3) points to several: (1) political capacity measured in terms of strong authoritarian executive dominance; (2) the availability of policy instruments and resources; and (3) bureaucratic capacity, such as competent and meritocratic bureaucratic agents, unity of bureaucratic purpose, and minimization of bureaucratic infighting. Neither of these scholars, though, emphasizes society's acceptance of state power as a motivating force.

These authors focus only on the authoritarian characteristics of the military regime while ignoring the country's pre-military and predevelopmental origins of the power of state being embedded in society. Completely absent from their consideration is the historical fact that Confucian ideology in the Joseon Dynasty prescribed that either the state or politics take precedence over the economy for the benefit of all. For instance, Korea's developmental state would sometimes deliberately distort prices in order to boost exports. Once export targets were met, losses could be recovered through sales in the protected domestic market. Furthermore, Korean politicians would often protect bureaucrats by holding off special interest claimants who threatened to deflect the state from its main developmental priorities and also legitimate and ratify the bureaucrats' decisions.

Korea's centralized system is not simply a result of authoritarian rule under the Park regime. Historically speaking, Korea has always been a centralized country, but the power of the state (*kukka*) was not exercised by the king alone; a large portion was wielded by Confucian scholars and bureaucrats (*sadaebu*), who often challenged the king's power. During the Joseon Dynasty, Korea's official land distribution and tax system directly reflected the interests of this gentry class. By the end of the Joseon Dynasty, however, poor economic performance in general had eroded the material basis of this ruling class and caused the collapse of its political authority. Later, under Japanese colonial occupation, this class system was completely destroyed by land reallocation and subsequent civil war. Consequently, no dominant class was left to challenge Park Chung-hee's ambitious Five-Year Economic Development Plan in the 1960s. In this way, Park's regime stepped into a preexisting centralized state position from which his regime could better accomplish its goal.

Moreover, state-society relations in Korea are not monolithic. Some industries (e.g., steel, petrochemicals, electronics, shipbuilding, machinery, nonferrous metals) received heavy subsidies and direct "guidance" from the state (cf., The HCI Plan, South Korean Government Policy Paper, 1973), while others experienced only intermittent policy intervention. The rest have been more or less left to take care of themselves within a broad framework of regulation. It is not that the government has attempted any significant prevention of investment in nonstrategic projects; it has simply not given such projects much help. In this way, the market is guided by the concept of a long-term national rationality of investment as formulated by government officials, and the content and pace of industrialization is not left entirely to the aggregate decisions of individual businessmen.

In addition to paying insufficient attention to the balance of state and economy, the developmental literature also neglects the impact of local-global interaction on state-society relations during internationalization and its effect on state hegemony. Researchers tend to treat economic development as a discrete and modern phenomenon without adequately scrutinizing the dynamic factors that legitimize and sustain state power. Korea's postwar development, for instance, was highly conditioned by a world economic system framed by US power. Due to this interaction between US geopolitical power and local developmental needs, Korea in the 1960s promoted two groups under internationalization that previously had been considered unimportant: the military and the merchant/manufacturing classes. This change in class structure and state power seems unusual, but it reflects a realignment of societal forces in the traditional context of state hegemony. The reproduction of Confucian state hegemony and its interaction with global hegemonic forces reflect a dynamic heretofore unrecognized within Korea's internationalization and industrialization.

Development theorists, in contrast, tend to overemphasize the role of external factors in the formation of the developmental state. While Cumings (1984, 1988) rightly considers the East Asian economic success within the geostrategic context of Japanese and then American hegemony, many ignore the sources of internal threat—i.e., the communist North for South Korea and Mao's China for Taiwan. This internal insecurity fueled both countries' nationalistic vision and commitment to a long-term transformation of the economy; it also enabled political leaders and bureaucrats to suppress increasing demands for equitable income distribution and social welfare from below in order to facilitate economic development (Castells, 1992; Grabowski, 1994). Additionally, development theorists offer little insight into how power relations transform internally as a result of these external interactions. Japanese colonial control from 1910 to 1945 actually eradicated the hegemony of the traditional ruling class, and thus Confucian class structure largely disintegrated. The US military occupation after World War II and the Civil War from 1950 to 1953 directly contributed to the establishment of military hegemony and the introduction of the entrepreneurial class in Korean society. Thus, the two social classes that had been looked down upon under the Confucian ideology—military officers and merchants—became two major social forces leading traditional society toward modernization and economic development. Also, the modernized bureaucratic system was followed by the introduction of a military administrative process.[7]

Without considering the external factors that led to the collapse of Confucian state structure and the emergence of a new domestic power structure, it would be impossible to obtain a comprehensive understanding of the state's role in economic development and its interactions with the economic sector (civil society) and the public (people) in general. Lacking this perspective, both Western and non-Western scholars limit their analysis of the source of state autonomy in the presence of a strong military regime, thus reifying the power of the military regime as a physical power only. The Park regime's weak political legitimacy was evident in the presidential election of 1963, which Park barely won by a margin of around 30,000 votes against Kim Dae-jung. The Park regime, despite its weak political legitimacy, successfully mobilized the nation toward economic development largely by playing the economic development card against opposition forces.

Scholars, in their interpretations of state power in Korean society, diverge in two major directions—strong state and weak state. One extreme regards Korea's state as a prototype of a strong state, based on the reasoning that a military dictator ruled modern Korea. They attribute the authoritarian features of the Korean state to traditional Confucian culture, and their views on this issue are somewhat static in that their analyses are largely confined to the scope of the state itself, ignoring the fact that state power becomes comprehensive only when society grants its full consent.

The other extreme describes the Korean state as traditionally weak, for power was divided between the king and the Confucian scholar bureaucrats during the Joseon Dynasty (Amsden, 1990). The problem with this description of Korea as being traditionally weak but strong enough to successfully discipline the private sector is that it is somewhat self-contradictory. For example, Amsden (1990: 24) argues that "the Korean state was traditionally weak, but in the 1960s the military regime of Park Chung-hee succeeded in consolidating its power over finance, commerce, industry and agriculture. Despite its supremacy over these sectors, however, the power base of the Park regime severely suffered from its weak political legitimacy due to the way Park seized power, military coup in 1961." Amsden's analysis fails to explain, though, how the politically illegitimate Park regime was able to tame the private sector to accomplish economic development.

In the search for a better explanation, several theoretical perspectives are worth considering. First, state-economy relations should be incorporated into any understanding of the dynamics of state power as they relate to power configurations among major social forces during Korea's development. Approaching this from the perspective of the three major social influences (i.e., hegemony, hierarchy, and heteronomy) on the Korean state's role in economic development puts into sociopolitical context the question of how the military regime was able to discipline the private sector. At the same time, it explains how relations among major social forces leave room for the state to pursue its goals by sacrificing the rights of the oppositional minority for the economic benefit of the tacit majority.

Second, to better articulate state-economy relations, local-global interaction should be considered. As briefly mentioned above, Japanese colonial rule, which was the first modern global force interacting with Korean society, destroyed the old class structure of the Joseon Dynasty and created a new power configuration among the old Confucian elites, the managerial class, and the dissenting social voices. This new configuration among social forces strengthened state hegemony by weakening the previously dominant class structure. American influence after national liberation from Japanese colonial rule also had a tremendous impact on relations between state and economy and on the composition of major social forces in modern Korea. Throughout the three major periods of Korean history, one major social force has been consistently influential in Korean society: the bureaucracy. This finding provides a historical context for the institutionalist observation of the autonomy that bureaucrats have possessed in maneuvering the private sector. Institutionalists such as Johnson (1982) and Deyo (1987) indicate that the central characteristic of the developmental state is its bureaucratic maneuvering of public-private cooperation and the coexistence of unusual degrees of bureaucratic autonomy. These two features of the developmental state in general, and of Korea's state in particular, make the long-term rationality and effectiveness of an industrial policy possible despite various pressures and interests from societal sectors (Amsden, 1989, 1990; Deyo, 1987). In other words, institutionalist analyses generally rest on the premise of an effective economic policy, which, this school believes, is created by a cohesive and well-organized bureaucracy capable of maneuvering public-private cooperation.

In order to avoid a static description of state power and gain a full picture of the dynamic nature of power relations between state and economy and among social forces, a historical approach is necessary. Moon (1990: 25-26) observes that state strength vis-a-vis society is not fixed but varies over time and across sectors, depending on the character of the regime and underlying coalitional dynamics. He further claims that, in the long run, authoritarian states face legitimation problems and, in order to deal with this lack of political legitimacy, may "seek not just to control but also to co-operate with key social actors."

This book, however, investigates the issue of the developmental state "historically" through the lens of state-society relations, analyzing the sociopolitical power configurations of social forces. In addition, another significant variable in examining how interactions with global forces influence relations between state and society is the impact of such interactions upon the domestic power configuration of major social forces. Understanding the workings of state-society relations and local-global interactions will help to illuminate the concept of state hegemony as dynamic and varying over time within its sociopolitical context.

CRISIS IN COMPARATIVE POLITICS

Rapid economic successes in Asia, such as those of NICs or CDSs in the 1980s, compel comparativists to pay attention to the question of what factors contributed to such remarkable economic growth. In order to avoid the same error that was made by the neoclassical, institutional, and late developmental arguments—i.e., oversimplification—comparative scholars should admit that there is no single process by which development occurs. Instead of a grand theory, a configurative middle-range theory is needed that is capable of explaining "a process actively modeled by different and vivid cultures and traditional institutions" (Dogan & Pelassy, 1984: 11). In *The Sociological Imagination*, C. Wright Mills referred to two tendencies that he viewed as inimical to the progress of human science. The first of these tendencies is grand theory, which Mills defined as a systematic theory regarding the nature of man and society. Characteristics of grand theory are to be found in efforts to construct abstract and normative theories of human nature and society. In this effort, the level of thinking, abstraction, and determinism are so general and high that its practitioners have difficulty shifting toward observation and rarely come down from their lofty generalities to analyze concrete problems grounded in particular historical and structural contexts. This absence of a firm sense of genuine problems, in turn, makes for the sense of unreality so noticeable in their writing. As a result, grand theory fails to address genuine human problems and, in extreme cases, even functions as legitimation for the sociopolitical status quo. Grand theorists tend to be preoccupied with syntactic meanings, unimaginative about semantic references, and rigidly confined to such high levels of abstraction that the typologies they create often seem more like exercises in conceptualization than efforts to systematically define the real problems at hand and guide our efforts toward solutions. One great lesson that can be learned from the systematic absence of real problems in the work of the grand theorists is that a self-aware thinker must at all times be aware of the levels of abstraction on which he is working. The capacity to shift between levels of abstraction, with ease and clarity, is a mark of an imaginative and systematic thinker. To clarify the syntactic and the semantic dimensions of such conceptions, we must be aware of the hierarchy of specificity and be able to consider all hierarchical levels.

The deterministic tendency is another crucial aspect of grand theory as, for example, in Wallerstein's world capitalist system theory. From the radical and world system view, capitalism is a system of global production and exchange, particularly the sort of exchange in which the center seeks to grow by exploiting the periphery. The possibility that capitalism might promote the development of the Third World is rejected as absurd due to the function that the South must play in the system. A precondition for peripheral development is thus a disengagement from the capitalist world system (Corbridge, 1986: 10). This view also rejects the idea that development and underdevelopment are dual aspects of capitalism because this contradicts the vision of capitalism set forth by Marx, Lenin, and Luxemburg. Instead, the Third World is considered underdeveloped as a result of its not being capitalist enough. It is believed that the metropolitan powers preserve precapitalist relations of production in the periphery because they can best secure and reproduce cheap labor in this way (Corbridge, 1986: 10-11). This theoretical system does not, however, consider the possibility that it might be challenged at certain points. Similarly, it overlooks the possibility that the relationship between capitalism and the Third World could be conceived in terms less teleological and deterministic. Another weakness of the grand paradigm is its tendency to conceive of the capitalist world system in terms of North versus South or core versus periphery. Placing exclusive emphasis on just two spatial blocs obscures many other important features that developed in the postwar international economic and political system.

This section has discussed the inadequacies of grand theory in terms of its abstractness, lack of historical and structural context, and failure to address genuine human problems. Any approach that makes up for these shortcomings should possess a willingness to emphasize the importance of the local and contingent, a desire to emphasize the extent to which our own concepts and attitudes have been shaped by particular historical circumstances, and a correspondingly strong aversion to all overarching theories and singular schemes of explanation. Based on these premises, I will briefly examine the shortcomings of three grand theories: the world capitalist system, modernization theory, and dependency theory.

There are two main approaches to understanding Korea's modernization of its economy and political system: modernization theory and dependency theory. A broader way to characterize these two phenomena is to explain both development and underdevelopment. Theories of development and underdevelopment (i.e., modernization, underdevelopment, dependency, and imperialism) can generally be divided into two groups: Non-Marxist and Marxist. Modernization theorists belong to the non-Marxist tradition of development literature, whereas most dependency theorists adopt a more Marxist stance (albeit with some exceptions taking a non-Marxist perspective). Both non-Marxist and Marxist dependency theorists, however, adopt an anti-imperialist position. Therefore, if we posit both non-Marxist and Marxist dependency theorists in the category of anti-Imperialism, then we need another criterion to differentiate the modernization theorists from the anti-imperialists.

WEAKNESSES OF GRAND THEORIES

Wallerstein's World Capitalist System

Any theory of social change, Wallerstein (1979) insists, must refer to a social system—that is, a largely self-contained entity whose developmental dynamics are largely internal (Skocpol, 1977). To achieve self-containment, a social system must be based on complete economic division of labor. In "The Modern World-System," Wallerstein explains the structure and functioning of capitalism as a world economic system, viewing states as but "one kind of organizational structure among others within this single social system" (Skocpol, 1977; 1976). Such a world economy is based upon labor geographically differentiated into three main zones—core, semiperiphery, and periphery—and tied together by world market trade in bulk commodities that are necessities for everyday consumption. Each zone has an economic structure that is based on its particular mixture of economic activities and its characteristic form of labor control.

In an attempt to avoid the intellectual dead end of ahistorical model building, Wallerstein grounds his theorizing in an analysis of the historically specific emergence and development of capitalism since the 16th century; however, he provides no theoretical explanation for why developmental breakthroughs occur. Similarly, in his 1974 article "Rise and Demise," the momentous consequences of the technological innovations achieved in the Industrial Revolution are much discussed, but the causes of the Industrial Revolution go unmentioned. Also, Wallerstein employs an amalgam of historians' arguments about reasons for the crisis of feudalism and then a series of teleological arguments about how the crisis must be solved—i.e., through the emergence of the capitalist world system. In other words, even though he intends to avoid taking an ahistorical approach to the social sciences, his analysis touches upon the surface by mainly appending the emergence of capitalism in Europe to the oversimplified and extremely reduced logic of his world system theory.

The most critical shortcoming of this theory can be found in its reductionism: first, a reduction of socioeconomic structure to determination by world market opportunities and technological production possibilities; and second, a reduction of state structures and policies to determination by dominant class interests. Relying upon arguments about economic conditions and world market interests, Wallerstein largely ignores other potentially important variables, such as historically preexisting institutional patterns, threats of rebellion from below, and geopolitical pressures and constraints. Without a hierarchy of dominating and dominated states corresponding to the existing pattern of economic differentiation, there is no worldwide unequal exchange, according to this theory. In "The Inadequacy of a Single Logic," Rapkin (1983) criticizes Wallerstein for his failure to take account of political-strategic factors that undermine his initial conceptual specification of the world system, which results in misleading empirical conclusions regarding its actual formation and operation.

Wallerstein's critics focus on his teleological explanations of the emergence of both capitalism and states—a crude instrumentalism in viewing the state largely as political machinery that exists to be manipulated by dominant capitalist classes for the purposes of maximizing their share of the world product. The main failure of Wallerstein's conception of the state is his neglect of the security motive in the formation and strengthening of states as a mode of political organization. Wallerstein's inattention to this fundamental dimension of statehood blinds him to the security dilemma and the other principal lessons of the classical paradigm. Consequently, all of materialist theory seems blinded to the logic of interstate politics and the crucial role it plays in world system processes.

Accordingly, grand theory must rely heavily on auxiliary theories to fill in gaps, repair tears, and more generally account for the diversity and complexity of human affairs apprehended at the world system level; however, auxiliary theories imply some measure of messiness and a loss of parsimony, and the criteria for assessing auxiliary theories and their bearings on the main theory at issue are rather problematic. Clearly, a theory cast strictly at the world system level is incapable of providing an adequate understanding of the dynamics of world leadership.

Wallerstein also argues that the modern world system is an economic but not a political unit and that the basic linkage between the parts of the system is economic. The point is not that the interstate political system plays no role in Wallerstein's theory; in fact, the political pluralism represented by this system is regarded as essential for the expansion of capital accumulation and hence for the functioning of world capitalism, but this is a rather static conception in which the interstate system is reduced to a structural constant.

Rapkin (1983) fills the gap of the grand theory's inadequacies in his examination of Modelski's political approaches to the world capitalist system. Modelski posits that the global political system has exhibited a pattern of cyclical fluctuations between (1) periods wherein a single world power has assumed responsibility for the provision of the public good of systemic order and security and (2) periods that lack the leadership of a single world power and in which order-keeping functions are either jointly managed in an ad-hoc fashion by several major powers or simply left undone. Five such long cycles are identified, each associated with the leadership of a particular world power: Portugal in the 16th century, the Netherlands in the 17th, Great Britain in the 18th and 19th, and the United States in the 20th. Modelski addresses the questions of how order is attained in an anarchical system and why it is impermanent. Rather than regarding an anarchical order as a structural constant, Modelski takes as the primary object of his investigation the variable extent of order within anarchy. He then turns this questionable premise on its head, thereby making it an explanatory consent by postulating that global order depends on functional specialization—that is, the world power assumes a variety of functional responsibilities for which ordinary states lack the requisite capabilities and incentives. The control of strategic space, for example, requires a functionally specific type of capability, which in turn is utilized for the maintenance of order, the provision of security, the organization of the world economy, as well as other system maintenance and infrastructural tasks. Modelski's political approach clearly exposes the problems in Wallerstein's world system theory and reminds us of the dangers of simplistically applying grand theories to reality. Here, the mechanical application of world system theory to the process of Korea's successful industrialization is incapable of explaining why only Korea and a few other CDSs succeeded in economic development where other countries in the same or similar situations in the world economic system did not.

Modernization Theory

Modernization theory and diffusionism are based on Eurocentricism, a view which differs radically from that of most dependency theorists who focus on the dynamics of development and underdevelopment. Modernization theorists and diffusionists argue that underdeveloped countries can become developed and can follow the Western model by emulating the capital flow, technology, and economic development of Western developed countries. That is, they imply that the path taken by Western society should be followed by underdeveloped countries too; in seeming to ignore other development models or paths, they thereby fail to consider the specific historical conditions that each underdeveloped country might face.

Most dependency theorists, on the other hand, claim that underdevelopment in the periphery is generally the historical outcome of development in the center. So, an in-depth analysis of the differences between anti-imperialistic non-Marxist and Marxist theorists of dependency is needed in order to resolve the confusion regarding the mixture of seemingly convergent but clearly opposing arguments on the simultaneous phenomena of development and underdevelopment. Further, such an analysis will contribute to our understanding of the rapid economic development and simultaneous democratization that occurred during Korea's process of modernization.

In *The Politics of Modernization*, David Apter (1965) distinguished between development and modernization:

Development, the most general, results from the proliferation and integration of functional roles in a community. Modernization is a particular case of development. Modernization implies three conditions—a social system that can constantly innovate without falling apart . . . ; differentiated, flexible social structure; and a social framework to provide the skills and knowledge necessary for living in a technologically advanced world. Industrialization, which is a special aspect of modernization, may be defined as the period in a society in which the strategic functional roles are related to manufacturing (67).

Indeed, there are as many definitions of "development" as there are scholars, and they vary from field to field. Institutionalization and democratization can be taken to be the representative criteria for political development. Furthermore, increases in income and national wealth can be utilized as an index for economic development. Most theories equate levels of development with levels of economic growth. Here, however, it is important to compare the concept of development with the concepts of modernization and diffusion.

According to Agnew (1982), modernization theory can be divided into two categories. The first category is stages-of-growth theory. Identifying five stages of economic development in mid-19th-century European societies, Rostow (1960) suggested that these stages be used as a model of development by other underdeveloped countries; however, his theory completely ignores the unique historical context and specificities of other countries. Thus, the paths that Western societies have taken are assumed to be universally applicable and of great use for late-developing countries to follow. In this view of social Darwinism, Western societies represent the center of the world in terms of development, and their experiences are to be diffused and ideally adopted by the rest of the world. The term "diffusion" should be understood in this context. The second category of modernization theory is the dual economy approach, which originated from an attempt to understand the coexistence of a traditional sector and a modern sector in the Western colonies, and to suggest the best model for colonies to use when transferring from a traditional to a modern society. In this approach, all things traditional are regarded as indices of underdevelopment.

What are the problems of such premises in modernization theory? Pieterse (1991) points out dilemmas of development discourse. According to Pieterse (1991), developmentalism is limited by the overall assumption that social change occurs according to a preestablished pattern, the logic and direction of which are known. Privileged knowledge of the direction of change is claimed by those who declare themselves furthest advanced along its course. Specifically, developmentalism is the truth as perceived from the center of power; it is the theorization of its own path of development, and the comparative method elaborates this perspective (Pieterse, 1991: 6). In most of the developmentalist approaches, dichotomous theories conceptualize social change in terms of a bipolar process—from status to contract, from mechanical to organic solidarity (Durkheim), from *Gemeinschaft* to *Gesellschaft* (Tonnies).

Thus, dichotomous conceptualizations of modernization are teleological. Modernization theory ignores the possibility that multiple paths may all lead toward the goal of modernity—democratic or totalitarian. Christian metaphors such as glory, transcendence, and mission, as well as the adoption of Western political institutions, are also strongly implied (Pieterse, 1991: 11). With regards to political modernization, democracy is often presented as formal democracy—in effect, the exercise of citizenship rights by the propertied class. Thus, indigenous forms of democratization remain unconsidered. The most important point here is that the key American theories of political modernization view democracy as contingent upon economic growth (Pieterse, 1991: 11-12). Furthermore, stage theories of political modernization could accommodate any form of authoritarianism as a necessary step in the progression toward transcendence—provided they were not communist (Pieterse, 1991: 12). Most of all, modernization theory, based on Western experience and history, posits that economic development should precede political development. In this linear view of development, the application of modernization theory and a diffusionist approach to the case of Korea fails to explain how this authoritarian or hierarchical Confucian and geomantic political culture was able to achieve economic development and democratization at the same time.

Dependency Theory

Non-Marxist approaches to dependency theory can be grouped, according to Chilcote (1981), into three categories: (1) structuralist and nationalist autonomous development (Prebisch, Furtado & Sunkel); (2) internal colonialism (Casanova); and (3) poles of development (Andrade). Marxist approaches to dependency can also be divided into three groups: (1) monopoly capitalism (Baran & Sweezy), (2) sub-imperialism (Marini), and (3) new dependency (Dos Santos). Chilcote posited Cardos' theory halfway between non-Marxist and Marxist perspectives. The Economic Commission for Latin America (ECLA) approach represents the first category of non-Marxist approaches to dependency.

The ECLA argument is based on two essential propositions. The first proposition holds that developing nations are structured into dual societies—one that is advanced and modern and the other that is backward and feudal. Furthermore, the underdevelopment of the backward side can be industrialized through state planning and control under the leadership of a nationalistic bourgeoisie. Here, the assumption is that the petty bourgeoisie would support national economic autonomy, which includes the diffusion of development into underdeveloped areas and restrictions on foreign interests. The second proposition divides the world in two: an industrial center and a periphery.

Under the scenario of unrestrained competition in world capitalism, the center appropriates most of the growth in world income at the periphery's expense. ECLA's preference for autonomous capitalist development was supported by the democratic leftists or social democratic politicians of the times, including Haya de la Torre of Peru, Romulo Betancourt of Venezuela, and Arturo Frondizi of Argentina.

Furtado (1963) examines inequalities in Brazil throughout the nation's history, tracing the shift of major economic activity and production from the Northeast to the Center-South region where Sao Paulo is situated. In his analysis, the state is intended to serve the masses by preventing a concentration of income in the privileged sectors, which it attempts by widening the market to include all segments of the population and by enhancing technological change. Sunkel (1966) seems to assume that underdevelopment is part of the process of world capitalist development and that manifestations of underdevelopment are normal. He further argues that planning and control can result in structural transformation and make development possible.

In the non-Marxist approaches to dependency theory, Casanova (1965) argues that the conditions of traditional colonialism are found internally in nations today. These conditions include monopoly and dependence, where the metropolis dominates over isolated communities; they also cause a deformation of the native economy and decapitalization, where exploitation despoils the land and discrimination is rampant. These are the conditions of marginal peoples who suffer from low levels of education, underemployment, unemployment, and malnourishment. Casanova believed that external conditions no longer have a great impact in Mexico, such that a national solution is possible. Thus, resistance can be mounted against monopoly capitalism turned inward and capitalist exploitation; however, his belief that autonomous development under capitalism may resolve the contradiction of dependency in backward nations overlooks the force of international capital, technology, and markets.

It is important to note that there is no unified body of thought called "dependency theory." Lenin might be the most important and original scholar to refer to the concept of dependency as such. In his theory of imperialism, he clearly differentiated between colonial powers (imperial countries) and colonies. At the same time, he mentioned the existence of diverse forms of dependent countries that formally may seem independent but in fact are inextricably bound up in nets of financial and diplomatic dependencies. Among very diverse and contrasting definitions of dependency, the Brazilian social scientist Santos (1970) suggests that "dependency" describes a situation in which the economy of a certain country is conditioned by another country's economic development and expansion.

The phenomenon of dependency, which is seen as a historic outcome associated with the origins of capitalism and the emergence of the international division of labor, includes several important concepts. According to Caporaso (1978), author of "Introduction to the special issue of *International Organization* on dependence and dependency in the global system," the umbrella concept that overarches both sets of articles is that of relational inequalities in the transactions among actors. These relational inequalities, which are different from attribute inequalities (e.g., differences in national literacy, wealth, or development), include unequal trade exchanges, power inequalities, and structural inequalities. In examining these relational inequalities, there are two separate levels of analysis: bargaining and structural relations. The bargaining approach is actor-oriented, focusing on differences between the capabilities of each country, and leads to an analysis of specific contexts among actors based on clashes among national interests; dependency theory, however, concentrates on structural power, which is a power of a higher order because it manipulates the choices, capabilities, alliance opportunities, and payoffs that actors may utilize. The creation of a producer cartel is an example of structural power because it decreases the number of independent supply sources in importing countries. In addition to the issues of unequal relations and structural power, approaches to dependency theory should grasp the central insight of the nation-state model as well as transnational relation perspectives.

Thus, "dependence" signifies what is commonly meant by "external reliance"; "dependency," however, cannot be defined so easily because it cannot be reduced to a single variable. It is a syndrome of related characteristics centering on a transnational alliance between local and foreign technology and capital, restricted developmental choices, and domestic distortions caused by the incorporation of less-developed societies into the international system.

Duvall (1978) sees the differences between dependency theorists and positivist social scientists as deeply pragmatic, separated by different languages, epistemological foundations, and conceptual views of the world. After identifying a number of serious obstacles to testing dependency theory that stem from deep philosophical differences between *dependentistas* and *non-dependentistas*, he suggests caution in the formalization and empirical evaluation of dependency, along with some very concrete suggestions on how to create dialogue.

Since so much of international relations is predicated upon the assumption of interdependence, mutual responsiveness, and cooperation, researchers should focus on the asymmetries that exist in the global economic system. Therefore, in the analysis of the global economic system, the importance of both bargaining and structural viewpoints cannot be overemphasized. In addition, an adequate treatment of dependence and dependency cannot be provided without drawing out the methodological implications of the transnational relations perspective. Thus, a more disciplined empirical evaluation of dependency theory is needed.

In summary, grand theories such as modernization theory and dependency theory generally fail to draw connections between the higher generalities and the historical specificities of Korea's simultaneous achievement of economic development and democratization. Modernization theory makes the flawed assumption that economic development must precede democratization, based on the Western experience of transformation from traditional to modern society. This theory's teleological or ideological inclination also hinders researchers from considering Korea's indigenous sources of cultural and historical context that have significantly shaped the course of Korea's economic development and democratization. Confucianism and geomancy are too traditional to be analyzed in this paradigm. Dependency theory, on the other hand, fails to explain Korea's ability to achieve miraculous economic performance while deepening its interdependence with a Western center. Korea's trading relations with the West have been mutually beneficial rather than lopsided or based on exploitation. Latin America's experiences with Western centers and their own military dictatorships during their attempts to achieve industrialization do not explain how Korea was able to accomplish both economic growth and political democratization under the military regime of Park Chung-hee and Chun Do-hwan from 1960 to 1987. Thus, these two grand theories fail to provide theoretical elements relevant to the analysis of Korea's simultaneous economic and political development. Problems and approaches to solutions are oversimplified and biased by these theories' political and ideological agendas. Most of all, these two theories were developed on the basis of Western and Latin American contexts. Modernization theory since the 1970s and dependency theory in the 1980s were widely adopted by Korea's academic community to explain the rapid industrialization and political instability in Korea; however, various approaches based on these two theoretical paradigms were rejected for the reason that they do not explain Korean cases. For all of these reasons, this book attempts to investigate this phenomenon from an indigenous perspective, which will be discussed more fully in the next chapter.

The central focus of the next chapter, where both the unit of analysis and the method of the analysis will be laid out, is the integral power of the state and its relations with society, including the economy. It also discusses Korea's state-society relations with regards to the role of state in the rapid economic development and the formation of the heteronomical forces that ultimately resulted in democratization; however, before proceeding to those matters, the next section will draw on Gramsci's notion of integral state as the model most closely resembling the centrality of state power in Korea. Gramsci's notion of the consensual aspects of political control is the key to understanding Korea's prototype of state centrality and the legitimacy crisis caused by the emergence of aggressive heteronomical forces in Korean political history.

INDIGENOUS APPROACH TO STATE-SOCIETY RELATIONS IN KOREA

Based on a dichotomous view of state and economy as being mutually opposed, Western liberalism upholds the virtue of the least intervention of political power in the economy; however, in Confucian political culture, where the rule of politics takes a position of precedence over the economy, political intervention is a given. Such practice is based on a non-Western and non-liberal notion prevalent in Asian countries strongly influenced by Confucianism, such as China, Taiwan, Hong Kong, Singapore, Japan, and Korea. In these countries, it is expected that the state, like a paternal presence, will lead and intervene in the economy for the good of all. In liberal thought, however, there is a neutral area within which each individual is believed to possess an inborn right to pursue his own development and advantage.

The Asian notion of state-society relations, favoring collectivism over individualism, opposes the Western notion. The main argument of this book is that Asian experiences of economic development are the result of closely interwoven relations between state and society with politics taking a position of precedence over the economy, especially in Korea. It is recognized in Korea that the current crisis stems from collusion, i.e., a corruption of traditional ideals. Under state leadership, five conglomerates were in the process of sorting out their overlapping investments in major industries, such as the semiconductor industry, each surrendering some market share with the goal of restoring the economy to solid footing.

As an illustration of ordinary people's attitudes, a recent survey (Cho, 1992: 84-85) asked: "If the government imposed a one-year freeze on wages in order to promote economic development, how would you respond?" Respondents chose between the following answers:

a) Though it causes a great disadvantage to my economic situation, I would support the government's decision so that our nation may benefit; or
b) Though it would contribute to the nation's economy, I oppose it because it causes a disadvantage to my economic situation.

Of the total respondents, 72.5 percent chose the former, while only 27.2 percent chose the latter (0.3% did not answer). Also, the so-called Five Mores campaign launched in 1991 by all major business organizations with the backing of the government urged citizens to work more, save more, export more, and live a more frugal life (Clifford, 1994: 8).

Further support for this argument is provided by the following items from a questionnaire administered to 296 students at Yonsei University in Seoul in 1987 (Wilson, 1988: 1077-1078) focusing on issues of equality.[8]

These survey results demonstrate a non-Western and non-liberal relation between state and society in Confucian Korean society. Clearly, the relation between state and society in Confucian culture, especially in Korea, differs significantly from that in the West, which is dichotomous and views them as mutually opposed. In Korea, state and society are felt to be parts of an organic whole where individual interests are incessantly coordinated and oriented toward the community's goals. This explains why 72.5 percent would approve of a government freeze on wages for the sake of the economic growth of the nation, despite the economic sacrifice each individual would have to make. More importantly, this cooperative attitude of community members would remain the same regardless of whether the regime in place was a military dictatorship or legitimate civilian government. In other words, citizens' cooperation with government economic policy does not stem from state coercion but rather from the people's consent. Thus, it would be misguided to argue that the presence of a strong military dictatorship in Korea was the main factor contributing toward the people's submission to

Table 2.1 Cross-cultural Survey on Rights of Community and Individuals.

A Cross-cultural Survey on Rights of Community and Individuals		
	Yonsei Students	American Public
The way property is used should mainly be decided:		
a. By the individuals who own it	39.5%	58%
b. By the community since the Earth belongs to everyone	58.8%	22%
c. No answer	1.7%	20%
If workers are not receiving equal treatment in terms of jobs or housing:		
a. They should strive harder so that they will receive better treatment.	26.7%	24.8%
b. The government should step in to see that they are treated the same as everyone else.	69.9%	52.8%
c. No answer	3.4%	22.4%

Source: Richard Wilson (1988, Wellsprings of Discontent, *Asian Survey*, 28, 10, October, pp. 1077-78)

the government's coercive economic policy and its resultant economic development.

Highly socialized individuals who are sensitive to the opinions of family, friends, colleagues, and the public represent the ideal in Confucian society. Such social relations make possible the national mobilization for economic development at the expense of individuals' political freedom and equitable distribution of resources. Confucian heritage provides a historical legacy of an economically interventionist state, a tradition of social and political hierarchy, and a strong nationalist sentiment underpinned by cultural homogeneity that is reinforced by external threats. Koo (1992: 18) claims that "the Park regime inherited a complex mixture of government interventions in the markets; its response was primarily to rearrange and adjust this mixture to ensure improved economic performance." Ever since the Joseon Dynasty, politics has taken a place of precedence over economy; it also produced a legacy of well-organized bureaucratic decision-making. Thus, this bureaucratic system, which many scholars identify as an element in Korea's modern industrial success, stems from its precapitalist, Confucian past. Thus, in order to be accurate, definitions of the "developmental state" need to include its source of power for national mobilization—namely, social consent. Such a historical, cultural focus helps us to avoid the error of "sweeping policy generalizations based on the alleged economic omnipotence of either state planning or markets" (Leeson & Nixon, 1988: 65). It compels us to examine the organic nature of state-society relations, especially in Confucianist societies.

To Weber, Confucianism, like Puritanism, is rational, but while Puritanism seeks control over the world, Confucianism accommodates itself to the world as it is. Thus, Confucianism prevents the emergence of modern capitalism in China, according to Weber. In *The Religion of China*, Weber argued that a lack of tension in the Confucian ethic accounted for the failure of the East to industrialize and to produce capitalism (Morishima, 1982: 1-2).

Despite differences of scholarly opinion on the impacts of Confucianism and Puritanism on capitalism, one point on which most scholars agree is that cultural characteristics related to the work ethic are the most important factors in economic success; also, they both identify such cultural characteristics as originating in Confucianism. Scholars who take a cultural approach tend to consider their approach as an alternative to existing paradigms (e.g., neoclassical, developmentalist, and institutionalist approaches); however, this cultural approach based on Confucian cultural characteristics has a critical flaw in that its level of analysis tends to be reductionist and culturally deterministic. Accordingly, these interpretations fail to rise above the psychological, sociological, and journalistic level of analysis. Clark and Chan (1992) argue that this recognition should make us wary of simplistic explanations focusing on cultural determinism, especially given the ability of non-Confucian nations like Thailand and Malaysia to follow the path blazed by Japan and the Four Tigers (Clark & Chan, 1992: 212). In addition, this approach fails to consider the relations between politics and the economy. Since the concrete historical and institutional dynamics of the specific societies are ignored, there is no mediating mechanism to bridge the cultural aspects with the sociopolitical and economic bases of this region. For instance, such descriptions do not account for the high levels of internal political opposition and mobilization found in Confucian South Korea today.

Certainly, the cultural influence of traditional Confucianism on rapid development in this region cannot be denied; however, without an analysis of precisely how this Confucian cultural legacy affected the complex interactions between state and economy, there is no escape from the charge of cultural determinism. Indeed, culture alone does not fully account for the success of high-performing economies, as the presence of differences within the spheres of Confucian cultural influence and unsuccessful economies in this region attest. At the same time, the research focuses of the three main approaches (i.e., neoclassical, developmentalist, and institutionalist) on either state or market principles is still appropriate even though they are incapable of explaining the complex interactions between state and economy due to their extreme views on either side of the developmental phenomenon. For all of these reasons, we need a political economic theory that can epitomize non-Western, non-liberal Confucian relations of state and society based on Confucianism.

In fact, some scholars wonder whether Confucianism is an appropriate variable in explaining the unprecedented phenomenon of economic development in East Asia, for even though Joseon Dynasty Confucian policy elevated agriculture over other economic pursuits, the agriculturally oriented economy remained relatively poor. Accordingly, Confucianism is often blamed for the poor agricultural economy of the old dynasty. Harris (1989: 411) claims that the "Confucian tag is just silly, a word to divert the search for real explanations into vanity." He suggests: "If Confucianism explains high economic growth today, it must equally explain the lack of it yesterday."[9] Harris presumes that Confucianism remains essentialist and unchanged over time; however, such a perspective is inappropriate, for the Confucianism of the Joseon Dynasty differs from that of modern Korea; it changed in response to both internal and external challenges. Kuah (1990: 375) aptly points out that "Confucianism is not just an ancient school of thought that has remained static since its inception. On the contrary, it is dynamic, evolving to suit changing circumstances and conditions, . . . which takes it out of the realm of cultural artifact and into the realm of functioning theory. It is this adaptability that has enabled Confucianism to remain relevant throughout the ages."

Another point to be considered is that the main economic activity which Confucian ideology supported was not commerce or industry but agriculture. Believing that commerce/industry would corrupt human nature, Confucians tightly controlled commercial and industrial activity. Nowadays, though, Confucianism no longer conceives of agriculture as the backbone of the nation. What is important in this Confucian ideal is not which specific economic sector Confucianism supported but rather the ideological roots of state intervention in the economy and the government's position of superiority over the economy. Taylor (1985: 197-198) defines the political culture of a country "as the *dominant ideology* . . . a moral framework of ideas and values that endorse the existing system." He differentiates this approach from the conventional political culture approach—namely, the theory of political socialization (Almond & Verba, 1963).

Interestingly, Almond and Verba find that a key to the stabilization of the political system in Britain, for example, was the process of political socialization involving the learning of the necessary political values through family, school, mass media, religion, and other communication. Through this process, consensus regarding the ruling dominant ideology was reproduced and sustained; however, the critical flaw of Almond and Verba's version of political socialization theory is that by limiting their focus to the system's stability as originating from coercive political control, they fail to account for that aspect of political stability which stems from social consent. Accordingly, they (1963) found it "deviant" for many working-class voters to support the Conservative Party, thereby prescribing the deferential characteristics of British civic culture.

Parkin (1971) identifies, within the paradigm of the dominant ideology, three different sets of values that belong to the dominated class: deferential, aspirational, and accommodative. All accept the status quo, but there are differences between the first two sets of values—the deferential also accepts his low status, while the aspirational strives individually to raise his position within the system. In this case, the status quo is accepted but within a moral framework that emphasizes communal improvement as defined by the system. This is an accommodative set of values which amounts to a negotiated version of the dominant ideology (Parkin, 1971: 92). These three sets of values contrast with the value of opposition, which aims to counter and replace the dominant ruling ideology. The concept of the aspirational and accommodative values of the dominated class provides us with clues as to how the dominant ideology maintains its ruling legitimacy: these two values of the dominated class become the source of social consent to the dominant ideology. Therefore, as Parkin (1971: 92) aptly notes, "we no longer have to subscribe to Almond and Verba's rather simplistic notion of Britain's deferential civic culture." Thus, the stability of a system can be maintained without coercion—that is, through aspirational and accommodative value systems as well as deference.[10]

This paradigm explains how Confucian state hegemony during the Joseon Dynasty was strengthened by its policy of highly valuing agriculture while scorning and limiting industry and commerce. Most who were involved in agriculture were easily co-opted by this policy and saw themselves as gaining an advantage by supporting Confucian ideology. The majority of these aspirational and accommodative classes later transformed into forces of opposition against Japanese colonial rule. During the Seoul era, though, the majority of people remained silent in regards to the military dictatorship, tacitly signaling that they consented to the sacrifice of their political freedom for the sake of economic development. The existence of this tacit majority was then used by the Park regime to oppress militant oppositional social forces.[11]

Theoretical Issues in the Indigenous Approach

Recently, in a rejection of the basic developmental models and paradigms that originated in the dominant school of modernization theory in the 1950s and '60s, new perspectives on the problems of Third World societies have emerged that are based on their own experience and an attempt to overcome the Eurocentricism that has occupied a central position in the theoretical literature on development. This rejection of the Western model of development is widespread, and new efforts are being made to establish a theory or paradigm (i.e., indigenous models of development) to properly explain real phenomena of development in the Third World (Wiarda, 1991 [b]). Ake (1979: 106) also argues that "There is a tendency to explain the problems of Third World societies in terms of their lack of the characteristics of Western societies." Indeed, sociology scholarship tends to foster a conception of development as the acquisition of the ideal characteristics of Western societies.

The timing, sequences, and stages of development in most Third World nations are so different that virtually all Western percepts require fundamental reinterpretation when applied there. The percepts include the so-called "demographic transition," the role of the emerging middle classes, military behavior and professionalization, the role of peasants and workers, the presumption of greater pluralism as societies develop, and notions of differentiation and rationalization (Wiarda, 1991 [b]: 134). In the case of late development theory, the role of state and the essential relations between the state and society causes economic and political developmental paths very different from those projected by Western standards.

The search for indigenous approaches has been spurred by the limitations inherent in "the extent to which sociological theories as forms of conclusions arising from empirical studies of facts of social life in European and American society can be regarded to be valid and reliable for the study and understanding of the facts of social life and social problems in African, Asian and Latin American societies" (Akiwowo, 1988). In this regard, Akiwowo (1988: 155) raises some important questions. To what extent do these conclusions apply to developing countries, and to what extent can generalizations from empirical studies of Third World societies be accepted and extended to European and American societies?

From this perspective, indigenization can be seen as "the development of national social science communities that are self-reliant, self-sufficient and self-directing, in other words, autonomous and independent, with respect to all aspects of the vital functions of the community, including its ability to relate to other communities on an equal, reciprocal basis" (Loubser, 1988: 179). Akiwowo (1988: 158) defines "indigenization" as "an empirical, culture-bound but emancipatory approach to the subject matter, including the recognition of anima in nature. Indigenisation also is the view that the study, analysis and explanation of the phenomenon called society must take into account, as much as possible, several elements which either make up society, or which account, in full, for social realities."

Based on the general lack of such indigenous interpretations in the literature on the late development and democratization of Korea, this book recognizes the need for a reformulated understanding of the developmental state. More specifically, the new direction of inquiry should begin with the fundamental concepts underlying the developmental state. Castells' definition of the "developmental state" provides insightful clues as to how the developmentalist literature on Korea's developmental state can be re-interpreted toward this end: "a state is developmental when it establishes as its principle of legitimacy its ability to promote and sustain development" (Castells, 1992: 56). By "development," here, Castells means the combination of steadily high rates of economic growth and structural change in the productive system, both domestically and internationally. He argues, though, that this definition is misleading unless we specify the meaning of "legitimacy" in a given historical context. If the indigenous approach is in fact the key to explaining the cases of Third World countries, including Korea, then the typical notion of state-society relations based on the Western path of economic and political development deserves a second look.

State-Society Relations

Habermas (1991) uses the term "public sphere" in two different ways. First, he uses it in reference to the bourgeois public sphere, which began in late

17th-century England and 18th-century France. Those phenomena accompanied the rise of a market economy, capitalism, and a bourgeoisie. The structural transformation of the public sphere is the process whereby a public forum emerges as a place for citizens to govern themselves from below through informed discussion and reasoned argument. Second, Habermas uses "public sphere" to refer to a more generalized and expanded public realm of life in modern society (of which the bourgeois public sphere is one type) with a wide variety of power relationships between state and society.

Habermas' notion of the public sphere plays an important role in this chapter's discussion of indigenization, specifically in discussing relations between state and society, which constitutes this book's central framework. Habermas places the public sphere squarely in "the tension-charged field between the state and society" (Huang, 1993: 219). At the same time, however, his bourgeois public sphere is a sphere that evolved in opposition to the state. Thus, the trinary conception of state, society, and the public sphere collapses once more into a binary conception that juxtaposes society and state. In other words, in Habermas' scheme, the public sphere becomes merely an extension of (civil) society in its democratic development against the state monopoly of power. In Onuf's scheme, state power is represented by the rule of hegemony and hierarchy, while civil society (including the public sphere) is represented by the rule of heteronomy as discussed in chapter 1.

Huang (1993), Madsen (1993), and Solinger (1993), in their search for ways to institutionalize a public sphere under modern circumstances in Chinese political history, raise an interesting question regarding the binary concept of state-society relations. In their view, it is possible to have a public sphere with a distinctively Asian cultural style, and many Chinese intellectuals seem to agree. There have been noticeable scholarly attempts to understand state-society relations in China from an indigenous perspective. Specifically, Madsen (1993: 187) points out that the concept of public sphere can provide the focus of a productive cross-cultural debate on this issue. The concepts of bourgeois public sphere and civil society as they have been applied to China presuppose a dichotomous opposition between state and society. If we adhere to such a presupposition, then we run the risk of reducing the debate to little more than an argument over whose influence was greater in the phenomena under discussion—that of society or state.

According to Huang and Madsen, such a dichotomous understanding of the relationship between state and society is an ideal that has been abstracted from Western experience and thus is inappropriate for the Chinese case. They argue instead for a trinary conception, with a third realm between state and society, in which state and society both participate. This third realm, Huang and Madsen explain, adopted characteristics and institutional forms over time that must be understood on their own terms; this is an indigenous understanding of the power dynamics by which political issues were resolved in China with regards to state and society. Based on an investigation of formal civil lawsuit cases, Huang found that (1993: 228), from the 1760s to the end of the Qing Dynasty in 1911, only 221 of 628 civil cases from three counties progressed all the way to a formal court session and adjudication by the magistrate. The majority of the remaining cases were resolved during the middle stages (i.e., after the filing of the complaint but before a formal court session) through the interaction of formal and informal justice systems. The mechanism for those settlements was a semi-institutionalized dialogue between magisterial opinion and community/kin mediation. This indigenous understanding of state-society relations in China can serve as a model for the state-society relations which this book attempts to explain in Korea's democratization and economic modernization.

Civil Society

Civil society is another conceptual framework where such an indigenous debate could occur. The mainstream view in Western social science seems to be that political backwardness in Asian countries is generally attributable to the lack or absence of civil society. Wakeman (1993) described how civic organizations in former East European countries were able to topple communist regimes in contrast to the absence of civil society in the occasions like the Tiananmen Massacre of 1989 in Communist China. Asian countries have been criticized as having "no dissident intellectual circles, no Catholic church, no autonomous labor unions, no old democratic parties" (Cheek, 1992: 127).

But what is "civil society"? In the late eighties, usage of the term suddenly became popular among American scholars; however, the looseness with which it is currently being used is also partly due to an inherent ambiguity in the traditional formulation of the concept (Madsen, 1993: 187). Although it was widely used in Western social theory during the 18th and 19th centuries, the term "civil society" had all but fallen out of use by the mid-20th century. Usage was revived, however, in the late '70s by Eastern European intellectuals and dissidents. Thus, for Adam Michnik in Poland, "the spontaneously growing Independent and Self-governing Labor Union Solidarity" was an indication that, "for the first time in the history of communist rule in Poland, 'civil society' was being restored, and it was reaching a compromise with the state" (originally from Michnik, Letters from Prison and Other Essays, quoted in Wolfe, 1989: 17, requited from Madsen, 1993).

In Hegel's view, for example, civil society was a kind of society formed by individuals who had become independent of traditional loyalties; this was a sphere of life concerned not with the fulfillment of traditional loyalties but rather with the reciprocal meeting of needs. Concretely, and for most other classical Western political theorists, civil society consisted in the utilitarian, contractual relationships so characteristic of the bourgeois society that had been created by a modern market economy. In Hegel's *Philosophy of Right* and Marx's *The Jewish Question*, civil society included economic relations as well. Similarly, theorists like Tocqueville emphasized the importance of premodern religious and political traditions for imparting stability, solidarity, and moral discipline to modern civil society. In Tocqueville's view, although civil society was modern and market-based, it also had to retain premodern and nonmarket foundations if it was going to play a role in preserving democratic liberties; however, modern Western social theory has never resolved the issue of how to reconcile the modern market with the premodern moral traditions that have somehow made it function. The term "civil society" carries all of the ambivalences toward modern market society bequeathed to us by our wisest social theorists (Madsen, 1993).

Eventually, the development of this bourgeois public sphere led to the creation of a new kind of state that depended for its legitimacy on the assent of a rationally constituted public opinion. This was the origin of liberal democracy in Western Europe and North America, but in the twentieth century, even in the West, the public sphere had been emptied of much of its content. Under the power of the modern mass media, corporate capitalism, and the powerful bureaucracies of the modern state, "public relations" and propaganda (of various levels of subtlety) had overwhelmed the capacity of an increasingly atomized citizenry to develop an informed understanding of the public good through rational discussion. Accordingly, Habermas' account of the public sphere explains the rise and fall of democracy in the modern West. In his view, even though modern Western societies retain forms of constitutional government that were developed in the 18th and 19th centuries, they are in danger of losing the moral capacity for democratic rule due to the erosion of their collective capacities for informed, rational public discussion of the common good.

Seeking indigenous forms of civil society similar to the notion of its Western origins, Madsen (1993: 189) enumerates a mélange of modern and premodern forms of social organizations in recent China: "some scholars are calling this whole range of associations—everything from democracy salons to organizations of *getihu* to clan associations to gong clubs—civil society." He further argues that these indigenous organizations and institutions might eventually contribute toward the creation of a democratic public sphere without which, he argues, China may be pushed closer toward anarchic fragmentation (Madsen, 1993: 190).

Despite scholars' efforts to identify alternative forms of organizations that have functioned similarly to the Western notion of civil society, Habermas' observation of civil society throughout Western political theory seems to differ drastically from the Confucian origins of civil society or the public sphere of dissenting voices in the Hanyang era, as explained in chapter 1. According to Habermas, civil society provides an opportunity for the creation of a democratic public sphere; that is, a democratic public sphere is not simply handed down from a benevolent state—it arises from a voluntarily organized citizenry. Civil society and opposition forces during the Hanyang era, however, actually did come from above or from within the Confucian power structure, unlike the Western case. For this reason, this book gives precedence to the indigenous understanding of the generic political concepts or institutions that caused Korea to have a historically and ideologically unique perspective of its own. In support of this approach, Wiarda importantly points out that the political development literature is largely biased and ethnocentric, derived primarily from the Western experience of development and, thus, of limited applicability to the Third World, whose culture and history follow entirely different logic. The political development literature has been accused of wreaking havoc on developing nations by denigrating and undermining local and traditional institutions before the modern ones had a chance to grow, thereby leaving many emerging nations with neither traditional nor modern institutions but rather an institutional vacuum (Wiarda, 1991b).

Emphasizing the importance of an indigenous approach, Madsen (1993: 190) suggests that "Perhaps the only way of assessing the significance of such groups would have been from the inside—from a perspective that could have gained insight not simply into the quantity of their material resources but the quality of the moral commitments that gave them their vision and their strength." Now that the rationale for an indigenous approach has been laid out, let us entertain some questions on the political aspects of such civilian groups. Specifically, what is their historical background? And what features distinguish them from the Western understanding of state-society relations?

Strong State and Weak Society

Another theory to examine with regards to the debate on the strong state in Korea and its role in the course of development is the debate on strong state and weak society—one of this book's central themes. During the 1970s and '80s, debates over the concept of states as strong or weak prevailed in the discipline of comparative and international political economy. Authors such as Dyson (1980), Katzenstein (1985), and Krasner (1984) used the dichotomous concept of strong and weak state capacity; however, as research progressed, the usefulness of this clear-cut way of classifying states' capacity soon became the subject of serious criticism.

Wilks and Wright (1987) and Sulieman (1987) demonstrated that, even within a single nation, significant variations occur across sectors in terms of the degree to which the state is able and willing to intervene in the economy. More specifically, contrary evidence is available for weak and strong states: Hall (1986) has shown the gradual breakdown of an étatiste approach to economic policy in France; also, Samuels (1987) pointed out how business sectors in Japan effectively resisted state control while regarding state regulation of markets as indispensable to economic growth. Also, there are many examples showing counterevidence in states that are generally regarded as weak. For example, the United States (Skocpol, 1980; Dyson, 1980) and Canada (Hall, 1986), which have traditionally been included in the weak category of state capacity, showed a strong will to intervene in their economies through policies such as federal R&D support and agricultural subsidies in the United States as well as centrally controlled monetary policy in Canada and Britain.

A growing amount of evidence suggests that the original conceptions of strength and weakness, offered almost exclusively at the macro level, are too crude to begin to account for the rich variety of state-society relations that are being documented. "Such founding has led to calls for a disaggregated view of the state, with more attention devoted to the different levels—micro, meso, macro—at which the state confronts the economy . . . What is required is a more precise specification of what Lehmbruch has called the interorganizational logic of relationships among macro, meso, and micro levels" (Atkinson & Coleman, 1989: 49). At the meso level, i.e., that of sectors of the economy, the matter of state strength cannot be explained by appealing to constitutional norms, the embeddedness of the party system, recruitment practices or the degree of state centralization. Atkinson and Coleman (1989: 50) argue that "Much greater attention must be paid to specific bureaucratic arrangements and to the relationships that the officials involved maintain with key societal actors."

In an attempt to bring some order to the wide range of relations that prevail between public and private sector actors in advanced capitalist systems, Katzenstein (1976) formulated the concept of policy networks at the sectoral level. He argued that the amount of centralization in society and in the state, and the degree of differentiation between the two, were the critical variables in the establishment of policy networks. What matters here, in regards to our discussion of the indigenous origins of Korea's developmental state, is to establish a list of criteria by which to measure the degree of centralization and to identify objects toward which we should direct our research. Atkinson and Coleman (1989), using Katzenstein's formulation, argue that "In evaluating weakness and strength at the sectoral level, it is critical to determine, first, the degree to which ultimate decision-making power is concentrated in the hands of a relatively small number of officials and, secondly, the degree to which these officials are able to act autonomously."

Overall, the problem with most approaches in the debate over the concept of weak and strong state is that the major analyses are confined to phenomenal boundaries. That is, they attempt to explain the various degrees of state strength more in terms of appearance than structure. Thus, they tend to overlook constitutional norms, the embeddedness of the party system, recruitment practices, and the degree of state centralization, focusing instead on the presence of military dictatorship and its state monopoly capitalist industrial policy, which became an easy target for later developmentalist studies on Korea's rapid economic development (1960-1980s). Without a specific historical case study on how Korea's strong state tradition was established and a study on the integral nature of the state power that was established through the Confucian state's moral and ideological hegemonic leadership, such a fixed approach on the notion of strong state and weak society will fail to discover the true source from which Korea's developmental state originated; rather, it will reify the role of the Park regime's military dictatorship in Korea's developmental phenomenon.

What is important in this book is to discover what creates a certain kind of constitutional norm, party system, and, more importantly, degree of state centralization. If we take for granted the degree of centralization in a country and attempt to account for the relations between its state and its economy, then it would be commonsensical to assume that a strong state can generally control its economy more than a weak state can. This view is nicely summarized by Atkinson and Coleman (1989: 52): "the more centralized, autonomous and elitist a state's bureaucratic-administrative core, the greater this capacity."

Migdal (1988) raises an important question in his examination of two former British possessions, Sierra Leone (a weak state) and Israel (a strong state)—he asks why only a few Third World states have developed the capacity to actually implement policies of any sort. One necessary condition, he concludes, for the development of a strong state is a rapid and generalized process of social dislocation—i.e., the evisceration of existing institutions of social control—brought on by the incorporation of peripheral societies into the capitalist world system.

However, this sort of dislocation characterized Sierra Leone as much as it did Palestine, so world-systemic forces alone, Migdal concludes, do not convey the whole story. The other requirement for the development of a strong state is a colonial power that channels resources to a more or less centralized state or state-like organizations that are thereby able to extend their control throughout the entire society. Such was the legacy of British imperialism in Palestine, astutely exploited by Zionist labor leaders via the so-called Jewish Agency.

By contrast, where the colonial power channeled resources to locally based chiefs, landlords, and other strongmen, social control became diffused through a web of non-state organizations, creating strong societies. This was the legacy of British rule in Sierra Leone and the typical progeny of colonialism more generally. Migdal suggests that social scientists need to examine the long-term intended and unintended effects of outside political forces—particularly the assertion of autonomous state interests—on colonized societies as well as the impact of the expanding world market.

Migdal's points and observations play a crucial role in the explanatory scheme that this book has set forth from the outset. Specifically, Migdal's point on the massive social dislocation caused by colonial power bears some relevance in our discussion of how Korea's colonial experiences under imperial Japan contributed toward the industrialization of Korea's economic infrastructure and, at the same time, caused the Confucian hegemonic and heteronomical forces to unite in nationalism. The Japanese colonial power channeled resources to a more or less centralized state apparatus in order to be able to extend its control throughout Korean society as a whole. There is no question that the Japanese colonial control was one of the most atrocious forms of colonial control in the 20th-century history of imperialism. Rather, it would be more relevant to recognize how Japanese colonial control motivated the consolidation of hegemonic, hierarchical, and heteronomical forces and resulted in the creation of aggressive nationalism throughout the entire colonial experience.

NEO-CONFUCIANISM AS GOVERNING IDEOLOGY OF THE JOSEON DYNASTY

Confucianism and Korea

From the early Three Kingdoms period (AD 343-668), Korea was ruled by centralized Confucian bureaucratic systems. During the Goguryeo Dynasty (37 BC-AD 668), a national university system for Confucian education was established (AD 372). In parallel with the national school, there were also many private Confucian academies (*kyong-tang*). During the Goryeo Dynasty (935-1392), two national institutions were devoted to Confucianism, thereby establishing it as the nation's official school of learning. One of these institutions offered a national civil service examination established in imitation of the T'ang Dynasty model during the reign of King Kwang-Jong (949-975), and the other was the National Confucian Academy (*Kukchakam*), founded in 992. Thus, "When Confucianism took over as the state ideology of Joseon Dynasty in 1392 [from Buddhism], the political system had already been developed as a bureaucratic state and for centuries government officials were selected through a civil examination system where the main subject was the Confucian classics" (Helgesen, 1998: 104). Indeed, the civil service exam served as a mechanism by which the court recruited national bureaucrats on the basis of individual proficiency in the literary skills of Chinese prose and poetry and scholarly mastery of Confucian texts. The recruitment of bureaucrat-officials through competitive examinations on Confucian literature and the state's support for Confucian educational institutions became the major impetus for the reform of the dynasty's bureaucracy as this exam officially introduced an achievement criterion. There were also provincial schools, the *Hyangkyo*, which performed that which the Kukchakam was accomplishing in the capital but at the level of the regional prefectures.

Starting in the 14th and 15th centuries of the Joseon Dynasty, the influence of Confucianism on thought, society, and government began gaining strength and remained dominant until the opening of the country in the late 19th century. In fact, even in contemporary Korean society, the legacy of Confucianism is impossible to ignore. Yang and Henderson (1958: 81) argue that "So closely were Confucianism and Korea intertwined during this latter long period that Korean history cannot be understood without Confucianism while the study of Confucianism itself will be greatly enriched by resorting to its Korean experience." Yet, the powerful ideology of Confucianism has never been recognized as the legitimate unit of analysis, even though it has been one of the most enduring sources of ideological influence on political, economic, and cultural aspects of Korean society. Most importantly, this book argues that Confucianism can explain how Korea recently achieved rapid economic development and democratization; yet, interests in Confucianism have largely featured in classical studies aiming to understanding the past.

References to Confucianism in Korean history actually date back even further to the Han Chinese colony in Pyeongyang (108 BC-AD 313). Confucianism first began gaining influence in the government in the Three Kingdom period (57 BC-AD 668). More specifically, in Goguryeo, a Confucian University (*Taehak*) was established (AD 372). The Goryeo Dynasty succeeded the culture of the Shilla Kingdom, bringing Confucianism; however, due to the prominence of Buddhism during the Shilla Kingdom, Confucianism seems to have made little impact upon Goryeo society until the end of that dynasty, by which point its influence had significantly increased. Yang and Henderson (1958: 85) point out that "With the Mongol conquest of Korea and of China, Korea's comparative isolation from China ended and a new era of close contact began." In 1290, An Hyang (1243-1306), a student of the classics, had an opportunity to learn more about Neo-Confucianism as represented by the Chinese scholar Chu Hsi, and brought Chu Hsi's "Collected Commentaries" to Goryeo, disseminating his teachings among the gentry class (Neo-Confucian literati) and re-establishing the National Confucian Academy, the *Seongkyungam*, which later turned into *Seongkyunkwan*.

Neo-Confucianism involved the reinterpretation of Confucius' original tenets by Chu Hsi, a leading scholar in the period of the Sung Dynasty in China. Accordingly, it is essential to understand Chu Hsi's fundamental philosophical perspectives, including those pertaining to nature and human beings. He formulated a theory of the "Supreme Being" as a source of beginning and the way in which human affairs are governed. The Supreme Being was a theoretical concept whereby Chu Hsi explained how everything was formed and governed. In his theorization, Chu Hsi formulated a dualism where two basic elements—law and matter—work as the ultimate cause of all things (Bruce, 1923: 126). Chu Hsi's main goal, in his reinterpretation of the original Confucian classics, was to establish a unified, strongly centralized governing institution to recover the original model of the state. Also incorporated into Neo-Confucianism were other competing schools of thought, such as Buddhist metaphysics and the Taoist concept of the universe.

In the central institutions of the highly centralized state, Chu Hsi's Neo-Confucianism became dominant. The reasons for the wide acceptance of Chu Hsi's Neo-Confucianism in late Goryeo were manifold. Intellectually, late Goryeo saw a decline in the moral and spiritual legitimacy of Buddhism, whose monks had succumbed to court influence and neglect of their spiritual and moral duties. Moreover, Buddhism suffered from its association with the much-hated Mongols. Political factions played their part too. Against this historical and political background, many unemployed scholars and lower-level government employees advocated a Confucian renaissance in late Goryeo in order to come into their own within a more powerfully organized Confucian bureaucratic state. In this unsettled period, Confucianism appealed to Korean officials on many counts: as a vehicle for reconstituting a stronger, centralized, bureaucratic state in which scholar-officials could prosper; as a weapon honed through centuries of Chinese history for use against Buddhism; as a quasi-religion whose wide cosmogonic presumptions and metaphysical scope were an effective substitute for Buddhist philosophy; and as a great advance on the humanly and socially centered Confucianism of earlier times, providing some religious satisfaction and opening many intellectual and cultural doors as well. In short, for Confucianists like the group of civil scholar-officials that had been ousted from office in the military putsch of 1170, or those who had suffered from invasion, occupation, and Buddhist hegemony, Chu Hsi's Neo-Confucianism seems to have offered a much-needed institutional and intellectual home, conservative in instinct yet fresh and stimulating to the people of its era (Yang & Henderson, 1958: 86; Lee, 1984: 165-171).

The Foundation of the Joseon Dynasty and Neo-Confucianism

Facing the Red Turban marauders from the north and Japanese pirates from the south, two military commanders—Choi Young and Yi Seong-gye—rose to prominence and became influential factors in the politics of the late Goryeo Dynasty; however, these military heroes were markedly different from each other in terms of their social status and political orientation. And though they both came to enjoy great influence in the capital, they vehemently disagreed over Goryeo policy on China, where the Yuan and Ming Dynasties were vying for power.[12]

In the local provinces, Neo-Confucianism gave rise to a new literati comprised mostly of unemployed local scholars and lower-level local government officers. Their search for a new world based on Neo-Confucian tenets set them on a collision course with those who had vested rights in the Goryeo Dynasty. These local Neo-Confucian literati attributed the chaos of the socio-economic and political system of the late Goryeo Dynasty to the unregulated power of Buddhism and the aristocracy. Thus, their ultimate goal was to end Goryeo and establish a new kingdom based on Neo-Confucian doctrine. This local Neo-Confucian literati, also called the *sadaebu*, wanted a leader who could represent and execute their political ideals. General Yi Seong-gye was their choice, and the sadaebu supported General Yi in his rivalry with General Choi Yung, a loyal supporter of King U.

General Choi Yung, incidentally, was also the father-in-law of King U (1374-1388) and represented the royal family and governing aristocracy of the Goryeo Dynasty. His political orientation was based on old conservative forces that mostly favored the Yuan over the Ming Dynasty. In 1388, the Ming Dynasty claimed the Northeastern territory of Goryeo, which was occupied by Yuan's Sangseong Commandery. Choi was determined to strike at the Ming Dynasty by invading the Liaodong region of Manchuria. Unlike Choi, however, Yi Seong-gye was "not the scion of famous family with a long history" (Eckert et al., 1990: 102); his immediate family was comprised of military commanders stationed in the Hamheung, a remote Northeast area of the Korean Peninsula, and he had advanced his political status through military exploits in numerous battles. As a member of a new military class with an anti-Yuan and pro-Ming political stance, General

Yi was supported by the newly emerging Neo-Confucianist literati, the sadaebu. Denying the legitimacy of the Yuan Dynasty, members of this new literati class, such as Jeong Do-jeon and Jo Jun, conspired to reform society according to the political doctrines of Neo-Confucianism. General Choi, having grown suspicious of the true intents of Neo-Confucianist literati and Yi Seong-gye, began to seek means of removing Yi. Choi, who represented the existing power of Yuan China and Buddhist Goryeo, collided with General Yi, who represented a new Ming China and the Neo-Confucian sadaebu. Ultimately, General Yi won.

The momentum for Yi Seong-gye and his sadaebu followers to take action came when "Choi began to draw up plans to attack Liaodong as part of a wider campaign to conquer the Ming Dynasty after he received a report stating that Ming had established the *Cehollyeong* Commandery as a means of directly controlling the territory that had formerly been under the command of the *Sangseong* Commandery" (Han, 2010: 27). Yi had opposed the idea of attacking Liaodong from the start, believing that "such an action would not only undercut his political ambitions but also put the very future of the state at risk by fostering a hostile relationship with the newly rising Ming" (Han & Hahm, 2010: 27). Leading his army back from *Wihwa* Island, in a nearly bloodless coup, "Yi Seonggye finally ousted the King and Choi from power, seizing political control himself. Thus, he grasped the historic moment for the overthrow of [G]oryeo and the establishment of a new dynasty" (Eckert et al., 1990: 101).

Why was the Confucianism of Goryeo unable, despite official encouragement and the proliferation of private Confucian academies, to take root in the social consciousness and political culture of the time? In short, the influence of Buddhism had been penetrating all levels of society ever since the Three Kingdoms era. Shilla Buddhism was greatly secularized to meet the day-to-day needs of the time; 90 percent of the population was Buddhist. Wang Keon, founder of the Goryeo Dynasty, believed that his success depended solely upon the favor of Buddha. Buddhism had become the state religion and cultural legitimation of the polity of Goryeo. Due to the widespread influence of Buddhism, Confucianism in the Goryeo Dynasty had no opportunity to flourish or influence the cultural tradition of Goryeo society; however, by the time of the reign of Seong-Jong (1567-1608) in the Joseon Dynasty, Confucian scholarly bureaucrats had become a group that possessed unquestioned political power.

At this time, a divergence took place between the meritorious Neo-Confucian central bureaucrats and resistant Neo-Confucian scholars in the countryside, which shaped the factional political strife in the mid-Joseon Dynasty and the emergence of Confucian civil society and dissenting voices. Yang and Henderson (1958: 87-88) aptly summarize this divergence as follows:

> Jeong Do-jeon, politician as well as scholar, was General Yi's right hand during the establishment of the regime and was largely responsible for the Yi policy of elevating Confucianism to the role of national cult in place of Buddhism. Never before, probably not even during the great days of Shilla Buddhism, were the intellectual and political traditions of another culture to have such pervasive influence on the society, government, and thought of the peninsula. . . . It should first be noted that, under the influence of the scholars of late [G]oryeo and of the revolution they sponsored, Chu Hsi Confucianism became the official creed of government and the aristocracy relatively suddenly after its serious introduction to a Korea which had previously known only a rather modest Confucian tradition. . . . Scholars like Jeong Do-jeon and Kwon Keun supported Lee [Yi] Seong-gye in his revolt and in his claims of the legitimacy of the new dynasty. Many other scholars did not. The leader of these, Cheong Mong-ju (pen name *Poeun*), believing that Yi's revolt was immoral and that the new regime could never, in Confucian terms, represent the legitimacy that was [G]oryeo's, opposed Lee Seong-gye and was killed by one of Seong-gye's sons at Songdo as the [G]oryeo Dynasty fell. . . . Yaeun [Kil, Jai], retiring in 1389 to his home province of Kyeongsang-do, set up his own school and trained about one hundred students in Chu Hsi Confucianism and in his own interpretation of legitimacy [origins of the Sarim, the Neo-Confucian literati groups in the countryside that exerted great influence upon central government and education and recruitment of Confucian students and later contributed to Confucian civil society as dissenting voices]. . . . Yet in the meantime a tradition of dissent had been established which, although occasionally interrupted, proved lasting. Indeed, these scholars and their successors have been called, because of their retirement to the country, the *Sarim hakpa* or the "Mountain-Grove School." The private school in Kyeongsang-do was one of the first of its kind outside the capital and had many successors later in the dynasty.

Extraterritoriality of Confucianism

With the royal edict of Sejong of 1421, the new Chinese Confucian philosophy was declared the foundation of national governing ideology: "the Crown Prince himself should worship at the Confucian shrine and humble himself before the Confucian sages." Now, even the sons of kings had to bow before the sages and rule in accordance with the state philosophy. The edict was a striking symbol; for Korea almost as momentous (though different in character) as when the Divine Right of kings yielded to the concept of the rule of law in Europe (Yang & Henderson, 1958: 91), which had come to the fore in England under the reign of James I (1603-1625). This new adoption of a strongly centralizing and tightly organized governing ideology originated from China; however, it had the potential to create a power vacuum or power divide mainly because it was foreign-born. The power structure of the new Joseon Dynasty was composed of the royal family and "*kaekuk kongshin* [Dynastic Foundation Merit Subjects]" (Lee, 1984: 172) in the center and newly emerging power group of local Neo-Confucian scholarly bureaucrats in the periphery. As briefly mentioned before, it was widely believed that the mandate (or divine right) to govern was realized through the royal family, but the actual task of governing was given to Neo-Confucian scholarly bureaucrats who had learned how to govern through their studies of Chinese classical literature. Furthermore, the exclusive rights to manage the Royal Shrine and Confucian Shrine were given to the National Confucian Academy, the Seongkyunkwan.

Thus, there were three main stakeholders, each with subtly different perspectives on Confucianism. To the kings and royal family, Confucianism was the most important source of political legitimacy for the foundation of the Joseon Dynasty. To the meritorious subjects, Confucianism was a crucial tool to equip themselves with administrative powers and privileges, which were often used to check and balance the power of kings and the royal family. To the Confucian students in Seongkyunkwan, Confucianism was a source of learning in general but also a way of learning the manuals and principles by which the entire ruling class was to be judged, including the King and bureaucrats in the center; moreover, students were given exclusive rights to manage all operations of the Confucian Shrine. These three different perspectives and political agendas within the Confucian ruling system and structure produced subtle power dynamics during the Joseon Dynasty. In addition, though, there was originally an anti-dynasty group of Neo-Confucian scholars in the countryside. Thus, a political environment existed wherein four major forces were constantly competing for power.[13] As a result, Confucianism served as a governing/legitimizing ideology and a mechanism of checks and balances with a built-in voice of dissent.

This situation created extraterritoriality within the power structure—the Seongkyunkwan occupied the center, forming occasional alliances with the Sarim in the localities or kings and central bureaucracy. As descendants of high-level meritorious elites in the center, and as future elites themselves, students in Seongkyunkwan were given the exclusive right to voice their dissent with the behavior of the King, the central bureaucracy, and all aspects of state affairs. The highest academic institution, the Seongkyunkwan, worked as a major political tool for studying, upholding, and promoting the governing ideology of Confucianism and as a semi-loyal force of opposition against the Confucian central power and elites. Yang and Henderson (1958: 88-89) evaluate the impact of this power divide among ruling and opposition Confucian scholars and bureaucrats:

> [t]he tradition of the scholar aloof from the government which was the special mark of the [Joseon] Dynasty tradition of dissent is alive today. While a connection between the question of dynastic legitimacy and the factional struggles of later times has not yet been established, the *Sarim hakpa* tradition, the formation of literati groups around key national problems and the contest of these groups for central power provide an almost continuous leitmotiv to [Joseon] dynasty history and may later constitute one avenue of approach to some useful generalization on Korean socio-political phenomena.

This notion of extraterritoriality, or the power gap within the Confucian ruling structure, occupies a central position in the main arguments of this book because this power divide that was built into the Confucian ruling structure later expanded and intensified to become a national force of resistance under colonial Japanese control, which in turn later enabled an aggressive civil society to topple the military regime that had led the industrialization and economic development in modern Korea. Understanding Confucianism as both the source of political legitimacy and, at the same time, the origin of dissenting voices in Korea is the key to explaining the simultaneous phenomena of economic development and democratization in Korea.

The strong state tradition and the legitimacy of state intervention in the economy are the historical origins of the modern developmental state; the extraterritoriality within the Confucian political system is the origin of Korea's belligerent civil disobedience and civil society. This book also argues that these two seemingly opposite political principles have been thoroughly embedded in the beliefs and behaviors of the general populace and widely accepted as norms. The consensual aspect of Korea's strong state tradition originates from this historical background.

Confucianism and Modernization

Among scholars, interest in the role played by Confucianism in East Asia's economic growth and development has increased steadily: Confucianism is discussed as a main source of the cultural characteristics that contributed to the economic development (Bellah, 1957; Berger, 1988; Berger & Hsiao, 1988; Redding, 1990; Wong, 1986; Spengler, 1980; Song, 1990; Pye, 1985; MacFarquhar, 1980; Hofheinz & Calder, 1982; Kuah, 1990; Morishima, 1982; Almond, 1990; Drakakis-Smith & Bale, 1992; Zeigler, 1988). In particular, Zeigler (1988: 187) points out that it was neither the strong state nor bureaucratic dominance over underorganized business and co-opted labor that caused economic success in Asian regions; it was the cultural legacy of traditional Confucian culture that made such economic success possible under the guidance of state corporatism.

In the Japanese case, more specifically, Morishima (1982) examines how Confucian ethics were adapted and transformed over time under historical conditions that were unique to Japanese culture and society. This Confucian ethic, he argues, became the fundamental basis for the unique relationship between state and business that Western observers have identified subsequently with the Japanese formula for economic growth. Defenders of Confucianism also contribute to this East-West essentialism. In discussing the causes of Taiwan's booming economy, Gold (1986: 126) identifies several contributing factors that stem largely from Confucian culture: (1) ambition for self and family, (2) high valuation of education, (3) role of family as an economic unit, and (4) entrepreneurship. Hofheinz and Calder (1982) identify the following Confucian values as responsible for the rapid growth of NICs: (1) guidance from a paternalistic government, (2) the role of the family in society, and (3) an anti-legal tradition (Kuah, 1990: 381). Similarly, Kahn (1984) attributes their success to (1) the Confucian emphasis on education, (2) the need for accomplishment, (3) dedication to work, (4) family and obligations, and (5) de-emphasis of self. Kahn further sees the Confucian ethic as possibly better suited than Western liberalism in many ways to the pursuit of industrialization, affluence, and modernity. Further, Kahn (1979) identifies a "Confucian ethic" built on the values of hierarchy, discipline, control, and motivation that will defeat the West in economic competition, given the latter's excessive reliance on the values of egalitarianism, rivalry, pay-offs, and self-indulgence. Others treat Confucianism as an affective culture that offers an alternative to Western traditions of individualism, efficiency, and rationality as a basis for development. Tai (1989) describes Confucianism in terms the following features: loyalty to family, emphasis on education, diligence, investment, paternalistic management style, reliance on personalized business networks, respect for authority and government, and willingness of the political elites to forgo maximizing their own material benefits rather than engaging in crony capitalism and exploitation. In this perspective, Tai (1989) claims that the successful developmental states in East Asia succeeded due to such Confucian traits as harmony, patronage, this-worldy traditions, and "feelings." These traits provide a stark contrast with the West's dynamism, individualism, other-worldly religions, and rationality, respectively. This is how Confucianism was treated by scholars as a source of national characteristics but not as a source of unit of analysis for rigorous scholarly research. All of the above-mentioned studies contrast sharply with Weber's (1951) denunciation of Confucianism as a detriment to capitalism in Asia.

PLACE AND POWER

Considering that geomantic principles served as one of the most important factors in the foundation of the Joseon Dynasty, an indigenous approach toward understanding Korea's state-society relations as well as the origins of state power and heteronomical forces should be considered within the context of place and power. As mentioned in chapter 1 and in the sections above, Neo-Confucianism in its original form already embraced many elements of other philosophies, such as Taoism and Buddhism. In the process of mutual adaptation, these branches of thought were merged with geomantic principles where symbols of power were sought in the natural landscape—specific topological configurations and orientations—that corresponded closely to the celestial charts. The notion of "place" in the foundation of the Joseon Dynasty was as influential as Neo-Confucianism due to the long tradition of *pungsu jiri sasang,* or *docham sasang* (the Korean version of geomancy adopted from the early Three Kingdoms period). Such influence in the formation of Joseon's political symbols and power structure will be discussed more deeply in chapter 3.

Similar to the Roman belief that certain places manifested spirits "or *genius loci*, [that] reflected the uniqueness of a place, distinguishing one place from other places with which it might be confused . . . inhabit[ing] all places of significance" (Crowe, 1995: 75), people in Joseon society believed that geomantic principles significantly influenced various aspects of their everyday life. They located the Will of Heaven, and thereby the source of power, in the topological configuration that resembled an ideal astronomical chart. In addition, they considered geomantic principles when building architectural artifacts such as houses, political and religious institutions, and even tombs. Interestingly, this powerful ideology functioned as a critical means for legitimizing the Confucian ruling ideology. In fact, the location of Hanyang was chosen for the capital city because its topological configuration bore a striking resemblance to the sacred part of the astronomical chart. In other words, the state's positioning of itself in relation to the natural landscape greatly contributed to the people's perception of the state's political power as legitimate in the Confucian Joseon Dynasty. Together, Neo-Confucian political ideology and geomancy became the two main features that were most evident in the maps, architectural designs, and city layout of this historical era.

In this ancient method of locating the most ideal spot in the landscape, the concept of sacredness and profanity plays a vital role. In modern geography, contrasting concepts of center and periphery seem to have replaced this dichotomous concept of sacred and profane. Shils (1975) sketches an image of the modern center as a seamless integration of three components that govern the society: dominant values/beliefs, institutions, and elites. On the other hand, according to Wiarda (1991b: 48), "the periphery contains dissenting habits, values, and beliefs." Authority expands the center into the periphery. Through its institutions, the center uses a smorgasbord of rewards and sanctions to facilitate the acceptance of its decisions and values." As Wiarda points out, Shils failed to consider that the periphery can affect the very nature and capabilities of the center. In the case of Hanyang, for example, the fact that the dissenting voices and heteronomical social forces were also co-opted by the sacred space (the modern version of the center) actually contributed toward consolidating the Confucian state hegemony during the Joseon Dynasty. During Japanese colonial rule, heteronomical forces played the most significant role of a "Resistant National Movement" against the Japanese, moving the heteronomy out of the passive and co-opted position that it had occupied during the Joseon era; historically, though, all of these heteronomical forces have been centered in the capital city, not only during the Japanese colonial rule but even during the modern period of Korean resistance against the Park regime. The

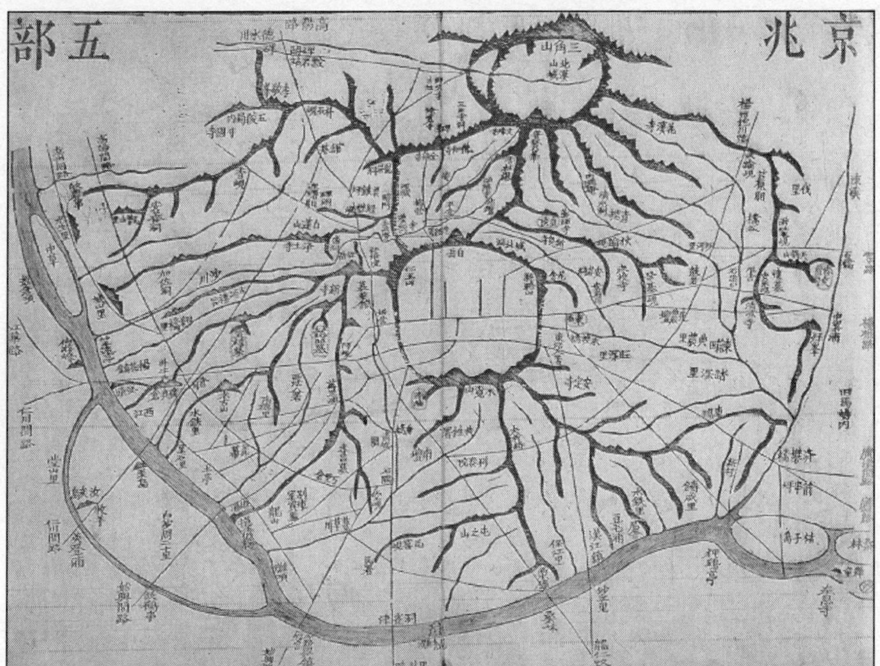

Map 2.1 The Five Districts of Hanyang: Representing Mountains and Rivers. Two major features expressed in this map are mountains and rivers pictured. Kyungjo oboo-do. Hand-colored Woodblock Print. Kim Cheong-ho, 1861. See, Hur (1994), p. 64.

heteronomical forces concentrated in the center capital, and the capital became the central area where political power was reproduced. Therefore, people viewed the capital city as the center of power and the source of state hegemony. This is a unique phenomenon in Korean political history whereby space is strongly related to the reproduction of components of the power structure.

Map 2.1, *Kyeongjo obudo*, [The Map of Five Districts of Seoul: Representing Mountains and Rivers], drafted in 1861 (Hur, 1994: 64), serves as a good example of this point. Two major codes incorporated into this map are mountains and rivers, the former in black and the latter in blue. This map shows how greatly the natural landscape mattered to the people of the Joseon Dynasty. The strong influence of geomantic principles is illustrated by this map's focus on mountains and rivers. As mentioned before, the people believed that the breath or Will of Heaven emanated from a certain type of mountain arrangement near a certain shape of river that possessed a certain ideal direction. This belief system explains why so many maps from that era only describe the forms of mountains and rivers. In these maps, nature was the main code, but the other important code was buildings of politically important Confucian institutions. Map 2.2 vividly demonstrates this tendency as well. All the locations described on these maps are Confucian political institutions—palaces, the Guardian Deities of the State, the Royal Ancestral Shrine, the Confucian National University, and the Six Ministries—institutions tellingly surrounded by mountains and rivers. These features provide us with a legible illustration of how the capital city of Hanyang consolidated Confucian monumentality and promoted Confucian political hegemony in society. Such is the knowledge that we can deduce from the maps created during this period. Here, we find good reason to utilize these maps as a way of reconstructing knowledge about the Joseon era from which they emerged.

Additional clues about the prevailing ideology and political purposes of the ruling social elites can be drawn not only from the distribution of landholdings but also from the entire system of spatial relations in city design (Safdie, 1984; Wheatley, 1971; Harvey, 1989; Creel, 1995; Lim, 1994a). Factors that influence a city's design relate to the social relations that function within it. The physical and spatial form of the city is itself "a representation of economic, social, political, and cultural relations and practices, of hierarchies and structures, which not only represent but also inherently constitute these same relations, hierarchies, and structures of everyday social life" (King, 1995: 218). Geographical representations of the capital city of the Joseon Dynasty (Hanyang) articulate the historically and culturally contextualized Confucian relations of state and society in

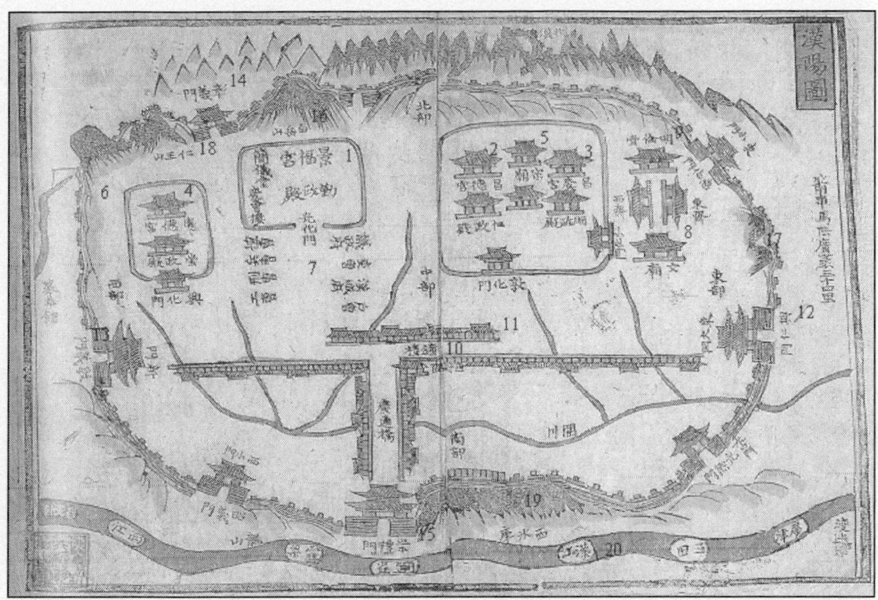

Map 2.2 Hanyang in the Joseon Dynasty: Representing Confucian Political Monumentality and Natural Integration. 1. Kyungbok Palace, 2. Changdeok Palace, 3. Changkyung Palace, 4. Kyunghee Palace, 5. Jongmyo (Royal Ancestral Shrine), 6. Sajik (Guardian Dieties of State, not shown in map), 7. Yukjo (The Six Ministries), 8. Monmyo (Confucian Shrine), 9. Seongkyunkwan, 10. Chonggak, 11. Sijeon (Market), 12. Heunginmoon (East Gate), 13. Doneuimoon (West Gate), 14. Changeuimoon (North Gate), 15 Soongryemoon (South Gate), 16. Mt. Baekak, 17. Mt. Nak, 18. Mt. Inwang, 19. Mt. Mokmyok, 20. Han River. Hanyang-do. Map of Seoul. Hand-colored Woodblock Print. Wi Back-kyu. Manuscript 1770 AD, Woodblock Print 1822 AD 24.3 x 35.3 cm. Private Collection. See, Hur (1994), p. 77.

Korean political culture that consolidated the central power of state over society and legitimized state intervention in the economy based on the sustained centrality of Confucian state hegemony. In addition to reconstructing those relations, this book aims to examine how Confucian state hegemony and the legitimacy of state intervention in the economy, which became the fundamental principles of the developmental state in modern Korea, were first realized in the choice of site for the capital city and the city's Confucian monumentality (i.e., city layout, architectural structures of important institutions, and their arrangements). On this point, Duncan and Duncan (1988) provide theoretical insight into the role of geographical features as descriptors of social relations. What this book owes to them is the belief that "virtually any landscape can be analyzed as a text in which social relations are inscribed." They go on to claim that:

> It can be argued that one of the most important roles that landscape plays in the social process is ideological, supporting a set of ideas and values, unquestioned assumptions about the way a society is, or should be organized. . . . If landscapes are texts which are read, interpreted according to an ingrained cultural framework of interpretation, if they are often read "inattentively" at a practical or nondiscursive level, then they may be inculcating their readers with a set of notions about how the society is organized: and their readers maybe largely unaware of this. If, by being so tangible, so natural, so familiar, the landscape is unquestioned, then such concrete evidence about how society is organized can easily become seen as evidence of how it should, or must be organized. (Duncan & Duncan, 1988: 123)

In line with this argument, Confucian political ideology was intensively reflected in the choice of this site as the capital city and in the city design, both of which took advantage of geomantic principles that had penetrated into the minds of the people even before the Joseon Dynasty was established. The sustained centrality of state power over society in general, and over the economy in particular, as represented in the capital city Hanyang helps us to understand how space is related to power relations in society. The fact that Hanyang features in one of the most famous folksongs, and the fact that the modern Korean government was planning to restore the Joseon Dynasty's Six Ministries Street, suggests that Hanyang has held more than just physical, geographical meaning for the Korean people since the Joseon period. The capital city was the political arena in which state hegemony was propagated and the people's recognition of that legitimacy was incorporated and identified. In turn, this identification with place contributes to the place's meaning. Indeed, it is through this process that the physical space becomes a political place.

The term "space" has more objective connotations than the term "place." King (1996: 188) sees space as a fossil that bears traces of past economic epochs. Agnew (1993: 252) views space either as a board/backdrop across which social processes move and are imprinted or a set of fixed containers for cultures and social processes. The concept of place, on the other hand, he categorizes into three different factors: locale, location, and sense of place. The paths and projects of everyday life, to use the language of time-geography, provide the practical glue for place in these three factors. A sense of place can be projected onto a region or nation and give rise to regionalism or nationalism, respectively. Thus, while "space" is generally regarded as a metric, compact area, "place" involves a conception of topological space in which diverse scales are brought together through networks of internal and external ties, thereby representing people's political and social identification (Agnew, 1993).

To the persistent voice of Henri Lefebvre, we owe the concept that command over space is a fundamental and all-pervasive source of social power in and over everyday life (Harvey, 1989: 226). As Lefebvre (1976: 33) explains, "There is a politics of space because space is political. It only appears to be politically neutral because the production processes going into shaping it are no longer in evidence." Spatial and temporal practices always express some kind of class or other social content, and are more often than not the focus of intense social struggle. Lefevbre (1976: 31) holds that "If space has an air of neutrality and indifference with regards to its contents and thus seems to be purely formal, the epitome of rational abstraction, it is precisely because it has already been occupied and used, and has already been the focus of past processes whose traces are not always evident in the landscape." Giddens explains how the reproduction of structures of domination and power are closely related to "the spatiotemporal extension of activities, so that what happens within a society or locale is shaped in part by the forces operating at the extremes of its extensions" (Shapiro, 1992: 89). Indeed, the space of the capital city was highly ordered and controlled, as were the times when it was accessible; thus, the city can be read as a sort of text. Harvey (1989: 226-227) argues that ideological and political hegemony in any society depends on the ability of the ruling class to control the material context of personal and social experience. For this reason, the materialization and meanings given to money, time, and space are clearly connected to the maintenance of political power.

These theoretical perspectives put forth by Agnew, Lefebvre, and Harvey aptly explain why, at the beginning of the Joseon Dynasty, a new social elite class, the sadaebu, implemented a new policy of land reform that included a new tax system. This reform began with the undertaking of a cadastral survey—an official register of the quantity, value, and ownership of real estate—which was used in appropriating taxes on landholdings throughout the country. Then, in 1390, all existing registers of public and private land were set aflame and destroyed. The next year, the basic statute governing the new land system, the Rank Land Law (*Kwajeonbeop*), was promulgated. Its terms provided for stipend land, taken only from the Kyunggi region around the capital, to be allocated to members of the official class in accordance with the rank that each had attained. This land reform symbolized the downfall of the Goryeo Dynasty itself, and the increase in state land brought about a corresponding increase in government revenues, which secured the economic foundation of the new dynasty of Joseon (Lee, 1984: 164).

The Joseon government implemented this cadastral survey of landholdings to strengthen the power structure of the dynasty and sadaebu. Comparison with the experiences of other nations reveals that such a cadastral policy in different circumstances can be used to bring about stabilization of the power bases, according to the desires of the state. Lefebvre (1976: 385) observes that one of the ways in which homogeneity of space can be achieved is through total pulverization and fragmentation into freely alienable parcels of private property, to be bought and traded at will upon the market. In fact, Turgot, French Minister of State and an eminent economist with physiocratic and liberal leanings, commissioned the accurate cadastral mapping of much of France precisely because he sought to support private property relations, to disperse economic and political power, and to facilitate the free circulation of commodities both within and outside of France (Harvey, 1989: 255).

Maps from Korea's past provide clues as to the relations between power and place in those eras. Such a map is not simply a copy of an objective reality but a product of social construction; there is a way in which the map reveals the world by code. More specifically, a map is a cultural artifact constructed by series of accumulated "choices made among choices, every one of which reveals a value" (Wood, 1992: 108). For a map to be made, some degree of selectivity is necessary; the cartographers cannot include every object that exists in the physical world. Logically, a map is inevitably shaped by the intentions and purposes of those who make it. In the Confucian Joseon Dynasty, the government monopolized the right to produce maps. The technology and tools were also in the hands of a few educated Confucian scholars. Thus, it was mainly the Confucian ideology that was reflected in maps of this period.

Another significant factor in mapmaking during this period was the ideology of geomancy (*pungsu jiri sasang* in Korean)—the art of adjusting the features of the cultural landscape to the cosmic breath (*gi*) so as to minimize bad luck and maximize good luck through the creation of a topological configuration similar to that of the sacred part of the astronomical chart. The concepts found in the ancient Chinese pseudo-science of *feng-shui* were not limited to China alone; indeed, as mentioned earlier, the Romans also believed that certain places manifested spirits, and such were the geomantic principles that significantly influenced the everyday life in Joseon society. They located the Will of Heaven, a source of power, in topological configurations resembling the ideal part of the astronomical chart. Leading the elites to choose Hanyang as the capital city, this pervasive belief functioned as a crucial means for legitimizing the Confucian ruling ideology. Most importantly, by situating the capital city, which was a symbol of their power, in a natural landscape resembling an ideal astronomical chart, the ruling elites greatly enhanced the legitimacy of their rule in the eyes of the masses. Together, Confucian political ideology and geomancy became the two main features to be represented and highly emphasized in the maps of this epoch.

The hierarchical structure of a society or political community can be expressed in many forms of spatial organization. For example, the most salient feature of Hanyang in terms of spatial organization is that a dichotomous concept of sacred and profane space was intensively applied to various aspects of its spatial organization. Interestingly, the history of Western cities features a similar dichotomy. Shapiro (1992: 92) finds that "the Middle Ages . . . was a hierarchical assemblage of places. There was the sacred and the profane, the celestial and the supercelestial, and, what was most important for church authority, the earthly world was to be read as a symbolic reality with referents in the transcendent, heavenly world."

To obtain a full picture of where this city layout originated, we must look back into the distant past. Since Hanyang, as a center of power, authority and material production, was located on a site believed to be an earthly realization of the ideal archetype of Heaven, this functioned as a source of infrastructural power for the centrality of Hanyang in national affairs. Western culture tends to have a similar attitude toward its cities. According to Crowe (1995: 111), the *polis* was a man-made cosmos, whole and complete unto itself, with its own intrinsic order, rules, laws, balances, place, history, and nature. Although the term *polis* refers to the place where a city resides, together with its hinterland, its essence was every bit as historical and human as it was locational. The original design used for the capital city Hanyang underwent two stages of major transformation, in terms of its dominant social and political ideology as well as its layout, before arriving at the current configuration that today is known as Seoul. These changes stemmed from local-global interactions. The first global influence came from Japan, which introduced imperial capitalism, thereby modifying traditional Confucian relations between state (politics) and society (economy). The city layout of Kyeongseong reflected those transitions. The second global influence was US geopolitical influence after World War II, which brought an international or multinational context to the capital city Seoul.

Generally, such interaction with global forces is believed to bring a process of cultural and social homogenization on a global scale, reducing particularization; however, as King observes, this local-global nexus is a process of dialectic nature. Quoting McGrew, King (1995: 221) argues that "as globalization universalizes different spheres of modern social life, it simultaneously encourages particularization, by relativizing both place and locale, so that the construction of difference and uniqueness results."

In sum, our sense of place and city provides us with a foundation upon which we have constructed culturally related meanings to make sense of the natural and the built worlds in which we live. While the origins of our sense of place may seem remote to us today, they continue to be reflected in ordinary experience (Crowe, 1995: 90). This is the starting point from which this book inquires into the origins of non-Western, non-liberal Confucian relations between state and society in Korean history, which served as infrastructural sources of the principles that gave birth to the developmental role of the state in modern Korea. For this purpose, this book approaches state hegemony and the role of the developmental state in an indirect and symptomatic way through relations among power and spatial organization, city monumentality, and architectural structures.

Confucianism, Geomancy, Taoism, and Ancient Cities

What is geomancy, and how exactly does it relate to Chu Hsi's philosophy of Neo-Confucianism? Answers to these questions will address the main point that this book seeks to explain: namely, how did geomantic principles, combined with the state ideology of Joseon's Neo-Confucian doctrine, contribute toward the formation of state centrality in Korean history? In order to answer these questions, this section starts with the notion of Heaven. In Chu Hsi's Neo-Confucian philosophy, "Heaven" is identified as the ultimate element in the dualism between law and matter. Neo-Confucians also describe Heaven as the "Supreme Ultimate" or "First Cause." In Neo-Confucian belief, Heaven or the Supreme Ultimate is the infinite First Cause and the Supreme Ruler (Bruce, 1923: 283), and this manifests in the form of a personal and righteous Being who rules and judges in the affairs of men as the Law (Bruce, 1923: 294).

Chu Hsi spelled out the way in which Heaven, the Supreme Ultimate, is the Law of the Universe and Final Cause. He believed that this Final Cause, which is inherent in matter, is realized in the politics of Earth. Bruce (1923: 190-191) explains that "The Decree of Heaven," according to Chu Hsi, "is like the command of a sovereign." Heaven itself was considered as being like an Emperor which mankind is obligated to obey even though its will may run counter to his own bodily desires (Bruce, 1923: 191). *T'ien*, the Chinese word for Heaven, is equated with the Ruling Power, the Empyrean, the Law or Heaven's Decree. Such was the view of Nature in relation to human and political affairs. Geomancy meets with Confucianism and produces synergic effects in that both find the Final Cause or the Way from Heaven. Confucianism, as a governing ideology upheld by the ruling class, had long been widely accepted in Asian culture throughout the land. It was given to the masses as a moral hegemony and regulatory and legal framework of governance. Within this ideological system, people's status, roles, and functions—as well as their options—were significantly regulated. Geomancy was popular beyond the categories of class; both ruling and ruled accepted geomancy as a *modus operandi*. Confucianism was formal and official, while geomancy was informal. When these two combined, they not only produced synergic effects upholding the state power based on the mandate of Heaven but also internalized the regulatory aspects of the governing ideology of Confucianism: geomancy softened the official, formal, and regulatory frameworks of Confucianism for the ruled and internalized the Confucian regulatory belief system into a part of their lives. Geomancy played such a role in state-society relations throughout Korean history, as will be explained more fully in the coming sections.

Geomancy

Whereas Neo-Confucianism interpreted Heaven (i.e., Nature) as the Ultimate Cause of everything, geomancy was the technology that explained how Nature articulates Heaven's will. As an old saying states: "Feng shui [geomancy, *kanyu*] is a combination of *tian* (天) *ling* (靈), *di* (地), *li* (利), *ren* (人) and *he* (和)" (천, 령, 지, 이, 인, and 화 in Korean, respectively). This means that the *feng shui* is auspicious if the heavenly influences are auspicious, the geographical features are beneficial, and the actions of man are in harmony with the social, cultural, and political situations. This phrase consists of just six words; yet, its implications are very complex and significant. To enjoy *tian ling*, several things are required: an understanding of the influences of cosmology on the earth, a knowledge of the way in which astronomy and astrology influence the orientation of man's dwellings, the beneficial disposition of the stars and the cycle of changes, an understanding of the Confucian classics as well as the *I-Ching*, and an awareness of the weathering processes and the forces of nature (e.g., wind, rain, snow, sun, tides) upon buildings and their surrounding environment. "*Di li*" refers to knowledge regarding the magnetic fields and their effects on man, the appropriate site for buildings in order to tap the *qi* or energy of the earth, the characteristics of various topographical and geographical features of land forms (e.g., hills and valleys, flat land and undulating land), the influences of physical environmental factors on buildings both internally and externally, and the orientation of buildings for maximum comfort and conducive physical environment. "*Ren he*" refers to man's relationship with others and to his surrounding environment; thus, it is affected by social, cultural, and political influences.

Lip (1995) explains the origins of geomancy by way of the term *kanyu* (堪輿, meaning heaven and earth), an abstract term used to represent the pseudo-physical science of climatology and geophysics. *Kanyu* is the art of placing, siting, and orienting a building in harmony with its surroundings; however, *kanyu* also involves the search for balance in nature and the creation of harmony in the home and work environment. In addressing the cultural and social issues of a particular society, *kanyu* makes reference to a wide range of natural, metaphysical, and cosmological influences: "*ming* (命, fate), *yun* (運, lucky and unlucky spells), *feng shui* (風水, geomancy), *daode* (道德, virtue) and *dushu* (讀書, education, experience, exposure, upbringing, cultural and social contacts, actions)" (Lip, 1995: 61).

The practice of *kanyu* originated in the West Han Dynasty (3rd century BC). People believed that the earth, being a living thing, had *qi* (energy or life) (Lip, 1995: 61). Exactly how much *qi* a site possessed depended on its topography and surrounding physical conditions. An undulating site with revitalizing *qi,* or *shengqi* (生氣), was thought to be good for those who dwell upon it. In contrast, a site with little *shengqi,* or one that had some *siqi* (死氣, harmful energy), would have an undesirable influence on the dwellers. In north China, a desirable building site was one facing south with hills behind and a lake in front, because the hills would protect the building during winter from the cold and dusty north winds. By facing south, the building would receive the warmth of the sun and a view of the lake. This was considered desirable, and in this way, surrounding physical features were thought to exert favorable or unfavorable effects on buildings either directly or indirectly (Lip, 1995: 62).

Geomancy played one of the most significant roles in the emergence and demise of political power in Korean history even as *feng shui* "increasingly became a private practice during the Yuan (1271-1368) and Ming (1358-1644) dynasties" of China (Bruun, 2003: 34). In light of how extensively this belief system impacted every realm of political affairs and the formation and demise of political power in traditional Korean society, geomancy, or *pungsu jiri sasang* (*pungsu* = wind and water; *jiri* = geography; *sasang* = thought), must be included in any effort to construct an indigenous model of political theory that explains the developmental state and democratization in modern Korea. There is certainly considerable validity to this perspective, for the ruling monarch was a member of a lineage that was believed to coexist ontologically on earth and in the heavens above, and was the pivotal figure in all ritual procedures. The royal ancestors themselves were believed to possess supernatural power, and divination of their wishes was in the hands of a group of priestly augurs, experts in scapulimancy who were sufficiently important in the administrative hierarchy to warrant the recording of their names on the oracle scapulae and plastra (Wheatley, 1971: 55-56). Originally, this had been a prerogative of the Son of Heaven, who alone could offer to Heaven the supreme sacrifices and thus maintain parallelism between the macro- and microcosmos, without which no state could prosper (Wheatley, 1971: 116).

Taoism

According to Chu Hsi's interpretation, there are endless forms of law and matter, which are the two basic elements. "These transformations are traced back to two modes of Matter represented in the symbols by the two I (儀), which are the divided line, thus, – –, and the undivided line, thus, — " (Bruce, 1923: 127). This is how Taoism understands the constant changes of the universe.

"However, these ceaseless rounds of changes originated from 'a Final Cause,' which makes the cosmos finite and at the same time generates an endless 'Flux' of combinations of changes born of the Infinite. This is the infinite as the ultimate cause beyond which thought itself cannot reach, and which is therefore termed the 'T'ai Chi', or 'Supreme Ultimate (Being)'" (Bruce, 1923: 128).

For the purposes of this book, it will be useful to comprehend the ideologies underlying this culture's sense of cosmic order. Further explanation on this order is provided by Bruce:

> The Supreme Ultimate by its energy produces the positive ether. Once energy reaches its limit, inertia follows. By inertia, the Supreme Ultimate produces the negative ether, and when inertia reaches its limit, energy returns. Thus, energy and inertia, in alternation, become the source of each other; the distinction between negative and positive ether is pre-determined; and the Two Modes stand revealed. By the transformation of the positive ether and the union therewith of the negative ether, Water, Fire, Wood, Metal, and Earth are produced. These five ethers are diffused in harmonious order, and so the Four Seasons proceed in their course. The Five Agents are the one negative and the one positive ether; the negative and positive ethers are the one Supreme Ultimate; and the Supreme Ultimate is essentially the Infinite. Each of the Five Agents are endued at its birth with its own nature-principle. The substance of the Infinite and the essence of the Two Modes and Five Agents unite in mysterious union, and consolidation ensues. The heavenly principle becomes the male element, and the earthly principle the female element. The two ethers by their interaction produce All Things, and universal production and reproduction follow in an unending stream of transformation. (Bruce, 1923: 129-130)
>
> "The Five Agents, therefore, correspond to the five cardinal virtues on the one hand, and to the four seasons on the other." (Bruce, 1923: 155)

This cosmic order was wide-reaching and comprehensive, as best explained by Lip:

> Everything under the sky can be classified by its nature or element. There are five elements and they are called Wuzing (五行, the five Elements: Gold, Wood, Water, Fire, and Earth). Colors, seasons, orientations, and tastes are classified under the Elements. . . . It is important to note that the relationship of elements, orientations and numbers is not to be taken literally but rather as hidden meanings and unseen cosmological influences. It must also be stressed that the theory and balance of yin, yang and the Five Elements is central to Chinese thinking. (Lip, 1995: 63)

As Lip proceeds to explain, the concepts of balance, harmony, and discord were fundamental to Chinese thought at that time. "China's ancient philosophical approach to numerology is found in the *I-Ching*. The word *yi* (易)

Table 2.2 Relationships between the Virtues, Elements, Seasons, Colors, and Directions.

Virtues	Elements	Seasons	Colors	Directions
Reverence	Gold (Metal)	Autumn	White	West
Love	Wood	Spring	Green	East
Wisdom	Water	Winter	Black	North
Righteousness	Fire	Summer	Red	South
Sincerity	Earth		Yellow	Center

represents the changeability of the state of all things and the interaction and relations of the negative and positive qualities of things in nature. Confucius used the ancient numerals (Eight Trigrams) of negative (*yin*, 陰) and positive (*yang*, 陽) signs to form the sixty-four hexagrams for making reference to the Chinese system of cosmology" (Lip, 1995: 62). In turn, "these two 'Forms' produced the four Symbols, which, again, produced the eight Trigrams, the eight Trigrams served to determine the good and evil issues of events, and from this determination was produced the successful prosecution of the great business of life" (Bruce, 1923: 126-127). This is how Chu Hsi understood the formation of this world and the way in which things occur. Such understanding of the universe and "Supreme Being" seems to be based on Taoist philosophy and *I-Ching* (classics on the ever-changing phenomena of nature and experience) (Bruce, 1923: 137).

The essence of geomancy is that the relative configurations of landscape and water flows are regarded as directing the flow of the universal *qi*, or "cosmic current," which with the help of a specialist—namely, a geomancer—can be brought to realize in society, the optimum advantage for a person in terms of wealth, happiness, longevity and procreation as well as the prosperity of a country and political system; similarly, a malicious flow of *qi* may bring disaster. "In geomancy, the world was conceived as a continuum in which all acts, natural and supernatural, conscious, and unconscious, were linked in a subtle manner, each with the next. In this worldview, the incorrect performance of an act, such as the misorientation of a building, was not merely doomed to fail in achieving its desired objective but also would bring unforeseen and uncontrollable consequences. Conversely, if the correct manner was applied at the right place and time, then the procedures would reflect not only what had gone before, but also what was about to happen" (Pennick, 1979:8). The flow of *qi*, an ultimate source of power and righteousness to humans, is influenced by all natural bodies and human constructions, which either repulse, redirect, or catch the *qi* depending on several variables (Bruun, 2003: 3).

The concept of the earth having a center has been embraced by cultures throughout the world. This center point was commonly believed to serve as a pivot about which everything revolved. It was thought to remain fixed despite the spinning of the heavens, even during earthquakes. The Omphalos at Delphi, as the oracle of Apollo, was seen as the center of the Greek world. As legend has it, the site was found by Zeus, who had sent out two eagles—one to the west, the other to the east—and where their paths crossed, the center of the world was identified. That was "Omphalos," a word originally meaning "navel" but now generally used to refer to any divined geomantic center (Pennick, 1979: 44).

Interestingly, the Chinese origin of *feng shui* draws much of its philosophy from the Neo-Confucian learning that arose with Chu Hsi and his contemporaries in the 12th and 13th centuries (Bruun, 2003: 5). The rise of geomancy as a political technology in China relates to the increasing intolerance of state power and its penetration into local society in China. Thus, geomancy effectively worked as a political technology for reading and realizing the will and power of Heaven, the Righteous Way. As Bruun (2003: 7) confirms, "[A]t a general level, [these alternatives] act as competing rationalities offering alternative explanations of causes and effects." Geomancy is a complex outcome of both remarkable historical unity and great cultural diversity, affecting a radical encounter between state rationalism and popular cosmology, and thus both diffused and in a continuous process of change (Bruun, 2003: 9).

In conclusion, Neo-Confucianism, Taoism, and geomancy all together significantly contributed to the establishment of a new political regime in 1392 in Korea. These three philosophical or ideological belief systems had been extensively ingrained into the minds of the masses as well as political elites and thus formed the fundamental basis of political culture. While Neo-Confucianism sought the Will of Heaven as the mandate to govern, Taoism sought to explain the fundamental principles by which cosmological events and human affairs occur. Geomantic knowledge and beliefs were human ways of finding and locating those topological and environmental configurations where the Will of Heaven is manifested and to comprehend the way in which the world is composed and operated. The complex combinations of these three belief systems played a critical role in the construction of important political institutions and their buildings, which symbolized the power of the center, government, elites, and state. The basic method of singling out the political power was to dichotomize the sacred and profane through city layout, architectural monumentality, and major changes in governing ideologies. Ancient cities in Asia, compared to those in the West, clearly reflect such principles. This book will examine how these principles were adopted to reflect the centrality of state power and its relations with society, thereby revealing the real aspect of state power and its relations in Korea during the developmental period and process of democratization.

Ancient Cities

"As the city was built in the image of the cosmos, so, in reverse, the image of the city was taken as the enduring symbol of God" (Pennick, 1979: 152). Thus, the ancient technology or pseudo-science of finding the landscape that most closely resembled the most sacred part of the celestial chart was favored by rulers in ancient regimes. Many scholars and practitioners (e.g., astrologers and geomancers) have spoken of the long-lasting influence and effectiveness of such practices in early England. Pennick (1979: 153) observes:

> The positioning of cities was always deemed of utmost importance, not merely from the admittedly vital considerations of trade, transport, water supply and agriculture, but also from the geomantic criteria of spiritual value, horizon landmarks, sacred springs and holy hills. Cambridge, for example, was set like Rome upon seven 'hills'. Durham's blind spring, indicated by the famous Dun Cow, formed the nucleus of the city. Dunstable was founded at the crossing of the four Royal Roads of England. . . . The abandonment of existing cities and the resettlement of their populations in a more favorable place upon an alignment is on record as having been performed on several occasions. The most celebrated instance was that of the removal of the city and cathedral at Old Sarum to a new site in the nearby river valley, New Sarum or Salisbury.

Indeed, from the beginning of human civilization, place and power have been inseparable. Kings and ruling elites believed that they could maximize their political legitimacy by locating the palace and the capital city in a site where the *axis mundi* was realized. Here, the *axis mundi* is an abstract line where the so-called Will of Heaven or mandate to govern is realized in a landscape where such sacredness is manifest as a visible reflection of the most sacred position in the celestial chart (i.e., the Pole Star). Generally speaking, the line of the *axis mundi* originated from the North and extended to the South, which is the direction that the kings, emperors, and the palace all faced.

Chapter 1 raised the question of how Korea's successful economic development could be understood in terms of the integral power of the developmental state and the state's legitimacy to intervene in economic affairs. Any inquiry into that phenomenon eventually leads to the state's centrality in Korean history and how such centrality could have so deeply penetrated Korea's politics. As mentioned previously, such successful development cannot be explained solely from a contemporary perspective but must be examined from a historical approach of the factors that made Korea's developmental regime in 1960s and '70s possible. Indeed, the main features of the successful developmental state cannot be comprehended without explaining the state-society relations in which political power of the state's rights to control economic and other societal issues has long been legitimized, entrenched in political culture, and taken for granted in the minds of the masses. In seeking an answer to this overarching question, three elements of Korea's political ideologies or thoughts—Neo-Confucianism, Taoism, and geomancy—are important to examine. This book argues that a key component of a developmental state's legitimacy to intervene in the economy and central power was inherited from Confucian political hegemony, to which the majority gave their consent. More importantly, this book argues that the two components of geomantic and Taoist belief systems popular in Korean society contributed to the consolidation of Neo-Confucian state tradition and government superiority over society, including economic sectors. What this book highlights is that the tacit consent of the majority in the Korean population can be explained within this context. As claimed in chapter 1, the combination of a Confucian concept of political power, the geomantic belief system, and a Taoist understanding of nature and life all need to be reconsidered together in order to gain a better understanding of Korea's developmental state in a non-Western and non-liberal context, reconstructing its historical origins and the changes it underwent as a result of local-global interactions. The vital relationship between the consolidation of political power and geomantic philosophy is grossly overlooked in the context of Western political culture.

For this very reason, in chapter 3, our historical investigation will begin its exploration of this topic in the classical period of the capital city, Hanyang (1392-1910), at a time when the state hegemony and the state's legitimacy to intervene in the economy were just beginning to become firmly established. Chapter 4 will then proceed to examine Japan's occupation of the city, Kyeongseong (1910-1945), as a period reflecting both major changes and continuities in the relations between the state and the economy. Together, the Hanyang and Kyeongseong eras formed the foundation for the emergence of the developmental state in Korea, bequeathing their tradition of strong state intervention in the economy. Seoul (1945-present), as a symbolic center and a physical place, embodies those legacies today.

As a microcosm of Heaven or the Ultimate Cause, the capital city served as a symbol of ultimate power and legitimacy. In that view, the geomantic skill of locating sacred spaces and building palaces and major political institutions was regarded as the most precious political technology in the process of establishing the Joseon Dynasty. In Korea, as in many old civilizations, the city, and especially the capital city, was regarded as the center of the universe embodied in earthly form, and accordingly was treated as the most sacred place where the Will of Heaven was realized. Pennick (1970: 150) explains:

> The city, fundamental unit of human civilization, has always been a microcosm of its immediate world, containing within its boundaries the hierarchical structure of the society. The rituals and sacrifices which attended the foundation of cities in ancient times reveal the geomantic nature of their design. Owing to the terrain, to the political, economic and social development, few cities have retained their cosmologically based format intact, having been enlarged or rebuilt according to different schemes. Despite these failings, an enduring theme throughout human civilization has been the concept of the Ideal City, a concrete expression of a cosmological idea which has been planned, founded, constructed and destroyed at many places and in many periods throughout recorded history. . . . Each city was the hub of its own world; each capital incorporated its own particular omphalos which was the center of that world. From this center radiated religion, trade, culture and directives, for, by its very nature it was centralist and authoritarian.

From the choice of the site to the details of the city layouts, the ideal city type of both Confucian and geomantic principles were clearly visible and served as a hub of Joseon's political, cultural, and economic worlds. At the same time, the hierarchical structure of the relations between Confucian bureaucracy and economy was clearly reflected in the location of Joseon's Six Ministries Street and market. The capital city of Hanyang exemplifies an ideal city archetype that Pennick (1979) describes above.

In China, emperors were given supreme power and were thought to deserve the utmost dignity, prestige and praise as they were believed to be the sons of Heaven. Since it was their role and duty to co-ordinate the cycles of the seasons with those of agriculture, emperors functioned as intermediaries between the gods and men, offering sacrifices during official religious rituals to ensure the maintenance of order in nature as mandated by the heavens. The extreme importance of the Emperor's role as political and religious leaders justified the grandiosity and lavishness of the palaces that housed and represented their imperial function. In accordance with the widely embraced tenets of *feng shui*, the design of these environments also sought to embody a balance between the forces of nature and influences of man (Lip, 1995: 7).

The architecture of the Forbidden City of the Ming and Qing Dynasties of China illustrated in its physical forms the magnitude of the Emperor's power, and expressed the hierarchy of authority in the shapes of the architecture as well as the etiquette it set forth. Such is the case in the tiers of marble terraces in the great quadrangles of the imperial grounds: "only the high Mandarins and officials were allowed on these terraces. Lower officials were permitted entry to the areas south of the main gateway." Throughout the architecture of the Forbidden City are visible manifestations of the status of *li* (理, principle), the existence of *qi* (氣, earth's energy), the balance of the *yin* (陰, negative) and *yang* (陽, positive) forces, and the harmony of the Five Elements as well as man's relationship with the cosmos. As Lip (1995: 8) explains, "The buildings constructed in the Forbidden City . . . confirm the political as well as the spiritual position of the emperor in China . . . represent a repository of imperial power . . . Just as Confucian principles are expressed in the planning of houses, palaces and cities, Taoist philosophy is demonstrated in the landscape of palaces and cities."

In Chinese and other cities around the globe, the people's understanding of Heaven as the origin of sovereign power and of the city as a symbolic replica and manifestation of that power required a mixture of geomantic beliefs and indigenous philosophies and played an essential role in the establishment of political regimes (Pennick & Lip, 1995).

What were the symbolic requirements for a royal city? As prescribed in the ritual manuals and tradition, a royal city according to Chinese city archetype of *Gugong* should have the following characteristics: orientation to the cardinal points; a square shape girdled by walls; twelve gates in the walls to represent the twelve months; an inner precinct to contain the royal residences and audience halls; a public market to the north of the inner enclosure; a principal street leading from the south gate of the palace enclosure to the central south gate of the city wall; and two sacred places—the royal ancestral temple and the altar of the earth—on either side of the principal street.

The meaning of this design is clear. The placement of the royal palace in the center allows it to dominate the city and, symbolically, the world. Such placement separates the center of profane activity, i.e., the market, from the centers of religious observance and political functions. The ruler faces south in his audience hall, where he receives officials and conducts public business, his back literally turned to the market.[14] Such an ideal plan has never found complete architectural expression though. Some elements are very old, such as the principles of proper orientation; others are relatively recent, such as the clear demarcation of spaces. An inner palace city set apart from the market and non-royal residences first came into existence, it would seem, only with the construction of Lo-yang as the capital of the Northern Wei Dynasty (AD 495-534). The magnificent city of Ch'ang-an did not strictly comply with the ideal pattern. During the T'ang period, the city was a vast rectangular enclosure measuring six miles from east to west and five miles north to south (Tuan, 1974). It displayed the proper orientation and had three gates on each of three sides of the enclosure; its altar of earth and royal ancestral temple were correctly located in relation to the central north-south axis; however, the palace quarter was backed against the north wall instead of being placed at the center; and this departure preempted the space for the official market, which in T'ang Ch'ang was divided into two sections and established in the eastern and western parts of the city, respectively. In China, the ideal pattern had broken down repeatedly in the past; yet, a distinctive fact of Chinese urbanism was the persistence of the "cosmicized" city as a paradigm of design (Tuan, 1974: 167).

China's archetype of the palaces followed the principles laid out in the manual, the *Gugong*, for designing and building the city and palace, which had greatly influenced the major shapes and principles in the choice of the capital city for the Joseon Dynasty and the construction of major political institutions as well as its main palace, the *Kyeongbok.* As an illustration of how critical Confucianism, Taoism, and geomantic principles and beliefs were in the establishment of *Gugong*, a thorough investigation of the construction of Joseon's main palace and major city layouts as well as its important political and economic institutions will reveal the relative positions of state-society relations in the Joseon Dynasty as well as the dynamics between political concerns, power, and economic affairs. This will facilitate a more comprehensive understanding of the successful developmental state in Korea's economic development and the sources of anti-state political forces or civil society in the Confucian and authoritarian political culture of Joseon Dynasty. The next section will lay out the principles by which this book will explain the nature of state in general and Korea's developmental state in particular.

Integral State: Antonio Gramsci and Michael Mann

To trace Korea's original prototype for state-society relations and the changes it experienced over time as a result of global interactions, it is useful to adopt Onuf's concept that a political society is composed of three different types of rule: hegemony, hierarchy and heteronomy. "Hegemony," as an assertive-rules Onuf explains, is the "promulgation and manipulation of principles and instructions by which superordinate actors monopolize meaning which is then passively absorbed by subordinate actors," i.e., Neo-Confucianism as an official governing ideology of Joseon Dynasty and Taoism and geomancy as an unofficial supporting mechanism of Neo-Confucianism and upholding political power of Confucian elites. He then goes on to say, "These activities constitute a stable arrangement of rule because the ruled are rendered incapable of comprehending their subordinate role" (Onuf, 1989: 209-210). "Hierarchy" he defines as the "paradigm of rule most closely associated with Weber because, as an arrangement of directive-rules, it is instantly recognizable as bureaucracy," i.e., unprecedentedly thorough rules of bureaucratic governance and organization as well as the well-established governing manual of Joseon Dynasty's Confucian bureaucracy and the power of Confucian scholarly bureaucrats. Onuf continues: "The relations of bureaux, or offices, form the typical pattern of super- and subordination, but always in ranks, such that each office is both subordinate to the one(s) above it and superordinate to the ones below . . . These hegemonic and hierarchical relations are mutually supporting" (Onuf, 1989: 211) the new official governing ideology of Neo-Confucianism of the Joseon Dynasty. Lastly, "heteronomy" as an arrangement of commitment-rules is the background condition of rule against which episodes of hegemony and hierarchy are set. "Heteronomy" refers to groups that are not autonomous but rather are dominated by others. The "rules of heteronomy" provide a place for elements in society that are not in keeping with the rules of the dominant group, i.e., the voice of dissent raised by students of the National Confucian Academy as the heirs of the Confucian patriarchal society of Joseon (i.e., the first sons), and by the Confucian scholars in the provinces (Sarim), against king and the meritorious subjects in the court of Joseon. Even though the place provided for this voice of dissent is a subservient one, an area for differences is reserved and the relationship of those differences to the dominant groups is officially recognized. In other words, "heteronomy" refers to dissent in Onuf's conception of political society.

Several scholars have discussed the integral notion of state power relative to consent from society. Differentiating between despotic and infrastructural state power, Mann (1986) defines the concept of the "despotic state power" as being associated with the extensive regulation of economic and political activity by highly centralized and authoritarian states combined with a lack of routine institutionalized negotiations with groups in civil society. "Infrastructural state power," on the other hand, signifies the ability of the state to "penetrate" society, organize social relations, and implement policies through a process of negotiation and cooperation in society. In other words, a state can be said to have infrastructural power when the legitimacy of the state has penetrated into the society and the minds of the masses through various socialization channels such that the state can secure consent from society without deploying forceful means in state affairs.

This infrastructural state power operates as a fundamental basis that enables states to elicit consent for political causes and policies, to organize and coordinate society, and to mobilize resources for long-term development. Consequently, it becomes the most important element in binding state and society and providing institutional channels for the continuous negotiation and renegotiation of goals and policies. The specific nature of this "embedded autonomy" is the key to understanding the economic success of

East Asian countries. In this perspective, Mann's notion of infrastructural state power is very similar to that of integral state power proposed by Antonio Gramsci (1971; Femia, 1981). Both of these notions, however, can be understood in terms of Foucault's notion of the relations of power that exist in every point of a society, which makes states function in the way that they do, as explained in detail in the section titled "Purpose, Scope and Methodology" in chapter 1.

Krasner (1978) also emphasizes the autonomous aspects of state power in international politics. His discussion revolves around the central concept of the state (defined as the central decision-making institutions and roles, i.e., the presidency and those bureaus relatively insulated from societal pressures). State is an autonomous actor whose objectives cannot be reduced to a summation of private desires. The state enhances its autonomy by engaging in goal-directed activity (i.e., the preferences of central US decision-makers) and distinguishing the goals of state from those of societal actors—that is, pursuing goals related to the well-being of society as a whole rather than the needs of particular elements within it. State, according to Krasner, is neither a simple instrument of class domination nor merely resultant from the vectors of social forces. This view also combats the structural Marxist concept of state in its claim that ideology, and not direct material interests, is the immediate motivating factor in several cases of state action.

Hegel's notion of state (i.e., political society) and civil society provides us with a deeper understanding of the concept of hegemony. Hegel divided the world of social reality into two categories: civil society and political society. Civil society, according to Hegel, is the complex of commercial and industrial life with no "Reason" to control itself. He saw the highest level of "Reason" as being possessed by the state, which is located in the final stage of the evolution of history. Hegel argued that only the state can guide and order this complex and chaotic civil society, where individual interests, mainly individual aspirations for commercial financial benefit, conflict with each other, thereby causing public interests mostly to be ignored.

Gramsci (1971, 1990) draws a distinction between "'political society' (or dictatorship, or coercive apparatus of a state, for the purpose of assimilating the popular masses to the type of production and economy of a given period) and 'civil society' (or hegemony of a social group over the entire national society exercised through so-called private organizations, such as the Church, the trade unions, the school, etc.)" (Femia, 1981: 25-26). The realm of "civil society," as identified by Gramsci, which contains the ideological superstructure, the institutions, and the technical instruments that create and diffuse modes of thought, is generally absent from the current literature on late developmentalist approaches, especially in regards to the case of Korea.

Gramsci's distinction between political and civil society is usually associated with Hegel's notion of state and civil society. In Hegel, civil society is a special, independent realm of knowledge and activity, and it connotes the complex of commercial and industrial life (e.g., corporations, trade associations), the totality of economic instruments and relations, together with the public services needed to maintain order within them (e.g., civil courts, police). Gramsci's contribution is that he departed not only from Hegelian usage but also from Marx's equation of civil society with the material substructure (i.e., the structure of economic relations). What Gramsci contributed, then, was to use traditional terminology in order to highlight an important, though generally neglected, theoretical distinction within the Marxist conception of superstructure, "a distinction whose relevance for explaining the structure of power and dynamics of revolution the wished to illuminate" (Femia, 1981: 26-27). The Gramscian notion of hegemony sheds light on the nature of state's infrastructural power (Mann, 1986) and helps us understand the nature of the developmental state in Korea. It also widens and deepens the understanding of the power in state and interwoven relationships with civil society and the rule.

In fact, Marx's idea draws a clear-cut and dichotomous distinction between civil society and political society with a radically different perspective from Hegel. Focusing on the domain of the material world, Marx claims that the superstructure (i.e., Hegel's political society) is merely a reflection of this material domain (i.e., economic infrastructure), and the political society (i.e., the state) is the apparatus of state coercion that legally assures the discipline of those groups that do not consent to state control. Consequently, it has been tacitly acknowledged that people are ruled and dominated by the coercive machinery of political society, which in turn is manipulated by the interest of the bourgeoisie. Gramsci, however, recognizes a different social reality. Finding the limited autonomy of state in ruling and the consensual aspects of political control (i.e., consent of the people), he focuses on the complex processes of how the political society or the state elicits the people's consent. He rediscovered and emphasized the fact that government is able to obtain the people's consent by mobilizing the support of the mass media and other ideological instruments, reconfirming Mann's notion of infrastructural power of a state. Such a consensual aspect of political power is partly because the various elites share similar worldviews and lifestyles and partly because the institutions of civil society must operate within a legal framework of rules and regulations.

According to Gramsci (1971, 1990), as well as Femia's (1981) interpretation of the Gramscian notion of state hegemony, the state is "the entire complex of political and theoretical activity by which the ruling classes not only justify and maintain their domination but also succeed in obtaining the active consent of the governed" (Femia, 1987: 24). Gramsci's comprehensive understanding of the generic sources from which state power originated provides this book with its theoretical basis on state centrality in Korean political history and culture in general as well as on the success of the developmental state during Korea's economic development period from the 1960s to '80s. From this perspective, Gramsci claims that the supremacy of a dominant social group or class will be one of two kinds: (1) "intellectual and moral leadership," which constitutes the central part of Gramsci's concept of hegemony, or (2) "domination or coercion" (also, interstate relations have been described as a phenomenon of dominance and dependency in this context). Gramsci's concept of hegemony refers to an internal control (i.e., consensual aspect of political control) that is based on the major prevailing order in society in terms of ideology. This order—namely, intellectual and moral leadership—penetrates and influences all modes of thought and behavior, and acquires consent from the ruled through various institutions (e.g., school, church) in the realm of civil society.

The predominance of hegemony is acquired not just from the physical form of state coercion but from ideological, moral, and behavioral forms of political legitimacy obtained by consent rather than by the force of one class or group over the others. The fundamental sources of such ideological and moral leadership in Korea's developmental state, and the heteronomical forces as well, seem to have stemmed from the historical evolution of Confucian governing ideology and the interrelation of place and power. As chapter 1 explained in regards to Foucault's notion of dispersed power, "The process of getting consent is done through the myriad ways in which the institutions of civil society operate to shape, directly or indirectly, the cognitive and affective structures whereby men perceive and evaluate problematic social reality" (Femia, 1978: 24). These "myriad ways" and "the cognitive and affective structures" whereby the masses perceive and consent to the political reality comprise the focal point of this book.

As Gramsci (1971: 239) aptly notes, "error occurs as a result of an inaccurate understanding of what the State (in its integral meaning: dictatorship + hegemony) really is." His notion of the "integral state" consists of two main features: political domination (i.e., rule through coercion, alternatively "command," "direct domination," or "dictatorship") and ideological domination (i.e., rule through "spontaneous consent"). Gramsci (1971: 171) further states that "therefore if one excludes all voluntarist elements (spontaneous consent), or if it is only other people's wills whose intervention one reckons as an objective element in the general interplay of forces, one mutilates reality itself." Here, Gramsci draws a contrast between coercion and consent and discusses the latter in terms of ideology. He argues that the spontaneous consent given by the masses to the general direction imposed on social life by the dominant fundamental group is historically conditioned by the prestige (and consequent confidence) which the dominant group enjoys due to its position and function in the world of production. The apparatus of state coercive power legally enforces discipline on those groups that do not consent either actively or passively (Gramsci, 1971: 12).

The dominant group is coordinated with the general interests of the subordinate groups, and the life of the state is conceived of as a continuous process involving the formation and superseding of unstable equilibria between the interests of the fundamental groups and those of the subordinate groups—equilibria in which the interests of the dominant group prevail but only up to a certain point, i.e., stopping short of narrowly corporate economic interest (Gramsci, 1971: 182).

The emergence of fascism or military bureaucratic regimes in the Third World is a kind of essential reality as an effort to survive in the world economic order and to control political crises within national boundaries at the same time. For example, South Korea achieved its economic miracle under repressive political control. In the course of Korean economic development, which is widely considered a very successful case of late development, Korea underwent several serious political crises. This means that the world hegemonic order contradicts the political and economic dynamics of the peripheral countries.

In light of the above-mentioned issues, research should focus on what legitimized the developmental state in Korea and permitted its successful ideological mobilization, pervasive political control, and social engineering. More specifically, it is essential to understand the origins of the legitimacy of state intervention in the economy and cooperative relations between state and society (i.e., economy). Of equal importance is that the common understanding of the developmental state be revised by recognizing the dialectical nature of the developmental process rather than affixing static definitions of what constitutes development.

Toward this end, we should recognize the dual sources of state hegemony in Korea—namely, state and civil society. State power is not the exclusive domain of either state apparatuses (e.g., bureaucracy, military, parties) or social forces (e.g., interest groups, civil institutions) but rather is mutually (re)constructed and (re)produced by both state and society. Korea's state power, for example, stems from a Confucian model of non-dichotomous and mutually constructed state-society relations (cf. Ling, 1994; Ketcham, 1987). Most scholars tend to focus on only one side of the developmental coin (i.e., dictatorship) and overlook its flip side (i.e., social hegemony or state hegemony over society).

Whereas current analyses fail to account for the essential source of state power in intervening and promoting the economy, the conceptualization of state hegemony based on consent from the dominated class aptly captures the fundamental source of state capabilities in taming the economy in the developmental state. Here, Gramsci's notion of hegemony provides valuable insight for understanding the nature of power and hegemony, especially as it is exercised through the state. His major contribution lies in pointing out that the system's real strength does not stem from the coercive power of the ruling class and state apparatus; rather, the comprehensive and effective strength of the state should be found in the acceptance by the ruled of a worldview created by the ruling class. Gramsci seeks to understand precisely how the ruling class was able to acquire the consent of the subordinate classes. Chapters 3, 4, and 5, which examine the emergence of the developmental state in relation to Neo-Confucianism and the two supporting belief systems of geomancy and Taoism, may serve as a case study of the point raised above—that is, "how the ruling class was able to acquire the consent of the subordinate classes." People during the Joseon era cherished and believed in these three ideologies. In other words, these ideologies earned the acquiescence of the masses.

The power of ideology was the only feasible explanation for the consent that production achieved from the subordinate classes—it could be adequately explained by neither force nor the logic of capitalist production (Carnoy, 1984: 69-70). The way in which this has come about deserves further attention. Rather than imposing its own ideology upon the dominated class, the dominant class articulated a hegemonic principle that drew elements from the interests of the group to be dominated. Also worth noting, this was a relationship between the two classes. To achieve hegemony, the dominant class had to establish its worldview as a universal truth and shape the interests and needs of subordinate groups through successful political, moral, and intellectual leadership. The dominant class moved on a terrain that constantly shifted to accommodate the changing nature of historical circumstances and the demands and reflexive actions of people. Buci-Glucksmann (1980) argues further that Gramsci's hegemony is expressed in society as the complex of institutions, ideologies, practices, and agents that comprise the dominant culture of value.

For Gramsci, cultural dominance was essential to complete the ruling power and state hegemony because the ruled could thereby be co-opted to embrace the dominant system of beliefs and moral and social values in a form of cultural identification, which in turn reduced the resistance from heteronomical forces in society.

Gramsci deepened our understanding of the integral meaning of the state, especially the power of ideological domination co-opting consent from subordinate groups. More specifically, his conceptualization of ideological domination helps to illuminate the nature of mutually inclusive state-society relations and the centrality of state hegemony in Korean society. His analysis, however, does not extend beyond the stage of elaborating upon the conception of the integral state. He provides no methodological framework for researchers to illustrate and reconstruct the integral meaning of state-society relations. In order to operationalize Gramsci's concept, this book takes a constructivist approach based on Onuf's three rules of political society.

Confucianism, one of the most influential forms of thought and worldview in Korea, has long pervaded every realm of daily life in Korean society, including all facets of social reality, culture, economy, and politics. No realm has escaped its influence: it exists "between every point of a social body," to borrow Foucault's phrase (Gordon, 1972: 187). As the official governing ideology of the Joseon Dynasty, Confucianism shaped the fundamental thoughts, systems, and structure of politics in Korea for about 600 hundred years. Despite the longer presence of Buddhism (i.e., since the 4th century) and the short but intense impact of American liberalism (starting in the late 19th century), Confucianism has remained the most influential source of power—overcoming challenges both materially and ideologically whenever met with global sources of influence—even to the present day.

Despite its centrality in the philosophy of Asia in general and Korea in particular, Confucianism has never received the consideration it deserves in scholarly research or international politics. Similarly, in discussions regarding Korea's economic development and democratization, the most important sources of the ideologies that shaped the nature of state and its relations to society have not been included as major units of analysis. Scholars who take a traditional approach to studying Confucianism have never come together with social scientists to assess the impacts of this ideology on Korea's rapid economic development and democratization. Understandably, some scholars assume that these two phenomena have nothing to do with Confucianism because Confucianism is typically regarded as antithetical to all that is modern and democratic. For a similar reason, geomantic principles should be reconsidered in that they permeated the thinking of the Korean people for over a thousand years as another generic source of political ideology that deeply affected relations between state and society. This book, however, argues that the common tendency of scholars to overlook the influence of Confucianism on Korea's unique experience of simultaneous democratization and economic development is largely due to the early and widespread influence of great Western thinkers such as Max Weber as mentioned earlier.

In any discussion on the role and positions of Confucianism in the process of modernization, one must inevitably turn to what still stands as the best theoretical explanation of why and how these patterns developed in the first place—Weber's thesis of the Protestant ethic (Levy, 1992). To Weber, the Protestant ethic played a powerful role in orienting people toward what he called "this-worldly asceticism" and toward continuous striving for mastery over the material environment. His Protestant belief was that humans had been created for the express purpose of carrying out God's will on earth. Whatever material gain might be generated by man, he believed, should be taken only as a basis for further striving to carry out God's will. The implication of this view, as far as economic development is concerned, was the continuous investment and reinvestment of capital with consequent continuous increases in material productivity. Though this summary admittedly necessitates some degree of oversimplification, this was essentially how Weber explained the Western origins of capitalism. Weber seemed to acknowledge the pragmatic aspect of Confucianism; however, he held that Confucianism and other Asian philosophies "lacked the vital motivation for this-worldly asceticism that constituted so large an element in his theory" (Levy, 1992: 16). His argument does not apply to Korea's late development, to say the least. Weber's deterministic view may have influenced the reasoning of intellectuals, not just Western but also Asian, on why modernization never developed in regions where Confucianism held sway; however, Levy (1992) seems open to the concept that aspects of development may indeed stem from Confucianism when he calls attention to the interesting issue of "why so many intelligent and thoughtful people think the Confucian ethic or philosophy is highly relevant to modernization in East Asia today."

Often, when journalistic approaches describe the Confucian work ethic or the characteristics that are typical in nations where Confucianism prevails (e.g., obedience, diligence, frugality, self-sacrifice), it is only in direct contrast to the Western ideal of individualism; however, by juxtaposing such Confucian characteristics with Western virtues and traits (e.g., responsibility, a pioneering mind-set, a penchant for abundance, leisure-oriented behavior, an attitude that challenges of authority), most reports imply that the Confucian characteristics are inferior, tainted, or immoral. The by-product is to either deny the self or be ignored by others. Despite the lack of economic development at the time when Confucianism was first formulated, this book argues, the Confucian philosophy on the centrality of state and its relations to society and the economy has been the most important factor in Korea's successful process of catching up. In addition, as mentioned throughout chapter 1, the power dynamics among the hegemonic, hierarchical, and built-in heteronomical types of rule evolved as a by-product of local-global interactions and ultimately came to play a vital role in the Korean process of democratization. This process in Korea could have taken a different course than in the Western experience; however, if we understand Korea's democratization as a process whereby the masses gain power, then the application of Onuf's three rules of political society over the course of Korea's three main eras should help to recognize how such co-opted dissenting voices contributed first toward the national resistance against colonial Japan and then later against the military regime and its repressive political power in modern Korea.

Several main principles comprise the Confucian understanding of the nature of governing as well as the relationships that exist among state, society, and members of the Confucian community. The first and by far the most important principle that affected political affairs of the Hanyang era was the Confucian belief that political power originates from Heaven, the ultimate source of not only physical power but also of righteousness and the so-called Way of Things. Sovereignty was abstract in that it originated from Heaven or the mandate to govern. Within this context, astronomy and geomancy functioned as an ancient sort of technology that aimed to discern the Will of Heaven. Eliade's time-honored studies *Cosmos and History* and *The Sacred and the Profane* both discussed how ancient humans thought about their relation to the cosmos and how this thinking shaped their religious, cultural, and political realities.

Wheatley's epoch-making studies on the origins of Chinese cities and capitals, described in his book *Pivot of Four Quarters*, provide another basis for this book's main claims. Guided by geomantic principles, people looked to the skies for a celestial model then sought topological configurations in the landscape that bore close resemblance to those of the ideal chart, seeking out mountains and rivers of specific shapes and directions as well as certain arrangements thereof. For both the governing elites and the masses, elements of Confucianism and geomancy laid the groundwork for the centrality of state and for society's consent; this is captured well in the notion of integral state and moral or ideological leadership from Gramsci's (1971) study on the Italian communist movement and in the notion of infrastructural state power or autonomous aspects of state power from Mann's (1986) studies on world history in general.

Levy (1992: 17) points out that, according to the doctrine of the Will of Heaven, the legitimacy of a regime relied on natural and sociopolitical phenomena when things were out of "proper adjustment" as "the best evidence that a regime was no longer legitimate. A regime lacked the Will of heaven if social affairs were out of kilter." Confucianism laid out the main ideology and codes of conduct for the good of society in general, reflecting the abstract Will of Heaven, but it was Neo-Confucianism that articulated a more sophisticated governing ideology that was based on the Will of Heaven. Neo-Confucianism indoctrinated people with the belief that the ultimate power of the king and the actual governing rights that were given to Confucian scholarly bureaucrats actually originated from the Will of Heaven. Based on Weber's interpretation of modern bureaucracy, Levy holds that Confucian government was not a modern corporate state with a monopoly on the legitimate use of force. This book disagrees with Levy's view in that the bureaucratic system of the Joseon Dynasty was systematically hierarchical and tightly organized with rigorous legal codes and manuals concerning every aspect of society, even dictating what uniforms should be worn by people of each vocation and rank. This bureaucracy was heavily centralized compared to the Western feudal political system, a difference that will be analyzed in this book's close examination of the Hanyang era in chapter 3.

With regards to the impact of Confucianism upon late developments in a few successfully modernized Asian economies, Levy views Confucianism as a kind of "corporate membership in general" and raises questions as important as those of this book. The spectacular success of modernization in East Asian societies (with the exception of Japan), which causes us to be concerned with the relevancy of Confucianism, postdates World War II. What then of the relevancy of Confucianism to these developments in the period between 1870 and 1945? In the countries with which we are concerned (except for Japan), why did these developments not occur until the aftermath of World War II? Answers to Levy's questions can be provided by tracing the prototype of state-society relations and the changes brought about by global interaction with colonial Japan and post-WWII international and bi-polar Cold War politics; these questions link directly to the overarching goal of this book—i.e., to explain the simultaneous phenomena of unprecedentedly rapid economic development and democratization in Korea. Many saw the vital role of Korea's strong developmental state in its intervention in the economy and find the source of its power as stemming either from military dictatorship, efficient bureaucrats, or Cold War politics; however, no major scholarly works have focused on Confucianism or geomancy as fundamental sources of explanations for the simultaneous processes of economic development and democratization in Korea. Many foreign-born theories on economic and political development have been temporarily adopted to explain these phenomena, but all have failed to do so, as mentioned in chapter 1's section on grand theories. Accordingly, this book attempts to view these Korean phenomena in relation to Korea's history and in light of its indigenous ideologies.

The Role of Geomancy in the Formation of Integral and Infrastructural State Power

As explained previously, the most important factor in achieving a complete understanding of state power in general and Korea's developmental state in particular is to analyze Gramsci's "integral," Mann's "infrastructural," and

Foucault's "dispersed" power of state. This task sheds light on the relative aspect of state power: state's coercive and repressive power and apparatuses as well as people's and societal consent to the state power. Mann argues that state's power can be described as "infrastructural" when it has the capacity to penetrate into society and the minds of the ruled, to organize social relations, and to implement through cooperation and negotiation; whereas Gramsci describes state power as being "integral" when the state can obtain the active consent of the governed. In Gramsci's scheme, the leadership of the state in intellectual and moral realms is the core component that makes state power integral. In integral or infrastructural state power, the consent or acceptance on the side of society and the masses needs to be spontaneous and voluntary. The interests of the dominant and subordinate groups need to be coordinated and internalized in such way as to produce political legitimacy of the community, which seems to be the dual sources of state hegemony in Korea: state and society.

The important questions to ask are as follows. What reasons and factors make such integral and infrastructural state possible? Why do society and the masses accept the state's regulation of their freedom and various rights? What makes such voluntary and spontaneous consent possible? By what mechanisms does such coordination occur between the dominant state and subordinate society and the masses? What made such authoritarian and repressive or exploitative ideology of Neo-Confucianism more acceptable in the minds of the ruled? Surely, there was a reason why the masses saw such state ideology as acceptable. In Korea's integral and infrastructural state power, the widely accepted, respected, and deeply embedded belief systems of geomancy and Taoism played a catalytic role in making Neo-Confucian state doctrine more tolerable, acceptable, and understandable to the subordinated.

What features allowed these two ways of thinking to function as a coordinating mechanism for the coercive state ideology of Confucianism? First of all, these two sources of belief systems had to be the *modus operandi* in every aspect of the everyday lives of the masses. Geomancy was the most popular technology and belief system guiding the people's decisions about where to locate their houses, buildings, and even tombs. It was a comprehensive knowledge system, as explained previously, for every aspect of the common people's lives. All of the successes and failures, health and sickness, prosperity and poverty, and ups and downs in people's personal life and state affairs were believed to be caused by geomantic and Taoist principles. Taoism was also very influential in the lives of the masses during the Joseon era. Most natural phenomena were interpreted according to Taoist principles. The principles of the yin and yang described the ways of the cosmos as well as the ways in which things happened in worldly matters, including relationships between men and women. Faithful adherence to those principles was strongly regarded as the way to bring about good fortune and avoid bad fortune. Due to their popularity, these two ways of thinking and living were able to play the role of softening the repressive and coercive sides of the state ideology of Joseon—i.e., Confucianism—since there were some common denominators between them.

As explained before, Neo-Confucianism adopted the main tenets of geomancy and Taoism in its process of evolving from classical Confucian doctrine. The most important common denominator in these three ways of thinking is that they share the belief in the First Cause of everything: Heaven (Neo-Confucianism and geomancy) or the Way (Taoism). Chapter 3 will explore how all of these ideologies contributed to the foundation and consolidation of state power in the early Joseon period. Due to this shared belief in the First Cause of everything and in the origin of political power and authority—including the right to govern and the duty to obey—the exploitative, repressive, and regulatory aspects of Neo-Confucian doctrine and the dominant elites groups became more acceptable and tolerable to the governed.

In turn, the state power became more integral and inclusive of the consent and agreement from the ruled and infrastructural; the Neo-Confucian state could opt for loyalty and support from the masses mainly because their belief system about the ultimate cause in both natural and human affairs corresponded to that of Neo-Confucianism. The repressive and exploitative nature of the controlling ideology of Neo-Confucianism was softened by the existence of a common ground between the moral and intellectual leadership and geomantic and Taoist thought. The source of the voluntary and spontaneous consent can be found in the fact that the everyday lives of the masses shared some core principles with the governing philosophy.

In our search for the sources of more autonomous and integral state power, specific contexts of history and political culture must be re-articulated across societies and countries. Our focus here should be on the foundation of dispersed power in terms of Foucault's argument on knowledge and power. In the Joseon era, Confucian, geomantic, and Taoist beliefs and principles constituted the fundamental background against which a specific political ideology was able to establish its own political agenda and power structure and systems. Neo-Confucian political doctrine rose firmly from the bedrock of geomancy and Taoism, deeply ingrained as they were in the everyday life of the governed, and as old as the Confucian influence. Joseon state power and its relations with society and the masses were products of the syncretism of Neo-Confucianism, geomancy, and Taoism.

In order to operationalize the concept of both integral and infrastructural notions of state power, a constructivist approach based on Onuf's three rules of political society will help us to re-articulate those three rules as they were embedded in Korean history and political culture through interactions among Neo-Confucian state ideology and the two widely respected philosophies of geomancy and Taoism. Importantly, this research scheme does not to claim to analyze the causal links between spatial arrangements and state power; rather, it claims that Korea's autonomous developmental state and its role in the process of miraculous economic development and the challenges from civil society can be better understood by re-constructing the integral and infrastructural aspects of Joseon state-society relations.

Chapter 3 will examine the core principles of the Neo-Confucian political ideology and geomantic and Taoist belief systems and how these principles were reflected in the city layout, architecture, spatial arrangements, and major political institutions. Also, chapter 3 will delve into evidence of hierarchical and heteronomical aspects of state power and its relations with economy and society, which will help us to understand the integral and infrastructural state power as well as the seeds of democratization in the Confucian context.

NOTES

1. Perkins (1994: 660) also points out that "much less attention is given to why the Highly Performing Asian Economies (HPAEs) were able to carry out effective policies when so many other developing countries have failed. But one cannot really decide whether the HPAE experience is relevant for another country unless one comes to grips with this 'why' question."

2. According to World Bank research reports (1993: 39), Singapore, Hong Kong, Taiwan, and Korea had ratios of total trade to GDP in 1970 of 2.12, 1.50, 0.53, and 0.32, respectively; in 1980, 3.70, 1.52, 0.95, and 0.63, respectively; and in 1988, 3.47, 2.82, 0.90, and 0.66, respectively.

3. (4) and (5) from World Bank (1993), p. 9.

4. "Hard states" are those that can resist the influence of social forces such as interest groups so as to define their own goals and policies. "Soft states," in contrast, are generally considered to be responsive or vulnerable to such social forces. In "soft states," interest groups play an important role in defining national goals and policies. See, e.g., Grabowski (1994), p. 415.

5. Gourevitch (1986) examines the responses of five countries (i.e., the United States, United Kindgom, France, Germany, and Sweden) in three different periods of crisis. He argues that the crises led to the development and realignment of coalitions among various economic actors and that differences in policy response arose from differences in the institutions that mediated the mobilization and application of power.

6. "Internationalization" refers to a process whereby the state restructures its "internal policies and institutions to accommodate the external exigencies of internationalized production." See, e.g., Ling, 1996, p. 4.

7. Clifford (1994: 47, 64) refers to POSCO (a giant state-owned steel company), the Korea Highway Corporation, and the Korea Cement Industry Association as examples of the application of a military logistical system to business.

8. This survey is based on two different status groups: the highly educated group in Korean society and the general public in America. Despite such a problem in the qualification of respondents, this survey is included here due in part to the lack of statistical data concerning the differences between Korean and American people on issues of public affairs.

9. See, Harris (1989), p. 411. On relations between Confucianism and economic success in East Asian NICs, see also Levy (1992) and Han (1984).

10. Lyotard (1984) also points out that "This overlooks the fact that in the context of the narrative of freedom, the State receives its legitimacy not from itself but from the people." See Easthope and McGowan (1992), p. 184.

11. Taylor (1985: 198) holds that "Ideological dominance will be reflected in various mixes of deferential, aspirational, and accommodative value systems. The particular mixture in any one country will depend upon the strategies of the dominant classes in the past and the concrete experiences of dominated classes in their day-to-day activities."

12. "Mongolian and Tartar tribes invaded the Song (宋) Kingdom and the ruling government had to abandon the capital at Kaifeng and move to Hangzhou. A period of turmoil ensued, and China fell into the hands of the Liao, who were later defeated by the Manchurians, who in turn began the Jin (金) Dynasty. The Chinese kingdom was conquered by Kublai Khan, the grandson of Genghis Khan, who established the Yuan (元) Dynasty (1279-1368). The Mongol capital was set up in Beijing. The Mongolians were unpopular and, after a period of unrest, were overthrown in a revolt led by Zhu Yuanzhang, who founded the Ming (明) Dynasty (1368-1644). In 1421, Emperor Cheng Zu moved his capital to Beijing and the Forbidden City. The Zi Jincheng was laid out and enclosed with high walls. During this period, one of the Chinaigh walls were constructed. During this period, period dodiodans were unpopular and after a period of (淸) emperor, the successor of the Ming rulers, it was based on the concept of symmetry, with all its principal buildings and gateways facing south" (Lip, 1995: 12).

13. Later Korean Confucianists thought only two Goryeo scholars were worthy of enshrinement as permanent Confucian sages: An Yu, founder of Chu Hsi thought in Korea, and Jeong Mong-ju, who, on the stone bridge at Gaeseong (which is said to be still stained with this blood), gave his life for his cause and became a lasting example of Confucian principles and loyalty for the emulation of later Korean youth (Yang & Henderson, 1958: 89).

14. This principle of having the market at the back was not applied in the design of the Hanyang in Korea. The market was on the East-West axis. Chapter 3 will provide more detailed explanation of this topic.

Chapter Three

The Hanyang Prototype of Hegemony, Hierarchy, and Heteronomy

In the previous chapters, we examined two generic sources of thinking that fundamentally contributed toward the political establishment of the Joseon Dynasty. Despite the fact that Neo-Confucianism and geomancy (including Taoism) played vital roles as sources of such thought, they have not received their fair share of scholarly attention. Interest in Confucianism has generally been confined to the area of classical studies, and few researchers have examined how Korea's most enduring political philosophy affected its modernization processes of economic development and democratization; this lack of scholarship is due to the fact that, from a Western perspective, Confucian doctrine has been deemed anti-democratic and anti-capitalistic. Since geomancy is often considered a pseudo-scientific, unsubstantiated folk belief or superstition, geomantic thought has also been excluded from scholarly consideration as a factor in state centrality and political power or as a principle affecting power politics in Korea. As chapter 2 explained, the philosophy of Neo-Confucianism was a belief that located the Ultimate Cause of everything in the Will of Heaven, and the practice of geomancy was the human technology utilized to locate those landscapes where the Will of Heaven was realized in earthly form. In addition, as chapters 1 and 2 made clear, the capital city was built in that sacred place where the mass believed the Will of Heaven to be realized, an effective hierarchical way for a regime to maximize and demonstrate the power of the governing elites, while upholding its political legitimacy. The integral power of such a regime originated from the fact that the masses and society at large had accepted both Neo-Confucian political doctrine and geomancy as norms in their everyday life and political culture, which seemed to function, to use Foucault's term, as "the concrete, changing soil in which the sovereign's power is grounded" (Gordon, 1972: 187).

Thus, the consensual aspect of state centrality that was established during the Hanyang era helps to explain the success of the developmental state in Korea's economic development. As pointed out in chapter 2, geomancy and a formal Confucian ideology of governing and control came together in the major spatial and architectural arrangements of the Joseon Dynasty and in the consolidation of state hegemony and its relations with society and economy.

The other important element in the Confucian political system that affected Korea's democratization was the notion of extraterritoriality within the Confucian power structure of the Joseon Dynasty. As the dissenting voices allowed within the Confucian power structure, the students of the National Confucian Academy (Seongkyunkwan) and the Neo-Confucian literati (Sarim) constituted the origins of civil society; and during the Kyeongseong era, this limited element of heteronomical forces expanded in opposition against colonial Japanese forces and then went on to play the most critical role in the democratization of the 1980s. This study re-constructs such state centrality and the origins of heteronomical force from the capital city of Hanyang, as laid out in chapters 1 and 2, by utilizing Onuf's three types of rule of political society and the changes that occurred during the Kyeongseong era.

Building upon these premises and focusing on the contributing factors of geomancy and Confucian political ideology, chapter 3 treats the Joseon Dynasty and its capital city Hanyang as the prototype within which the centrality of state hegemony over society and economy was founded. To examine the extent to which state hegemony penetrated into every realm of society, this chapter examines the symbolism of state hegemony as reflected in the architectural monumentality of major Confucian institutions and in the design of the capital city in the Hanyang era. In addition, this chapter examines the hierarchical nature of the highly centralized bureaucracy of the Confucian Joseon Dynasty and its tight grip over economic activities. Finally, the origins of extraterritoriality will be analyzed as the Korean roots of the public sphere, civil society, and voices of dissent.

POWER FROM HEAVEN AND EARTH

The Neo-Confucian political ideology upholding state centrality[1] in the Joseon Dynasty was represented in the geographical arrangements, the legibility of the city through architectural monumentality, and administrative law—all of which manifested the dynamic relationships that existed among the ruling principles of hegemony and hierarchy. Moreover, the extraterritoriality of the heteronomy was instituted within the hegemonic Confucian political center of the capital city. An accurate representation of the

Confucian state and its complete control over the economy can be viewed through three structural parallels—(1) between Hanyang and provincial castles, (2) between the main palace and the houses of the *yangban* (Confucian bureaucrats and literati), and (3) between the National Confucian Academy (Seongkyunkwan) and provincial Confucian schools (*Seowon*). Each of these parallels reveals the all-pervasive nature of the state's physical and moral influence and actual power to penetrate into all aspects of social life, thereby providing support for a non-Western, non-liberal Korean model of strong state and dependent economy.

During the Joseon Dynasty, the people's attachment to the capital was intense. They felt a strong sense of attachment to and admiration for Hanyang, as the following folksong vividly demonstrates.

> When I die, bury me in the earth beneath the tide,
> Where I will enter the mouth of the sea bass
> To be placed on the table of a Hanyang gentleman
> And raised by his golden spoon.[2]

As expressed in this popular song, the people viewed the capital city as a sacred space more lofty and mysterious than that of their daily lives, as a center toward which they projected their loyalty, and as existing on a greater scale of importance than they would ever experience. So, how did the state, which was represented by the capital, become and remain so central in the minds of the people? And what role did Hanyang play in creating and sustaining such state centrality in Korea? How did the voice of dissent assume its position within the scope of such strong state hegemony? These questions provide the foundation upon which this book reconstructs the rules of hegemony, hierarchy, and heteronomy that were reflected largely in the capital city of Hanyang and in the administrative code of the Joseon Dynasty. The actual technology and knowledge utilized to locate the sacred space for major symbolic state institutions came from geomancy, while the governing ideology and political power structures and principles came from Neo-Confucian statecraft. Confucian political and state symbols appeared in spatial contexts where the Will of Heaven was realized as identified by geomantic beliefs and technology. These two pervasive and widely upheld ideologies mutually reinforced overlapping principles from artificial and natural sources of power and authority.

Interestingly, the practice of considering the capital city as the nation's most important symbol of political power, in fact, was borrowed from ancient China. There, capitals became relatively permanent foundations at an early date, but fairly reliable traditions record at least five moments of the capital under the *Shang* (Wheatley, 1971: 448).

The capital of Siang (Shang) was a city of cosmic order,
The pivot of the four quarters.
Glorious was its renown,
Purifying its divine power,
Manifested in longevity and tranquility
And the protection of us who come after. (Wheatley, 1971: 450)

The actual model that Hanyang drew upon was the archetype of the capital city of China's Han Dynasty, the *Ch'angan*, which Tuan (1974: 145) describes as one of the earliest landscaped enclosures to be based on Taoist magical beliefs. Eliade (1954: 15) sees China's capital city as the center of the universe where Heaven, Earth, and Hell all came together.

In general, China's capital cities had the following characteristics. First, the most central position in the city was designated as the ceremonial center. Since it was primarily used as an altar to the god of the soil, it was left open to the elements in order to "receive the hoar frost, dew, wind, and rain, and to allow free access by the influences of Heaven and Earth" (Wheatley, 1971: 175), which played a dominant role in the political, social, and economic organization of its locality.[3] Inseparable from the religious authority exercised by the ritual experts who mediated between god and man was the political and social power that they wielded. This was abundantly clear in the massive constructions undertaken at the ceremonial centers, many of which still extend over many acres and square miles.

The other essential feature of the capital city was its symbolic role as the patrimonial center. There, as the Son of Heaven, the king received the mandate of Heaven. At the temple, royal families worshipped their ancestors, where the tablets of the agnatic ancestors and their wives were kept. This practice was essential because it was widely believed that no state could survive without the favor and intercession of its former rulers who, in turn, traced their lineage back to the sage emperors or cultural heroes of antiquity. When the ancestral sacrifices were discontinued, it was believed, ruler and state would go extinct as well. It was this temple of the ancestors which served as the focus for all of the important state functions, whether religious, political, diplomatic, or military. In ancient times, these two religious and patrimonial centers were the main features of the palace, legitimizing the royal family's rights to govern and to continue the succession of power. The third feature of the capital city was comprised of the palace, i.e., the king's residence and office, which together served as a symbol of political power.

Wheatley's case study of China's capital city in the *Pivot of Four Quarters* is theoretically based on Eliade's epoch-making studies on archaic people's beliefs regarding the interaction between nature and humans. According to Eliade's observations:

> This same symbolism of the center explains other series of cosmological images and religious beliefs. Among these, the most important are: (a) holy sites and sanctuaries are believed to be situated at the center of the world; (b) temples are replicas of the cosmic mountain and hence constitute the pre-eminent 'link' between earth and heaven; (c) the foundations of temples descend deep into the lower regions. . . ; the remarkable consistency of these traditional conceptions of the world will then appear with greater clarity. The capital of the perfect Chinese sovereign is located at the center of the world. (1957: 39)

As mentioned in chapter 2, Eliade has systemized four basic modes of symbolism in the ideal city type: (1) reality is a function of the imitation of a celestial archetype; (2) the parallelism between the macrocosmos and the microcosmos necessitates the practice of ritual ceremonies to maintain harmony between the world of gods and the world of men; (3) reality is achieved through participation in the symbolism of the center, as expressed by some form of *axis mundi*; and (4) the techniques of orientation needed in order to define sacred territory within the continuum of profane space involve an emphasis on the cardinal compass directions (Wheatley, 1971: 418).

These four basic modes of symbolism in the design of the ideal city were extracted from the celestial archetype and reflected in almost every capital city in China and Korea, as this chapter explains in regards to the design of Hanyang. The celestial archetype lends legitimacy to the political authority of any regime that builds its capital city based on constellations and stars in the Heavens. Such an effort to discern the Will of Heaven and the mandate to govern corresponds with the philosophical core of New-Confucianism, as discussed in chapters 1 and 2. The parallelism between the macrocosmos (i.e., the celestial archetype) and the microcosmos (i.e., the capital city) is applied similarly between the capital city and cities in the localities; the actual realization of the celestial symbol on Earth becomes possible through orientation to the *axis mundi*, where it manifests.[4] The zoning of the sacred and profane spaces follows as result. The capital, which was situated directly on top of the *axis mundi*, was also believed to be the point of ontological transition where divine power entered the world and diffused outward through the kingdom.

Eliade's four basic modes of symbolism in the ideal city type can be interpreted as humanity's efforts to realize a cosmic archetype on earth and in its social systems. These four basic modes all come together as a principle guiding the design of the capital city and thereby producing the legibility of the city, which is categorized as follows:

> . . . a perceptible order, a sense of location for the people within it, a sense of structure, and a much needed hierarchy. This legibility comes from monumentality in the city, which is formed by the articulation of a network of spaces and significant buildings, public places, and the connections between them. The specific design of a city reflects the will of the designer or the ideology of the major social forces strengthening the city's legibility. In striving for legibility and in their desire to give significance and importance to certain buildings, the builders of cities have relied on their visual imagination. From time immemorial, they were concerned with two closely related issues: the choice of what to single out and the means by which to make it significant. (Safdie, 1984: 87)

If spatial and temporal experiences are primary vehicles for the coding and reproduction of social relations, Harvey (1989: 247) claims, then a change in how the former gets represented will almost certainly generate some kind of shift in the latter. For example, he points out that maps drafted in Renaissance England upheld the values of individualism, nationalism, and parliamentary democracy at the expense of dynastic privilege. Two elements that Safdie (1984: 75) pointed out—political intention and natural integration—are clearly visible in the maps made during the Joseon era. These maps do not fail to illustrate the legibility and architectural monumentality of Hanyang, as pointed out in maps 2.1 and 2.2 in chapter 2.

The two most salient features represented in most of the maps that were produced during the Joseon Dynasty were nature and political institutions, as Safdie observed. In map 2.1, the part depicted in black connotes the mountains and the part in blue connotes the Han River (*Han Gang*). In maps 2.1 and 2.2, Eliade's following points are clearly reflected: "1. The Sacred Mountain—where Heaven and Earth meet—is situated at the center of the world; 2. Every temple or palace—and, by extension, every sacred city or royal residence—is a Sacred Mountain, thus becoming a Center; 3. Being an *axis mundi*, the sacred city or temple is regarded as the meeting point of Heaven, Earth, and Hell" (1954, 12). Political institutions appearing in map 1 include the palaces, the *Jongmyo* (Royal Ancestral Shrine), the *Sajik* (Dynasty Guardian Altar), the Six Ministries Street, the Seongkyunkwan (National Confucian Academy), the Four Gates, and several other government buildings. Korean maps of that era typically highlight the relationships among political institutions within the natural setting. Eliade (1957: 37) expounds upon how the sacredness and city's monumentality are realized:

> Here, then, we have a sequence of religious conceptions and cosmological images that are inseparably connected and form a system that may be called the 'system of the world', prevalent in traditional societies. These conceptions are as follows: (a) a sacred place constitutes a break in the homogeneity of space;

> (b) this break is symbolized by an opening by which passage from one cosmic region to another is made possible (from heaven to earth and vice versa or from earth to the underworld); (c) communication with heaven is expressed by one or another of certain images, all of which refer to the *axis mundi*, e.g., a pillar (cf. the universalis columna), ladder (cf. Jacob's ladder), mountain, tree, vine; and (d) around this cosmic axis lies the world (our world), hence, the axis is the located 'in the middle,' at the 'navel of the earth', as the Center of the World.

Furthermore, evidence of the great importance that the people attached to Hanyang can be seen in the disproportionately large size of its depiction in map 3.1.

During the Hanyang period, Confucian political ideology and geomantic principles contributed toward the consolidation of state hegemony and the precedence of politics over economy. As a traditional Asian body of knowledge concerning the relations between space and power, geomancy assigned political meaning to the capital's location and thereby empowered Confucian political ideals. Confucian codes of law regulating economic activities provide the main evidence for the principle of political priority over the economy. More specifically, buildings created during the Hanyang period reveal how the Confucian state hegemony was successfully established as a hierarchically centralized bureaucracy that embraced its heteronomical social forces.

The legibility of the city also makes it possible to see how Japanese colonial rule during the Kyeongseong period (1910-1945), in recognition of the bond between power and place, attempted to dismantle Confucian political power bases and subtly appropriate the strong state tradition of the Joseon Dynasty. First, the occupation forces defaced mountains that had been considered heavenly sources of state hegemony in the Joseon Dynasty, driving iron spikes into certain hills and mountain ranges to demoralize the Koreans, who believed that such regions of the landscape contained sacred spiritual energy. Then, the Japanese constructed their colonial headquarters directly in front of the main palace in order to block the people's view of that powerful symbol of confucian Joseon and supplant it in people's minds as the source of authority. These are just a couple of the many ways in which Japanese colonial authority destroyed, supplanted, and appropriated Confucian state hegemony. New rules added by Japan transformed Korea's political and economic prototype through this period and later deeply affected the process of economic development during the 1960s and '70s.

The geographical layout of present-day Seoul illustrates the operation of social forces, grounded in the inherited rules, upon the modern city. Still visible are the politically important institutions that occupy the core of the sacred zone near the palace and the major economic institutions that are concentrated

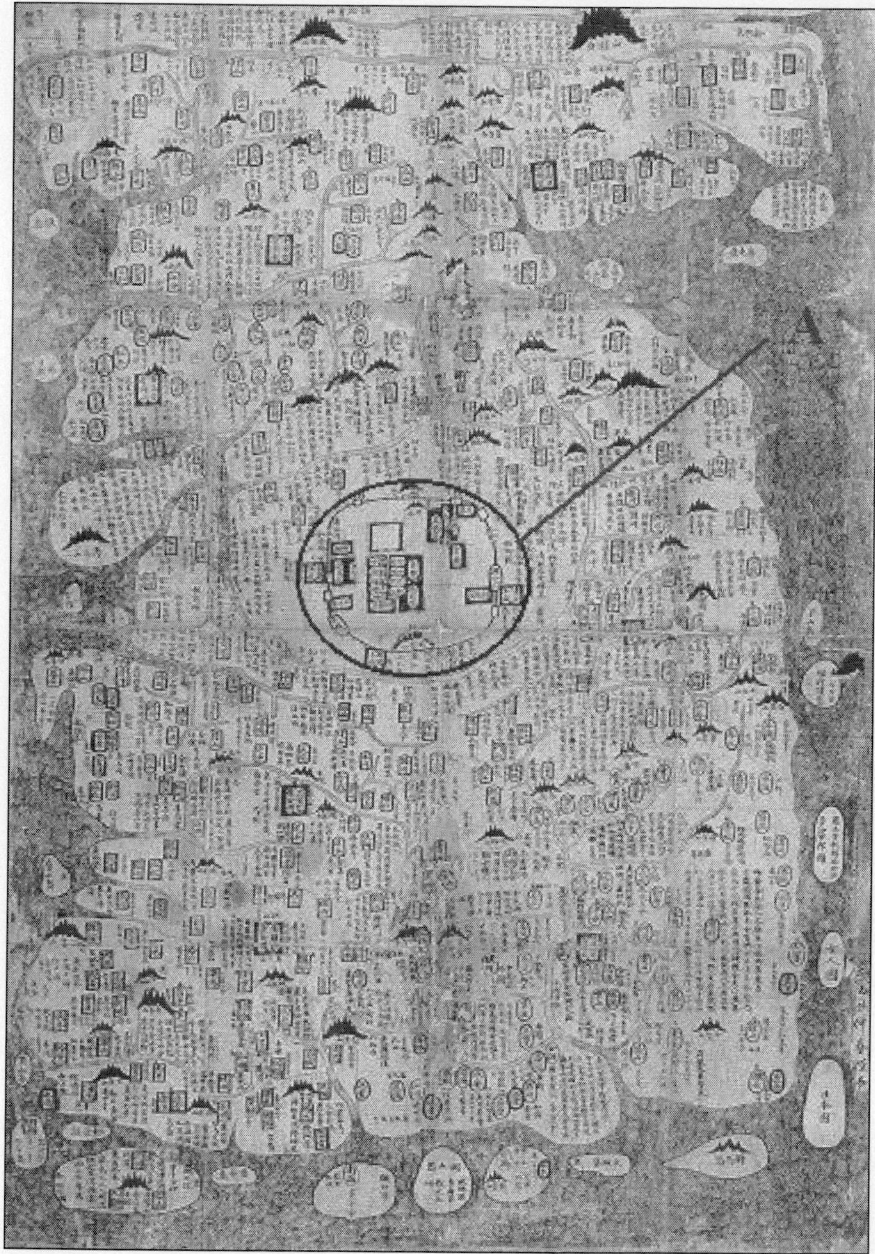

Map 3.1 Disproportionately Large Representation of Hanyang on the National Map. A: Nation's most sacred ground, encircled by the castle wall. Choson Paldo Koum Chongnam-do. Map of Korea, Past, and Present. Manuscript map in color. 1673 AD 127 x 88.4 cm. Private Collection. See, Hur (1994), p. 12.

in the profane zone farther off toward the periphery. The dependency of economic institutions upon political power remains legible from the fact that the basic city layout situates political institutions along the north-south line of the *axis mundi* and economic institutions in the lower profane zone that runs from east to west. To consolidate the autonomy of the modern regime, the Japanese colonial headquarters were demolished in November 1996.

By summarizing the dynamic interactions among the three categories of rule—hegemony, hierarchy, and heteronomy—this book reviews the benefits of the constructivist approach that makes use of evidence from a broader range of sources, including three assertive-, directive-, and commitment-rules and three types of rule hegemony, hierarchy, and heteronomy in the spatial arrangements manifested in the city's layouts, monumentality, and architecture. More importantly, this approach opens up a productive way to investigate the Confucian political culture in developmental state inquiries and indicates how this applies to economic development in countries where the Western liberal model is less appropriate. This book concludes by suggesting an indigenous approach to unearthing the roots of a country's state-society relations and applying the insights thus gained to a holistic analysis of that country's political and economic challenges.

Eliade claims, "What enables mankind to recognize the sacred is the fact that it takes forms markedly different from those of the profane" (1957: 11), and proposes to use the term "hierophany" to conceptualize "the act of manifestation of the sacred" which "expresses no more than is implicit in its etymological content, i.e., that something sacred shows itself to us." The term "hierophany" denotes:

> 1. Facts which show us that, for archaic man, reality is a function of the imitation of a celestial archetype; 2. Facts which show us how reality is conferred through participation in the "symbolism of the Center": cities, temples, houses become real by the fact of being assimilated to the "center of the world; 3. Finally, rituals and significant profane gestures which acquire the meaning attributed to them, and materialize that meaning, only because they deliberately repeat such and such acts posited aborigine by gods, heroes, or ancestors. (Eliade, 1954: 5-6)

In Eliade's definition of "hierophany," the sacred space itself automatically manifests awe or grandiosity without any artificial additions. Nature reveals the unusual characteristics of the spot as compared to the mundane landscape such that humans revere the space itself as well as the architecture built thereupon. The frame of reference for such spatial uniqueness comes from the sacred part of the celestial body. In addition, due to the scarcity of such sacred spots, the political power and legitimacy of whatever regime occupied that space could be easily secured. In that perspective, the capacity to locate such sacred space has always been the most important task for a new political regime.

THE CHOICE OF HANYANG AS A CAPITAL CITY

This book's main purpose is to provide evidence of the strong role played by the state in the economic development of Korea as well as evidence of the origins of the power configurations that later served as the foundations from which heteronomous voices initiated the process of Korea's democratization in late 20th-century Korean history. A brief survey of Korea's history—from the era of the Three Kingdoms of Goguryeo (37 BC-AD 668), Baikje (18 BC-AD 660), and Shilla (57 BC-AD 935, the united kingdom of Shilla in 676), through Goryeo (918-1392), to Joseon (1392-1910)—will be necessary to explain how the capital city changed over the three major periods of Korea's history: Hanyang (1392-1910), Kyeongseong (1910-1945), and Seoul (1945-present).

The simplest way to characterize the sociopolitical system of the Three Kingdoms is as a group of aristocratic societies brought together under a monarchical rule. Buddhism was introduced into Goguryeo in 372 from the earlier *Chi'in* Dynasty of China and spread into Shilla by approximately the mid-5th century. Buddhism spread to Baikje directly from East Chi'in in 384. The common characteristic in the acceptance of Buddhism in the period of Three Kingdoms was that the royal families in each kingdom were eager to adopt it as a state religion in order to protect the country and generate patriotism. Their intention was to centralize the political power of the royal family and "to undergird the new governing structure centered on the authority of the throne" (Lee, 1984: 59). This is by no means to argue, though, that the aristocracy was completely controlled by the royal family or the state religion of Buddhism. The governing structure of the Three Kingdoms period was based on a dynamic system of checks and balances between the royal family and aristocracy. As Buddhism was established as the state religion, it began to influence court politics, and some Buddhist monks even became directly involved in state politics as advisors to kings and powerful aristocrats. For example, the Buddhist monk Doseon (827-898), serving as a private advisor to King Heon Kang of the late Shilla, is widely credited with establishing the tradition of political geomancy. His *Doseon Bigi* (i.e., Secret Records of Doseon) tremendously affected the rise and fall of Goryeo as well as the foundation of the Joseon Dynasty.

Doseon greatly enhanced the appeal of geomancy because he managed to integrate it into the Buddhist idea of achieving merit through good works, as well as the Taoistic theories of the yin-yang and the Five Elements. According to Doseon, the natural features of a land area and their configuration deeply affect the fate of the country and its inhabitants. In the lay of the land, there is prosperity or decay (i.e., favorable or unfavorable), and by selecting a flourishing or propitious site for the construction of a building or tomb, a country or individual can enjoy good fortune. On the other hand, since an inauspicious site brings misfortune, one might forestall calamity by constructing temples to remedy topological defects just as one might apply a poultice to the human body. Doseon is said to have wandered all over Korea divining the auspiciousness and inauspiciousness of its topographical features (Lee, 1984: 107).

In 1394, just two years after the foundation of the Joseon Dynasty, King Taejo decided to move the capital of Gaeseong, which had previously been the capital of the Goryeo Kingdom, to Hanyang, which has remained the physical location of the capital city for more than seven centuries. In fact, King Taejo succeeded King Kongyang of Goryeo in its capital Gaeseong in 1392 and renamed the kingdom "Joseon" in 1393. As soon as he ascended to the throne in 1392, he asked his subjects (Jeong Do-jeon and Ha Ryoon) and the greatest geomancer of the time (Muhak) to find a location for the new capital. Proposed sites included locations near Gyeryong Mountain, Muak Mountain, and Hanyang. According to the *Annals of the Joseon Dynasty*, Taejo personally visited the site near Geyryong Mountain in 1393 to make the final decision on the location which had been recommended by Monk Muhak for the new dynasty's capital; however, his subject Ha Ryoon objected that the location was too far from the geographical center of the peninsula, unlike Hanyang. Most critically, based on *docham sasang*, Ha argued that the new kingdom would fall if Joseon were to choose that site for the new capital. Facing such stark opposition, King Taejo withdrew his initial approval of Monk Muhak's recommendation and weighed the two remaining options—namely, the sites around Muak Mountain and Hanyang. Finally, in 1394, Taejo decided to relocate to Hanyang since the Muak site was not spacious enough and the mountain to its north was too small to be a manifestation of the North Star. Even Ha Ryoon, who had initially recommended it, acknowledged these facts (Kim, 2006: 26-28). Finally, in 1394, King Taejo declared that Hanyang would be the capital, motivated greatly by the fact that Hanyang was located in the center of the country, possessed a topological configuration similar to the forms of the ideal celestial charts of a sacred space, and enjoyed easy access to maritime transportation. In addition, he was greatly swayed by the fact that this recommendation came from Jeong Do-jeon, with whom he was closest.

Hanyang—located in the center of the Korean Peninsula, surrounded with mountains in the north, east, and west, and bordered by the Han River along the south—was regarded as one of the most strategic locations for a political capital. The city was originally built as a Southern Capital (*Namkyung*) of the Goryeo Kingdom in the mid-11th century under King Munjong. Geomancers never missed pointing out Hanyang as the most desirable location for a political center. The most important motivation leading King Taejo, the founder of the Joseon Dynasty, to build a new capital city in a new location was to confound the political loyalty being projected toward the old capital city of the previous kingdom and to make a clean break from that era.

In choosing a new location, King Taejong had to find a new source of geomantic legitimacy to justify his military coup against the former ruler as well as the founding of a new Confucian dynasty. Geomantic principles were the most important factor in the choice of the location for a capital city, and they strengthened the political justification for the birth of the new regime. As a new political group in a new political regime, their territorial base had to be revered as a better alternative to the old capital, which in turn had to be degraded as a place that had lost all sacred mandate to govern. Lee (1984: 107-108) aptly explains this point:

From the standpoint of this sort of geomantic theory, the gentry of each locality regarded their own home ground as auspicious, and they appeared to have sought to legitimize their standing as gentry on this basis. The case of the Wang family in Gaeseong may be said to be a prime example of this, for Wang Keon's unification of the Later Three Kingdoms was believed to be the result of Gaeseong's virtuous topography. Specially, we are told that Wang Keon's ancestors believed implicitly the geomantic forecast that if they planted pine trees on Mt. Songak, thus making the mountain green, and then moved their house to a site near the southern slope, a hero who would unite Korea's ancient *Samhan* would emerge from among their descendants. They proceeded to carry this out and Wang Keon's unification was the result. Wang Keon himself was a sincere if ingenuous believer in such geomantic theories, so much so that he asserted in the fifth of his Ten Injunctions: I carried out the great undertaking of reunifying the country by availing myself of the latent virtue of the mountains and streams of the *Samhan*.

Later, Chu Hsi, the founder of Neo-Confucianism, adopted geomantic principles in his political thought. Thus, despite the general perception of geomancy as superstitious, esoteric, and mystic, an identification of topological configurations and landscapes reflecting the ideal celestial charts with the mandate to govern from Heaven served as one of the most important factors in political affairs in ancient Korea, including the Shilla, Goryeo, and Joseon kingdoms. Just as original geomancy instructed, the shapes of landscapes and topological configurations had a great deal to do with the fate of kingdoms and individuals, according to Doseon's idea of *docham* (*do* = "signs," *cham* = "foretelling") *sasang* (idea).

Doseon was the first political geomancer to predict that the military general Wang Keon of the post-Shilla Kingdom would establish a united Goryeo kingdom in 918. Doseon is commonly credited for having recommended that the house of Wang Keon's father be moved to a site near the southern slope of the Songak Mountain so that his descendant, Wang Keon, could unite the ancient Samhan. Later, Doseon also foretold that Hanyang would be the capital city that would replace Gaeseong.

In his "*Yuki*," Doseon predicted: "Wang Keon's Goryeo will be succeeded by the king whose family name is Yi, and his kingdom will be located in Hanyang." Further, based on this belief, "he ordered *Yukwan* during the mid-Goryeo period to plant the Oyat tree (*Prunus domestica*, 李[*yi*]) on the South of Baekak Mountain (Hanyang) and to prune it so that it does not grow thick" (Kim, 2006: 6). Doseon ordered Yukwan to prune the Oyat tree because the Chinese character for this tree was 李 (*yi*), the same character as the family name of the founder of the Joseon Dynasty—Yi Seonggye. This episode demonstrates how important the symbolism of geographical and geomantic elements was in the demise of the Goryeo Dynasty and the foundation of the Joseon Dynasty as the *Annals of the Joseon Dynasty* devote numerous pages to describing the process of selecting the site for a new capital city and debating the importance of geomancy.

Doseon's prediction was inherited by his student geomancer, Kim Wije, who claimed that "Hanyang would become the center of the world, and that all the auspicious fish of the world would gather in the Han River, while the dragons and fish of the Han River would spread out to the world. He also stressed the fact that merchants from all over the world would come to *Hanyang* to offer up their treasures" (Han, 2010: 33). The most important point made by this geomancer was that "it would be a man of the Joseon clan, and not Wang clan, that would start a new age in Hanyang" (Han, 2010: 33).

This was not the first time that such geomantic principles served to cause political upheavals in the foundation of the Joseon Dynasty. A Buddhist monk named Myocheong urged Injong of the Goryeo Kingdom to abandon Gaeseong and move the capital to Pyeongyang in 1135, arguing that the virtue of the Gaeseong topography was depleted while that of Pyeongyang was full of vigor. Moving the capital to Pyeongyang, he claimed, would reinvigorate the dynasty (Lee, 1984: 137). Therefore, the new rulers had to convince the masses of their political legitimacy. Moreover, their seizure of power from existing power groups had to be justified by choosing a new capital city, which would serve as proof that Heaven had abrogated its mandate to govern.

In this perspective, the importance of geomantic technology and philosophy in the political transformation of ancient Korea cannot be overemphasized. The relocation of the old Goryeo capital from Gaeseong to Hanyang was a fundamental way to debilitate the aristocratic ruling class whose economic base was concentrated there and to promote the beginning of a new dynasty in a new capital. Nonetheless, the role of geomancy has received scant attention in scholarly analyses on traditional Korean politics. The literature on Korean traditional politics tends to treat the elements of geomancy in a journalistic manner: for example, geomancy may be mentioned briefly as a side story but never as an authoritative source of explanations for Korea's political culture. The people's deep-seated and continuously reproduced belief in the impact of geomantic principles upon politics has significantly contributed to the centralized hegemonic power of state in Korean political history; thus, it is essential to re-construct how this has affected the emergence of the developmental state during Korea's modernization and the expansion of the heteronomical forces throughout the eras of Kyeongseong and Seoul.

Korea's capital city, which has remained in the same spot for almost a thousand years, is a microcosm of state-society relations that today bears traces of each era's major political and economic ideologies and dominant political culture. In reconstructing the state-society relations, this book re-articulates three distinctive yet integrally related principles of polities—hegemony and hierarchy (as origins of state centrality and bureaucracy) and heteronomy (as the origin of the previously small but contemporarily expanded civil society)—by reading those principles as reflected in the architectural design, city layouts, and monumentality of the Confucian capital city of Hanyang, Kyeongseong, and Seoul. My interpretation of Kant's "heteronomy" in the context of power dynamics in the Joseon political system is more like a way of being "heterogeneous" to the hegemonic royal family and hierarchical Confucian bureaucracy. Geomancy contributed to the rise and demise of political forces, emphasizing the changes of political power configurations, while Neo-Confucianism reified the power of the Confucian literati. Thus, this book will retrace how this prototype of state-society relations was modified and adapted during the Kyeongseong and Seoul eras in order to provide a theoretical paradigm capable of explaining the simultaneous phenomena of rapid economic and political development in the 20th century.

SACRED AND PROFANE

In their search for the Ultimate Cause or Will of Heaven, archaic people looked to the sky for a model that they could replicate on earth and promote as the center of the world. Such efforts to symbolize political legitimacy by constructing a replica of the celestial archetype were recorded in a passage in the *Lun-Yu*: "Confucius is alleged to have remarked that, 'He who exercises government by means of his moral force may be compared to the Pole Star, which keeps its [central] position while all the [other] stars do homage to it [i.e., by revolving about it]" (Wheatley, 1971: 430). The characteristic that ancient people sought was constancy or immutability; so it comes as no surprise that they would identify Polaris as a symbol of that which deserved their complete reliance. Thus, the Pole Star became the center of the ideal city type for archaic folks, and the identification of the center of the Heavens became central in their search for the most sacred spot in their land.

Thus, geomantic technology and knowledge was revered by both the rulers and the ruled: kings and elites had to demonstrate their legitimacy to govern by locating the topological configurations and landscapes that most closely resembled the Heavens for their palaces and ceremonial and patrimonial centers. This is demonstrated by the Duke of Chou's address to young King Ch'eng: "'I report to you my son and bright sovereign. If the King will not settle in the place where Heaven founded the mandate and fixed the mandate [i.e., the western capital at Hao], I have . . . made a great survey of the eastern regions in order to find a place where he shall be the people's bright sovereign" (Wright, 1977: 36). The ruled were also likely to give their consent when they saw their rulers' capacity to choose those sacred spaces in which the symbols of sacred manifested themselves; this is what Eliade terms "hierophany," which he describes as follows:

> . . . there is not only a break in the homogeneity of space; there is also revelation of an absolute reality, opposed to the non-reality of the vast surrounding expanse. The manifestation of the sacred ontologically founds the world. In the homogeneous and infinite expanse, in which no point of reference is possible and hence no orientation can be established, the hierophany reveals an absolute fixed point, a center. (1957: 21)

Lacking the scientific knowledge and technologies that we have today in geology, geography, and astronomy, the people of that era looked to the pseudo-scientific knowledge of geomancy as "the ultimate political technology" for linking Heaven with rulers and for mystifying the power of kings and aristocracy. Within that context, Hanyang was chosen during transition from the Goryeo to the Joseon Dynasty for several reasons. The geomancers' contributions were not confined to merely locating a few resemblances but to sacralizing and cosmicizing the places as well. "Its consecration signified its 'reality' and, therefore, sanctioned its habitation; but its establishment as an imitation of a celestial archetype required its delimitation and orientation as a sacred territory within the continuum of profane space" (Wheatley, 1971: 417). On the other hand, being profane means being homogeneous, monotonous, and neutral; there is no break that "qualitatively differentiates the various parts of its mass" (Eliade, 1957, 22), so that "No true orientation is now possible, for the fixed point no longer enjoys a unique ontological status" (23).

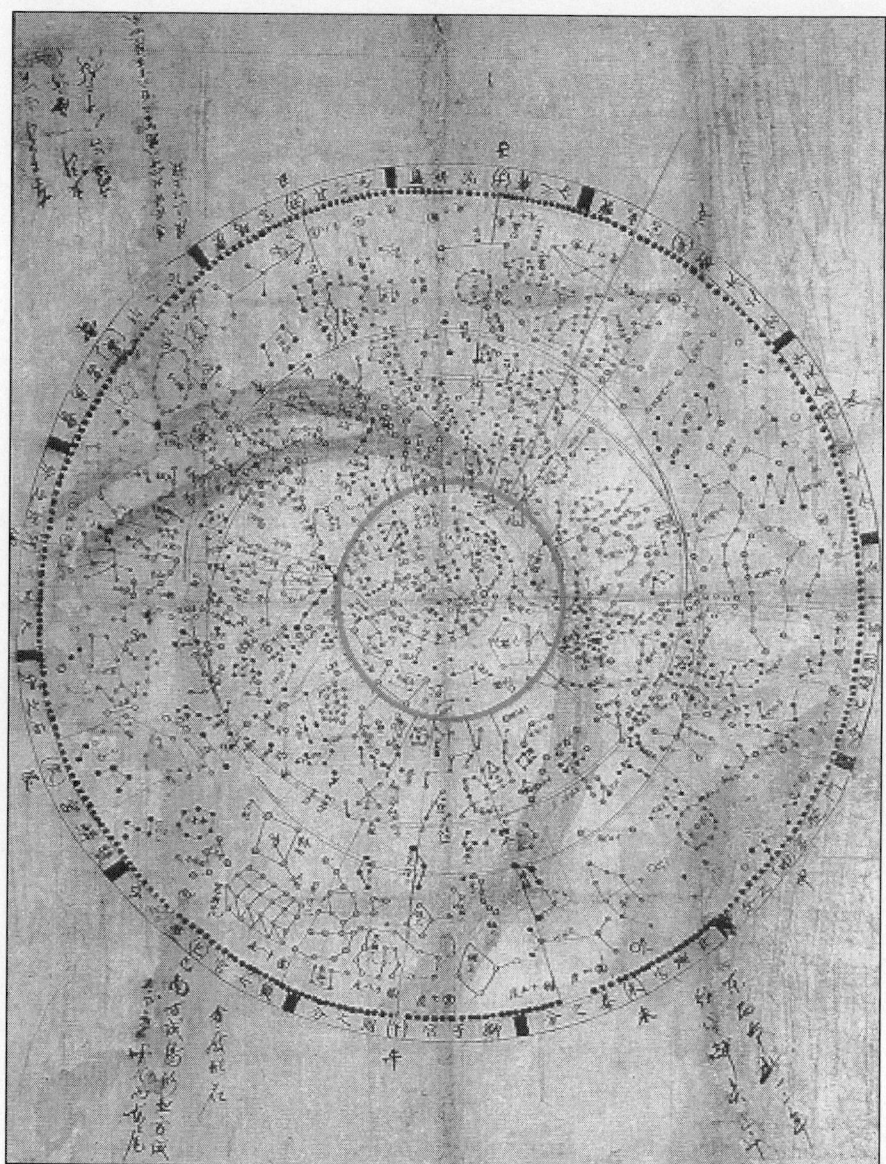

Map 3.2 Cheonsang yolcha boonya jido in 1395: Astronomical Quadrants Centered on Polaris. A: Celestial Origin for Circle A in Map 2, and Figures 3.1 and 3.2. Korea's Astronomical Chart, see Korea's Astronomical Association (1995), p. 33.

The development of astronomical charts in Korea went hand in hand with the development of maps. The *Cheonsang yolcha bunya jido,* an astronomical chart produced in 1395 for the purpose of displaying monarchial power,[5] included 1,463 stars, constellations, and formations such as the Milky Way. This chart evinced a high level of astronomical information as well as topographic skill. In the epilogue to this astronomical chart, Kwon Keun, who had played a critical role in founding the Joseon Dynasty, emphasized that "the King must observe the Will of Heaven to govern well" (Noh, 1996: 225). The divine, in other words, is abstracted from the rites re-actualizing the specific event which sanctioned comparatively little direct effect on the landscape. On the other hand, those religions which hold that human order was brought into being at the creation of the world tend to dramatize the cosmogony by creating on earth a replica of the cosmos. Sacrality (which is synonymous with "reality") is achieved through the imitation of a celestial archetype, as a result of which such religions can powerfully transform the landscape, sometimes to a very extreme degree.

Throughout Asia, where this latter category of religious dramatization was widespread, there was a tendency for kingdoms, capitals, temples, and shrines to be constructed as replicas of the cosmos. Eliade (1957) has illustrated this with examples drawn primarily from the architecture, epigraphy, and literature of the ancient Near East and India, and numerous others could be adduced from Southeast Asia and the Americas. In the astrobiological mode of thought, irregularities in the cosmic order could only be interpreted as misfortunes, so that, if a city were laid out as an *imago mundi* with the cosmogony as its paradigmatic model, it became necessary to maintain this parallelism between macrocosmos and microcosmos by participating in the seasonal festivals that constituted man's contribution to the regulation of cyclic time, and by incorporating an abundance of symbolism into the planning.

This central axis of the universe, kingdom, city, or temple could be moved to a more propitious site or duplicated whenever circumstances rendered that desirable, for it was an attribute of existential rather than geometrical space. From this line, which was the holy of holies at whichever hierarchical level it might occur, the four horizons projected outward in the cardinal directions of the compass, thus assimilating the group's territory—whether tribal land, kingdom, or city—to the cosmic order, and constructing a sanctified space or *habitabilis*. The sacred space delimited in this manner within the continuum of profane space provided the framework for conducting all of the rituals necessary to ensure intimate harmony between the macro- and microcosmos; without such harmony, no prosperity could exist in the world of men. As the *Li-Chi* puts it, "Rites obviate disorder as dikes prevent inundation."

A capital city, in order to establish and maintain the credentials for its sacredness, had to satisfy the following conditions. First, its topographical configuration had to be identical with the shape of a constellation. Second, it had to be in a place where great mountains came down to meet a river. Third, it

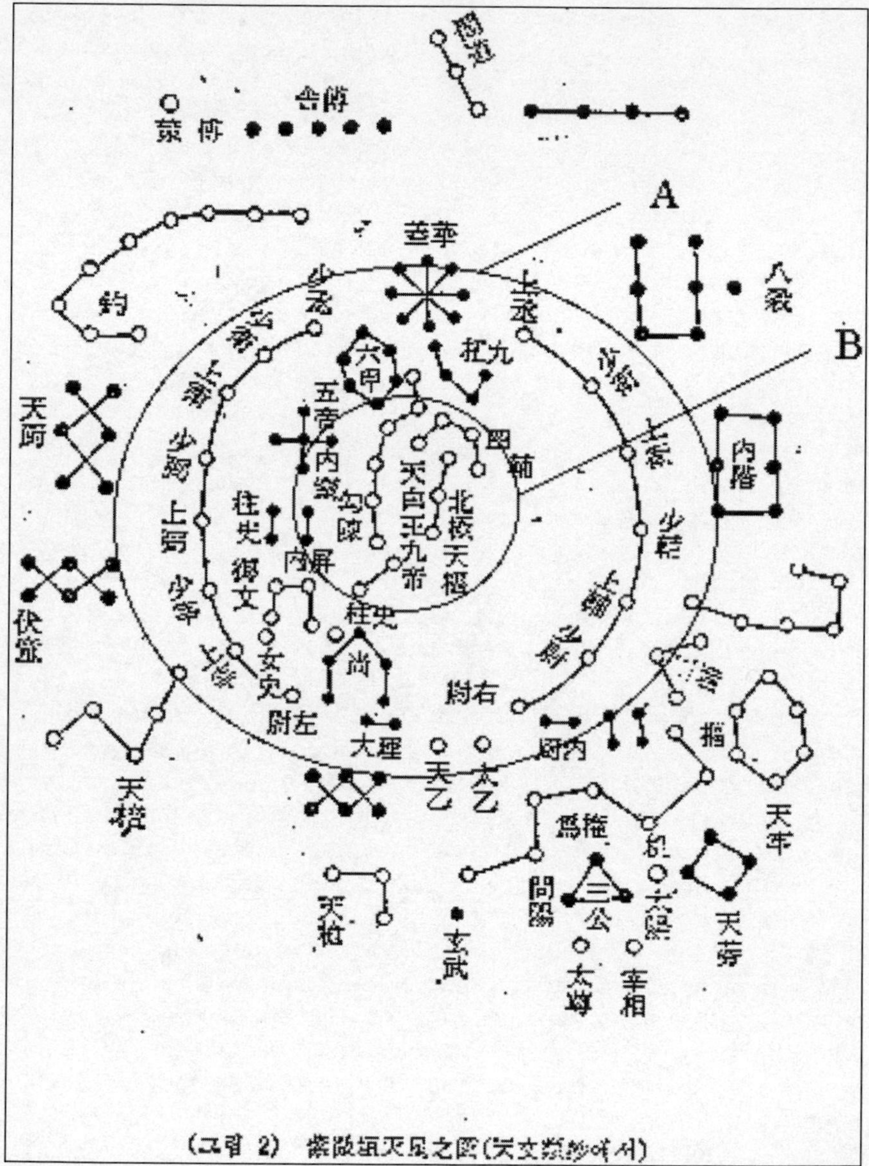

Figure 3.1 Celestial Chart of Jamiwon, the Astronomical Quadrants Centered on Polaris: Expanded Map Corresponding to Circle A of Map 3.2. According to ancient Chinese astrology, the sky is comprised of four quadrants each with its own fixed star. The quadrant of Jamiwon, with Polaris at its center, is where the Lord of Heaven resides. All of these inner circles in figures 1, 2, and 3 mark the core-sacred space where the Kyeongbok Palace is analogously located. The outer circles in figures 1, 2, and 3 mark the encircling sacred space. Celestial Chart of Jamiwon. See Kim, Dong-Kyu (1991), p. 294.

had to be in the country's center (Kim b, 1991: 289). Indeed, the more closely the arrangements of mountains and rivers in an area resembled the arrangement of the stars, the more auspicious the spot was deemed. At the same time, as can be clearly seen on various maps, cities were placed in their natural environments for more than just the convenience of borders. Furthermore, the shape of mountains and the direction of rivers were considered as important factors for the well-being of the people and the success of the dynasty.

Figure 3.1 shows a very complex celestial archetype that would be hard to replicate on earth. In the Joseon Dynasty, the Kejesa, a highly regarded agency within the Ijo (Ministries of Personnel), took charge of geomancy, the calendar, weather prediction, and time measurement (*Kyeonggukdaijeon*, 1986: 214). By utilizing this effective government agency that possessed advanced geomantic skills, city planners were able to find the physical location most closely resembling the celestial chart, and there they built Hanyang. Figure 3.2 shows the ideal arrangement of mountains reflecting the sacred part of a celestial body. Specifically, an encircling wall[6] formed by four mountains marked the best spot for establishing the city. Thus, important buildings, such as palaces, the Royal Ancestral Shrine, and powerful government institutions, were placed on this spot.

CONFUCIAN CITY LEGIBILITY

Confucian virtues were integrated into the geomantic infrastructure. The 18-km castle wall ran parallel to the encircling wall of mountains formed by Mt. Baekak to the north, Mt. Nakta to the east, Mt. Mokmyuk to the south, and Mt. Inwang to the west (fig. 3.3). The city was designed also to be in accordance with certain widely held principles. Taoism held that the world was composed of five elements: fire, water, wood, iron, and earth.[7] Each of these elements was paired with a corresponding Confucian virtue: ritual, wisdom, benevolence, righteousness, and fidelity, respectively. In addition, a direction was associated with each element: east with wood and benevolence, west with iron and righteousness, south with fire and ritual, and north with water and wisdom, and center with earth and fidelity. Such syntheses of astrological, Taoistic, geomantic, and Confucian ideas are systematically embodied in the city structure of Hanyang.

Each of the four mountains was associated with one of the above combinations:[8] Mt. Baekak stood for water and wisdom, Mt. Nakta for wood and benevolence, Mt. Inwang for iron and righteousness, and Mt. Mokmyuk for fire and ritual. Moreover, a symbolic animal was added to each of these combinations: white tiger (*Baekho*) for Mt. Inwang, blue dragon (*Cheongryong*)

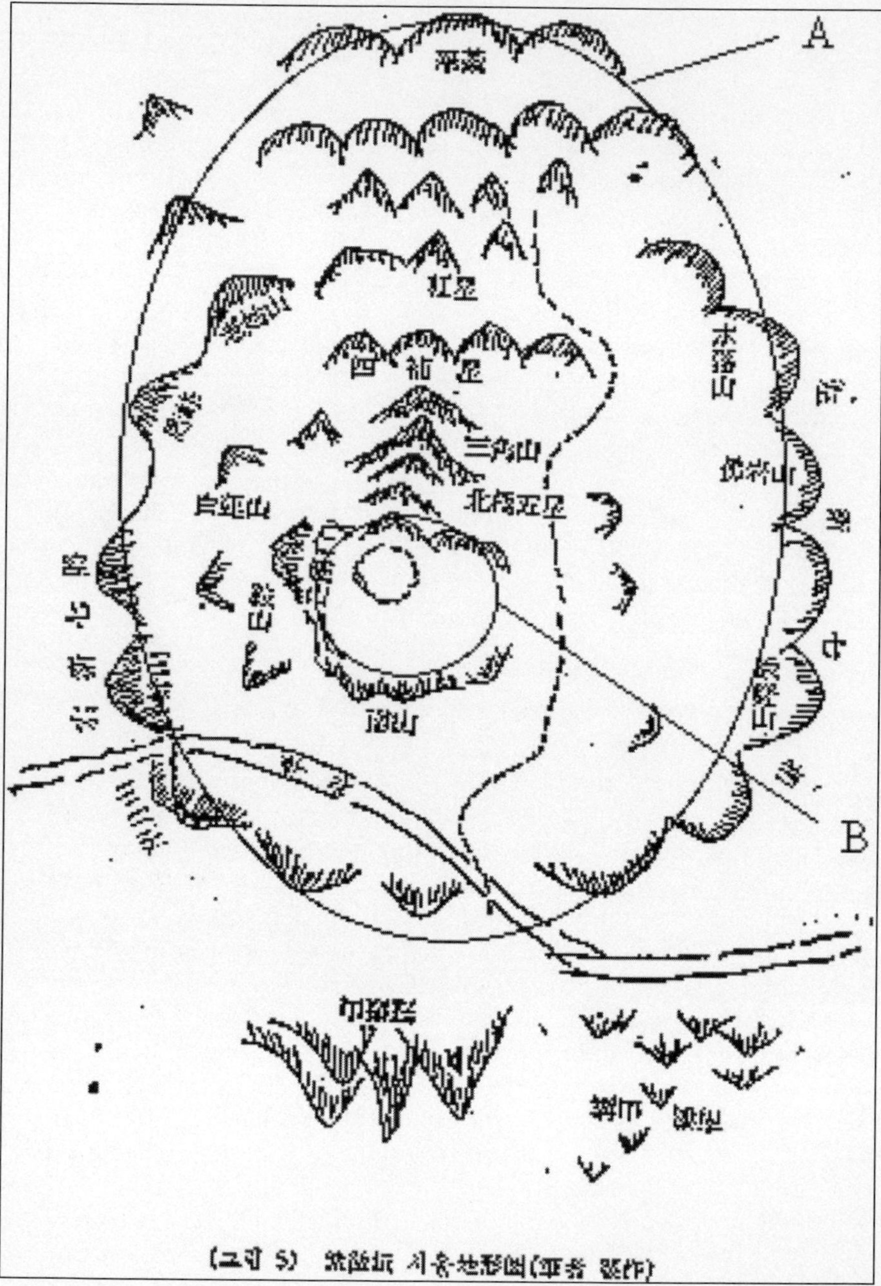

Figure 3.2 Idealized Topological Map Reflecting Configuration of the Celestial Chart of Jamiwon. See Kim, Dong-Kyu (1991), p.299.

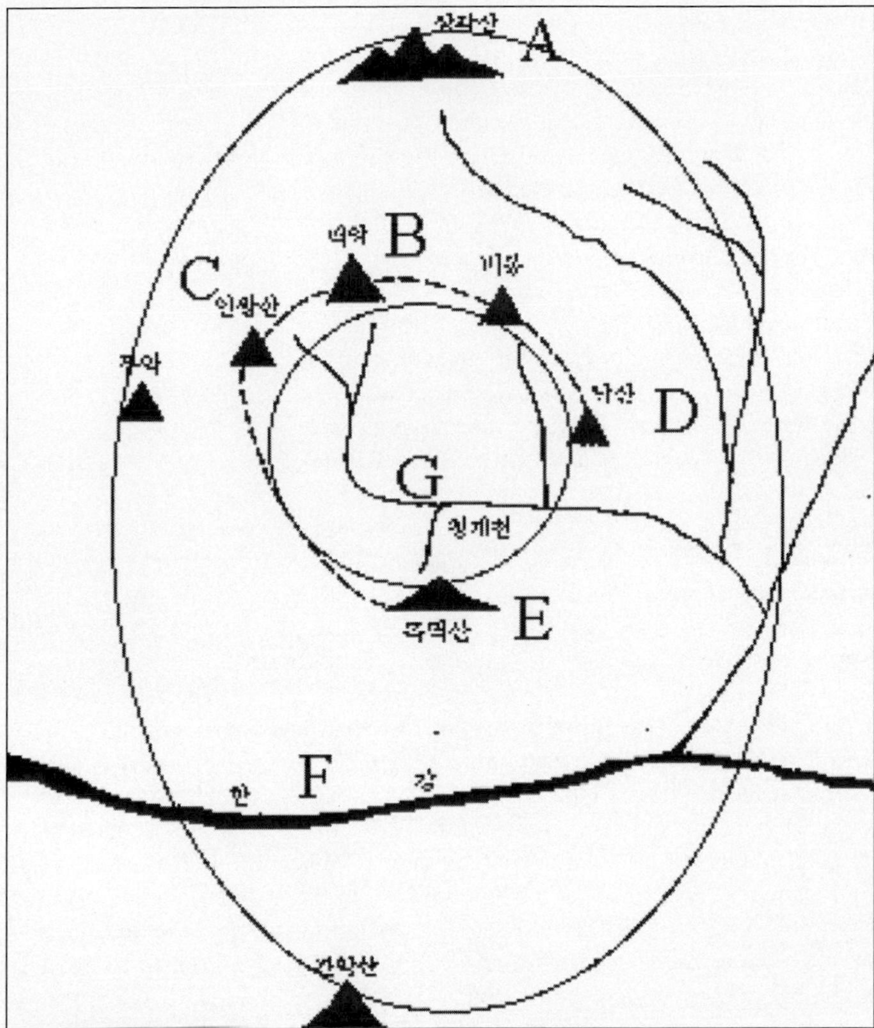

Figure 3.3 Actual Topological Map of Mountains and Rivers of Hanyang ("C" Type). A. Mt. Samgak, B. Mt. Beakak, C. Mt. Inwang, D. Mt. Nak, E. Mt. Mokmyuk, F. Han River, G. Cheonggyecheon, tributaries of Han River. See Lim, Deok-Soon (1994a), p. 51.

for Mt. Nakta, a mythological bird (*Joojak*) for Mt. Mokmyuk, and a mythological turtle/snake (*Hyunmoo*) for Mt. Baekak.

In the parallels that were created between the celestial archetype and the natural topological configurations of Hanyang, we can find a parallel between the macro- and microcosmos. This parallelism is further reflected in the architectural design of the capital. Each of the four perimeter gates was linked with one of the above-mentioned associations: the east gate (*Heunginjimoon*) with wood and benevolence, the west gate (*Doneuimoon*) with iron and righteousness, the north gate (*Sookjeongmoon*) with water and wisdom, and the south gate (*Soongryemoon*) with fire and ritual; the bell tower (*Boshingak)* in the very middle of city was associated with earth and fidelity[9] (Lim, 1994a: 51-52). Furthermore, such parallelism is also found between the layouts of the capital city and those of the provincial capital cities, as shown in map 3.3. In this way, both natural and artificial elements were incorporated extensively into the symbolic significance of the city's monumentality.

Prominent among the morphological features that the ideal type Chinese city shared with the majority of the great capitals of Asia were the use of cardinal orientation, cardinal axiality, and a more or less square perimeter delimited by a massive wall. In China, this schema, which can even be found in the plans of some of the earliest cities (Wheatley, 1971: 135-150), was most apparent in the design of the imperial capitals; however, even the smaller *hsien* cities usually exhibited the rudiments of cardinal axiality and orientation (Wheatley, 1971: 423).

In the idealized city of the Western Chou, the ruler's palace was raised exactly in the center of the enceinte, and itself constituted a city within a city. At its very center, the hall of audience faced southward toward the axial avenue, which ran between the altar of the god of the soil and the temple of the ancestors. At the next lower level in the social hierarchy, the dwellings of the more powerful families, each grouped round its own great hall, reproduced on a smaller scale the residence of the ruler. As in all classical (which is synonymous with archetyped) literatures, the cities of the Western Chou are represented as splendid creations of Chinese architectural genius (Wheatley, 1971: 188).

By locating the main palace, the Kyeongbok, in the northern center of the archetype as a reflection of the position of Polaris in the sky, the designers established the preeminence of Confucian political power as that fixed point around which all human affairs revolve. According to Eliade and Wheatley, this centrality is further supported in the form of the *axis mundi*, the North-South axis on Earth. In Hanyang, this *axis mundi* is clearly expressed in the line connecting the main mountain Mt. Baekak in the north to the main palace (Kyeongbok) and further to the Six Ministries Street in the south. This North-South axis symbolizes the line connecting the macrocosmos (Heaven or Celestial Archetype) and microcosmos (Hanyang, Kyeongbok Palace, king). Based on this *axis mundi*, the cardinal orientation, including the East-West axis, is established. Within this ideal spot, a dichotomous concept of "sacred" and "profane" space is clearly embodied in the layout of the capital city. All of the important political institutions are located either directly on the *axis mundi* or parallel to it within the area north of the East-West axis;

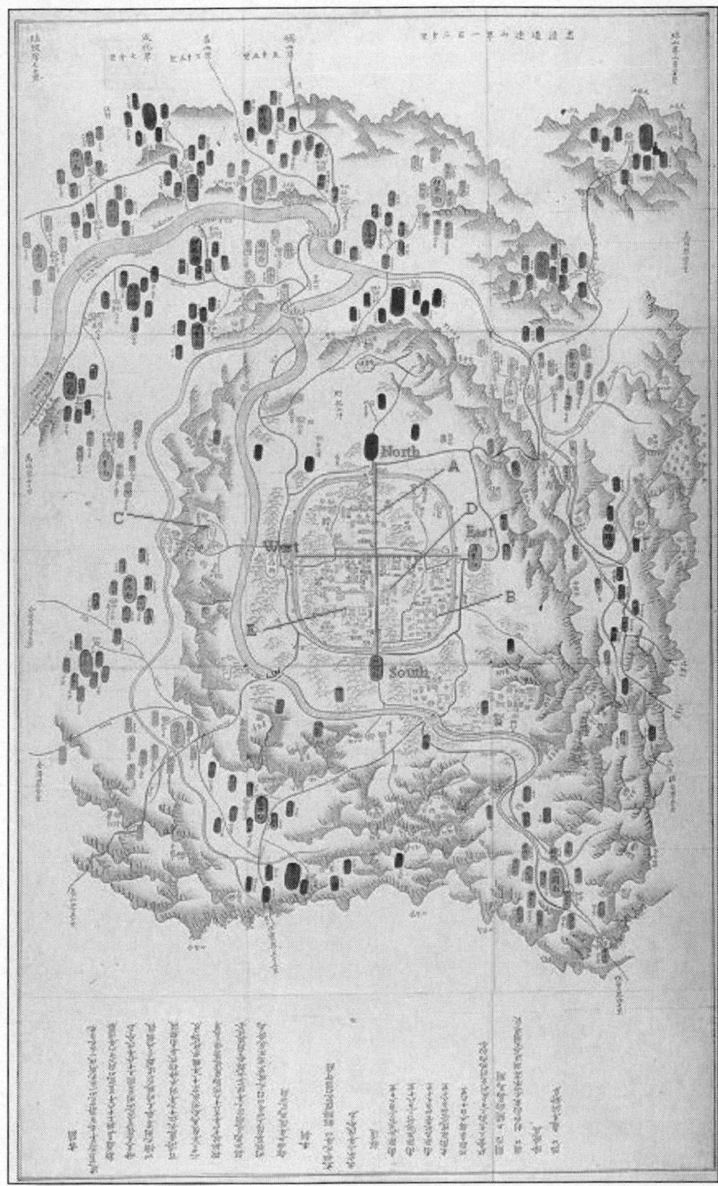

Map 3.3 Cheonjoo Booseong Jido: Map of Cheonjoo Castle in Cholla Province, with a Layout Analogous to Hanyang's. A. Gaeksa, B. Kyunggijeon, C. Sajik, D. Booyoung (Judge's Office), E. Gamyoung (Office of Provincial Governor) Booyoung and Gamyoung together make Kwana, meaning a collective government office building in the provinces. Copyright Kyujanggak Institute of Korean Studies. Kyujanggak (1995), Choson sidae jibangjido, p. 25. For an explanation of this map, refer to Chang (1994), p. 55.

these buildings include palaces, the royal ancestral shrines, and the Guardian Deities of the State, as replicas of the cosmos. The resulting configuration emphasized that these Confucian political institutions were to be highly esteemed, thereby strengthening Confucian state hegemony.

Chinese City Archetype: Gugong (Kao-Kung chi)

The capital city of the Joseon Dynasty was regarded by the masses both as the most auspicious spot on Earth and the place where the Will of Heaven was realized. In its design, the "Final Cause" was believed to be manifested through participation in the Symbolism of the Center, expressed by some form of *axis mundi*. It was important in Confucian ideology that the axial design of the main processional axis run north-south because ancient astrology believed that divine power originated from Polaris (Wheatley, 1971; Lim, 1994). So, it was due to the influence of geomancy and Confucian ideology that the king and the palace faced southward (*Seoul Yukbaeknyunsa* (1), 1978: 200). Since this *axis mundi* was also believed to be the point of ontological transition at which divine power entered the world and diffused outward through the kingdom, Wheatley (1971: 418) argues, the techniques of orientation necessary for defining sacred territory within the continuum of profane space involve an emphasis on the cardinal compass directions. Even more impressive is the symbolism of the four entrance gates facing the cardinal compass points (Wheatley, 1971; Lim, 1994a; Kim, Young-Sang, 1994). These gates, through which the power that was generated at the *axis mundi* flowed out from the ceremonial complex toward the cardinal points of the compass, possessed a heightened symbolic significance that was expressed through the massiveness of their construction, far exceeding that which was necessary for the performance of their mundane functions of granting access and affording defense (Wheatley, 1971: 435).

As a whole, the design of the Joseon capital represented a strong ideal type of Confucian state ideology in many ways. Although, at a glance, the layout may seem irregular in terms of the design of the city functions, such as the roads and positions of houses and walls, the seemingly irregular compositions of these components is infused with Confucian ideology as shown by the articulation of networks of significant spaces and buildings, public places, and the connections between them. Through these forms, the factor of monumentality in the capital city contributed to the establishment of the Confucian hegemony in the Joseon Dynasty. For all of these reasons, the city is seen as an entity that embodies and expresses certain values and ideals.

The principles that guided the construction of the ancient capital city in China were recorded in the form of a manual called the *Gugong* or *Kao-kung chi*, which is summarized in appendix 1.[10] By way of Neo-Confucianism, these principles found their way into Korea and guided the designers and builders of Hanyang. Thus, an examination of the beliefs contained in this original manual will help demonstrate the extent to which geomancy and Confucian values influenced the design of this symbolic city. The most important point to note here is that the view of the government as sacred and the market as profane planted seeds for the rationale underlying state-run economic growth and the developmental state.

CONFUCIAN INSTITUTIONS AND ARCHITECTURAL MONUMENTALITY

The Joseon Dynasty was established in 1392 on the solid bedrock of Neo-Confucianism, a new philosophical interpretation of Confucianism that explained the origins of man and the universe in metaphysical terms. The main social forces of the Joseon Dynasty—comprised of Confucian scholar bureaucrats or literati or sadaebu—might well have dreamed of achieving an ideal polity through the moral cultivation of the masses. Accordingly, they devised a corpus of administrative law[11] infused with the ideals of Confucianist government, a code embodying the cardinal principles of the Joseon Dynasty's political process.

This Confucian principle of governance can be found in the urban disposition of the Confucian political institutions. The principle of symbolic centripetality was also clearly manifested in the traditional Chinese city. "The essential Asian mode of urban design was refracted through the lens of a Great Tradition whose primary concern was with the ordering of society in this world. The centrally situated temple of the archetypal South Indians and Southeast Asian city was replaced in the Chinese realm by the seat of secular authority, royal palace" (Wheatley, 1971: 428).

First of all, the main palace (Kyeongbok) stands at the top of a pyramid of power, occupying the most ideal spots within the castle, just before the main mountain (Mt. Baekak). The other royal palaces (Changdeokgung, Changkyeonggung, and Kyeonghuigung) lie to the east and west of the main palace. King Chungjo described in *Hongjejeonse* how the palace should be placed. "*Goonggwol* [the palace] as the place where the king conducts affairs of state and rules the lives of subjects should look grand and beautiful to inspire the people's respect and loyalty" (Hong, 1994: 33).

The district of the main palace is divided into three sections (fig. 3.4)—the entrance, main office, and private quarters (Lee, Wha-Seon, 1993: 79). Located in the entrance section are the main gate (Kwanghwamoon) and Youngje Bridge (Youngjekyo). In order to display the grandeur of the palace, this Kwanghwamoon was constructed in the form of a castle gate. To signal the demarcation between the holy and worldly areas, the Youngje Bridge was built across Cheongkye Stream (Cheongkyecheon). Generally speaking, this

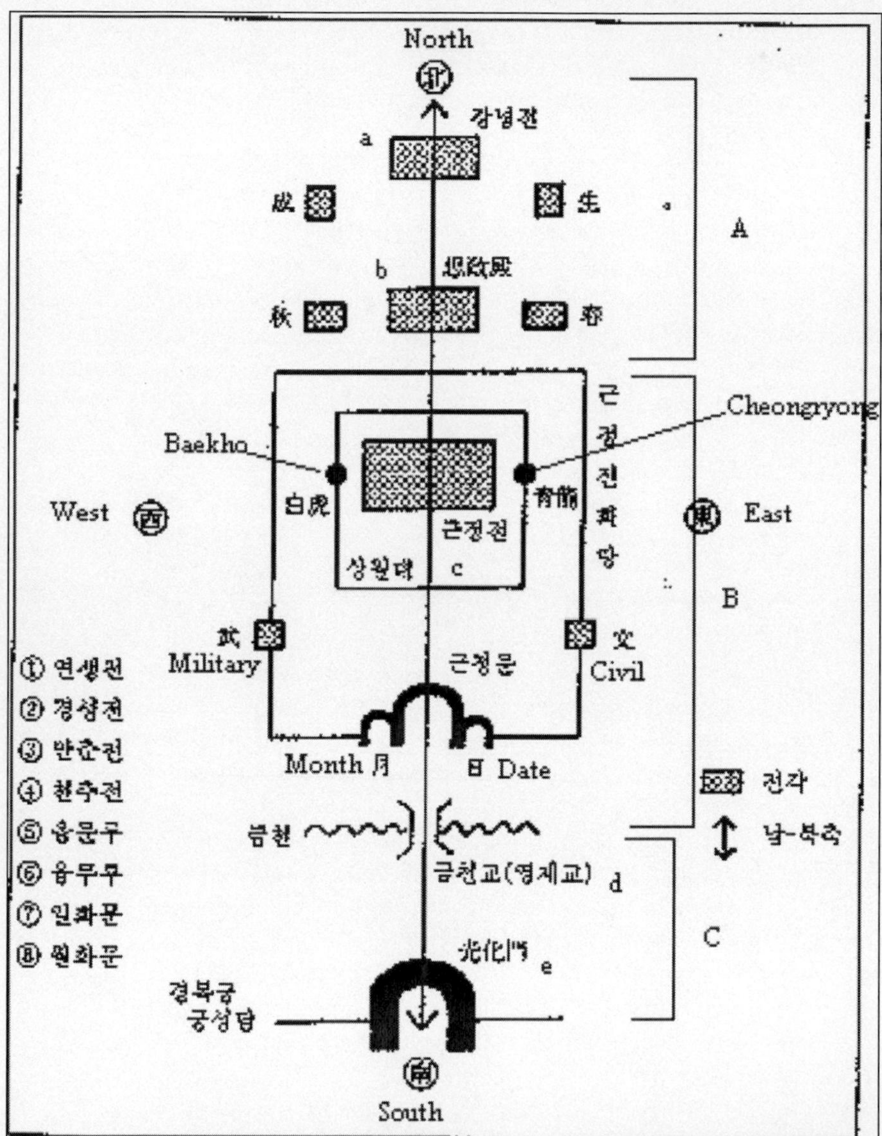

Figure 3.4 Aerial View of Main Buildings in Kyeongbok Palace. A. Royal Family Quarters, B. Main Office Area, C. The Front Gate Area, a. Gangnyunjeon (Royal Family Quarters), b. Sajeongjeon (Informal Office of King), c. Keunjeongjeon (Main Office of King), d. Youngjekyo, e. Kwanghwamoon. Lim, Deok-Soon (1994b), p. 59.

stream functioned as a geographical boundary separating the King and palace from that which was profane. More specifically, though, it separated the palace from the sacred Six Ministries Street, thereby glorifying the authority of the King even more in comparison.[12]

The next section to the north was reserved for the King's main office (Keunjeongjeon), which was built with proportions that reflected a sense of dignity and authority. The relationship of its side dimensions to its facade dimension was 1:1.33, according to tradition. Interestingly, this proportion is not far from the Western formula for such buildings, 1:1.42 (Park, 1977: 21). Keunjeongjeon and its sub-architectures, like gates, stairs, and small walls, were symmetrically built directly along the *axis mundi* or parallel to it.

There are various different lines for egress and ingress according to hierarchical order (Park, 1977: 19-20). For example, there was one stairway in front of the main office, divided into three sections: the middle for the king and the left and right for high officials. Lower bureaucrats had to use egress/ingress paths farther from the center. Behind the main office (Keunjeongjeon), in the private quarters, was an office unit called Sajeongjeon where the king would lead academic discussions with Confucian scholarly bureaucrats. Figure 3.5 shows all paths of egress/ingress in the Keunjeongjeon.

Another important function of this division relates to worship. Confucian elites believed that Confucian ideals could only be realized through rule based on *Ye* (rite). The *Kookjo oreui*, which was a book of protocol, divided the forms of worship and ceremonies into five major categories: good fortune, foreign guests, family affairs, bad fortune, and military affairs. Except in the case of rituals for good fortune, all rituals were conducted in the Keunjeongjeon. And since Confucianist rule was based on rite (*Ye*), institutions like Monmyo,[13] Jongmyo, and Sajik (where ceremonies related to good fortune were conducted), in addition to the palaces, were considered the most significant buildings in the Confucian Joseon Dynasty. The main palace in particular became a center for such rituals, thereby strengthening the ruling power of the dynasty. Prayers were offered up for the good fortune of the state in the Guardian Deities of the State and the Royal Ancestral Shrine. Small sub-branches of these institutions were spread throughout the so-called sacred space within the capital city, as shown in figure 3.7. These were the most important Confucian political institutions (Kim, 1991: 20-21). As can be seen in figure 3.4 (Lim, 1994: 57), around the King's main office there stood four stone statues of symbolic animals: Blue Dragon to the left, White Tiger to the right, *Hyunmoo* to the rear, and *Joojak* to the front.

The last section to the north was the private quarters of the royal family. Locating the office area in the front and the housing area in the back was in accordance with the rules set forth in the *Gugong*. This section was

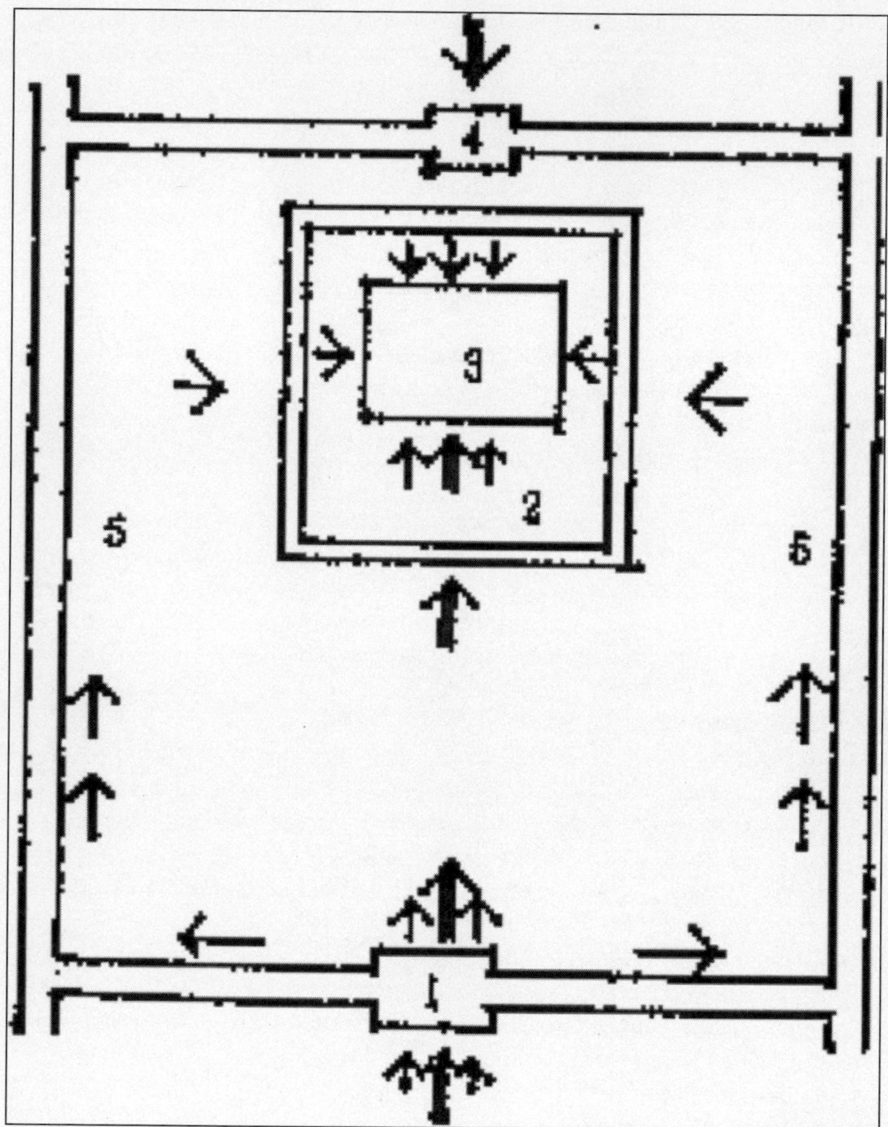

Figure 3.5 Arrows Showing Hierarchically Determined Paths of Ingress/Egress in Keunjeongjeon (Main Office for King). King in the center, high civil and military officials adjacent, and lower bureaucrats on the periphery. Park, Young-Ho (1977).

comprised of the main royal house (Kangnyeongjeon) and four more sub-branches for the royal family. Figuratively speaking, the King was Polaris, and these five units were the Five Emperors in the sky (Chin, 1995: 255;

Lee, 1991a: 33). Each palace comprised a centrally situated ceremonial and administrative enclave, which can be safely presumed to have afforded a habitation for members of the royal lineage, a priesthood, and a few selected craftsmen together with perhaps something similar to a praetorian guard (Wheatley, 1971: 47).

Shifting our attention from the palace to the Six Ministries Street (fig. 3.6), we can see that the main government offices, the Six Ministries, and affiliated government agencies around them were located in front of the main palace. It is no coincidence that the Ministry of Rites (Yejo) was placed closest to the main palace; such placement demonstrates the importance of this office in Confucian political thought. Confucius believed that the societal realization of the highest moral value of humanness must be channeled through the proper rituals of decorum—more specifically, ethical norms regulating social behavior (Fu, 1993: 31). Moreover, humanness could be inculcated in the people through education, persuasion, and moral example, and such was the holy function of this Ministry of Rites. The virtue of the ruler was believed to have direct bearing on the good fortune of his subjects, and Confucius taught that a ruler should govern based on moral principles—not by force. If the ruler himself were not righteous, then his command would garner no respect, Confucius said. In order to cultivate human nature, Confucius prescribed that decorum be incorporated into government functions. In government, consistent enforcement of the conducting of rites was more important than penal law: "Lead the people by administrative measures and regulate them by penal punishment, the people will not commit crimes but will have no sense of shame. Lead the people by virtue and regulate them by decorum, they will have a sense of shame and be upright" (Fu, 1993: 31-32). The most important business of government, Confucius believed, was to ensure the availability of food and provide moral education for the people. Furthermore, the government was regarded as a parent feeding and taking care of its children. The importance of decorum and ritual in Confucian culture was reflected in the location of the Ministry of Rites, which regulated and managed all kinds of ritual ceremonies and bureaucratic processes in the statecraft, along the line of the Six Ministries Street.

Placing the city hall in the midst of the Six Ministries (fig. 3.6) indicates that the political role played by city government was essential; this was the case not merely because this institution dealt with city government but because it handled the city government of Hanyang, the capital. From 1395, the city hall was located in the Chingcheong-bang District in the Central Section (Choong-bu) of the city, between the Yijo (Ministry of Personnel) and the Hojo (Ministry of Taxation). Its office was located along the Six Ministries Street in front of Kyeongbok Palace. The fact that it was located between powerful Yijo and Hojo attests to its importance in Joseon's political system;

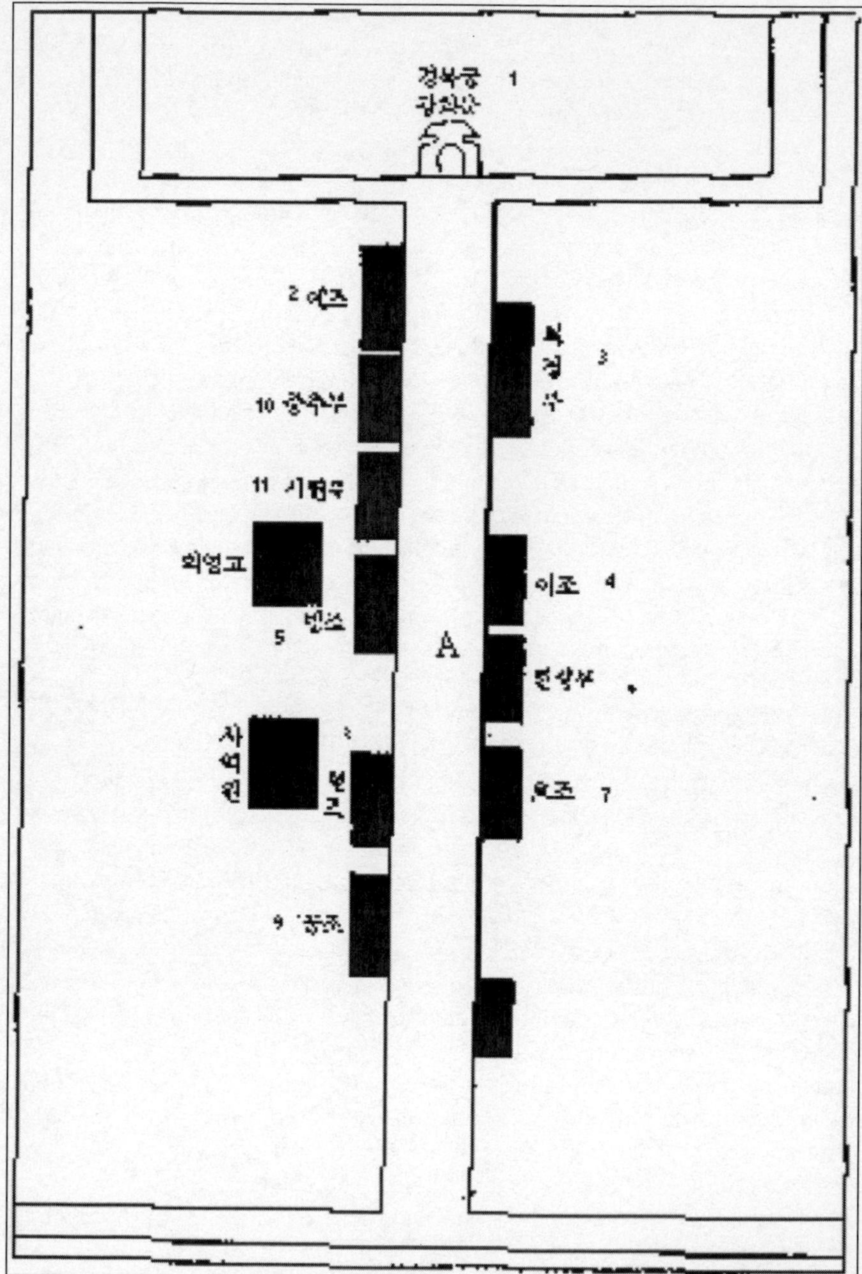

Figure 3.6 The Six Ministries Street. 1. Kyeongbok Palace, 2. Yejo, 3. Euijeongbu, 4. Ijo, 5. Byungjo, 6. Hanseongbu, 7. Hojo, 8. Hyungjo, 9. Kongjo, 10. Joongchoobu, 11. Saheonbu, 12. Kinoso. Lim, Deok-Soon (1994a), p. 76.

in fact, the function of the city hall was regarded as more important than that of the Ministries of Economics and Policing.

To the east of the main palace lies another important political institution (fig. 3.7), the Royal Ancestral Shrine (Jongmyo), which held the ancestral tablets and the bones of the King's forefathers. Furthermore, since the Joseon Dynasty followed Confucian ideology, the tablet of Confucius was kept there too. This shrine was considered the single most important building in Joseon society. Thus, the construction of the Royal Ancestral Shrine took precedence even over that of the palace, and significant state affairs were reported there first and then decided in the government (*Seoul Yukbaeknyunsa* [1], 1978: 227). "To achieve permanence, such power had to be validated by some form of authority," Wheatley (1971) explained. "The shrine, which had from the beginning assuaged man's deepest anxiety by providing assurances of the continuity of the world as he knew it, was able to draw on supramundane sources of authority" (304).

The bureaucratic structure was deigned to include the function of priests. A central government office (Kyejesa) was in charge of rites, civil service examinations, the school system, and national worship (*Kyunggookdaijeon*, 1986: 194); and there was an elaborate and strictly controlled calendar of rituals for the glorification of, and communication with, the ancestors (Wheatley, 1971: 56).

To the west of the main palace,[14] there were the Sajik (Guardian Deities of the State), the temple where the gods of soil and grain were venerated. Since these two gods formed the basis for the welfare of the state and the people, the government placed a high priority on this institution (*Seoul Yukbaeknyunsa* [1], 1978: 230). Worship in the Sajik involved the practice of ritual ceremonies to maintain harmony between gods and humans, as Eliade formulates. To the east of the main palace and just north of the Royal Ancestral Shrine was the National Confucian Academy[15] (Seongkyunkwan), a prime location that attests to the importance of its having access to the royal shrine and the presence of the King. This shrine was the country's highest educational institution, selecting young scholars from all over the nation to be educated as future Confucian scholars and bureaucrats and serve in the temple. The students who attended could sit for the Erudite Examination (*munkwa*) and ultimately a Palace Examination (*cheonsi*), which was held in the presence of the King (Lee, 1984: 180-181). The location of the Academy in the immediate vicinity of the temple and palace indicates the importance of nurturing future generations of Confucian scholars and bureaucrats to maintain the most important political institutions.

Wheatley (1971: 186) observes a spatial expression of the dichotomy between the two main sectors of society—the sacrally ordained elite and the

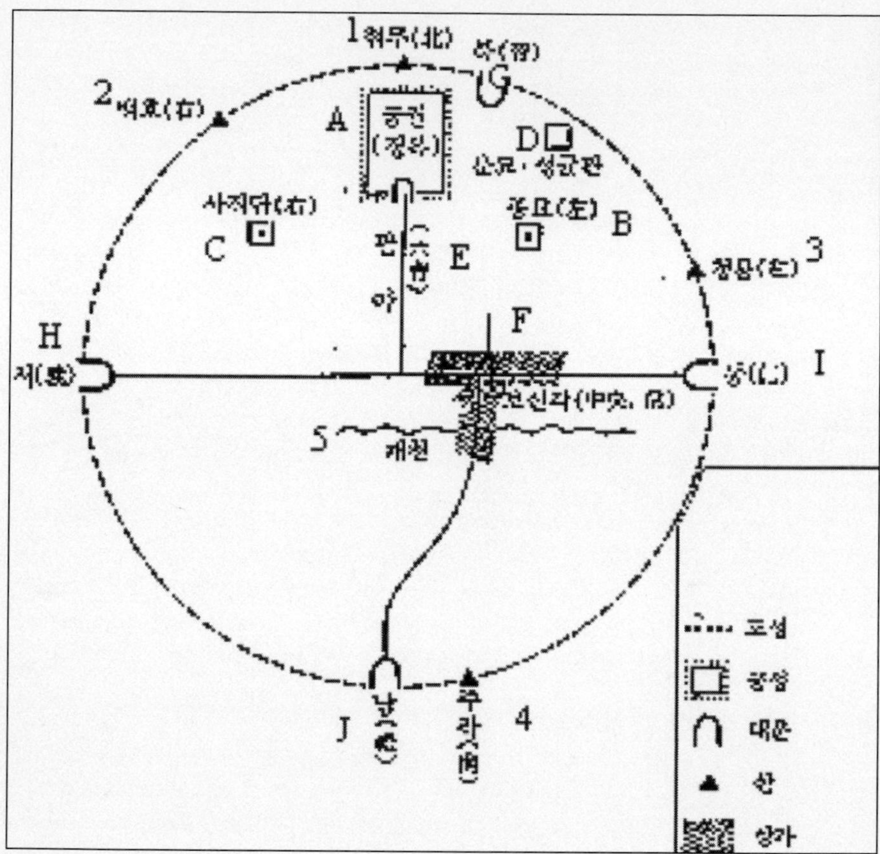

Figure 3.7 Simplified Layout of Hanyang. 1. Hyunmoo, 2. Baekho, 3. Cheongryong, 4. Joojak, 5. Cheonggye River, A. Kyeongbok Palace, B. Jongmyo (Royal Ancestral Shrine), C. Sajik (Guardian Dieties of the State), D. Monmyo and Seongkyunkwan (Confucian Shrine and National Confucian Academy), E. The Six Ministries, F. Chonggak, G. Changeuimoon, H. Doneuimoon, I. Heunginmoon, J. Soongryemoon. Lim, Deok-Soon (1994a), p. 73.

mass of the populace. In the city, the location of housing areas[16] reflected the prestige of scholars relative to that of non-scholars and of sacred areas relative to those that were profane. Thrupp (1963: 122) finds a tendency in the city design to cosmocize city areas by linking living spaces with this sacred space. If we look at the residences of *yangban* (the gentry class that was qualified to be appointed to both civil and military offices) in Hanyang, we can clearly see the truth of this observation (fig. 3.8). The yangban did not even live side by side with those who were not yangban (Lee, 1984: 174). The northern part of Hanyang between the main palace (Kyeongbok Palace)

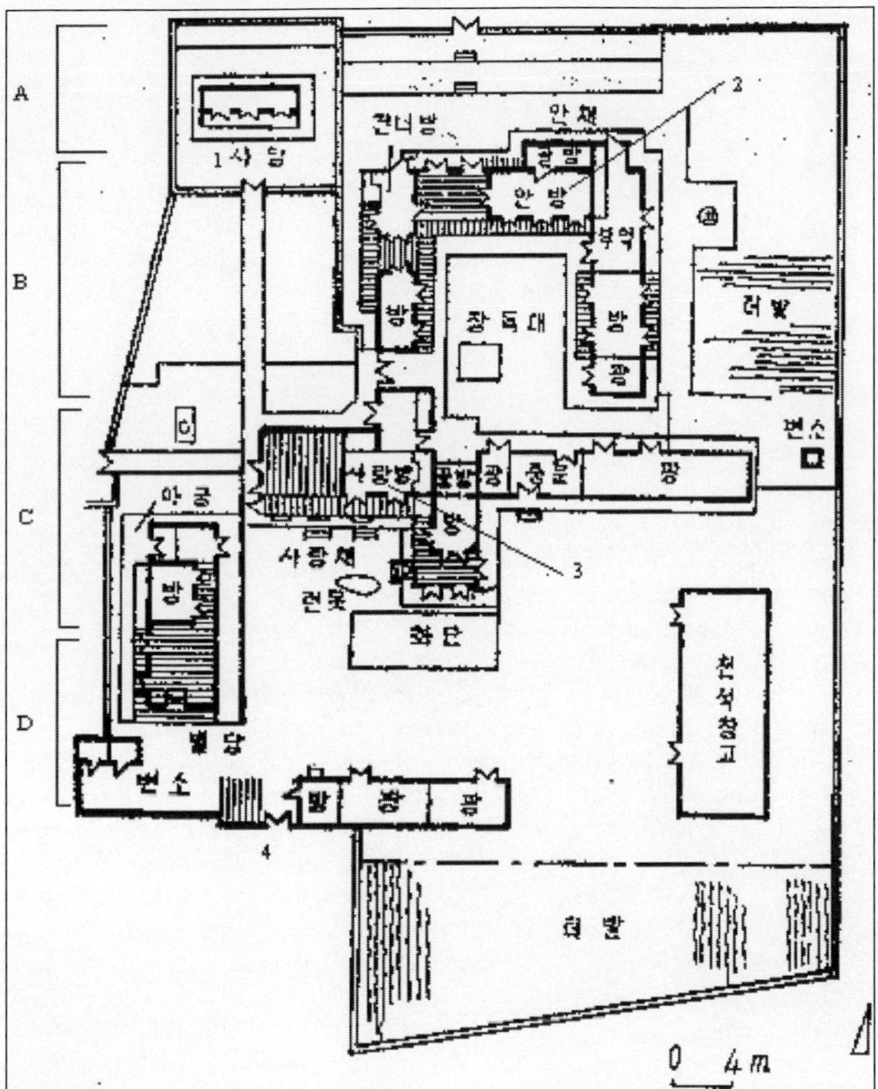

Figure 3.8 Layout of Typical Yangban House Copying Palace Layout. A. Family shrine area (1. Sadang), B. Family quarters (2. Anbang), C. Reception and office for the head of the family (3. Sarangbang), D. Front gate area (4. Daemoon). Lee, Wha-Seon (1994), p. 57.

and the Royal Ancestral Shrine was reserved for the housing of high-ranking bureaucrats and aristocrats. This northern part was considered the most prestigious region within the city in terms of topographical geomantic benefits. It was located above the parallel axiality of city, which was demarcated by a single wide road linking the West and East Gates. Around the South Gate, there resided bureaucrats of lesser prestige or Confucian scholars with no official post. Between these housing areas, and especially around the market place, there resided members of the lower classes, including merchants and craftsmen. This area had the disadvantages of bad drainage, crowdedness, noise, and narrow roads, which were dangerous in the case of fire. Middle-level bureaucrats such as medical officers, translator-interpreters, statute law clerks, scribes, and government artists constituted the hereditary preserve of the so-called middle people (*choongin*), who were allowed to live between the area reserved for the lower class and the area for the less prestigious Confucian bureaucrats and scholars. Most lower-level officers who worked in the palace resided in the western section of the capital, which was regarded as a less prestigious zone than the eastern section between Kyeongbok and Changdeok Palaces. A hierarchy of zones allocated to officers and people of various different social standings was clearly reflected in the city layout. Such allotments of housing areas for different classes were stipulated in the administrative law. This overview of the arrangement of housing areas aims to demonstrate how easily the hegemonic position of the ruling class and its ideology can be read in the hierarchical order of the city itself.

Over time, the market quarter became a venue for more than just commercial activity; it became a place for social exchange as well, a place where the businessman, stallholder, teamster, housewife, casual passerby, idler, and countryman who had come to town for just a few hours could all pass the time. "The western market was a busy, noisy and multilingual cluster of bazaars and warehouses. People came not only to buy but to meet friends and gossip; students argued philosophy and politics. In addition, visitors and clients were entertained by prestidigitators and illusionists of every nationality as well as by storytellers, actors, and acrobats" (Tuan, 1974: 177). In fact, the market resembled a hybrid between the *agora* from the Greek *polis* and the *forum* from the Roman city in terms of its economic and social functions, and there remained only a tenuous distinction between these facets of its activities. In China, however, there was—as far as is known—no Aristotle to advocate the separation of these functions on the Thessalian pattern (Wheatley, 1971: 178).

As mentioned previously, the four gates in the city walls were named after the Confucian virtues, and the usage of these gates was designed to reflect the hierarchical order of the bureaucracy itself: different gates were reserved for higher and lower officials. More specifically, though, the Kwanghwamoon (front gate of the Kyeongbokgoong) had three different openings: the middle gate was exclusively for the King and Queen, while the two side gates were for Moon (civil) and Moo (military) bureaucrats. Officials who lived and worked in the Palace were to use a separate gate in the west (Youngchoomoon). Other members of royal family and Sanggoong (women who worked in the palace) were to use a separate gate in the east (Geonchoonmoon) (Kim, 1994: 144).

The marketplace was located primarily on the street that led from the east gate to the intersection of the Six Ministries Street, but it also extended partly along a smaller street that intersected from the south.[17] The market's location, dominated by the government center directly to the north, illustrates the precedence of government over economic activities. This urban layout provides hard evidence of the socially constructed principles of the legitimacy of government intervention in the economy.

Commerce and industry were looked down upon by Confucian economic philosophy, which placed much higher value on agriculture as a national industry. In the Confucianist view, human morality could be ruined by individual self-interest in the pursuit of economic wealth; indeed, economic self-interest (*i)* was the antithesis of the fundamental moral principle of the Confucian ideal (*ei*). Furthermore, Confucianists believed, virtuousness could be fully cultivated and realized through agricultural activity. Interestingly, this attitude is not exclusive to Asian Confucian culture but can be found in the thinking of some of the Western architects of democracy as well. For example, Thomas Jefferson in his letter to John Jay on August 23, 1785, also pointed out that "Cultivators of the earth are the most valuable citizens. They are the most vigorous, the most independent, the most virtuous, and they are tied to their country and wedded to its liberty and interests by the most lasting bands."[18] However, just as Confucianism and Jefferson share the belief that agriculture is the best economic activity for cultivating virtuousness, they also agree that commercial activity aggravates human nature. We can find many examples in the *sangso*[19] of Confucian bureaucrats and scholars in their criticisms of mercantile activities. One such example is as follows:

> Groups of merchants sell their items at higher prices than real value, potentially disguising the actual value of substandard products. In this process, merchants compete with each other. As a result of this selfish behavior of the merchants, the consumer price surprisingly increases and the people (*Baekseong*) suffer from the merchants' immoral pursuit of economic self-interest. (Lee, 1993: 139)

In the macro-political context, Confucianists also argued that being a merchant and engaging in commerce produced no food but rather took advantage of the benefit of exchange. Thus, economic activity was regarded not as contributing to the Confucian social order but rather as damaging it. In addition, Confucianists viewed merchants as a class that challenged the Confucian hierarchical social order because merchants were wealthy, sometimes even wealthier than Confucian bureaucrats and scholars, producing nothing yet accumulating great amounts of wealth. Another remonstrance leveled the following criticism: "Merchants do not labor; they wear silk clothes without raising any silkworms, so to speak. Despite their low status, they eat good food and lead luxurious lives, which are at a much higher level of living than the *Yangban* enjoy. From this perspective, they are sinners" (Lee, 1993: 127-128). Similarly, Jefferson criticized commercial activity as "the panders of vice and the instruments by which the liberties of a country are generally overturned" (Peterson, 1975: 384).

In summary, Confucianists viewed the agricultural industry as contributing to the formation of good personality and as maintaining Confucian political authority because they believed that working in agriculture makes people more genuine and virtuous. This Confucian ideology, which esteems agriculture and scorns commerce and industry, served for the rulers as the perfect way to embrace the agricultural population and induce the consent of the majority, thereby consolidating Confucian state hegemony. Thus, the aspirational and accommodative values of the majority, which were based on Confucian economic ideas, became the major source of legitimacy for the ruling class, thereby making coercion less necessary. An effective mechanism to control the commerce/industry classes was reflected in the provisions of economic activity in the corpus of law. The privileges granted to classes involved in minor commerce/industry actually functioned as a means to strengthen the cooperative relations between state and economy because these commerce/industry classes recognized their marginal status within Confucian ideology, and thereby had to maximize whatever opportunities they were presented.

Similarly in ancient China, the low status of commerce left plenty of room for political motivations to take precedence over economic ones (Fu, 1993: 93). Rulers' underlying motive for establishing and enforcing various forms of state control over the economy was never purely economic; state intervention in the economy served the political objective of maintaining and strengthening state power; non-economic factors played a significant role in business operations. The Chinese state's tradition of discriminating against merchants and craftsmen was derived largely from its antipathy toward any potentially autonomous social force. In other words, the economic institutions of the traditional world have been subordinated to a greater or lesser degree to the moral and political norms of society (Wheatley, 1971: 282).

The extent to which politics was ingrained in the economy is demonstrated by the fact that economic status was based exclusively on political power. Lots for residences in Hanyang were awarded by the government in the name of the king; the size of the house, the materials out of which it was made and, to some extent, even the furniture within it were all regulated by the political rank or status of the owner. Less prestigious areas of the capital, far from the palace, were set aside for commercial activity by the government's "grace and favor." "Significantly, merchants were not allowed to own rice lands" (Henderson, 1968: 33) because Confucian sadaebu feared the rising power of the merchant class.

In addition, on the street, the physical presence of merchants and city inhabitants was strictly controlled. A bell (*inkyungjong*) that rang from the middle of the market street served to regulate the activities of everyday life. At around four in the morning, the bell would ring thirty-three times to signal the start of the day, and the eight gates in Hanseong opened. At around seven at night, twenty-eight rings signaled the end of the day and all gates closed. This functioned as an institution to regulate the presence and absence of the people. Symbolically, the entry and departure of people represented the breath of the city (Kim, 1994: 89, 91). Furthermore, the measurement of time had a greater significance in political life than the simple keeping of time. Harvey (1989) aptly points out how the control of time and space closely relates to power.

This control was at once a sign of newfound creativity and an agent and catalyst in the use of knowledge for wealth and power. Accurate maps and mechanisms for keeping time have long been highly prized throughout the world, and command over space and time plays a crucial role in any search for profit. Those who define the material practices, forms, and meanings of money, time, or space fix certain basic rules of the social game (Wheatley, 1971: 226). Symbolized by the clocks and bells that called workers to labor and merchants to market, separated from the natural rhythms of agrarian life, and divorced from religious significations, a new temporal net was created by which daily life was contained (Wheatley, 1971: 228).

HIERARCHICAL HANYANG

The rule of hierarchy in Confucian bureaucratic institutions maintained tight state control over all aspects of social life, including the bureaucracy itself and the economy. The arrangement of the directive-rules of Confucian bureaucracy in the political and economic realms of Joseon society is delineated in the corpus of administrative law,[20] which reveals how the dominant Confucian economic ideal prescribed relations between state and economy and how tightly Confucian government maintained its grip over its government organizations, economy, and every aspect of the masses' everyday lives. The Central Government Officials in the Gyeongguk daejeon (appendix 2) and the Local Civil Officials Table (appendix 3) serve as examples of the centralized and tightly organized bureaucracy that was in place throughout the nation.

The central government's firm hold on the economic and industrial sectors is also clear from the List of Craftsmen in Central and Local Government Offices (Appendix 4). Finally, the Students in Capital (Appendix 5) serves here to demonstrate Joseon's educational policy. All of these examples vividly illustrate the degree to which the government exercised control over the bureaucracy, the economy, and education. There were other regulations as well, over industry and various aspects of people's everyday life, and the details of these controls are examined below.

Before examining the case of Korea, though, it would be useful to look more closely at the ranking system used by Chinese government officials during the Western Chou (1046-771 BC) Dynasty and the system used by other classes that formed the power group in the state. The Chinese ranking system was different from the Korean system in that the former allowed a few positions to be hereditable; however, considering that this ranking system was developed from such ancient times, the practice of allowing positions to be hereditable is hardly surprising. In fact, a tightly stipulated hierarchical system of government officials existed even in the old Asian regimes. Paul Wheatley (1971: 124) observes:

> There were two grades of ministers, the *k'iang* (*ch'ing*), those of higher rank whose offices were hereditable and who were relatively few in number, and the *t'ad-piwo* (*tai-fu*), who were more numerous and functioned as assistants to the *k'iang*. There were, in fact, several grades of *t'ad-piwo*, some of which seem also to have been hereditable. Together, a ruler and his ministers constituted the power group in a state and, at least in the idealized texts of later times, were classificatory kin to one another. On the lower fringes of the power group, . . . was a class of *dz'ieg* (*shih*), men who were descendants of rulers or ministers and trained in the six arts of propriety, music, archery, chariot driving, writing, and arithmetic, but who were often, perhaps predominantly, unlanded. Although ranked among the *kiwen-tsieg* (*chiin-tzu*) or gentlemen of good birth, such *dz'ieg* might be no more than officials in the bureaucracy or in a noble household. . . . Apart from a few of the *dz'ieg*, none of the ruling classes engaged in agricultural or artisan activities, so that virtually the whole society structure was supported by the labors of the peasantry, who were referred to variously as *mien* (*min* = people), or *siag-nien* (*shu-jen* = the masses), or *dz'ian* (*chien* = plebeians), or simply as *siog-nien* (*Hsiao-jen* = the mean [i.e., average] people).

Appendix 2, The Central Government Official Ranking System, presents a much more detailed delineation of Joseon's central government offices and officials. According to Yun (1986: 552-556), the North Korean scholar who first translated the *Kyeongguk dajeon* into Korean, a total of 4,090 government officials were classified according to the eighteen ranks of *pumgye*, a hierarchical ranking system for Joseon's Confucian government officials. These officials were assigned to fifty-three central government offices. The Uijeongbu (Supreme State Council) and Yukjo (the principal administrative institution) comprised the basic system of the government, under which 51 offices existed with roles and responsibilities prescribed according to strict bureaucratic rules. To the Office of Special Counselors for the King (Sagan-won), for instance, five officials were assigned: one *jeong 3 pum* official, one *jong 3 pum* official, one *jeong 5 pum* official, and two *jeong 6 pum* officials (refer to note on *pumgye* in appendix 2). In Gwansang-gam, the Office for Observance of Natural Phenomena, there were twenty four officials: one *jeong 1 pum*, one *jeong 3 pum,* one *jong 3 pum*, one *jong 4 pum*, two *jong 5 pum*, four *jong 6 pum*, two *jong 7 pum*, two *jong 8 pum*, seven *jeong 9 pum*, and three *jong 9 pum* officials. Hyeminseo, the Office of Medical Service for Commoners, had a total of ten officials: three *jong 6 pum*, one *jong 7 pum*, one *jong 8 pum*, one *jeong 9 pum*, and four *jong 9 pum*. Clearly, the hierarchical system of government officials was highly organized and controlled.

Appendix 3, the Local Civil Officials, demonstrates that the grip of central government over public administrations in local areas and provinces was strict as well. According to *Kyeonggkuk daejeon* (Yun, 1986: 560-561), 807 government officials worked for local government offices in eight provinces, all assigned and appointed by the central government. Their *pumgye* ranks were *jong 2 pum, jeong 3 pum, jong 3 pum, jong 4 pum, jong 5 pum, jong 6 pum,* and *jong 9 pum*. For example, in Chungcheong-do, there was one *gwanchalsa* (a governor of a province; *jong 2 pum*), four *moksa* (country magistrates ruling *mok*; *jeong 3 pum*), and a *gunsu* (a local magistrate of a *gun*; *jong 4 pum*). There were seven officials of *jong 5 pum,* including twelve *1 dosa* (inspecting local magistrates), four *pan-gwan* (administrative assistant of *gwanchalsa*), and one *hyeollyeong* (a local magistrate of a big *hyeon*); there were forty-four officials of *jong 6 pum* of three *chalbang* (in charge of a transportation and communication between the capital with local areas), including thirty-seven *hyeon-gam* (country magistrates for a small *hyeon*) and four *gyosu* (in charge of education); and there were another fifty-eight *jong 9 pum* officials of two *chambong* (assistant caretakers), including fifty *hundo* (educators), two *simnyak* (examiners of medicinal material), one *geomnyul* (law clerk), and three *yeokseung* (in charge of transportation station).

The Confucian government's firm command of industrial activities of craftsmanship both in the capital and the provinces (appendix 4) far surpassed the list of government officials (Yun, 1986: 498-514; 579). For example, 2,841 artisans and craftsmen worked in the thirty central government offices. The types of jobs amounted to 129. To the government arsenal (*Gun-gisi*), 644 craftsmen are assigned: 12 *chiljang* (varnishing with lacquer), 12 *majo-*

jang (making millstones), 6 *gunghyeonjang* (making bowstrings), 2 *yuchiljang* (making varnish), 20 *jujang* (casting weapons), 4 *saengpijang* (treating rawhide), 35 *gapjang* (making armor), 90 *gung-in* (making bows), 150 *si-in* (making arrows), 11 *jaengjang* (making percussion instruments), 4 *mokjang* (carpenters), 130 *yajang* (blacksmiths), and so on. In the office of government publication (*Gyoseo-gwan*), there were 102 craftsmen: 8 *jogakjang* (sculptors), 2 *mokjang* (carpenters), 6 *yajang* (blacksmiths), 8 *jujang* (type casters), 40 *gyunjajang* (type spacers), 20 *inchuljang* (book printers), 14 *gakjang* (letter carvers), and 4 *jijang* (papermakers). In the *Kyeongguk daejeon*, these numerous kinds of jobs and government offices are listed individually along with the numbers of craftsmen for each.

In the capital as a whole, the number of craftsmen and artisans amounted to 2,841, but throughout the rest of the country—i.e., in the local areas—there were only 3,652. The number of crafts jobs enlisted in the capital amounted to 129, but there were only 27 in the local regions. This shows that while the government-run handicraft industries centered on the capital, the local industries did not develop with as many specialties as in the capital (Yun, 1986: 139).

Appendix 5 provides a full picture of the enrollments assigned for each school and each curriculum that was regarded as essential to government operation: 885 students studied 13 subjects in 10 central government offices. In the Seongkyunkwan, for example, there were 200 students studying Confucianism. In Sayeogwon, there were 80 in total—35 devoted to Chinese classics, 10 to Mongolian studies, 20 to Jurchen studies, and 15 to Japanese studies.

Appendix 6 provides a full list of the Joseon Dynasty's central government offices. In addition to a king and the royal family, there was the highest deliberative political institution, the Uijeongbu (State Council). Comprised of the three highest Confucian bureaucrats, the Uijeongbu discussed important state affairs, conveyed their consensus to the king, and transmitted the king's final decisions to government agencies. Under this State Council, there was the main administrative body of the Joseon Dynasty—namely, the Yukjo—which was comprised of the Six Ministries: Personnel (*Ijo*), Taxation (*Hojo*), Rites (*Yejo*), Military Affairs (*Byeongjo*), Justice (*Hyeongjo*), and Public Works (*Gongjo).* All the other government agencies listed in appendix 6 were under the direct control and supervision of the Six Ministries or the royal family. All military agencies were supervised by the *Byeongjo,* including five *Wi* (military commands), which were under the five *Wijang* (Commanders) of the five *Wi Dochongbu* (military command headquarters). A total of eighty-eight central government agencies are listed in appendix 6, with the exception of the State Councilor and the Six Ministries, according to the *Gyeongguk daejeon*. The *Gyeongguk daejeon*—The National Code of Joseon, promulgated in the reign of *Seongjong* in 1471—compiled previous statutory codes, such as the Administrative Code of Joseon (*Joseon Gyeonggkuk jeon* compiled by Jeong Do-jeon) and the Six Codes of Governance (*Gyeongjeyuk jeon* prepared by Jeong Do-jeon with Cho Jun), and provided the fundamental administrative structure and functions of the Joseon Dynasty. Names of government agencies listed in appendices 2 and 4 refer to those in appendix 6. The city of Hanyang was divided into five *bu* (administrative districts) with four *hak* (public school districts in the capital city). A complete list of government agencies both central and local appears here along with their functions and jurisdictions; also included are the numbers and kinds of craftsmen listed according to the functions of these government offices, which serves as clear evidence of the centrality and highly regulatory nature of the Joseon state and its relations with society and economic activities.

As clearly presented in the Appendices, the central Confucian government stipulated how many officials and craftsmen were needed both in the center and periphery. More specifically, the government determined what kinds of craftsmanship and how many craftsmen were required and tightly controlled the numbers. The government's complete control over jobs and personnel also affected the numbers of students allowed into each school in the capital city, including the highest Confucian educational institution, the Seongkyunkwan.

To control the portion of the population capable of working as soldiers, the Joseon central government adopted a national identification system—every third year, the family registration system was updated. In both the capital and the localities, five households were considered one unit, which was required to have its own superintendent. In the local regions, one leader was appointed for each group of five units, and an agricultural advisory officer (*gwonnong-gwan*) was appointed for each *myeon* (a bigger administrative district including five units). If the regions were big enough and had many lakes, more leaders would be appointed. In the capital, a *gwallyeong* (an officer) was appointed for each *bang* (an administrative unit specific to the capital and some other important local areas) (Yun, 1986: 271-272). In addition, all lands were rated on a scale from one to six. Every twenty years, the lands were surveyed, and the land registers were kept in the royal court, local provinces, local towns (Yun, 1986: 272).

At the lowest stratum of Joseon society, there were both official and private slaves, which were also tightly controlled by the central government and high-level government officials (appendix 7). Across eighty-three government agencies, two categories of slaves—2,416 *chabino* and 1,480 *geunsuno*—were listed in the *Gyeongguk daejeon*. The former worked for the palace and central government offices, while the latter served the royal family and high-level government officials. As illustrated in appendix 4, specific numbers of chabino and geunsuno were assigned to various government and royal offices for specific purposes. The existence of slaves during the Joseon Dynasty was nothing new; however, what is most noticeable from this fact is that the central government maintained thorough organization, assigned the functions and duties of each government agency, and kept tight control over slave labor and the economic activities of civil society. Clearly, the central government firmly controlled major portions of the population, including craftsmen and slaves. In addition, by highly defining and organizing public offices and educational institutions (as well as their functions, rights, and duties), the ruling elite was able to establish and maintain the hegemony and hierarchy of Confucian state centrality and political superiority over economic sectors and activities. All of this evidence supports the claim that the developmental state's legitimacy to intervene in the economy in the Park regime was drawn from the Confucian legacy.

Next, by examining the placement of government institutions in the capital city, we will analyze the ways in which both Confucian and geomantic principles were involved in the hierarchies of governing structure and embedded in Joseon state-society relations. For our exploration of this issue, it will be useful to divide this analysis into two categories: political and economic. As seen in the previous section on the reconstruction of the rules of hegemony, Confucian and geomantic philosophy sought to distinguish between two different realms: the political as sacred and the economic as profane. Through such a division, the superiority of political over economic considerations was maintained. This distinction played an important role in the establishment of the Confucian state's hegemony. Even though the main bureaucratic institutions were included in the sacred space (i.e., the Six Ministries Street), the same distinction between sacred political and profane economic institutions existed even among the bureaucratic institutions. For example, the Ministries of Taxation and Public Works were located farther from the sacred space than were political ministries, such as the Ministries of Rites and Personnel. A tendency to be close to the sacred space is also apparent in the arrangement of the ministry buildings relative to each other. Despite the importance of the material bases for state and society, the Ministry of Taxation was located closest to the profane space of the market. Thus, the design of the city itself provides some clues as to the directive-rules of the bureaucratic system in terms of its political and economic aspects.

The organization of the Joseon government must be explained first in general terms. The highest organ of the government was the Euijeongbu (State Council), and important matters of state were discussed by the three

High State Councilors, who conveyed their consensus to the King, received his decision, and transmitted it to the appropriate government agencies. The Yukjo, the Six Ministries,[21] came to have the authority to memorialize the King directly on matters under their purview and then to execute his decisions. The Joseon Dynasty's political structure might aptly be termed a "ministries system," which in turn suggests that the political structure of the Joseon was more bureaucracy-centered than the Goryeo had been (Lee, 1984: 175). Another agency that performed a vital role was the Seungjeongwon (Royal Secretariat), the organ through which documents were transmitted to and from the King, and which at times ignored other agencies and exercised an authority of its own.

Economic Hierarchy: State Intervention in the Economy

Hanyang's treatment of the market differed starkly from that of the Chou Dynasty:

> . . . early Chou cities were primarily administrative and military foundations. Such industrial activities as they generated were restricted to crafts producing prestige items in bronze, jade, lacquer, pottery, and bone for the Chou nobility, while village workshops continued to manufacture the stone and bone implements used by the peasantry in farm and field. . . . in this almost wholly self-contained, manorial-style economy, commerce played only an insignificant role. With the political, social and economic transformations of the Ch'un-Ch'iu period, however, the city often became a locus for the enterprises of the new merchant class. The representative Eastern Chou capital never lost its ceremonial functions, but not a few cities developed their commercial activities to a high level. In the ritualized schema of the K'ao-kung Chi, the market was located behind, that is to the north of, the royal palace. (Wheatley, 1971: 177)

As discussed in the previous section on hegemony, the state's intervention in the economy was legitimized by the Confucian value of politics taking precedence over economic affairs. As early as the Eastern Zouh period, a form of state-controlled manufacture and trade of salt was instituted.[22] The selection of salt and iron for the state monopoly was based on the universal utility[23] of these commodities in an agrarian society (Fu, 1993: 94). The institutionalization of the state monopoly conformed with the legalistic principles of encouraging agriculture, inhibiting commerce, and preventing the formation of associations among the people. The Hojo (Ministry of Taxation and Economy) took charge of the monopoly of salt and iron production. In each province, weirs and salt kilns were rated, registered, and copies of this list were kept by the royal court, the province, and the town. Those whose names were missing from the list were flogged eighty times for punishment, and the profits they had taken were forfeited to the authorities. In the case of individual occupation of weirs, the same rules and punishments were applied. Weirs were given to the poor subjects and had to be exchanged every third year (Yun, 1986: 289). In towns that were located far from salt kilns, salt storage bins were built, and the salt that had been collected as tax revenue was brought and exchanged for grain or cloth, which in turn would be used to replenish military supplies. The salt that was collected as tax revenues in Gyeonggi, Chungcheong-do, and Hwanghae-do was to be sent to *sajaegam*,[24] *gunjagam*,[25] and salt storage facilities (Yun, 1986: 289).

The Confucian scorn for commerce led to strong state intervention in every aspect of commercial activity in the early Joseon Dynasty. Only one category of market was legally permitted by the government: the *sijeon*. As shown in figure 3.9, each site was designated by the government for the sale of a specific item. The government implemented a policy to support this sijeon. With the exception of this legally permitted market, the government prohibited all other small markets, which were called *nanjeon*. Furthermore, the government gave the sijeon exclusive rights (*kumnanjeonkwon*) to exercise control over nanjeon. In 1791, though, King Chongjo rescinded these exclusive rights, allowing the nanjeon to do business but still requiring it to pay tax to the sijeon. In other words, government continued to subordinate the nanjeon by letting the sijeon impose taxes upon it. Because this law was enacted in the year of *shinhae* (in 1791), it was called the *shinhaetongkong* (Jeong, 1992: 55).

From an early time, there were shops in Hanyang along the main thoroughfare of Chongno, but these had been established by the government and the premises were leased to merchants. Somewhat later, the so-called Six Licensed Stores (*yukuijeon*)—purveying silk, cotton cloth, thread, paper goods, ramie cloth, and fish products—came to typify this pattern of commercial activity (Lee, 1984: 187).

All of these articles that were sold in the yukuijeon were very popular in both domestic and international markets. Most of the paper goods were used in the government. Luxury items, including silver, silk, and fish for sacrificial ceremonies and the National Academy, were primarily intended for use by the government or dominant elite groups as well. Interestingly, all of these items (except for fish) were popular in China. Considering the silver standard in the Chinese monetary system, it is clear that the yukuijeon were exclusively for government procurement and international trade (Lee, Tae-Jin, 1995: 33).

Granted the monopolistic privilege of dealing in designated articles, these stores operated in effect by government license, in exchange for which they paid a tax in the form of delivery on demand of items required

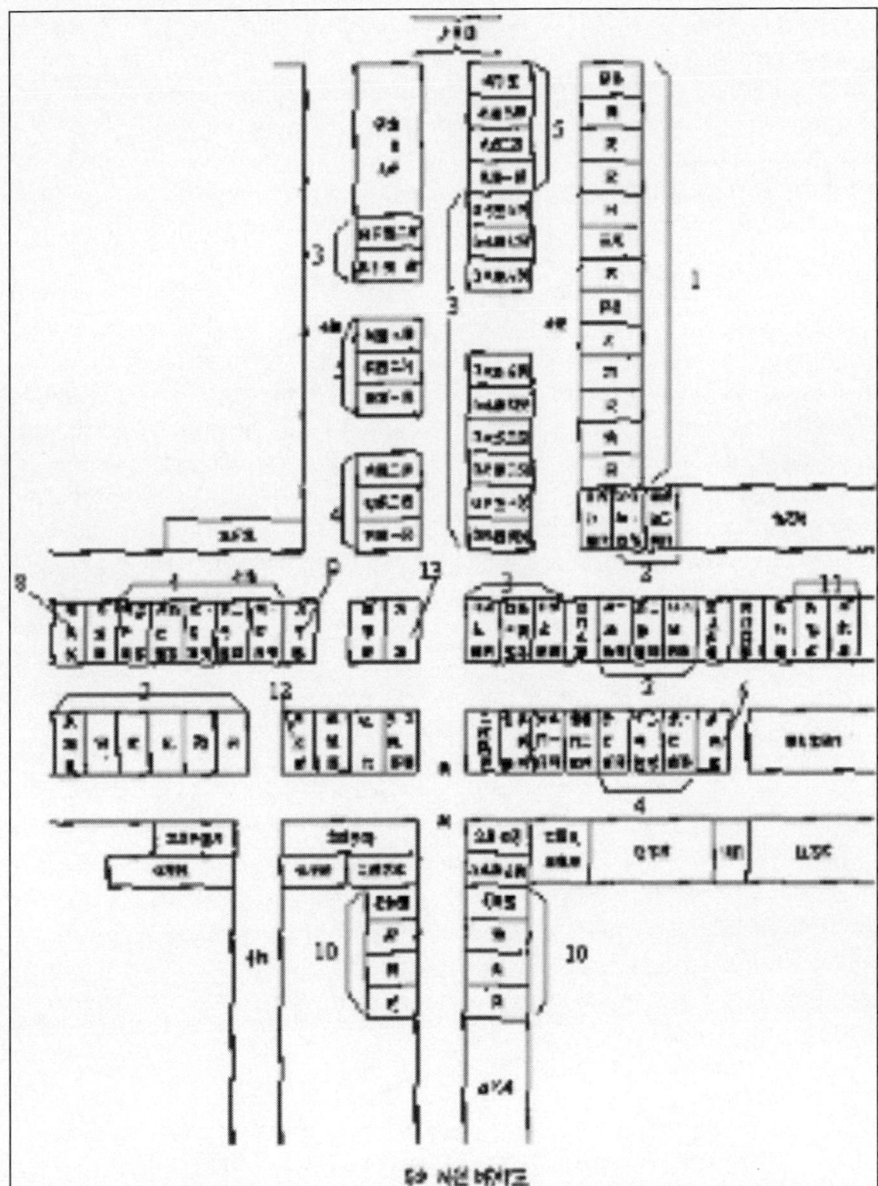

Figure 3.9 Market Plan with Prescribed Sections for Trading in Each Commodity. 1. Silver, 2. Silk, 3. Cotton, 4. Ramie cloth, 5. Paper, 6. Thread, 7. Fish, 8. Meat, 9. Knife, 10. Fur, 11. Fruit, 12. Hats, 13. Chonggak. Jeong, Seung-Mo (1992), p. 140.

by the government; however, there were some small shops that were free of any tax obligations, and markets were opened in numerous other places too. In the local areas, starting in the early Joseon Dynasty, permanent markets called *jangmun* (market gate) began to develop. These were established by peasants who had fled their land either due to famine or to avoid the burdens of military service or taxation. Such markets were deemed to constitute a threat to the Joseon Dynasty's order, and so they were suppressed (Lee, 1984: 187).

As in the Goryeo period, the work of craftsmen and artisans in the early Joseon Dynasty was performed preponderantly under the aegis of the government. As a general rule, all workers with special skills were listed on separate rosters as "government artisans" and were attached to the various agencies in Hanyang or to the provincial and local governments and the military garrison commands. Thus, some 640 artisans were assigned to the Government Arsenal to make weapons, 590 to the Bureau of Royal Attire to make court robes, 380 to the Palace Kitchen Management to produce utensils for the royal table, and 91 to the Paper Manufactory to meet the government's needs for paper. Altogether, some 2,800 such skilled workers were employed in Hanyang, and more than 3,500 were employed in the provinces (Choi, 1971: 154).

In Hanyang, the metropolitan craftsmen were assigned to 30 government agencies, including the Kongjo (the equivalent of the Ministry of Commerce and Industry), and were specialized in 129 classifications. Totaling 2,841, they included 386 ceramicists, 192 blacksmiths, 171 arrow makers, 110 weavers, 105 silk weavers, 104 tile makers, 85 paperware specialists, and 74 carpenters among others. In the provinces, by contrast, there were 3,656 craftsmen but only 27 job titles. The paperware specialists were the most numerous with 698, followed by 466 blacksmiths, 392 seat makers, 350 arrow makers, 340 carpenters, 313 tanners, 311 painters, and 255 bow makers (Choi, 1971: 164). Metropolitan or provincial, the craftsmen who were engaged in the government industry during the period under discussion were under the exclusive control of the government.

HETERONOMY IN HANYANG: LOYAL OPPOSITION AND SEMI-OPPOSITION

The term "heteronomy" literally means "the lack of moral freedom or self-determination or subjection to something else." Kant used this term in his *Foundation of the Metaphysics of Morals* to refer to the condition of lacking autonomy (Onuf, 1989: 212). From such a definition, it is clear that a characteristic of heteronomy is "the lack of autonomous power" whether for an individual or a social organization. Based on this phenomenon of lacking autonomy, Onuf (1989) developed "heteronomy" from its literal meaning into a term that has additional political connotations. After claiming that "heteronomy is the background condition of rule against which episodes of hegemony and hierarchy are set," Onuf (1989: 197) adds that it "refers to groups which are not autonomous but rather are dominated by others." Further, he argues that the "rules of heteronomy" provide a place for elements in society which are not in keeping with the rules of the dominant group. Even though the place provided is a subservient one, an area for differences is reserved, and the relationship of those differences to the dominant groups is recognized. For instance, in Onuf's conception of political society, "heteronomy" refers to rules in dealing with dissent. For Hanyang, the rule of heteronomy is a conceptual category that represents dissenting voices in society in general.

So, how has state power in Korea been mutually (re)constructed and (re) produced over time by both state and society? To pin this question down with a precise answer, it is necessary to illuminate what kind of state-society relations have been created and shaped by the three different types of rule (i.e., hegemony, hierarchy, and heteronomy), especially in terms of economic development. Also, how are these three different types of rule connected to state-society relations? And what does the rule of heteronomy have to do with state-society relations? If this analysis were based on a clear-cut Western notion of dichotomous state-society relations, then it would surely be unrealistic to expect a proper interpretation of state-society relations in a nation where a non-Western, non-liberal, Confucian, traditional ideology and culture has been dominant for so long.

Institutions of Heteronomy

During the Joseon Dynasty, the three main sources of dissenting voices were the institutions of Daegan, the Sarim, and the Seongkyunkwan. In light of the modern incarnations of these voices, it is useful to keep in mind that "the tradition of the scholar aloof from the government (group of Neo-Confucian literati in the countryside), which was the special mark of the Joseon Dynasty tradition of dissent, is alive today" (Yang & Henderson, 1958: 89). The Daegan—the term that was used to describe government posts in Saheonboo (Office of the Inspector-General) and Saganwon (Office of the Censor-General)—were important constituents of the state. From the Western liberal perspective of state-society relations, therefore, it may seem incongruous to locate dissenting voices within the state power structure.

This, in fact, is a unique phenomenon of the Joseon Dynasty as represented in the city layout of Hanyang, specifically in the placement of heteronomical forces within the center, embraced as they are by the power structure. This runs counter to the common assumption that dissent is peripheral and thus marginalized. In a community where the power of the King was significantly checked and balanced by Confucian bureaucrats, and where Confucian political ideology had made state-society relations into a seamless social network, an adequate explanation of how state and society interacted with each other simply cannot be achieved through the mechanical application of a Western-liberal notion of state-society relations.

An instrument designed to prevent abuses in the exercise of political and administrative authority was the *Samsa*, which was comprised of the Hongmunkwan (Office of Special Advisers), the Saheonbu (Office of the Inspector-General), and the Saganwon (Office of the Censor-General). Two of these agencies were designed to guard against the abuses of power by the King or influential bureaucrats: the Saheonbu was a surveillance organ, criticizing the political issues of the day, scrutinizing official conduct, and rectifying public mores; and the Saganwon was responsible for examining critically and censuring as necessary the conduct of the King himself, a function that imposed restraint on the arbitrary exercise of the power of the throne. Taken as a whole, the advising and censoring bodies of the Samsa and the policymaking and executive bodies of the State Council and Six Ministries were positioned so as to create a system of checks and balances, thereby preventing power from becoming overly concentrated in any one branch of government. The very existence of the Samsa, with its constant, keen scrutiny of the public and private conduct of the King and his high officials, adequately conveys the nature of Joseon Korea's literati-centered yangban society. For the convenience of working with the King directly, the Office of Special Advisers and the Office of the Censor-General were located within the palace. Moreover, the Office of the Inspector-General was located just west of the middle of the Six Ministries Street. Thus, all three of these government institutions were situated within Hanyang's sacred space.

Another vital Confucian government institution was the National Confucian Academy (Seongkyunkwan), located just beside the Royal Ancestral Shrine.[26] From the 14th century onward, the National Academy was maintained by a chief of staffs and a head, both of whom were career officials of the central government, the highest titular ones, holding Censorate or official literary positions. The official function of the Academy was to prepare yangban for their examinations and subsequent careers in bureaucratic service. Interestingly, this system has been largely retained in today's national civil service entrance examination system. The original academy students regarded themselves not only as a specially privileged elite but almost as if they had already become a part of the governmental system with semi-consultative rights. Academy students ruled much of their intramural affairs, could collectively memorialize the throne, and from the 15th century onward occasionally took to the streets in demonstrations (Henderson, 1968: 199-200). Students held an autonomous academy residents' meeting known as *chaehoe* in which they decided on actions by majority rule. These meetings could be used to determine punishments for fellow students or to take part in government politics by sending a memorandum in the name of the body (Henderson, 1968: 435). The student body of the Seongkyunkwan numbered about 200, and students were required to attend 300 times per year in order to be eligible for taking the national civil service examination. This was a national university, and the budget was based on royal endowment, which included grants for books, food, and buildings as well as about 400 slaves (Kim, 1981).

Throughout the Joseon Dynasty, students form the Academy repeatedly demonstrated against Buddhist tendencies, even when the country's greatest monarch, Sejong (who ruled 1418-1450), was friendly to Buddhism. Moreover, in 1492, hundreds of students made joint pleas to the monarch to exonerate a young official, Cho Kwang-jo. They had supported his extreme Confucianist reforms, and when he ultimately fell in the purge of 1519, they forced their way through the gates of the palace compound and up to the very door of the King's residence to offer their lamentations, protestations, and declarations that the accused was innocent. In many ways, students played an active political role in supporting justice, often in terms of the theory and dogma of a political system artificially adopted from another nation. Their zeal for implanting foreign values has, at least occasionally, set Korean students apart from those of China, the United States, and England, who tend to operate within the internal—or at least the more internalized—values of those powerful states (Henderson, 1968: 200). In the anti-Rhee and anti-Park struggles, for example, the role of these 15th-century students was visibly revived. Probably nowhere else in the world is there so ancient and continuous a tradition of student demonstration, memorializing, and active participation in national politics as in Korea. The extremeness of this tradition bespeaks the national focus on access to central power, the key role of the educational system therein, and the intellectual tensions aroused when a small nation adopts foreign systems (Henderson, 1968: 201).

What gave these students such a prominent status in the social and political hierarchies in Joseon Dynasty? Simply put, their status stemmed from the Confucian shrine. A Confucian shrine (*Munmyo*) was a temple for worshipping Confucius and saints, which included the disciples of Confucius as well as Korean saints. This institution was the place where all honorable lineages were memorialized, and this was the Joseon Dynasty's most sacred source of political legitimacy. Directly beside it, the government located the Confucian National Academy, where students learned the teachings of Confucian saints, royal ancestors, and kings. What is most significant here is that these Confucian students were the only group granted the right to be in charge of serving and operating the rituals of the shrine and to speak up against the King and senior Confucian bureaucrats, who were themselves mostly graduates of the Confucian National Academy. The government financially supported this academy by instituting a government agency, Yanghyungo, which was in charge of providing rice to the Seongkyunkwan students. Thus, in many ways, the state ensured a steady source of dissent for itself.

Within this complex, there were classrooms for students in the Seongkyunkwan. Sometimes, the students demonstrated against the King or government officers based on their conviction in the teachings of the saints enshrined in this temple. The sources of protests against existing power also sometimes came from abroad, and so the Academy became a buffer zone for both students and the state (*Seoul Yukbaeknyunsa*, 1978, (1): 268-269). Twice a year (in spring and fall), the King visited Monmyo in the Seongkyunkwan to perform *Jakheonrye*, a ceremony symbolizing the King's pledge to observe the supreme ideology of Confucianism. After the ceremony, *Alseongsi* was held, a special administration of the National Civil Service Examination (Cha, 1996: 97). To the students who carried on the Confucian tradition and tended the memorial tablet of Confucius, the King's visit and pledge symbolized their privilege and power in Joseon society even though they were merely students. The power of Confucian students and the National Confucian Academy is also exemplified by another event. Yeonsankun, the tenth king (1494-1506) ordered the dismissal of Confucian students from the National Confucian Academy and the removal of the tablets from the Confucian Shrine because the students had criticized his unseemly banquets for featuring royal harems and concubines. Possibly perceiving the students as a threat, the King ordered the Seongkyunkwan and Munmyo to be relocated to the Buddhist temple (*Wonkaksa*). Due to strong objections from high-level officers that the Confucian Academy could not be moved into a Buddhist temple since Buddhism was regarded as evil by Confucian doctrine, he ordered the National Confucian Academy and Confucian Shrine to be moved beyond the capital walls. If not for the fatal illness of the King, the order might not have been rescinded and the institutions returned to their original location (*Seoul Yukbaeknyunsa*, 1978, (1): 272-273).

Another example of student demonstrations against absolute power appears in the *Annals of the Dynasty of Joseon* (*Joseon Wangjo Sillok*, 1413-1910). When the King decided to expel a certain Confucian bureaucrat, approximately 150 students in the National Academy raised severe objections. According to *Sillok,* the court was shaken by the students' outcry (Kim, 1994: 121). This was the first demonstration against the government and King that *Sillok* officially recorded.

Since this dissenting voice was potentially formidable, the government made sure to filter and control it by means of an institutional mechanism—the civil service examination. This exam served multiple functions: enticing into government service the best talents and people who might otherwise encourage revolution; indoctrinating the intellectuals and making them more dependent upon the state; ensuring that government posts would be filled by loyal subjects; reinforcing the status of official orthodoxy; breaking down the hereditary privileges of the nobility; strengthening the emperors' control over the bureaucracy; and preserving autocratic traditions (Fu, 1993: 98).

Loyal Opposition and Semi-opposition

The concept of "loyal opposition" in Linz and Stepan's (1978) *The Breakdown of Democratic Regimes* connotes an opposition party or force that is more loyal than one that is purely opposed to a political system. Fernandes (2006: 4) views loyal opposition as "a commitment to maintaining a legal constitutional order, following parliamentary procedure, and rejecting other political actors who refuse to do so in a legitimate, democratic political system." As mentioned at the end of chapter 1, the concept of loyal opposition is relevant to our analysis of Korea's simultaneous developmental state and democratization, despite the fact that it is based on the analysis of contemporary democratic regimes, but how is this concept relevant to our analysis of hegemonic state centrality and the formation of civil society in the Hanyang era? Fernandes (2006: 4) provides a valuable clue:

> In parliamentary systems of government, the term 'loyal opposition' is applied to the opposition parties in the legislature to indicate that the non-governing parties may oppose the actions of the sitting cabinet—typically comprising parliamentarians from the party with the most seats in the elected legislative chamber—while maintaining loyalty to the source of the government's power. The concept thus permits the dissent necessary for a functioning democracy, as the policies of the governing cabinet can be challenged without fear of being accused of treason against the state.

With regards to the concept of loyal opposition, three elements of this observation deserve attention. First, the political group of loyal opposition takes a clear stance against that of the ruling group without denying the overall legitimacy of their ruling power; the loyal opposition only objects to specific policies or actions of the party in charge. Second, its stance of opposition aims to support the power basis of the ruling party, such that its allegiance remains meaningful. Third, its stance of opposition becomes necessary as a way to make the whole system function more healthily. Thus, despite their differences on specific political issues, the ruling party and the party of loyal opposition acknowledge each other in a mutually reinforcing and supportive way; that is, the loyal opposition does not pose any serious threat to the basis of the ruling party's political legitimacy. The governing party is well aware that the opposition party is in fact loyal to the fundamental basis of its legitimacy and, in some sense, even contributes to the sustainability of its fundamental power base.

The position and the function of the Seongkyunkwan clearly fits into this concept of loyal opposition: the collective actions that were allowed for students of the National Confucian Academy were never intended to overturn the royal crown and Confucian state of the Joseon Dynasty. In fact, in the beginning of the Joseon Dynasty, even though their collective actions and remonstrance were directed toward the King, their collective actions did not aim to remove the King but instead were directed against the remnants of Buddhist influence in Joseon; thus, the royal crown and Confucian government did not perceive the Seongkyunkwan's collective actions as a fundamental threat. The students did not consider the option of revolution; the Seongkyunkwan's initial role was to worship and maintain the Shrines of the Royal Family and Confucius, the founder of the governing ideology of Joseon, as well as to uphold Confucianism and serve as the source of future recruitment of Confucian scholarly bureaucrats. This function was critical for the power basis of Joseon; however, the Academy was given almost exclusive rights to make appeals and engage in collective actions on specific issues, taking a stance of visible opposition.

To the types of power dynamics that exist among parties, Linz adds one more concept—that of "semi-opposition." Simply put, according to Linz, a force of semi-opposition takes part in the governing party, but its goal is to transform the governing party into a democracy, especially when that governing party is autocratic. On this concept, Fernandes (2006: 4) says,

> Semiopposition is made up of those groups which control or are present in some of the regime's institutions and which initially were supportive of the regime, but with the purpose of attaining goals not shared by their coalition partners. The important thing to keep in mind here is that, in certain contexts, autocratic regimes may engender political groupings, present in the regime's institutions, who are simultaneously inside and out of the regime, and who seek the gradual and controlled evolution of the regime into a democracy. We call these groupings the democratic Semiopposition.

The concept of semi-opposition, despite the fact that it was formulated to explain the power dynamics in a modern democratic regime, is relevant to our analysis of the role of the Sarim during the Joseon Dynasty. Sarim (사림, 士林) literally means "a forest" (림 in Korean and 林 in Chinese) of Neo-Confucian scholars or literati (사 in Korean and 士 in Chinese). This term was commonly used to designate a group of high-class Confucian scholars who had their political and economic bases in the countryside. Lee (1984: 204) views them as "a force that had preferred to exert its influence, through the Local Agency, on administration at the county level rather than to seek to enter the capital bureaucracy."

This book argues that the Sarim fits more with the concept of semi-opposition than loyal opposition because the Sarim was mainly composed of Confucian scholars "who had remained faithful to the royal house of Goryeo by refusing to accept office under the Joseon" or were critical of Dynastic Foundation Merit Subject (*kaekukgongshin*) (Lee, 1984: 204). Their moral thrust and pursuit of idealistic politics in early Joseon differed significantly from the realistic stance taken by the meritorious subjects and elites in the central government in Hanyang. The latter, composed of power elites, was constantly being confronted by the Sarim, whose primary goal in the middle phase of the Joseon Dynasty was to replace the preponderant meritorious elites and seize power in the central government with the royal crown intact. "In the main, they held positions in the Censorate and in the Office of Special Advisors, where they had charge of remonstrance and the preparation of certain state documents" (Lee, 1984: 204). In general, the Sarim who took these government positions were close to the royal crown and challenged the power elites in the center. They were part of the governing structure, yet their main political basis was in the countryside. These features match well with Fernandes' criteria for semi-opposition. First, they were in "control or present in some of the regime's institutions"—the Sarim took positions in the Censorate and the Office of Special Advisors. Second, they "attain[ed] goals not shared by their coalition partners"—the Sarim challenged the meritorious elites in the center even though the Sarim shared the governing structure. Third, they were "simultaneously inside and out of the regime"—that is, though they were inside the government, they maintained their power basis in the countryside. And lastly, the Sarim were "seek[ing] the gradual and controlled evolution of the regime"—they were involved in a series of political convulsions known as the "literati purges" as a result of their attempts to weaken the power elites in the center. Eventually, in the 16th century, they were able to establish a Sarim government (Han, 2010: 146).

The Sarim as Civil Society

Do the Sarim of the Joseon Dynasty qualify as civil society? "Civil society" refers to "that arena of the polity where self-organizing and relatively autonomous groups, movements, and individuals attempt to articulate values, to create associations and solidarities, and to advance their interests. Civil society can include manifold social movements (e.g., women's groups, neighborhood associations, religious groupings, and intellectual organizations), as well as associations from all social strata (such as trade unions, entrepreneurial groups, and professional associations)" (Linz & Stepan, 1996: 17).

In many ways, the Sarim can indeed be regarded as a seed of civil society. By the end of the Goryeo Kingdom, there existed two groups of Neo-Confucianist—scholars and political elites. The former was composed of a radical sadaebu group of Neo-Confucianist reformists, including Jeong Dojeon, Jo Jun, Nam Eun, and Yun Sojong—all of whom supported General Yi Seongye's "withdrawal from Wihwa Island" in 1388, which had resulted in the collapse of the Goryeo Dynasty. These members of the radical sadaebu went on to become the founding power elites of the new Joseon Dynasty. The other was a moderate reformist group that was loyal to the Goryeo Dynasty and included Jeong Mongju and his followers. After successfully reorganizing the land distribution system of the old Goryeo Dynasty and the economic base of its powerful conservatives in 1390, the former meritorious sadaebu purged the opposition sadaebu in 1392, and Yi Seonggye ascended the throne to found the Joseon Dynasty.

Boasting that it had gained the support of the public and the Heavens, the new government justified this change of dynasty under the notion first advanced by Mencius of revolutionary dynastic change as decreed by the Heavens. The foundation of the Joseon Dynasty is regarded as a significant event in the history of politics in that it was achieved with minimal use of military power, and the new rules were able to cement the legitimacy of their rule by courting public support through such means as the reform of the existing system (Han, 2010: 30). It goes without saying that the *docham sasang*, based on China's geomancy or Korea's *pungsu jiri sasang*, should have significantly influenced the masses to believe that the political transformation from Buddhist Goryeo to Confucian Joseon was recognized by Heaven.

Thus, Neo-Confucianist scholars near the end of the Goryeo Dynasty were split between realist sadaebu who had helped found the Joseon Dynasty and idealist sadaebu who had opposed the military coup. The radical reformists were comprised of meritorious power elites in the center, and the opposition sadaebu established their sphere of influence in the local provinces (i.e., Sarim, local Confucian scholars, or literati). The latter strongly advocated reform as part of their effort "to establish the type of sage kingship called for under ideal Confucian politics," and the former was composed of "exiting meritorious subjects and royal in-laws who, in addition to wanting to maintain their power, promoted the need for worldly policies such as those related to the building of a strong army and economy" (Han, 2010: 136).

The power of the meritorious subjects in the center, however, declined as King Seongjong (1469-1494) recruited local sadaebu from the Southeastern province of Youngnam to posts within the three Censorate offices (Samsa) in order to curb the excessively centralizing power of these meritorious subjects, which peaked during Sejo's reign (1455-1468). The Sarim's successful rise to power began to check the power of the meritorious subjects. While the Sarim faction was attacking the concentrated power and wealth of the existing elites in the center, it was also attempting to consolidate its power in the local provinces by establishing autonomous local institutions, both political and economic, such as Yuhyangso (a local government committee charged with advising the magistrate) and Sachang (a village aid system to provide financial support for the poor). Han (2010: 137) argues that "In a sense, the rise of the Sarim can be regarded as a phenomenon which emerged alongside the historical transition from the establishment era to that of pursuing the growth and stability of local communities." As can be seen from the Sarim's actions, they possessed all of the ingredients essential to the concept of civil society.

Despite a series of purges, the Sarim had grown through "the private Confucian academies (*seowon*), the village code (*hyangyak*), and their landholdings. In the reign of Seonjo (1567-1608), the Sarim factions were able to enter government service in the central government and, in the end, to dominate the political process" (Lee, 1984: 206). The Sarim continued to grow and, by the end of Seonjo's reign in 1608, there were hundreds seowon nationwide. At one point, the number of seowon reached 679, but it dwindled to 47 by 1871 (Kim, 1981: 75). Receiving grants and royal endowments in the form of books, land, and slaves, the seowon came to occupy a position in Joseon society reminiscent of that which had been enjoyed by the Buddhist temples in the Goryeo Kingdom (Lee, 1984: 207). In addition, the local Neo-Confucian literati were able to establish a Sarim government in the 16th century, Han (2010: 146) explains, due to the Sarim's firm establishment of moral and economic hegemony within their provinces.

The Sarim as Political Society[27]

Linz and Stepan (1996: 17) define "political society" as an "arena in which political actors compete for the legitimate right to exercise control over public power and the state apparatus." They go on to explain: "Civil society by itself can destroy a nondemocratic regime, but democratic consolidation (or even a full democratic transition) must involve political society. Democratic consolidation requires that citizens develop an appreciation for the core institutions of a democratic political society—political parties, legislatures, elections, electoral rules, political leadership, and interparty alliances." There is good reason to argue that the Sarim spread across the countryside in the form of local civil societies and then emerged as a political society in the 16th-century Joseon Dynasty. Successful access to central power during the reign of Seonjo (1567-1608) led to a power struggle not only between central meritorious subjects and local literati but also among factions of the literati themselves. Both Lee (1984) and Han (2010) label such power struggles in the central government as factional strife, or *tangjaeng* or *boongdang Jeongchi* in Korean.[28] Lee (1984: 208) attributes this strife to the increasing inflow of local Confucian literati into the central political arena, which ignited competition among them for the limited number of government positions.

The most famous tangjaeng began as a personal clash between Shim Euigyum, who was representing the Seoin, a group of Sarim bureaucrats living mostly west of Hanyang with a practical emphasis on the pursuit of national wealth and defense capabilities, and Kim Hyo-won, who was representing the Dongin, a different group of the same bureaucrats living mostly east of Hanyang with an idealistic emphasis on self-cultivation and the moral regeneration of literati as part of an effort to heighten the morality of the political leader. The substance of the discrepancy centered around appointments to powerful positions in the Ministry of Personnel, known collectively as the *cheollang*, which was responsible for recruiting and selecting candidates for certain vital offices. Thus, this was a power struggle between two opposing political cliques for powerful positions in the central government, which perfectly fits the definition of "political society": that is, an "arena in which political actors compete for the legitimate right to exercise control over public power and the state apparatus" (Linz & Stepan, 1996: 17). There existed a strong sense of identification as a factional affiliation, and this tradition continued, generation after generation, throughout mid- and late Joseon. Behind such factional strife were seowon (private Confucian academies), which served not only as educational centers but also as seedbeds for partisan disputes. Moreover, these private academies began to compete with Hanyang's public schools as children of the yangban class increasingly enrolled in seowon. At one point, the Sarim began recruiting students who would have entered either the Seongkyunkwan or Hyanggyo (public school system) (Kim, 1981), which shows the increasing influence of the Sarim in court politics. Later, the Dongin clique split into hard-liners and moderates over the issue of punishing the Seoin faction. The hard-liners developed into the Bookin (Northerners), and the moderates developed into Namin (Southerners).

In this analysis, the Sarim are generally considered to be a civil society; thus, political strife among the different Sarim factions is interpreted as the emergence of political society during the Joseon Dynasty. The application of the concepts of civil society and political society to these early Asian phenomena must reflect the asynchronous differences between the advent of Western civil society and Confucian society in Korea; however, the characteristics of Sarim come close to matching those of civil society in general; and since collective actions were allowed only by students in the National Confucian Academy, the Sarim later became seedbeds of intelligentsia that resisted Japanese colonial control as well as General Park's capitalist monopoly dictatorship. The next subsection will examine the role of the Seongkyunkwan as a unique source of dissenting voices within the hegemony of the Confucian state.

Seongkyunkwan and Collective Actions

As soon as Japan colonized the Joseon Dynasty in 1910, Japanese colonial headquarters shut down the National Academy of Seongkyunkwan. In 1911, they went a step further and replaced it with the Kyunghwakwon, which was in turn replaced by Kyeongseong Imperial University in 1926. The main reason for this replacement was to control Confucian civil society, including the Sarim, and to put the Sarim under Japanese influence as well as to promote Japanese colonial policies. Overall, the aim of the Kyunghwakwon was to convert Confucian intelligentsia into a pro-Japanese social force (Jeong, 2007: 25).

That the National Confucian Academy represented the heteronomical force in Korean politics during the Joseon period (1392-1910) and contributed to the formation of dissenting civil society is supported by the school's dual aspects: by recruiting the brightest students and bureaucrats, it remained the highest educational institution, teaching and upholding the governing ideology of the Joseon Dynasty; however, it also functioned as a group of the highest intelligentsia to check and balance the power of the King and his established subjects while also serving as a public sphere where the opinions of the local Confucian scholars and retired high-level government officials were reflected. Whenever the King or his officials infringed upon the fundamental principles of Confucian governing ideology or the Academy's internal matters (Kim, 2008), these students would engage in collective actions. Thus, the Seongkyunkwan served as a legitimate source of dissenting voices within the Confucian governing structure, and this was widely recognized by the ruled in general; in fact, whenever people came to know that the Seongkyunkwan was opposed to a certain government policy or was engaging in collective actions, they would recognize in the least that a problem existed in the court.

During the Joseon Dynasty, there were several kinds of demonstrations. The Bokhap was utilized by high-level government officials to make appeals against the King's decisions. The Bokkweol, Kajeonsangeon, and Kyukjaeng were for the people to voice their concerns. The Seongkyunkwan, though, had more types of demonstrations, each geared toward a particular purpose, with well-established rules of engagement (Kim, 2008: 182). Kongkwan, which literally means "emptying the building," was the students' strongest method of expressing their discontent with the King; this form of demonstration involved deserting the Academy, which was a potent symbolic gesture since the Academy was nation's highest educational institution of the governing ideology. Such a demonstration would seriously tarnish the legitimacy of the Confucian state and morality of the King (Kim, 2008: 187). Another form of collective action, Kwondang, involved the students' refusal to enter the official cafeteria of the Seongkyunkwan. Each student was required by the school to have a certain number of attendances at the Seongkyunkwan in order to qualify to take the national civil service examination. When students did not enter the school's cafeteria, they were counted as absent. If a student's total absences reached a certain amounted, then he would lose the opportunity to sit for the national exam; however, if all of the students missed the daily meals that were provided by the school cafeteria, then this would function as a collective threat that all of the students might refuse to participate in the national civil service examination, which in turn would cost the government the opportunity to recruit more government officials. Therefore, students' collective action of absenteeism during this daily roll call was a strong method of expressing their dissent against the King and their seniors. To their seniors, these students in the government-funded National Academy represented the future of the state and governing structure as well as the vanguard of the governing ideology of Confucianism. As the Academy was the highest educational institution, the guardian of the Confucian shrine, and a place of recruitment for high-level government officials, the royal family and the established power elites treated Academy students as representatives of the future of the nation and accordingly granted them the right to raise voices of dissent. Such an attitude was also based on the idea that these students comprised the backbone of the nation; thus, their mistakes were treated with a generous dose of lenience. At the same time, students' sense of independence and resistance against injustice or unrighteousness was encouraged by kings and meritorious subjects as a valuable source of corrective feedback (Kim, 2008: 183).

Thus, the Seongkyunkwan's extraterritoriality, which stemmed from serving the Confucian shrine, also functioned as a kind of Achilles' heel to the Confucian power elites because it enabled the Academy to voice opposition against the central power of kings and Confucian scholarly bureaucrats. In addition, Seongkyunkwan students could present a collective remonstrance called *Yooso* against the government, and they communicated to each other through a referendum called *Tongmoon*. When Seongkyunkwan students initiated a remonstrance with joint signatures, they marched to the main gate of Kyeongbok Palace (Kwanghwamoon) with Seongkyunkwan slaves ahead of them in order to display their political status and, kneeling down before the gate, handed their remonstrance to the King. Even high-level meritorious subjects were not allowed to block Confucian students who knelt to appeal to the King, and the students would continue demonstrating until the King responded (Shin, 2005: 27). Also worth noting, established power elites would sometimes coax students to use this exclusive right to raise a dissenting voice as a way of bringing up issues that the power elites felt unable to raise on their own. For example, in early Joseon, elites urged students to demonstrate against Buddhism, which gave the government some justification to implement the anti-Buddhist policy it had long been yearning to initiate. In many cases of students' demonstrations, the students' opinions were respected (Kim, 2008: 184).

The Seongkyunkwan's role as a heteronomical force built into the Joseon Dynasty intensified as the descendants of prestigious families began to acquire government jobs without passing the national civil service exams. The Seongkyunkwan soon filled with students from local provinces who did not come from powerful families. Those who were unable to secure jobs in the government through merit became a source of constant discontent regarding those who possessed power in the center, and these students expressed this discontent through various forms of demonstration. This phenomenon began to surface toward the end of the Dynasty. In late Joseon, the number of Kongkwan and Kwondang dramatically increased, as shown table 3.1 below (Kim, 2008: 195).

According to Kim (2008: 196), the two main forms of collective actions that were utilized by National Confucian Academy students—the Kwondang and Kongkwan—were uncommon until the end of the middle of the Joseon Dynasty. According to the official record, the average rate of these demonstrations remained less than one per year until Hyunjong but dramatically increased after Sookjong and toward the late phase of the Joseon Dynasty in the mid-18th century. In particular, Youngjo's Policy of Impartiality (*Tamgpyunchaek*) produced unprecedented numbers of collective actions—37 (i.e., 35 Kwondang and 2 Kongkwan) to be exact. This Policy of Impartiality was

Table 3.1 Number of Kwondang (Kd) and Kongkwan (Kk) per Regime/King

King	Sejong	Seongjong	Joongjong	Myungjong	Kwanghae	Injo	Hyojong	Hyunjong	
	Early Joseon (1392-1567)				Mid Joseon (1567-1724)				
#	1 (Kk)	1 (Kk)	1 (Kk)	3 (Kk)	2 (Kk)	3 (Kd 1; Kk 2)	3 (Kd 1; Kk 2)	3 (Kk)	
Years of Reign	32	25	39	22	15	27	10	15	
# on Average	0.03	0.04	0.02	0.14	0.13	0.01	0.3	0.2	
King	Sookjong	Kyungjong	Youngjo	Jeongjo	Soonjo	Heonjong	Cheoljong	Kojong	Total
	(1567-1724)		Late Joseon (1724-1897)						
#	32 (Kd 19; Kk 13)	5 (Kd)	37 (Kd 35; Kk 2)	24 (Kd 23; Kk 1)	41 (Kd 38; Kk 3)	8 (Kd)	12 (Kd)	6 (Kd)	182
Years of Reign	46	4	52	24	34	15	14	43	518
# on Average	0.7	1.25	0.71	1.0	1.2	0.53	0.86	0.14	0.35

Source: (Kim, 2008: 196)

designed to reform factionalism and partisan politics based on region and different branches of Confucian school of thought, and to appoint moderate and conciliatory scholars and officers to government posts. It aimed to strengthen the power of the royal family, remedy the kingship, and reform faction-based politics that had been activated during the reign of Sookjong by recruiting high-level officials from various factions (Han, 2010: 196). Due to the length of his reign (i.e., 52 years), the average number of students' collective actions reached almost one per year despite the fact that the largest number of demonstrations was recorded during his reign. This number increased during the reign of the last king, Kyungjong, in the middle phase of Joseon, with more than one demonstration per year—1.25. Immediately after the low point of the demonstrations during the reign of Youngjo, two consecutive regimes (Jeongjo and Soonjo) experienced almost the same level of demonstrations as the Youngjo period—24 (23 Kwondang and 1 Kongkwan) and 41 (38 Kwondang and 3 Kongkwan), respectively. The reign of Soonjo signaled the waning of strong royal family and kingship. During his reign, the Kim family from Andong of the Southeastern province seized power in the government, which in turn decreased King Soonjo's power. This was called *Sedo jeongchi*, which refers to the politics of the royal in-law clan that significantly limited the power of kings in court politics (Han, 2010: 269). The two kings who ruled prior to him, Youngjo and Jeongjo, exemplified the heyday of the King's strong central power, whereas Soonjo's reign was recorded as the beginning of the decline of the King's central power.

Ironically, strong royal authority during these three reigns did not decrease the number of collective actions made by the Confucian students, which means that despite the strong kingships that had been maintained by Youngjo and Jeongjo, the Joseon Dynasty entered an era of faction-based politics in the last phase from 1724 onward, and the royal in-law clan politics significantly weakened the authority of the crown after these two powerful kings. Back at the beginning of the Joseon Dynasty, a consensus existed between the King and the Confucian subjects over the balance of power; however, the power balance between royal authority and high-level subjects began to fall considerably into the hands of high-level government officials as a result of their loyalty to their factions and their relations with the royal family.

Over time, the form of demonstration or collective actions utilized by Academy students clearly shifted. Among Kwondang and Kongkwan, the latter was a stronger expression of opposition against the royal authority because it involved the future ruling elites literally leaving the school. The possible interruption to the recruitment of Confucian scholarly bureaucrats severely threatened the state, which relied completely upon Confucianism as the state's ultimate governing ideology and as the organizing principle of the government bureaucracy, the relations between government and market, and the codes of conduct for the ruled. The Kwondang, on the other hand, was a softer form of collective action as students remained in the Seongkyunkwan while expressing dissent. Table 3.1 above shows that there was a stronger form of Kwondang demonstration in the early phase of the Joseon Dynasty. Up until the late middle phase of the Dynasty, the majority of the students' collective actions took the form of Kongkwan when the power balance between the King and subjects was shifted toward the King or balanced.

Were student demonstrations much stronger when the King's power was strong? The answer to this question can be found in table 3.2 below. Most Kongkwan were directed against Buddhism. As is well known, the Joseon Dynasty purged the Buddhism of the previous kingdom of Goryeo. In the early Joseon era of the late 14th century, both royal authority and Confucian sadaebu made every effort to eradicate Buddhism's influence on general culture and politics as a means of legitimizing the foundation of the Joseon Dynasty, consolidating the power of Confucianism, and securing their own political and economic interests. Accordingly, in the early days of Joseon, the Kongkwan were directed against remnants of Buddhist power and influence rather than against the King. To both royal authority and Confucian government elites, the Seongkyunkwan was considered the best way to control Buddhist influence in politics without tarnishing their hands with blood. At the same time, the Seongkyunkwan was able to establish itself as the most legitimate source of public opinion and as a powerful political institution in its own right. Because it served as a cat's paw for the central power, which was eager to remove all remnants of Buddhist influence that had sprung up from Confucian origins, the Seongkyunkwan was protected by kings and Confucian power elites in the center and thus could make itself an ultimate balancer of power. Therefore, the highest form of the collective action, the Kongkwan, which was the most popular form of demonstration in the early phase of the Dynasty, posed no real threat to hegemonic central power. Rather, it served as both a political tool for ruling elites and a self-promotional tool for strengthening their legitimacy as an institution of checks and balances, not just in relation to central power but also to the masses.

It is interesting to note that as the Dynasty entered the middle phase, there was an increasing number of Kwondang, the softer form of demonstration. As briefly mentioned above, in the middle phase of the Dynasty, the Seongkyunkwan lost its function as a major recruiting institution for future bureaucrats because the descendants of privileged families were allowed to secure good government positions without passing the national civil service examination. Those who replaced students from powerful political families

Table 3.2 Causes of Collective Actions by Seongkyunkwan (SKK) Students

King	Sejong	Seongjong	Joongjong	Myungjong	Kwanghae	Injo	Hyojong	Hyunjong
Phase	Early Joseon (1392-1567)				Mid Joseon (1567-1724)			
Anti- Buddhism	1	0	1	2	0	0	0	0
Factions	0	0	0	0	2	1	2	2
Insult at SKK, Saseup	0	0	0	1	0	1	0	1
Internal Issues	0	1	0	0	0	0	0	0
Total	1	1	1	3	2	2	2	3

King	Sookjong	Kyungjong	Youngjo	Jeongjo	Soonjo	Total
Phase	Mid Joseon (1567-1724)		Late Joseon (1724-1894)			
Anti- Buddhism	0	0	0	0	0	4
Factions	10	1	0	1	0	19
Insult at SKK, Saseup	3	1	1		2	10
Internal Issues	0	0	1	0	1	3
Total	13	2	2	1	3	36

Source: (Kim, 2008: 196)

came from local provinces and were frustrated because their pathway to the government had been significantly narrowed. Factions of the Sarim were behind newly recruited Seongkyunkwan students, and the Sarim's role as a balancer of power and an ultimate source of righteousness in Confucian criteria was diminished as it became an arena for political power struggles among different factions (Kim, 2008: 195-197; Han, 2010: 143-149).

In the 18th century, though, as Joseon politics became increasingly controlled by factions of Sarim and high-level and royal in-law politics, the Seongkyunkwan's function of leading public opinion shifted to that of a mouthpiece for factional interests. Table 3.2 clearly shows such a trend of increasing collective actions by Seongkyunkwan students, which meant the weakening power of the King and increasing power of high-level officers.

Seeds of Civil Society: Combined Hegemony and Heteronomy

The fundamental basis of the heteronomical force in the Hanyang era contained two main elements: the Sarim as the emergence of civil and political society, and the Seongkyunkwan as the origin of the loyal opposition. In addition, there were Confucian bureaucracies that worked to check and balance the central government organizations, the Daegan. The combined presence of these institutions and their rise to power as factions from the mid-Joseon Dynasty contributed to the formation of an aggressive civil society, which then transformed into strong nationalist resistance against Japanese colonial control after Japan occupied Korea in 1910. The next chapter will examine how hegemonic forces subsequently joined the heteronomical base when faced with a common enemy during the Kyeongseong era, thereby expanding their power.

NOTES

1. "[T]he symbolism of Chinese cities became a part—if only a minor one—of the imperial ideology with its emphasis on the centrality of China in the world and on the Son of Heaven as radiator maximus of civilizations" (Wright, 1977: 73).

2. Kim, Young-Don (1952), "Seoul Reflected in the Folksongs of Cheju Island."

3. "Some of these ceremonial complexes, those of Lower Mesopotamia in Proto literate times, for example, the great cult centers of the Indus valley and of classical Cambodia, Teotihuacan in the Valley of Mexico, and some of the later Mayan centers of Yucatan, had attracted permanent settlement to the fringes of their sacred enceintes; but other ceremonial sites, notably Tiahuanaco, perhaps Chavin de Huantar, some of the Mayan shrines (particularly Monte Alban, where no source of water has been discovered) and, say, those erected on the Dieng Plateau in Java during the 8th

century, were either so remote or in such agriculturally unproductive locations that it is to be inferred that they accommodated no permanent populations of any size. In fact, it would seem that, apart from a corps of priests and a limited number of resident craftsmen, such a ceremonial complex was in all probability starkly empty during most of the year. Only during seasonal festivals, when cultivators were presumably drawn in from the surrounding countryside, would it have sheltered a more numerous and less specialized population" (Wheatley, 1971: 257).

4. "Examples are Meru in India, Haraberezaiti in Iran, the mythical 'Mount of the Lands' in Mesopotamia, Gerizim in Palestine—which, moreover, was called the 'navel of the earth.' Since the sacred mountain is an *axis mundi* connecting earth with heaven, it in a sense touches heaven and hence marks the highest point in the world; consequently the territory that surrounds it, and that constitutes 'our world,' is held to be the highest among countries. This is stated in Hebrew tradition: Palestine, being the highest land, was not submerged by the Flood. According to Islamic tradition, the highest place on earth is the *kaaba*, because 'the Pole Star bears witness that it faces the center of Heaven.' For Christians, it is Golgotha that is on the summit of the cosmic mountain. All these beliefs express the same feeling, which is profoundly religious: 'our world' is holy ground because it is the place nearest to heaven, because from here, from our abode, it is possible to reach heaven; hence our world is a high place. In cosmological terms, this religious conception is expressed by the projection of the favored territory which is 'ours' onto the summit of the cosmic mountain. Later speculation drew all sorts of conclusions—for example, the one just cited for Palestine, that the Holy Land was not submerged by the Flood" (Eliade, 1957: 38-39).

5. See Hur (1994), p. 257.

6. In figures 1 and 2, this encircling wall is marked by red circles. "In China, for example, where they appear together as an architectural complex, the circle represents heaven or nature, the square the earth or the artificial world of man" (Tuan, 1974: 153). "Man constructs according to an archetype. Not only does the city of his temple have celestial models; the same is true of the entire region that he inhabits, with the rivers that water it, the fields that give him his food, etc." (Eliade, 1954: 10). "The fundamental role of the inner wall enclosing the administrative and ceremonial focus of the territory, the axis about which revolved the microcosm of the state, is reflected in the etymology of the word *dieng* (*ch'eng*), which came to denote both 'city' and '[the] wall', whereas *kwak* (*kuo*), the outer wall, acquired overtones associated with fortification and subsequently developed the secondary meaning of 'suburb'" (Wheatley, 1971: 187).

7. See Lim (1994a), pp. 51-52.

8. *Ibid.*

9. The Chinese character *In* (Benevolence) literally means "East." Similarly, *Eui* (Righteousness) means West, *Rye* (Rite) South, and *Ji* (Wisdom) North. Originally, the name of the North Gate was *Sojimoon*. In the name of the Bell Tower that is located in the center of Hanyang, the Chinese character *Shin* means "center." Refer to Lee Kyu Tae's column on the "The Names of the Four Gates" in *Chosun Daily News*, December 3, 1996.

10. *Kao-kung chi* [考工記] was a part of *Chou li* [周禮], a classical source that described how the ancient Chinese built their capital city and palace buildings. Serving as a manual for building, it prescribes Confucian ideals that the Chinese believed needed to be represented in the capital city and palaces. It combined Confucian governing ideology with ideas from the school of Taoism and geomancy. Important excerpts of the *Kao-kung chi* that closely affected the construction of Hanyang and major political institutional buildings are included in appendix 1. This compilation is from the chapter that Arthur A. Wright wrote in 1977, "The Cosmology of the Chinese City" in *The City in Late Imperial China* edited by G.W. Skinner.

11. The Administrative Code of Chosun (*Choson Kyeongguk Cheon*) and the Six Codes of Governance (*Kyeongje Yukcheon*) were prepared by the two important Dynastic Foundation Merit Subjects, Chong To-jon and Cho Chun, around 1388, just before the Joseon Dynasty was founded in 1392.

12. The Japanese authorities during the colonial rule from 1910 to 1945 destroyed these architectures that were symbolic of Confucian authority, thereby damaging the authority of the Korean king and degrading the symbolism of the main palace.

13. In 1592, Japan invaded Joseon, destroying three palaces—Kyeongbok, Changkyeong, and Changdeok—as well as Monmyo (Seongkyunkwan), Jongmyo, and Sajik. In 1602, the reconstruction began. The first building restored was Moonmyo (the Confucian Shrine and the National Confucian Academy), and then Jongmyo (the Royal Ancestral Shrine) and Sajik (the Guardian Deities of the State). The fact that these repairs came first shows how important "rite" was in the Joseon Dynasty. See, Kim, Bong-Ryol (1991), pp. 24-25.

14. Refer to figure 3.4.

15. Refer to figure 3.7.

16. See figure 3.7.

17. Refer to figure 3.7.

18. See Peterson, M. D. (1975), p. 384.

19. Sangso was the institution through which subjects reported injustice or inappropriate policies to the King for improvement in the Joseon Dynasty. See Lee, Jong-Ko (1993), pp. 139, 127.

20. The Confucian central government devised a corpus of administrative law upholding the ideals of the Confucian governing system. Several major laws were enacted by the court embodying the cardinal principles and practices by which the Joseon Dynasty's political process would operate. Jeong Do-jeon was the major contributor in completing the major corpus of administrative laws, including the Administrative Code of Joseon (*Joseon Gyeonggukjeon*) and the Six Codes of Governance (*Gyeongje Yukjeon*) compiled by Cho Jun even before the beginning of the Joseon Dynasty following the march back from the Yalu in 1388. King Sejo endeavored to complete a statutory code that would define the governing structure and system of Joseon. As a result, the National Code (*Gyeongguk Daejeon*) was promulgated in the second year of Seongjong's reign, in 1471. See Lee, (1984), pp. 172-173.

21. Yejo (Rites), Ijo (Personnel), Hojo (Taxation), Byungjo (Military Affairs), Hyungjo (Punishment), and Kongjo (Public Works).

22. In 119 BC, Emperor Han Wudi decreed a state monopoly of the manufacture and trade of salt and iron, and placed their management under the jurisdiction of the Grand Minister of Agriculture. See, Fu (1993), p. 94.

23. In the Roman Empire, salt served as salary for soldiers. The Latin origin of the word "salt" is *salarium,* meaning a soldier's salary. See, Kim, Eui-Whan (1996), p. 186.

24. A government office in charge of some food items that were offered to the palace, such as fishes, meat, and salt.

25. Military provisions agency.

26. See figure 3.7.

27. It is important to understand the materialistic basis of the Sarim community. The Gwajeon (land distribution system based on rank) in the early Joseon, in fact, eased the concentration of land in aristocratic class of the Goryeo Dyansty and solidified the economic basis of new meritorious subjects and farmers. Together, they functioned as both the political and economic bases of the *Joseon* Dynasty; however, the Gwajeon system began to collapse as political elites in the center accumulated land beyond the regulations. Agricultural productivity increased, though, due to improvements in cultivation and technologies, and market-based agricultural economy dominated the controlled market, which provided the Sarim with a sound material basis in the provinces. This study does not focus on the materialistic basis of the Sarim economy and their landholding situation.

28. Yang and Henderson (1958: 93) summarized the emergence of factional strife as follows: "During the first century and a half of the dynasty, it may have worked to this effect and it is in this period that factional strife was least apparent. About the beginning of the sixteenth century, however, beginning with the reign of Myeongjong (1545-67), the administration of the examination system became corrupt, its effectiveness declined and did not recover. Passing the examination became more dependent on the political background of the aspirant than on his intellectual attainment. Moreover, tutoring at the house of the right official in Seoul proved more efficacious than study at even a government school; if the official were highly enough placed, the subject matter he taught often proved rather closely related to the examination questions and it was frequently suspected that the questions themselves were sometimes divulged through such judicious contacts. This trend in the examination system played directly into the hands of the factions by encouraging personal favor, personal schools, personal favorites. It is precisely this corruption of the examination system which underlay the accusations of Shim Eui-gyeom against Kim, Hyowon; it is from the long struggle between these politicians in the 1560's and 1570's that the Tongin and the Seoin, the first factions universally recognized as such, emerged."

Chapter Four

Kyeongseong: Local-Global Interaction

This chapter recounts how Japanese colonial rule (1910-1945) sought to dismantle the basis of Confucian political power and appropriate the strong state tradition of the Joseon Dynasty in the Kyeongseong period, bringing major changes to the rules of hegemony, hierarchy, and heteronomy established during the Joseon Dynasty. The first rule—namely, the state's centrality and legitimacy to intervene in the economy—was pursued by two antagonistic agents for different goals of their own. For the Koreans elites, including the heteronomical forces, the centrality of the Joseon's Confucian state was an object that they sought to recover; in contrast, Japanese colonial headquarters sought to take advantage of the loyalty that was being projected toward the abstract notion of state centrality by the Korean masses in order to strengthen the legitimacy of its own colonial policy. In terms of hierarchy, the Japanese modernized and imperial bureaucracy replaced the traditional Confucian bureaucratic system. More importantly, though, the Kyeongseong era produced massive heteronomical forces by compelling the former Confucian hegemonic and hierarchical classes to join with Joseon's dissenting forces—all in a nationalistic reaction to Japanese imperial colonial policy. Thus, in addition to introducing capitalism into the agricultural and Confucian economic system of old Korea, the Kyeongsong era greatly contributed to the emergence of modern civil society and the achievement of democratization through such nationalistic expansion of the heteronomical forces. New rules added by Japan transformed Korea's political and economic prototype in ways that would later affect the economic development process in the 1960s and '70s as well as the formation of strong civil society.

THE MEANING OF THE KYEONGSEONG ERA WITHIN THE RESEARCH FRAMEWORK

This book's ultimate goal is to provide an alternative explanation to existing literature of late developmentalist approaches as well as grand approaches, such as modernization, dependency, and bureaucratic authoritarianism theory, on how South Korea was able to accomplish economic development and democratization at the same time. Rather than focusing on the physical power of the developmental regime of the Park Chung-hee administration, the efficiency of his bureaucracy, the Cold War strategic contexts of the US influence on Korean economy and politics, or numerous indicators for modernization in Korean society, this book approaches the topic from the perspective of the state-society relations that have resulted in the formation of factors central to the birth of the developmental state. In that perspective, the role of state in economic affairs and the centrality of such state power in the government's intervention into economic affairs are relative phenomenan; in other words, societal consensus on the role and power of state is required in order for the functions of state to be able to meet the people's expectations of its positive roles and authority over the economy.

More importantly, without such societal consensus, the legitimacy of the state's centrality in the minds of people and society would not have been so firmly established. A state's power is always a relative phenomenon and can be accurately measured only through such a relative perspective. Without explaining how society has granted such legitimacy to the state's power over economic affairs and what made society recognize such power of the state as legitimate, we glean only a partial understanding of why some countries have succeeded in their efforts to catch up with developed economies while others have failed. To fully explain the late developmental phenomenon in countries under development, more holistic approaches to understanding the relative phenomenan of state-society relations and the state's power over economy and society, are required. This book sheds new light on Gramsci's notion of integral state and Mann's notion of infrastructural state power. Further, Foucault's understanding of power in dispersed knowledge of the whole social system enables us to develop more adequate explanations and theoretical insights into the late developmental phenomenon discussed in chapters 1 and 2.

Conventional approaches to late development seem incapable of revealing those elements that enabled such countries to successfully begin economic and political development in their late stages mainly for the following reasons: 1) a dichotomous understanding of underdeveloped countries confines researchers and scholars to the mere comparison of traditional and modern elements within each country, so that they cannot locate the seeds of success in efforts toward democratization and economic development, as discussed at length in the first two chapters; 2) grand theories, in their explanatory frameworks, tend to overemphasize the role of external environments or factors in both successful or failed attempts at economic and political development (i.e., Cold War international politics that resulted in abundant US aid and Korea's access to US market and technology); 3) scholars, due to their linear formula for the modernization of society as a whole, tend not to notice the simultaneous phenomenan of both economic and political developments. In so doing, they tend to inadvertently distort the unique contexts of successful and failed attempts to develop the economies and political systems in late-developing countries: the lack of attempts to theorize and analyze the impact of Confucianism and geomancy in Korea's political system and Korea's unprecedented developmental phenomenon can be understood in this context. These two crucial resources in the formation of Korean state-society relations, state centrality, and political control of economic affairs have long been neglected as outdated, non-scientific, and unimportant sources for scholarship. An indigenous approach toward the country's own history and the use of other generic sources for the scholarly analyses of Korea's own political and economic phenomena have clearly not been the modus operandi for domestic and international scholarship. More seriously, such conventional perspectives and approaches lead us to the false understanding of the state-society relations in general and the theories on state in particular by singling out one or the other research unit or sources as the main paradigm for their scholarly analyses.

As quoted in chapter 1 (Schwandt, 1994: 118), this book sees the late development and the role of state in Korea's developmental period as a result of the social construction that was established in several historical and ideological contexts; that is, particular actors (i.e., Confucian scholarly bureaucrats and the masses who had been indoctrinated by the Confucian and geomantic belief system) in a particular temporal and spatial era (i.e., the Joseon Dynasty) and at particular times fashioned the relations between state and society through prolonged, complex processes of global and local interactions involving Japan's colonial control and American influence in Korea's developmental periods. The main goal of this book is to re-articulate such historical construction through geographical, architectural, and textual evidence.

There is, however, a concern with the application of the constructivist approach in regards to whether it can provide "a causal explanation between spatial arrangement of capital city and power configurations between the state and society and resulting impacts on political system and economic development."[1] As explained in chapter 2, the combination of Confucianism and geomancy produced the synergic effect of consolidating the state hegemony and typifying state-society relations. Especially, geomancy seemed to play a role of softening and internalizing the regulatory and governing framework of Confucianism as natural and taken for granted among the masses. In analyzing those two main ideologies, along with the attendant influences of Taoism, in terms of how they influenced state-society relations in spatial and architectural arrangements in the Joseon era, the constructivist method provides useful tools to re-articulate such power configurations in state-society relations; it may not, however, be suited for a causal analysis because, by directing us to culture-bound, context-specific realms, and reconnecting the agents and their principles of interpretation, it attempts to extrapolate rather than locate the causality of any social construction completed in the past. In fact, this book does not aim to explain the causality between spatial arrangements and power configurations in the developmental state and among hegemonic and hierarchical and heteronomical forces. Rather, this book shares hard evidence of the main ideological paradigm and belief system that prevailed in each of the three eras and thereby contributed toward the successful late development and democratization of Korea. In other words, the spatial arrangements are both outcomes and evidence of the state-society relations that the two main ideological paradigms disseminated during the Hanyang era.

One way to complement the shortcomings of constructivism is to design a research framework in such a way as to trace the continuities and changes in state-society relations in the historical processes of the developmental phenomenon in Korea. In chapter 3, by looking into spatial order and arrangement, architectural monumentality, and various visible aspects of the state's centrality, we examined how the formation of state-society relations in the Joseon Dynasty had been based on Neo-Confucian and geomantic belief systems. Building upon such analyses, chapter 3 explored the integral and infrastructural aspects of state power and society's acceptance of such state authority and influence. Constructivism is a useful method for unearthing those relationships and examining how their articulation is reflected in the layout of the capital city in fossilized form, so to speak. In addition, by tracing the continuities and changes of those features in the state-society relations that formed the political basis of the developmental state, this constructivist approach helps researchers to create an operational framework for examining the underlying types of rule that account for the sustained centrality of state power over society in Korea's process of the late development. Thus, identifying the explicit and implicit system rules that existed during major historical epochs elucidates the underlying logic of events and the order in which they occurred.

Based on this philosophical understanding of social constructivism, the previous chapter illustrates why it is necessary to examine non-conventional sources for the state-society relations—(1) Neo-Confucianism and geomancy as new sources for the state centrality and (2) the design of the capital city and architectural monumentality as evidence of such relations. Chapter 3 laid out the most important rules that would later contribute toward the success of Korea's developmental state and the political development—(1) the establishment of state hegemony (politics) over society (economy) and (2) the legitimacy of state intervention in the economy—and strove to re-construct evidence according to Onuf's three types of rule.

Having examined the original aspect of the developmental state and the seeds of democratization in the previous chapter, let us now turn toward the question of how such a prototype of state-society relations can be interpreted as core elements in the late development and democratization of modern Korea. This question might be the most relevant way to address the issue of causality in our basic research framework, i.e., whether there are any causal links between geographical evidence, state-society power configurations, and the impacts of these power configurations on Korea's simultaneous phenomena of development.

The era of Kyeongseong can serve as evidence of continuities and changes in the established state's centrality and its influence over the economy as well as the co-opted heteronomical forces, both of which would become critical elements in the simultaneous phenomena of the so-called Miracle on the Han River and democratic movements from the 1960s to the '80s. How can we find evidence of state centrality? More specifically, how can the main argument of state centrality in previous chapters be substantiated by evidence of continuities and changes in the geographical layout? The Japanese colonial headquarters' policies on the layout of the capital city, as well as new spatial arrangements for its important political, military, and economic institutions, support the fact that important power configurations of state and society were represented in the capital city. In other words, new additions and adjustments to the original Hanyang city layout and architecture suggest possible motivations for such revisions to the geographical and architectural designs and construction. In this context, this chapter serves to demonstrate how the phase leading up to modern Seoul provides evidence of the factors that contributed toward late developmental success in Korea's economy and simultaneous democratization.

This chapter will elucidate continuities and changes in the constructed meanings of state-society relations, the state's legitimacy to intervene in economic affairs, the hierarchical orders among governmental institutions, and anti-Japanese political forces—all as a lived reality of the transition from Confucian Joseon to modern Korea and Seoul. It will reveal how the Japanese colonial period re-constituted the interplay between agents and society as well as global-local interactions in a way that impacted the prototype of state-society relations in terms of economic affairs and political power configurations between external rulers and domestic power groups. Geographical, architectural, and spatial evidence are more reliable than textual sources because they reveal dominant ideological paradigms, prevalent belief systems, and living patterns without intentional fabrication, manipulation, or persuasion. In this sense, as mentioned before, the city itself bears traces of the dominant rules of state-society relations. Again, it would be beyond the scope of this book to ask whether the spatial arrangement caused a certain type of state and society. Rather, here, it is most valuable to inquire how changes and continuities in state-society relations were clearly reflected in the spatial arrangements. Such evidence suggests that the core principles of the developmental state and democratization were established well before the era of modern Korea, which explains the indigenous aspect of Korea's simultaneous phenomena of successful economic development and substantive democratization from the 1960s to the 1980s.

Before we begin the second of our three case studies, a brief glance at the overall trajectory of this book's argument may prove useful. As a whole, this book aims to compare how Onuf's three distinctive yet integrally related types of rule in a political society—hegemony, hierarchy, and heteronomy—are all present to different degrees in each of three different eras of Korea's capital city: (1) Hanyang (1392-1910), as a prototype of Korea's state hegemony and the state's legitimacy to intervene in the economy, with a limited and co-opted dissenting voice of heteronomy; (2) Kyeongseong (1910-1945), a period reflecting major changes and continuities in the relations between state and society (economy) through interaction with Japanese colonial control; and (3) Seoul (1960s-'80s), the symbolic center and physical place containing those legacies of the developmental state and successful democratization by civil society. Together, the Hanyang and Kyeongseong eras formed the foundation for Korea's developmental state and democracy in the Seoul era, bequeathing a tradition of strong state intervention in the economy and the seeds of expandable loyal opposition forces.

FROM CONFUCIAN HANYANG TO COLONIAL KYEONGSEONG: LOCAL-GLOBAL INTERACTION

The Kyeongseong colonial period brought significant alterations to the contents of state centrality and state-economy relations that had been established during the Hanyang era. The legacy of the Hanyang era underwent three major transformations. First, Confucian state hegemony was supplanted by Japanese imperial authority such that the Confucian principle of civil priority over the military was reversed; however, the strength of the state itself and its institutional power were reinforced. Legal codes and regulations were added to those of the Joseon era through Japan's modernized governing system. The military imperialism of Japan was introduced strongly in the colony and overpowered the civil superiority of Confucian Joseon values with modernized military and police institutions. Thus, the state centrality of the Joseon era was supplanted with stronger versions of state power, rather than reversing the superiority of state over society and economy. Second, with the introduction of the Japanese version of capitalism, the formerly low-status industrial/commercial sector was granted higher status, leading to the establishment of close relations between state and business rather than state and agriculture as had been the case during the Joseon era. This was the direct outcome of combining a local production system (Joseon's agricultural industry) and global capitalism (Japan's industrialized and capitalistic economic system), and the change was graphically reflected in the modifications to the city layout, including the locations of new institutions of great importance in the Kyeongseong era. Lastly, in reaction to the supplanting of Confucian state legitimacy by Japanese imperial authority, the formerly co-opted heteronomical forces multiplied in strength and activity, joining forces with the hegemonic and hierarchical forces of the Hanyang era in order to face a common enemy—the Japanese colonial authority and military. In this way, the originally authoritarian and seemingly anti-democratic ideology of Confucianism could help to explain the late democratization of Korea—not based on the Western notion and experience of democratic evolution of the political system but as changes in power configurations among hegemonic, hierarchical, and heteronomical forces, i.e., as a domestic response to external power. These features of the Kyeongseong era were clearly reflected in the city layout and visibilities, which will be detailed in the coming sections. This chapter views these changes and continuities as the means by which the major principles of the developmental state and the seeds of stronger civil society were cultivated.

The loyal opposition and semi-opposition, which served as the seeds of civil society in Korea, this book argues, transformed into a force of belligerent nationalism against Japanese colonial control. Consequently, civil society combined with Joseon's hegemonic and hierarchical classes, and its capacity and scope of opposition vastly expanded in Korean politics. During the Kyeongseong era, this expansion was mostly led by the sector of education, a tradition inherited from the Seongkyunkwan and Sarim tradition of giving voice to dissent, this book claims. Overall, the three major rules of hegemony, hierarchy, and heteronomy that originated in the Hanyang era responded to the stimuli introduced during the Kyeongseong period by re-ordering and reshaping their contents. This chapter will seek evidence of the continuation and expansion of such heteronomical forces as well as supplanted aspects of hegemony and hierarchy.

The above-mentioned transformations are reflected in modifications to the city layout, major institutional buildings, architectural structures, the hierarchical order of social classes, the emergence of liberal educational institutions, and heteronomical forces that spoke out against Japanese colonial rule. When the Japanese colonists seized power, the name of the capital was changed, but the capital itself was not moved, thereby allowing Japanese imperial authority to draw upon the hegemonic state power and centralized bureaucracy inherent to that space that had been established during the Hanyang era. This is how the capital city can serve as a reliable repository of the changes and continuities that occurred over time, thereby revealing the elements that factored in the state's superiority over society and economy and the growing power of dissenting voices first against the King, then against Japanese colonial authority, and later against the military dictatorship. While seeking to repress national resistance, Japanese colonial occupation of Korea brought a new modernized bureaucracy and capitalist economic system. Immediately upon colonizing Korea in 1910, Japan identified the Seongkyunkwan as a major source of resistance against its colonial policy and shut it down, subsequently replacing it with the Kyunghakwon on June 15, 1911, which in turn was replaced by Kyeongseong Imperial University in 1926. The Seongkyunkwan had been the center of loyal opposition and extraterritorial sanctuary for different opinions against the dominant discourse in the royal court. The main reason for replacing the Seongkyunkwan was to control Confucian civil society, including the Sarim, and to place it under Japanese influence and promote Japanese colonial policies. An indigenous perspective makes it possible to identify internal sources of social forces as the seeds of a democratic political system and power dynamics. In the absence of the Western notion of democracy and power struggles in the transitional period from a feudal to a capitalistic system, the peripheral groups of Confucian scholars and their dominance in the local provinces, as well as the tradition of the Seongkyunkwan's exceptional rights to appeal against royal and bureaucratic decisions, can be understood as factors leading toward the formation of belligerent civil society in Korea. Overall, the Kyunghwakwon aimed to convert the Confucian resistance and intelligentsia into a pro-Japanese social force (Jeong, 2007: 25).

For the Japanese colonial authorities, the best way to maximize their colonial policy and minimize the insurgence was to take full advantage of Korea's existing political tradition and culture as well as the symbols of loyalty to central power and government that had already been embedded in the minds of the Korean nation. Even though Japan's policy had to face stark opposition from the Koreans, they made systematic efforts to appropriate and make use of the strong tradition of state centrality over economy and society that had been embedded in the minds of people during the Joseon era. To achieve this goal, Japanese colonial headquarters implemented extensive policies to exploit sources of state hegemony and hierarchy and thereby uphold and justify their own political authority. Inheriting this authority from the Hanyang era depended upon the colonialists' success in disrupting the people's sense of loyalty to Korea's state by destroying the natural symbols of state hegemony, such as symbolically meaningful topological configurations, or manipulating Confucian architectural monumentality, which will be discussed further in this chapter. Another policy adopted by Japan to facilitate its colonial policy was to eradicate the sources of insurgence. What institutions would the Japanese colonial headquarters target for this purpose? Clearly, their attention turned first toward the indigenous sources that worked as opposition or heteronomical forces under the previous governing institutions—the Confucian literati and students of the National Confucian Academy. Thus, Japan eradicated the bases of rebellions and domesticated them by enacting an educational system of its own, inculcating them to uphold Japan's governing ideology and to embrace its advanced socioeconomic systems. In this process of destruction, displacement, and re-institution, core elements in the developmental state and the emergence of opposition forces were either maintained or produced.

Similarly, the old Confucian social elites were replaced by Japanese bureaucrats to further advance the goals of the occupation. This had two implications. First, the modernized Japanese bureaucracy systematically carried out its mission to promote growth in the sectors of commerce and industry. Japanese colonists forcibly introduced capitalism and industrial production systems and structures into agricultural Joseon not for the economic development of Korea but for its own imperial expansionism in East Asia. Thus, Korea became an additional source of rice and other materials and products for the Japanese military, and Korea's new industrial system and structure were shaped according to those needs. Regardless of motivations, the capitalistic industrial economy became the main policy target of the colonial government, while maintaining from the previous era the strong legitimacy of the state to intervene in the economy. Second, the displaced Confucian scholar bureaucrats assumed a heteronomical role in the resistance to the occupation. In addition, two forces introduced from the West—liberalism and Christianity—became ideological resources for expanding heteronomical forces through their significant influence in schools and churches. Interestingly, the educational institutions that played a central role in resisting Japanese oppression were concentrated in the physical sphere of Korean domination[2] within the sacred space, proving the continuation of the old legacy of the Hanyang era. Thus, around the time of the 1905 Protectorate Treaty,[3] which the Joseon Dynasty was forced to sign, the old hierarchical and heteronomical forces banded together within the hegemonic sacred space, incorporating foreign ideals in order to resist Japan. This, in turn, re-invigorated the hegemony of the Korean state in the eyes of the people. This chapter on the Japanese colonial era addresses the third major issue of this book—local-global interaction and its impact on state hegemony.

The main goals of this chapter are to explain how Japanese colonial authority attempted to gain control by appropriating the state's hegemony and hierarchy as sources of authenticity and dislocating the tradition of centrally co-opted dissenting voices, which will serve as another piece of evidence reinforcing this book's argument about the Korean prototype of state hegemony and origins of heteronomical forces and civil society. With regards to state-society relations and Onuf's three rules of political society during the Hanyang era, the Kyeongseong period played a catalytic role of introducing modern Western social, economic, and political systems to Korea. Also, Japanese militarism supplanted the civil superiority of the Confucian Joseon era. The most important change, however, caused by the Japanese colonization of Korea was to give rise, though indirectly, to a strong nationalism that brought the hegemonic and heteronomical forces together. This heteronomical force that expanded during the Kyeongseong era continued on into the Seoul era where it functioned as a force of militant opposition against the military dictatorship of the developmental regime and played a vanguard role in Korea's democratization process, symbolically achieved in the June 10 Resistance of 1987.

This point deserves extra attention because although nothing is unusual about the formation of nationalism against colonial control, not every former colony has successfully achieved democratization through the forces of nationalism. In fact, most countries that gained independence in Asia and Africa at the end of World War II, and some newly in Latin America, are still under authoritarian regimes even though the seeds of anti-authoritarianism and dictatorship had been disseminated during the formation of their nationalism. A substantial amount of scholarship will be required in order to conduct a comparative analysis of how various forms of sociopolitical forces in each colony have reacted to colonial forces and how these forces have influenced the process of democratization. Interestingly, the Korean case—i.e., a tradition of dissent strongly embedded within the power structure followed by the emergence of nationalism, expansion into a strong civil society through global interaction under Japanese colonial control, and successful democratization—has not been duplicated by most former colonies.

Here, it may be valuable to ask what factors have made the difference between democratized and under-democratized countries. What stands out in Korea's successful democratization is the role played by university students (later joined by the intelligentsia) and their legitimacy as the most respected source of opposition forces or dissenting voice against existing power in politics. Indeed, university students have played a critical role in most of Korea's major political upheavals: the March First National Independence Movement in 1919; the June 10 Independence Demonstration in 1926; the *Kwangju* Student Movement in November 1929; the April 19 Revolution of 1960, which toppled the civil dictatorship of the Syngman Rhee regime; the demonstration against the normalization treaty between Korea and Japan on June 4, 1964; a series of student-led demonstrations against the Park Chung-hee regime from 1963 to his assassination in 1979; the May 16 Kwangju Uprising of 1980 under the Chun Doo-hwan regime; and the historic June 10 Resistance of 1987, which fundamentally transformed the military dictatorship into a democracy.

Even after the successful June 10 democratization movement, university student leadership has played a central role in Korean politics and has strongly impacted young generations who use networked information technologies like the Internet and online social media (OSN) in recent major elections with a surprising result: namely, strong gravitation toward liberal candidates and unprecedented mobilization of OSN users for voting (Han, 2012). For example, the legacy of the '386 Generation' in the June 10 Resistance of 1987 significantly influenced the political behavior patterns of the younger generations, such as the '2030 Generation' (i.e., those in their 20s and 30s during the early 21st century) through a series of test-run mobilizations in 2002 and demonstration effects (Han, 2012). Further studies are required, though, to more thoroughly compare Korea's student-led democratization process with the processes of democratization experienced in other countries.

HANYANG VERSUS KYEONGSEONG

During the period of Japanese colonial rule from 1910 to 1945, the physical layout and components of the capital city underwent extensive demolition and transformation. The most drastic change brought by the Japanese colonialists was to replace the monumentality of the Confucian hegemony of the Joseon Dynasty with that of Japan's imperial symbols, appropriating for their own purposes the Korean people's strong attachment to the sacred space that was the legacy of the Hanyang period. The first change made to achieve this goal was to destroy the monumental buildings of the Joseon Dynasty. At the same time, architecture was planned to reflect Japan's imperialism and emperor through political symbols. In the city design, this process replaced the major social classes, royal family, and Confucian scholarly bureaucrats of the Confucian hegemony with military and capitalist elements.

This transformation from Confucian hegemony to Japanese influence was a process designed to oust the old Confucian hegemony from the aforementioned sacred space and replace it with Japanese influence, thereby transforming Hanyang into Kyeongseong. Confucian hegemony, its hierarchical system, and the heteronomical factors that it embraced—which comprised the three main elements of the Confucian Hanyang—were erased, demolished, and cast out of this "sacred space." Ironically, the outcome of such destructive Japanese policy resulted in the formation of a massive force of heteronomy that strove to ultimately recover state power from Japanese colonial rule.

Hanyang was transmuted into Kyeongseong mainly by means of four major institutions of Japanese colonial rule: Japanese Shinto shrines, Government-General Headquarters, the Japanese Army, and the Oriental Development Company. As a result, the legitimacy of the Joseon Dynasty was denied. This process also denied the major principles of Confucian hegemony: 1) the Confucian principle of agriculture taking priority over commerce and industry was reversed through the introduction of a capitalistic economic system; 2) the Confucian principle of civil superiority over the military was reversed; and 3) in the process of Japanese intrusion into the Korean economy, the Confucian principle of government taking absolute precedence over the economy was overturned as more cooperative relations between politics and economy were established. Another important feature resulting from Japanese rule was the production of heteronomical social forces on a greater scale than ever before, which would affect the dynamics of domestic politics in modern Korea after liberation from Japan.

Japanese Alterations to Hegemonic Hanyang

The definition of "hegemony" provided in chapter 2 is based on Onuf's conceptual framework of explaining political society with three types of rule. It refers to the "promulgation and manipulation of principles and instructions by which superordinate actors monopolize meaning which is then passively absorbed by subordinate actors" (Onuf, 1989: 209-210). This definition highlights the dual aspects of how hegemony is established—through the actions taken by superordinate actors as well as the acquiescence to principles and instructions promulgated and manipulated by the subordinate actors. The power is a relative phenomenon, much like the power of state that is expounded in Gramsci's notion of moral and ideological hegemony and Mann's notion of infrastructural state hegemony. The essence of state power is composed of two main elements: (1) the state's regulatory and physical power and (2) the consent from the ruled and society. The hegemony of the Joseon era was, as examined in chapters 1 and 2, established through Confucian and geomantic monumentality in the choice and design of the capital city as well as in the Confucian architectural monumentality of major political institutions. These two ideologies and belief systems had played a fundamental role in legitimizing Neo-Confucian values—i.e., upholding the heavenly mandate and Confucian bureaucrats' rights to govern, and voluntarily consolidating such belief systems into their own way of life. Neo-Confucianism functioned as an active ideology upholding the authority of the royal family and the sadaebu, while geomancy worked as a passive system of self-indoctrination and Confucian way of life. The geomantic way of life made the Confucian political authority more concrete and real; it also reaffirmed existing political and socioeconomic orders. The political and socioeconomic orders established through Confucian and geomantic belief systems were systematically and advertently destroyed and distorted. Politically, the most important architecture in Hanyang included the offices for kings and high government officials and residential buildings for royal families. These were the Joseon Dynasty's symbols of political authority and hegemonic and hierarchical power. The main palace (Kyeongbok) and other palaces (e.g., Changdeok, Changkyeong, and Yeonhee) suffered extensive alterations, reduction from their original scale, mass destruction, and degradation. As mentioned above, Japan sought to disrupt the bonds of loyalty that connected the masses to the Joseon Dynasty in order to thereby overturn the authority of old Korea. At the same time, however, Japan wanted to take full advantage of the political symbols and architectural monumentality that were upholding state centrality in its governing structure. In other words, Japanese colonial headquarters wanted to exploit every artifact that had contributed to the hegemony of the ruling institutions while at the same time effectively detaching the bonds of loyalty that had connected the Joseon Dynasty to its subjects. Thus, Japanese colonial control did all it could to defame, destroy, and significantly reduce the original architecture and other artifacts that symbolized the legitimacy of the Joseon Dynasty, while at the same time placing its own symbols over those of the Joseon Dynasty so that Japanese authority could co-opt this majesty, loyalty, and respect for its own purposes.

Examples of this strategy abound. In 1915, the Japanese authorities held a Fair within the Kyeongbok palace. To make room for the more modernized buildings of the Fair, the Government-General ordered the sub-buildings of Kyeongbok palace to be destroyed. Consequently, the place that used to be both the actual and symbolic center of state power in the Joseon Dynasty was occupied and hidden by new modern buildings, showing the collapse of Confucian symbols of architectural monumentality (image 4.1). Through such a move as

Image 4.1 Kwanghwamoon (Main Gate of Hanyang Castle) Obstructed by Occupation Edifice. A. Kwanghwamoon, B. Special Exhibition Center for Railroad Built by Japanese.

this, the goals of the Japanese colonial authorities could have not been more effectively achieved. By damaging part of the palace, they successfully defamed the majesty of the architectural monumentality that had upheld the power and authority of kings and government as well as other ruling institutions of the Joseon Dynasty.

At the same time, by setting up a modern Fair that was completely new and wondrous to Koreans in the early 20th century, the Japanese impressed the minds of the Korean people with advancements in science and technology. Seeing such impressive modern structures juxtaposed with the outdated buildings of their past, Koreans would have likely felt discontent with the relative "backwardness" of their own society. Watching as the political symbols that had attracted their loyalty to the old political regime were damaged, and then seeing the impressive attractions of the Fair, which symbolized Japan's superiority over Korea, many Koreans likely felt too discouraged to resist Japanese colonial control and instead acquiesced to Japan's occupation. Significantly, all of these defamations and replacements of old political symbols and architectural monumentality were executed along the line of the *axis mundi* and within the sacred zone.

In image 4.1, the Special Exhibition Center for the Railroad, built by Japanese authorities, clearly obstructs the view of the main gate of Kyeongbok Palace.

Japanese colonial authorities made every effort to obstruct Joseon symbols by adding occupation edifices (Hong, 1994: 157). In so doing, Japan succeeded in damaging Joseon authority and upholding the superiority of its own power. Their goal was to reiterate how the Joseon had established the centrality of state power over society by creating architectural monumentality of their own within the sacred space that reflected the most revered celestial chart in the heavens.

The most striking example can be found in 1916, when Japanese imperial authorities built the Government-General Headquarters directly in front of the main office building of the Kyeongbok palace. This architectural manipulation, intended to weaken the legitimacy of the Joseon Dynasty's power base, aimed to build these headquarters larger than the former royal office building (Keunjeongjeon) by 10 meters to the right and left, so that the new headquarters building would entirely block the Keunjeongjeon from the people's view. In other words, Japanese headquarters would hide the most powerful building in the Joseon Dynasty's power structure, and so they hoped to blot it from the minds of the Korean people and thereby force the hegemony of Confucian Joseon to lapse into oblivion. By thus enshrouding the nation's most powerful symbol, Japan intended to make clear to Koreans that their political power had been completely defeated, thereby elevating its own power. The Confucian architectural monumentality and the most sacred space for the power of the Joseon Dynasty were now seriously damaged and tainted, and the bonds of loyalty between the rule and the ruled of the previous regime were symbolically broken. Image 4.2 clearly shows the motivation of the Japanese government for constructing the colonial headquarters building in front of Kyeongbok Palace.

In image 4.2, Kyeongbok Palace (B) is covered by the Japanese colonial headquarters (A), both of which face south (i.e., upward in image 4.2). By being

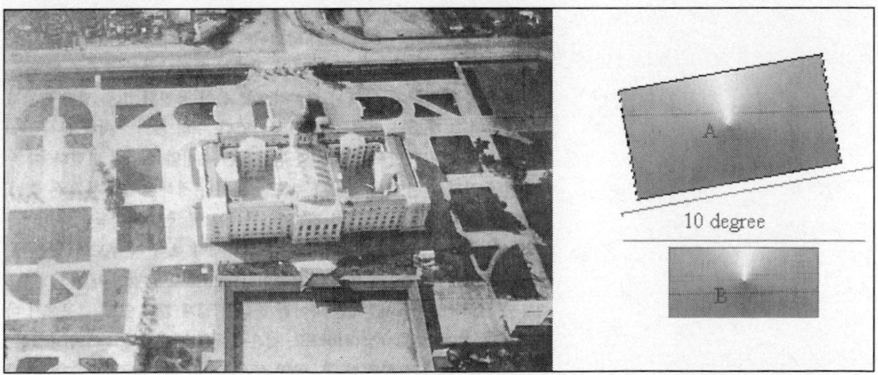

Image 4.2 Japanese Governor-General Headquarters Deforming the Axis Mundi of the Confucian Joseon Dynasty by 10 Degrees. A. Governor-General Building, B. Geunjeongjeon. Hong, Soon-Min (1994), p. 153. Right: figure created by author.

located 10º southeast of B, the colonial building (A) also intentionally distorted the *axis mundi* of the Joseon Dynasty. Ten degrees may seem like a conspicuous difference in image 4.2; however, 10º between these two edifices is much more difficult to consciously notice from a viewpoint on the ground, so its impact remained subtle though powerful. This 10º shift was reinforced by the corresponding placement of a building far away oriented in relation to this new axis. This represented a very skillful, well-calculated, and ill-willed tactic to evade, eradicate, and erase Korea's main sources of political power and loyalty.

Through such an effort to maximize the visible impact of Japanese power upon Korea's traditional symbols of state authority and centrality, Japan sought to distort the fundamental principles that governed the whole design of the capital city. How exactly did Japan accomplish this goal? In its construction of the headquarters, Japan defiantly thwarted the *axis mundi*, the line of orientation which had symbolized the legitimacy of government, originating from the fixed star in the Heavens. There were, again, two simple reasons for this placement: (1) to block the view of the symbolic architecture of the Confucian Joseon Dynasty toward which the legitimacy of state power was projected by the people, thus minimizing or diluting the legitimacy of Korean state power; and (2) to establish Japanese legitimacy by taking advantage of the geographical center of Korean society. Japanese authorities could remove physical buildings and objects that symbolized the power and legitimacy of the Joseon Dynasty, but they could not remove the space itself or the belief system attached to it. According to *pungsu jiri* ideology, this place possessed the best topological configuration within Hanyang where the Will of Heaven and mandate to govern, according to Neo-Confucian governing ideologies and government, could be realized. In the minds of the people, it was the *axis mundi* where the Will of Heaven and the right to govern originated. Both Confucian and geomantic beliefs reinforced the importance of this line that separated the sacred space from the profane, which produced synergic effects for the state hegemony and its legitimacy to intervene in societal and economic matters. Accordingly, there was no better space than this for Japanese colonialists to legitimize their rule by taking advantage of the people's strong attachment to the space. After the Protectorate Treaty in 1905 and before the Japanese annexation of the Joseon Dynasty in 1910, the highest headquarters of Japanese authority, the Residency-General, was located to the northeast of the Six Ministries Street. Later, this building was moved to the Japanese sphere of influence near Mt. Mokmyuk in the south. Then, the Japanese authorities decided to move their headquarters into the "sacred space" to enhance the legitimacy of their rule in Korea.

The destruction of the palace buildings and the construction of Japanese headquarters illustrated how spatial considerations can affect power relations in society and, more specifically, the extreme importance of the spatial factor in the establishing of power and to the people in general. In this context, Confucianism was replaced by Japanese imperial symbols, but geomantic beliefs were completely reinforced, which clearly demonstrates the impact and power of the geomantic belief system in the power configurations.

What the Japanese authorities did was not to simply replace palaces with the modern architecture of its headquarters but rather to insidiously change the basic framework of the spatial power structure of the Joseon Dynasty: bringing true distortion to the *axis mundi*. The Joseon Dynasty's main *axis mundi* was a North-South axis, originating from Mt. Baekak in the north, sweeping through the main palace Kyeongbok and the Six Ministries Street, and stretching south to Mt. Mokmyuk. The East-West axis intersects it for the convenience of dividing the space for markets and housing. All the arrangements of the important buildings of the Joseon Dynasty were framed vertically or horizontally parallel to these main axes. By distorting the fundamental basis upon which that power structure had been built, the Japanese intended to deny the Joseon Dynasty's right to rule and create a new axis in support of the legitimacy of Japanese imperial rule. The picture vividly shows the intentional distortion of the Joseon Dynasty's *axis mundi* and the creation of a new Japanese axis.[4] The new Government-General building was designed to face the Japanese Shinto shrine, which would later be built on Mt. Mokmyuk, shifting the axis of the palace 10º to the east as shown in image 4.1.[5] The line connecting the Government-General building with the Japanese Shinto shrine was to become the *axis mundi* of the new power structure and the Korean belief system. In this way, Confucianism and Confucian political forces were ousted from their sacred spaces and stripped of the architectural symbols of their power, while geomantic principles and influence were kept intact.

To emphasize the dignity of Japanese imperialism, the headquarters were built in a baroque style similar to Japanese headquarters in Taiwan. The bronze dome atop the headquarters building resembles the imperial crown upheld by six supports in the shape of (日) (Cheong, 1994: 31). Furthermore, from a bird's-eye view of this building, its shape resembles the first Chinese character of the word "Japan," (日本). Nearby, the city hall (Kyeongseong Bucheong) forms the second character (本). These combine with the shape of Mt. Baekak in the background, which forms the Chinese character (大) meaning "largeness." The juxtaposition of these two buildings and the mountain altogether can be read as (大日本): "Greater Japan." The monumentality of Kyeongseong can be found in the colonial efforts to implant the power and dignity of the Japanese Empire. In other words, Confucian monumentality was explicitly supplanted by Japanese imperial symbols on the basis of *pungsu jiri* ideology. Japan could not and would not eradicate the relationship between space and power, embodied in the history of Korea and the belief system of the people because it wanted to take advantage of that bond instead. In this sense, the geomantic aspect of political power was more influential than any political ideology, which also illustrates the argument of this book that the consensual of state power becomes the foundation for Gramsci's notion of integral power or Mann's infrastructural power of state. In other words, geomancy is not just a superstitious, psychological, and secondary matter. Rather geomantic principles deserve more scholarly attention and need to be treated as an important source in scholarly analyses of Korea's political systems and structures.

Furthermore, the Government-General vulgarized the image of other palaces. The second largest palace, Changkyeong, was turned into a zoo and botanical garden in 1909. Then, in 1911, the name was degraded to Changkyeongwon (Changkyeong Zoo). In a similar vain, most of Deoksu palace was destroyed. All aspects of this destruction were planned in detail and intended to weaken the dignity of the Confucian Joseon Dynasty. Other significant buildings that symbolized Confucian hegemony were the Royal Ancestral Shrine (*Jongmyo*) and the Guardian Deities of the State (*Sajik*). After annexation, Japan shut down the Shrine, replacing it with a Japanese Shinto shrine[6] in 1920, and restyled the Guardian Deities of the State into a park. Later, all of the regional Guardian Deities of the State throughout the nation were turned into parks as well. Moreover, Wongoodan, where the Korean Emperor used to worship the God of Heaven, was destroyed, and the Choson Hotel was built in its stead, symbolically replacing the Confucian system with a commercial entity.

A similar effort to manipulate symbols was launched against the natural environment. For three months, Japanese authorities drove iron spikes into the summit of Mt. Baekak, which was regarded as the main mountain of the Joseon Dynasty because the Korean people believed that the power and energy of Korea originated from it as the source of the *axis mundi*. Moreover, Japan defaced the peak and set fire to the summits of many other mountains that possessed symbolic meaning.[7] All of this destruction illustrates the importance of the spatial factor and natural environment in the power structure and Confucian hegemony during the Joseon Dynasty; it also shows that Japan considered geomancy to have great influence over the belief system of the Korean people and thus sought to capitalize off such deeply embedded beliefs when establishing the legitimacy of its own imperial authority. That was the most efficient way to achieve the masses' consent to Japanese colonial policy.

This widespread destruction of influential Confucian architecture and the erection of buildings symbolizing Japanese imperial authority aimed to replace traditional Confucian state hegemony with Japanese imperialism. The

Korean population, which identified itself with and consented to Confucian authority, had to face the Japanese strategic denigration of Korean symbols of Confucian state hegemony and traditional values. Thus, while the Japanese imperial authority was in power, loyalty to the ideal of the Korean state continued, though in diminished form, among the majority. Those who had given consent to the Confucian legitimacy with a mixture of deferential, aspirational, and accommodative values now became forces of extreme opposition against Japanese authority. In addition to feeling attached to their lost state, this majority began to identify themselves as legitimate successors of that state while faulting the old Confucian elites for allowing themselves to be divested of the state by Japanese imperialism. Japan adopted a series of policies to separate Confucianism from geomantic beliefs, to maximize the impact of their dethroning of Confucian political authority, and to capitalize on the influence of geomancy upon the minds of the masses in regards to the objective aspect of political power.

After liberation from Japanese colonial rule, this resistant majority would split into two different categories: an accommodative, aspirational tacit majority and a militantly oppositional minority. The former would tacitly consent to the Park regime, sacrificing their political freedom as long as the economy grew; in fact, the existence of such a tacit majority gave the Park regime room to oppress minority militant oppositional forces for the sake of the economic development of the tacit majority. Thus, changes made during the Kyeongseong era in the composition of social forces set the stage for new sociopolitical configurations in the Seoul period, which in turn helped to bring about the birth and success of the developmental state in modern Korea.

Changes in Hierarchy

In tracing the changes in Korea's state-society relations from the Hanyang to the Kyeongseong era of Japanese colonial control, Nicholas Onuf's analytical framework of three distinctive yet integrally related types of rule offers useful tools for decoding the centrality of state hegemony and the legitimacy of state intervention in Korea's economy. In addition, the constructive approach focuses on an economically interventionist hierarchical bureaucracy in civil society and the formation of militant heteronomical social forces. There is no clear-cut way to differentiate between hegemonic and hierarchical aspects of state power in terms of established spatial arrangements or architectural artifacts. As mentioned above, Onuf (1989: 211) defines "hierarchy" as an arrangement of directive-rules clearly exemplified in the organization of bureaucracy. The relations of organizations within the bureaucracy "form the typical pattern of super- and subordination, but always in ranks, such that each office is both subordinate to the one(s) above it and superordinate to the ones below." In general, these hierarchical and hegemonic rules are mutually reinforcing. This book further extends Onuf's definition of "hierarchy" into the more general principle of organizing societal actors hierarchically.

The hierarchical class order of the Joseon society, starting with the king and royal family at the top, followed by Confucian scholar bureaucrats, farmers, merchants, and slaves, underwent tremendous transformation during the Kyeongseong period. As collaborators with the Confucian bureaucracy, Japanese military and bureaucratic classes supplanted the Confucian elite classes, including that of the king. Accordingly, the Six Ministries Street was occupied by Japanese military police, the Telecommunication Agency, and other Japanese bureaucratic institutions. The housing area that was considered to be the best during the Joseon Dynasty, the *bukchon* (northern village between the Kyeongbok and Royal Ancestral Shrine) gradually lost its hegemonic position in the Kyeongseong era. Instead, the southern village where poor Confucian scholars used to live became a new power base full of Japanese political and economic elites. The lines of confrontation between the collapsed Confucian Joseon loyalists and imperial Japan were formed in several spaces along the former border between the sacred and profane.

Furthermore, the introduction of Japanese capitalism brought an important shift to traditional Confucian ideology, which had placed high value on agriculture and looked down upon commerce/industry. Thus, Confucian economic views and policy were supplanted with Japan's advanced industrial capitalistic economic system, which would weaken the political basis of the toppled Joseon Dynasty and make Japanese colonial control beneficial to the masses. The Government-General encouraged Japanese entrepreneurs to commence their business by taking advantage of Japanese colonial control over land, natural resources, cheap labor, and political power in Korea. This new phenomenon brought forth a new commercial and industrial town centering on Eulji-ro and Choongmoo-ro, and leaving Chong-ro, which had been the traditional Korean commercial center, stagnant. The area of Yongsan, which was the exterior of Hanyang Castle and thus a periphery, now came to the fore as the most important center of Japanese power—namely, the military.[8] Therefore, new economic centers emerged, challenging the traditional centers of economy—the markets situated along the East-West axis. The Headquarters of the Japanese Army came to be located in Yongsan as well, and the city sphere automatically expanded.

All of these changes together seriously damaged the Confucian hegemony and its hierarchical order in social structure, producing a new hegemony and hierarchical structure for Korean society. The large-scale reorganization of the city layout clearly confirms the changes inflicted upon the social structure. Among these changes, the rise of military forces as the most powerful social elite was most striking. For thirty-six years, there were ten Governors-General; with the exception of Samato Makoto, who was the 3rd and 6th Governor-General, all were generals of the Japanese Army or Commanders of the Japanese Army in Korea, mostly on active duty.[9] The Governor-General, formally appointed by the Premier, submitted his reports directly to the Emperor. Having made Korea its colony, Japan exercised its rule through a Government-General, which took the place of the former Residency-General, and all legislative, executive, and judicial powers resided in his hands alone (Lee, 1984: 314). This was reflected in the composition of government buildings on the Six Ministries Street during the Kyeongseong period. Figure 4.1, a simplified version based on the Maps of Kyeongseong,[10] shows that the Headquarters of the Japanese Army and Gendarmerie occupied the most prestigious location on this street where the Ministry of Rites (Yejo) had been located during the Joseon Dynasty.[11] In addition, Southern areas of the traditional *axis mundi* were mostly occupied by Japanese economic institutions, forming a line of confrontation between traditional Confucian hegemony and Japan's new economic power.

Moreover, although a reduction of police numbers was announced, the police organization actually expanded and the number of police personnel increased. Including the gendarmerie, police strength grew to about 15,000 in the immediate aftermath of the March First Movement in 1919, and reached 21,782 by 1938.[12]

The city hall, Hanseong-bu, located between the Ijo (Ministry of Personnel) and the Hojo (Ministry of Taxation), which indicated the importance of the city of Hanyang in relation to the political affairs of the Dynasty as a whole, was altogether removed. Instead, the Japanese placed the Office of Kyunggi Province[13] on the left side of the Six Ministries Street, which indicates the Japanese intention of demoting the position of Hanseong-bu in the political life of Korea, thereby weakening Confucian hegemony as well. Also, the Telecommunication Agency's occupancy of a site on the Six Ministries Street proves that industrial sectors were no longer of low prestige as they had been in the Hanyang era.

All other important buildings were located on the street connecting the Headquarters of the Government-General. Thus, the former sacred space of the Six Ministries Street was expanded.[14] All of these important buildings were located on Taepyung-ro, the street that stretched from the end of the former Six Ministries Street to Mt. Mokmyuk. Taepyung-ro had not been included as a part of the sacred space in the Joseon Dynasty and thus was not considered prestigious. By placing all of these important buildings on Taepyung-ro, the authorities diminished the prestige of the formerly sacred

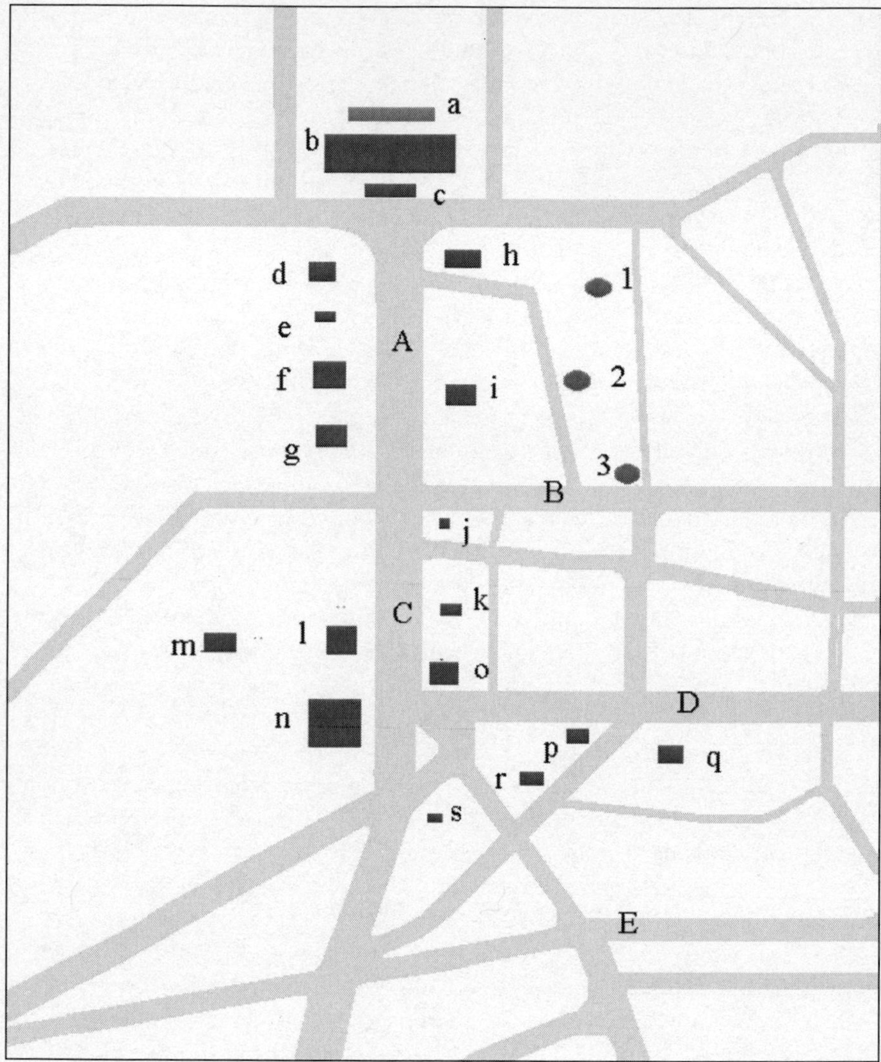

Figure 4.1 Locations of Major Buildings in the Kyeongseong Era. A. Former Six Ministries Street, B. Chongro, C. Taepyungro, D. Euljiro, E. Choongmooro. a. Keunjeongjeon, b. Governor-General Headquarters, c. Kwanghwamoon, d. Japanese Infantry Corps, e. Official Residency for Gendarmerie Commander, f. Gendarmerie Headquarters, g. Telecom Agency, h. Kyunggi Province Office, I. Law School, j. Post Office, k. Kyeongseong Daily News, l. British Embassy, m. Russian Embassy, n. Deoksoo Palace, o. Kyeongseong City Hall, p. Siksan Bank (Shokusan Ginko), q. Oriental Development Company, r. Choson Bank, s. Kyeongseong Chamber of Commerce. Created by author Han, Jongwoo.

street, and the area that had previously been regarded as unimportant came to the fore of the capital city under Japanese influence. To the masses, such contrasting pictures of the changes in the traditional Confucian monumentality and state hegemony must have been clear.

More specifically, the Headquarters of the Government-General, located in the main palace site (the best spot in Kyeongseong), had all the legislative, executive, and judicial powers in its hands alone. All the dynasty's institutions and buildings were no longer functional. Other politically important Japanese buildings—The Supreme Court, Kyeongseong Bucheong (City Hall), and Kyeongseong Buminkwan (City Assembly)—were on the new hegemonic street, Taepyung-ro. Locating the most powerful political institutions on this street established a new hegemonic site beyond the former sacred space. Thus, a dichotomous reorganization of the capital city took place (Japanese vs. Korean), reflecting Japanese superiority over Koreans. Such a phenomenon can be found in the composition of the bureaucracy; before annexing Korea, Japan insisted that Korea install Japanese advisers in strategic Korean ministries (Lee,[15] 1984: 308).

As Japan exerted more influence upon Korean society, Koreans observed a rising tide of governmental and economic modernization; whereas Koreans had once participated fully in both, they were now increasingly being separated by a thick layer of alien elite filling almost all of the important positions (Henderson, 1968: 75-76). Japanese colonizers swarmed in, increasing from 3,622 in 1882 to 42,460 in 1905, then 171,543 in 1910, and 336,812 in 1918, finally reaching 708,448 (or approximately 3.2% of the population) in 1940. As a ruling class, the Japanese outnumbered even the yangban, whom they displaced. Moon (1967) points out that official Korean bureaucrats numbered only 14 out of a total of around 3,000 in the Government-General, showing that Japanese hegemonic and hierarchical superiority over Korean bureaucrats had been established.

The majority of these new buildings located on Taepyung-ro were economic institutions. In the past, the commercial center (i.e., Chong-ro) was controlled by political institutions. The necessity for this commercial center had been admitted only for the demands of the Joseon Dynasty's political and administrative purposes. Now in the Kyeongseong era, all of these capitalistic economic institutions received their positions with the positive support of the Government-General and expanded their sphere of influence, establishing a center in the new economic hegemonic streets Eulji-ro, Choongmoo-ro, and Taepyung-ro. More support was given to these economic institutions since the colonial authority regarded them as ways of penetrating into Korean society as well as tools for imperial expansion not just to Korea but to China and Manchuria too. Geographically, the commercial center formerly located on the east end of the East-West axis moved to the southwest. This was the start of capitalistic economic development and modernization in Korean history even though Japan did not intend economic development for the Korean people.

This capitalization of the Korean economy reversed the Confucian principle of political priority over the economy; the new principle took the form of cooperation between political and economic forces for the sake of economic development itself. This was quite a transformation because, during the Hanyang period, the state had unilaterally controlled the economy in order to meet the needs of government operation, not for the sake of economic development. In 1920, the Government-General rescinded the laws regulating business concerns in Korea. As a consequence, the establishment of a company no longer required permission but simply registration, so that those who wished to launch new business enterprises were freed from the tedious procedures hitherto required for obtaining a permit. It would be erroneous, though, to assume that Japan took this step in order to encourage capital investment by Koreans; their intention was to develop a profitable market in Korea for the investment of Japanese capital, now swollen from the WWI prosperity that Japan enjoyed as a supplier to the Allied nations.[16] Also, these economic powers in Korea were aimed at providing logistical supports for Japanese military expansionist policy in China and Southeast Asia.

In fact, the Government-General itself was simply another, and by far the largest, Japanese entrepreneurial complex in Korea. The Government-General operated all railways, harbors, communications, and airports and possessed monopolies on products like ginseng, salt, tobacco, and opium; furthermore, the profits from these enterprises were enormous. In short, Japanese business, with the Government-General itself in the forefront, came close to monopolizing Korea's natural resources and, operating under such favorable conditions, reaped ever fatter profits (Lee, 1984: 321). Japan's great *zaibatsu*[17] competed with each other to build factories in Korea, and as a result, the proportion of manufacturing industries within Korea's industrial structure grew at a rapid rate. Specifically, in 1925, the proportion contributed by manufacturing industries to Korea's gross commodity product was 17.7 percent; in 1931, it had increased to 22.7 percent, in 1936 to 31.3 percent, and in 1939 to 39 percent (Lee, 1984: 351).

Under the political protection of Japanese imperialism, Japanese capital investment in a wide range of Korean industries was growing apace. War-related industry in particular was established in Korea by the great zaibatsu of Mitsui, Mitsubishi, and Noguchi, hand in hand with Japan's war ministry. In fact, the domination of Japanese capital investment in Korean manufacturing plants of 1938 was an overwhelming 87.7 percent, which is in contrast to the level of Korean capital at 12.3 percent (Lee, 1984: 354). At this point, Japanese entrepreneurs vied with one another to establish companies that seized possession not only of uncultivated state land but even the paddy lands that the Korean government had formerly set aside for the support of military and government agencies and such state services as the network of post stations (Lee, 1984: 318).

The fact that all of the important political and economic institutions were located within this triangular area connecting Eulji-ro, Choongmoo-ro, and Taepyung-ro supports the claim that the Confucian principle of separating economic institutions from "sacred space" had been broken down by the establishment of cooperative relations between them. Accordingly, this triangle zone became the center of finance, commerce, industry, and politics.

Above all, the Oriental Development Company, which was located in Eulji-ro, was the main tool by which the Japanese acquired land. It was established in 1908, and in its first eighteen months of operation, it acquired about 30,000 *cheongbo*[18] (73,500 acres) of land (Lee, 1984: 318). As a consequence, according to statistics for 1930, the combined total of agricultural and forest land held by the Government-General was 8,880,000 cheongbo, 40 percent of the total land area of Korea. A portion of the land thus taken over by the Government-General was sold at a fraction of its worth to companies under Japanese management, particularly to the Oriental Development Company, or to Japanese immigrants (Lee, 1984: 319). On Choongmoo-ro, the Japanese department stores were concentrated. To Koreans, many aspects of these stores were totally new: their grand scale, their diversity of merchandise, and their mode of sales, which was based on the manufacturing system. The traditional commercial center, Chong-ro, was incapable of competing with them (Sohn, 1991: 35). Thus, Japanese economic hegemony prevailed, and commercial activities were no longer scorned as they had been.

The financial center formed around Taepyung-ro. The largest bank in Korea at that time, Choson Bank, was located on this street. Japanese financial institutions appeared in Korea just after the opening of the ports. According to Lee (1984), by around 1900, a number of Japanese banks—the Daiichi Ginko most importantly but many others as well—had established branch or agency offices in Korea and began to play a leading role in the country's financial activities. Early in 1905, when the Korea branch of Daiichi Ginko was given authority to issue currency, it assumed the role of a central bank for Korea, buying gold and silver bullion, making loans to the government, collecting customs duties at the open ports, and undertaking a wide range of other central banking functions. With the establishment of the Bank of Korea in 1909, these functions became its responsibility, but the manager of the Daiichi Ginko's general offices in Seoul was concurrently appointed to the governorship of the new bank. After annexation, Bank of Korea transformed into the Bank of Joseon in 1911 and was given the duties of a central bank (Lee, 1984: 323).

Also, Siksan Bank (Industrial Bank, Shokusan Ginko in Japanese) was located on this street. It was originally established in 1906 under another name to assist in the development of agriculture and industry in Korea. After Korea became a colony, the Siksan Bank became an instrument for supporting mostly Japanese business and farmers (Lee, 1984: 323). The Oriental Development Company and Siksan Bank were the mechanisms by which the Government-General typically supported Japanese industrial and commercial activities; they represented the introduction of a new principle: a close relationship between political authority and entrepreneurs—a sharp reversal of the traditional Confucian prescription for the relations between political authority and economic sectors. Furthermore, Kyeongseong Chamber of Commerce, Kyeongseong Electric Co., and the Government-General Center for Commerce and Industry were also positioned here. Eventually, this triangle zone became the Street of Capitalism, the center of commerce, finance, and industry.

During the Joseon Dynasty, foreign presence in Hanyang had been very rare. China was the only country with which the Joseon Dynasty considered it worthwhile to have an official relationship. China was the center of Confucianism, so toadyism toward China was considered natural. At that time, all facilities for the Chinese delegation were located outside of the West Gate (Doneuimun) of Hanyang. Accordingly, the Chinese sphere of influence was concentrated on the west side of the capital city. At times, Japan and other small nations attacked the coastlines or requested trade. The official policy of the Joseon Dynasty was to maintain mutual relations with them. Thus, in some cases, they were allowed to settle in Korea; however, these cases were too rare to cause any change in demography or city layout.

In summary, Japanese authority capitalized off of Koreans' strong attachment to the sacred area of the capital city and symbolic center of power by destroying Confucian order and constructing Japanese imperial symbols in their stead. Japanese penetration into Confucian Joseon was achieved in various ways. After the systematic destructions, distortions, and deformations of Joseon's Confucian monumentality, substantive replacements were enacted through the introduction of a modern bureaucratic system. The strong establishment of Japanese hegemony in terms of politics and bureaucracy also forced the political activity of the Korean people to go underground despite the fact that such political activity had been the custom of a large class (Henderson, 1968: 74). This is how former governing Confucian elites joined the heteronomical forces, which thereby expanded and strengthened the basis for the future civil society. Furthermore, the Koreans who had been accustomed to broader access to rule and to checks on autocracy by government councils suddenly found themselves facing foreign bureaucratic and authoritarian centralism. Now, all government inspector institutions, such as the Censorate and Confucian memorializing, were gone. Oligarchic traditional and centralized bureaucracy and scholarly bureaucrats were replaced with a forceful and modernized bureaucratic system from Japan. "In the place of the fluid politics and endless discussion of issues that were once considered the aristocratic birthright came enforcement from capital to village by a bureaucracy equipped with arms, communication, efficiency, and ruthless purpose" (Henderson, 1968: 74-75).

In economy, this period brought two important changes: (1) a capitalistic system of commerce and industry came to the fore of economic activities in Korea, where they had long been regarded as lowly; and (2) relations between government and economy became much closer and more cooperative with each other than in the Joseon era. In fact, the introduction of a capitalistic industrial economic system would have been greatly delayed were it not for Japan's forced occupation of Joseon Dynasty. This does not mean, however, that there were no traces of commerce or industry in Hanyang. Such commercial and industrial economic activities were officially denounced in the Joseon era, but agriculture was theoretically regarded as the backbone of Joseon's economic foundation. With colonization, the overall relationship and power dynamics between state and economy remained largely similar to before; however, the basis of the main economic mode was forced to transform from agricultural activity to modern capitalistic industrialization. Even though such industrialization was not intended to benefit Joseon's economic development, the seeds of the late development strategy of modern Korea were germinated during this colonial period. In summary, the state's power and rights to intervene in the economic activities were kept intact but the content of economic activities was forced to change. That was the major outcome of local-global interaction between Joseon and Japan. Later, Japan's successful catch-up strategy in global market competition of the early and mid-20th century was adopted in Korea's late development.

Spatial evidence of the transformation can be found in figure 4.2, which will be discussed at length later in this chapter. A hierarchical order of political and bureaucratic superiority over the economy, represented by the emphasis on the North-South axis during the Joseon Dynasty, was superseded by the East-West axis representing the rising power of commerce, finance, and industry centered in the triangle zone in figure 4.2. Such a drastic change in the power distribution between government and economy, which was

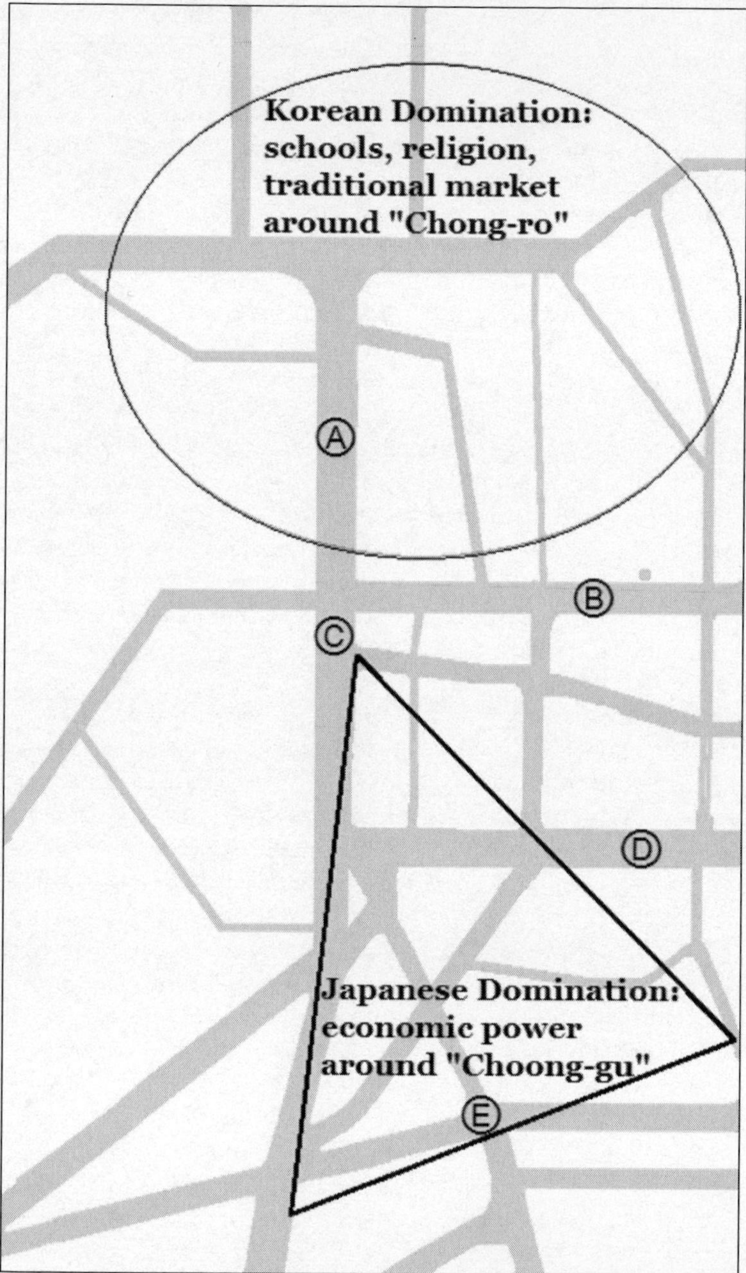

Figure 4.2 Confrontation between Traditional Korean and Japanese Occupation Spheres within the City. A. The Former Six Ministries Street, B. Chong-ro, C. Taepyeong-ro, D. Eulji-ro, E. Chungmu-ro. Created by author; Han, Jongwoo.

reflected in the expanded zone of economic centers in the Kyeongseong era, could mean more balanced and cooperative relations between economy and politics/bureaucracy. As discussed above, the symbols of Joseon hegemony in the sacred zone were mostly supplanted if not severely damaged or destroyed, while the southern areas under the East-West axis were occupied by Japan's new economic power as well as newly rising modern capitalistic centers. Such an analysis of the changes in spatial arrangement was applied in the previous chapter's examination of Joseon's state-society relations.

All of these changes during the Kyeongseong period have left a great impact upon modern Korea. The fundamental city layout in Seoul has been framed by the structural changes established during the Kyeongseong period. The government plan released in April 1995 aiming to restore the former Six Ministries Street and Taepyung-ro and rename them "National Central Boulevard" serves as further evidence of the relations between the spatial arrangements and power dynamics. The expansion of the areas that were not regarded as the core of the sacred space during the Joseon era was the result of Japanese penetration into the Korean economy and stood for the new economic ideas and systems of the Kyeongseong era. New modern Japanese corporations and other economic institutions naturally came to challenge the hegemony that was based on Confucian economic ideas, forming lines of confrontation between the conventional Confucian elites and the Japanese military and entrepreneurial power groups within the core of the capital city, as indicated in figure 4.2. Such a transformation from Confucian Hanyang to imperial and modern Kyeongseong paved the transition from an agricultural stagnant economy under a Confucian state to a modern and capitalistic economy under a developmental state in the mid-20th century in Korea.

From Loyal Opposition to National Resistance: Upsurge of Heteronomical Forces

What exactly does it mean to say that "heteronomy" is the background condition of rule against which episodes of hegemony and hierarchy are set? Simply put, this means that heteronomy is not independent of hegemony or hierarchy but rather is merely different from those two types of rule. "Heteronomy" refers to social or political forces that are not autonomous but rather are dominated by others. That is not to say, however, that heteronomy is completely subdued by hegemony or hierarchy; rather, it merely implies differences from those two types of rule. Onuf explains this difference as conditions that are not in keeping with the rules of the dominant hegemonic group. Even though the place provided to heteronomy is a subservient one, an area for differences is reserved, and the relationship of those differences to the dominant groups is recognized. "Heteronomy" refers to rules in dealing with dissent in Onuf's conception of political society. Here, the concept of heteronomy perfectly describes the nature of two dissenting voices during the Joseon era: the Confucian National University of Seongkyunkwan and the Sarim of local Confucian literati. The former was not completely independent of the Confucian hegemony in the center. In fact, from the mid-Joseon era, local Confucian literati or sadaebu emerged as strong factions in central politics. The latter played a significant role in court politics, which was under protection and supervision of the royal and central government offices; however, during the Kyeongseong era, the combined forces of the Sarim and Seongkyunkwan students formed a national basis of resistance against Japanese colonial control. This section details the process whereby these two relatively weak voices of dissent came to pose a serious challenge to the colonial forces of Japan.

The collapse of the Confucian hegemony and hierarchy brought about an eventual upsurge in heteronomy due to the special features of the heteronomical aspect of the power structure of the Joseon Dynasty. Government institutions such as the Samsa and National Confucian Academy played the role of checks and balances against the king, bureaucracy, and power elites. The Samsa was obviously a tool for the government to monitor and supervise any wrongdoings in the powerful government offices. In that sense, it would be unfair to categorize the Samsa as a typical voice of dissent; rather, these institutions were embraced within the Confucian power structure so that the Confucian social order could be more comprehensive and secure. Now, though, with the collapse of Confucian hegemony and hierarchy, the original heteronomical function temporarily became unable to operate publicly. As Henderson points out, all of these heteronomical activities had to go underground.

Japanese oppression, however, functioned as a catalytic conversion of previously hegemonic forces into a belligerent voice of dissent. Such an opportunity for various social forces to unite might have not presented itself under the rule of Confucian social structure alone; however, with newly shared interest, the royal family, bureaucrats, scholars, military, religious groups, students, and the masses all came together to form a broad social force with a clear political purpose—"Resistance Nationalism." The former ruling Confucian elites groups which had to control the dissenting voices and the heteronomical force despite its co-opted nature now came to form a united front of resistance against Japan and a basis of civil society that would later become a force of militant opposition against President Park's military and development regime. In this way, various social forces that would have been antagonistic to each other if not for the Japanese oppression eventually joined to form a tradition of powerful and legitimate dissenting voice, which would later play a significant role not only in standing up against military dictatorship but also accelerating the democratization process in modern Korean political history. The resistance nationalism that formed during the Kyeongseong era transformed the power configurations from the preeminence of hegemonic and hierarchical forces of the Hanyang era, expanded and bolstered the heteronomical forces, and nourished the seeds of both civil society and belligerent opposition forces against the ruling regime. At the same time, liberal influences from American missionaries began to dilute Confucian aspects of the newly formed alliance between Confucian ruling elites and subordinates. In this way, an indigenous historical approach sheds light on how democratization could occur in a Confucian, and therefore authoritarian, society with a strong state tradition; however, this book does not argue that these internal politics which resulted from the global-local interaction between Confucian Joseon and militaristic Japan were the only reason for Korea's democratization in the mid-20th century. Socioeconomic changes, including class composition during the rapid industrialization of the 1960s to '80s, and the consequent sociopolitical changes must also be accounted for, but such a task lies beyond the scope of this book.

As mentioned briefly above, Western liberalism[19] and Christianity also played a great role in the formation of mass heteronomical forces during the Kyeongseong era. The reason that students at the National Confucian Academy during the Joseon Dynasty could resist the king and scholar bureaucrats was that they served as a source of recruited officials and development of the Confucian ideology, which in turn served as the basis for the Joseon Dynasty's political legitimacy. In addition, students were given the right to take care of the Confucian tablets that the King and Confucian scholar bureaucrats worshipped as a national ideology and the source of their legitimacy to rule. Similarly, students were given the responsibility to maintain the Confucian Shrine (Monmyo), the center of Confucianism. The state ideology of Confucianism originated from China, which was the center of the Confucian world order in East Asia at that time. The King and senior bureaucrats who had graduated from that same academy would not do anything to deny the Chinese authority as that would thereby undermine their own Confucian legitimacy. Now, a Western educational system, political ideology of liberalism, and religion (especially Christian denominations) were changing the source of heteronomy in Korea from Chinese to Western, particularly American.

As the former Confucian elites and students faced the most atrocious form of colonial control that ever existed in human history, they began looking for a new source of ideology that could equip them with ideas and strategies to deal with the failure of old state ideology originated from China. To these people, China was the center of the world, and Korea was more civilized than Japan in that worldview of China as the center. Many former Confucian intellectuals were very frustrated by the fact that their center of the world had been defeated by the uncivilized Japan and had high hopes of American influence and its liberal educational system as an alternative to challenge Japanese colonial control. Now, failed and defeated Confucian elites began to view America as a new source of leverage and American liberalism as a source of power to overcome Japanese militarism; ironically, they were unaware that the United States had already agreed with Japan that the Korean Peninsula should fall under Japanese colonial control. This was made official in their 1905 secret agreement between Katsura (Prime Minister of Japan) and Taft (War Secretary of the Roosevelt administration). Such changes were clearly reflected in the locations of the new educational building.

The new educational institutions that started being established by American missionaries and old Korean elites in the late 19th century sprang up within the so-called sacred space such that the power of the students fit well with the Korean people's traditional belief of investing legitimacy in this geographical location. As figures 4.3 and 4.4 show, there is a clear overlap between old Confucian shrines that were concentrated in the sacred zone of the Hanyang era and new liberal educational institutions that were mostly influenced by American missionaries. This provides solid evidence that old Confucian elites who were still based in the sacred zone of the Hanyang era wanted to host new liberal educational centers in this space of dominance, which they considered as the last and fundamental bastion of hope in the fight against Japan. Later, in the Seoul era, universities became concentrated in this sacred region and served as a symbolic center of opposition against the military dictatorship of the Park regime. The transition from Confucian Hanyang to colonial Kyeongseong and finally to modern Seoul manifests traces of changes in the power configurations between hegemonic, hierarchical, and heteronomical forces in Korea. It also demonstrates how the interaction between domestic and foreign forces affected Korea's state-society relations. In the long run, the heteronomical forces newly formed at that time came to play a critical role even in modern Korean politics.

Resistance to Japanese aggression in Korea took many forms. First, there was the struggle of the royal house to restore its disintegrating sovereign power (Lee, 1984: 315). Among the Confucian literati, there were those who resisted Japan in a way hallowed by tradition—they attempted to bring about the adoption of a national policy of resistance by offering memorials to the throne. Then, there also were those who engaged in an active, armed struggle against Japan by forming "righteous armies" (Lee, 1984: 315-316). Considering that only 14 Korean officials worked in the Government-General in 1936 out of a total workforce of around 3,000, it should come as no surprise that the

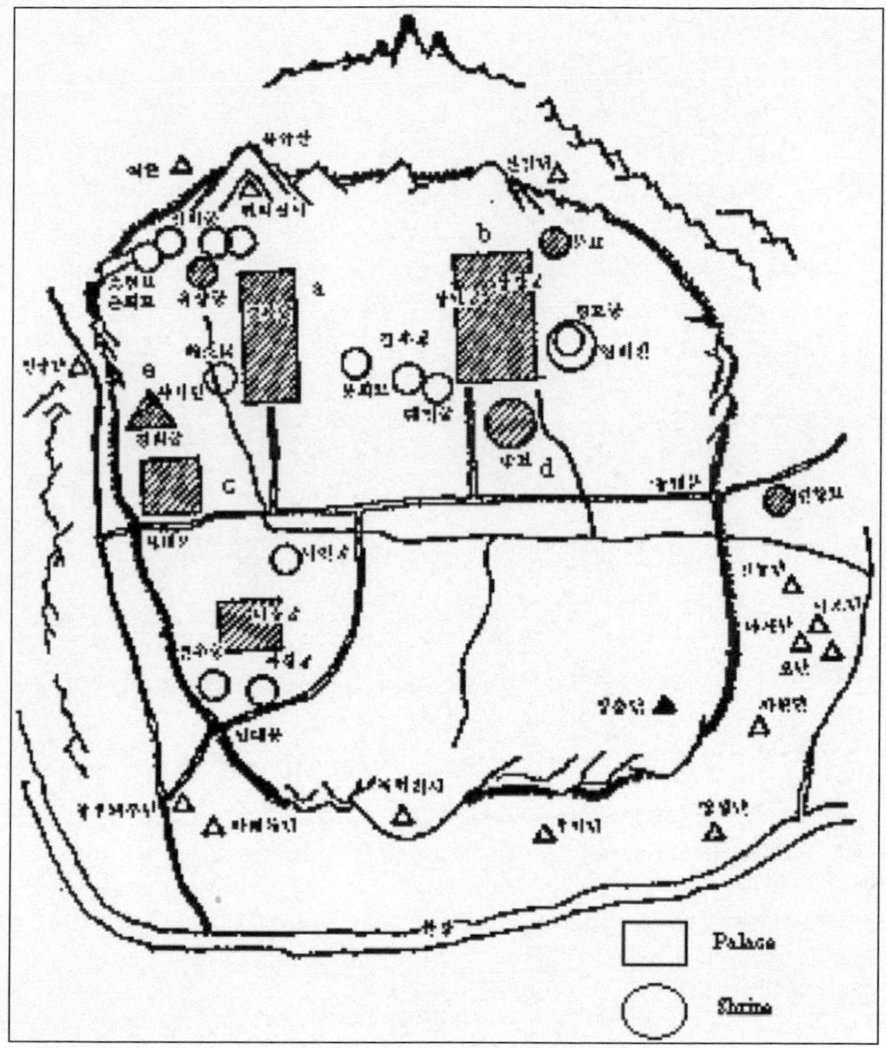

Figure 4.3 Locations of Confucian Shrines. Source: Kim, Dong-Wook (1991), p. 35.

remaining discharged Confucian bureaucrats resisted Japanese rule, forming a heteronomy on a massive scale with other social forces.

Those who played the biggest role in the resistance to Japanese aggression, however, were students. A salient feature of the Korean nationalist movement during Japanese colonial rule was the outbreak of student-led demonstrations focusing specifically on demands for independence. The beacon heralding the March First Movement in 1919 was lit by Korean students in Tokyo, and the

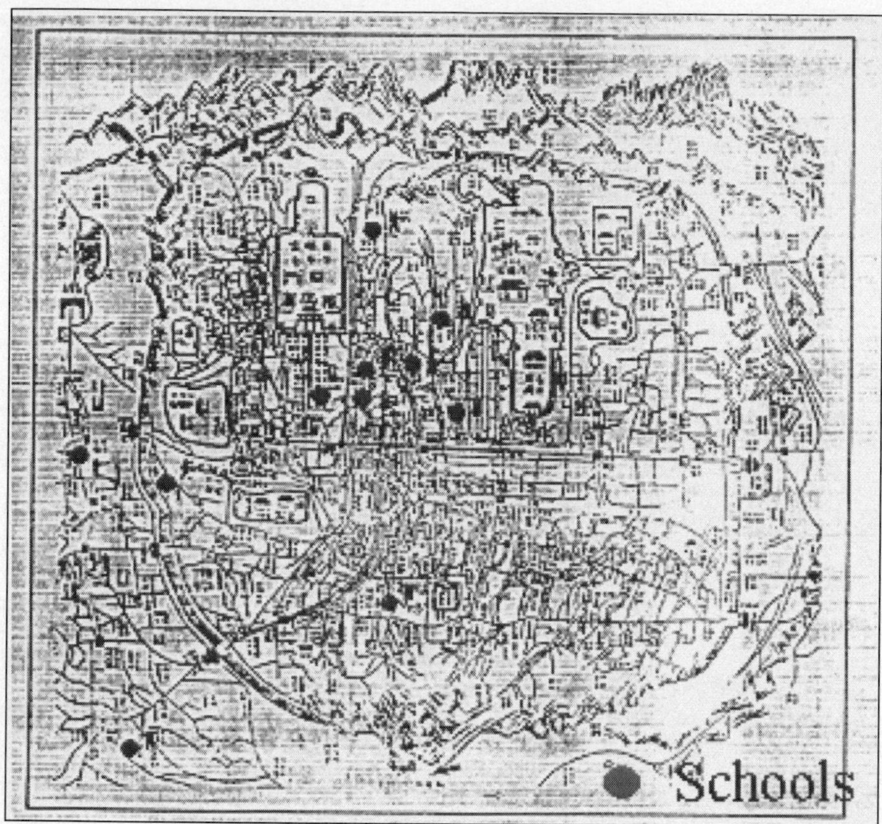

Figure 4.4 Locations of Liberal Educational Institutions in the Early 20th Century. Lee, Young-Han (1992), p. 101.

demonstrations in the streets of Seoul that transformed the movement into a nationwide struggle were also conducted by students. This was the case as well with the June 10, 1926, Independence Demonstration and the Kwangju Student Movement in 1929. The last ruler of the Joseon Dynasty, Sunjong, died in April 1926, and the deep sorrow of the Korean people combined with their hostility toward Japan to produce an outpouring of grief and discontent. With left-wing activists in the forefront, a plan was set in motion to seize this opportunity and hold a massive anti-Japanese demonstration on June 10, the day of the late monarch's state funeral (Lee, 1984: 363).

Although Confucian students had traditionally been granted the exclusive right to resist the ruling elites, the National Confucian Academy had closed under Japanese colonial rule. Instead, a Western-style educational system was officially adopted as a national educational policy. Farther back, in 1886, the

Korean government had established a special institute (*Yookyoung Kongwon*) to provide education and new knowledge from the West, and after the 1894 reforms, a new educational system had been created, with a new curriculum offered in government schools of several types—ranging from primary and middle schools to normal schools and schools for foreign languages.[20] Also, the passion for education during this period burned still more brightly among the public at large, and numerous private schools were established to serve the younger generation's growing interest in education (Lee, 1984: 331). Just as the ideology that had empowered Confucian students' legitimacy to criticize ruling elites during the Hanyang period came from foreign origins (i.e., Chinese Confucianism), the main framework of modern Korean education in the Kyeongseong era was foreign as well—Western liberalism. Interestingly, the power and legitimacy to criticize the ruling elites came from the extraterritoriality of foreign ideology during both periods.

Christianity, and Protestantism in particular, exerted tremendous influence on the political and educational activities of the intellectual class. In 1886, the *Baejae* school and several other private institutions were founded by American missionary organizations. In the scant few years before Korea fell completely under Japanese colonial domination, the number of private schools reached approximately 3,000. "The private schools of that day served not only to disseminate the new learning but also as renowned hotbeds of the nationalist movement" (Lee, 1984: 332). According to Lee (1984: 333-334), there were thirty major private schools in the late Joseon period. Among them, eleven had been founded by foreign organizations, all of which were American missionaries. Here, we can see the American influence upon the educational system in the beginning of Korea's modern period. Moreover, of these major thirty private schools, twenty were located in Seoul.

The Formation of a Public Sphere

Public opinion politics during the period of factional political strife in the late Joseon era did not extend beyond the scope of the private sphere of the Confucian literati and a few Confucian political and educational institutions such as the Daegan and Seongkyunkwan; the scope of lively discussion and debate on politics did not reach most of the population. Even though the Sarim covered vast areas of local provinces and their factional politics were called *kongron* (*kong* in Korean and 公 in Chinese meaning "public"; *ron* in Korean and 論 in Chinese meaning "debate") politics, the people were mostly excluded from the sphere of political discourse during the Joseon era, which should be understood as a "private sphere" since Habermas (1991: 5-7) clarifies that the private sphere of the feudal lord's house affairs was "public" only in name. The Western origin of the public sphere comes from capitalist commercial relations and the rising power of the bourgeoisie as well as their interest in forming a sphere of their influence to direct against the realm of the private sphere of the feudal ruling class. Accordingly, Habermas attributes institutions of communication, such as the postal service and press, to the formation of the public sphere for bourgeoisie interest in the traffic of commodities and news. While the origins of the public sphere in the Western hemisphere were based on changes in the materialistic world, its origins in Korea were politically oriented as explained above and in chapter 3. Furthermore, at the end of the Joseon Dynasty in the early 20th century, as Western imperial countries began to divide and rule Korea, the public sphere began to emerge in Korean politics. Surrounded by Western imperial powers and their aggression, the Joseon Dynasty's hegemonic and heteronomical forces merged to form a united front, and the public began to engage in the forum for national independence.

Interactions with global forces awoke the people's nationalism and produced various modern organizations engaging the public, the first of which was the Independence Club (*Tokriphyuphoe*), which, this book argues, constituted the first major public sphere in Korea's political history. In the midst of aggression from the Western imperial powers interested in colonizing Korea, King Kojong proclaimed the establishment of the independent "Empire of Great Han" (Daehanjaegook) in 1897. Despite King Kojong's efforts to be independent from the protection of Russia, America, England, and Japan, the Great Han Empire had to survive the competition among foreign forces in Korea: China, Russia, England, America, and Japan. The Independence Club was a specific reaction to the demise of the nominal Empire.

The Independence Club was the first modern political association in Korean political history that contributed to the formation of a public sphere. Most importantly, it was led by incumbent and former government officials, activists, and intelligentsia who were influenced primarily by Western liberalism; and though it was based partly on indigenous Confucianism, it did not limit its membership to those who had been leaders in the hegemony and hierarchy of the Joseon Dynasty. Membership was open to all, and, similar to the Sarim, the Club expanded its network of membership and activities into the countryside. Secondly, the main business of the Club operations, including the selection of Club officers and the conduct of its business, was handled democratically (Lee, 1984: 302). The Club demanded basic political and human rights for the citizens, such as freedom of press, property rights, and the establishment of a Western-style parliament.

The culmination of the Independence Club included the formation of a citizen assembly, the sponsorship of a forum for debate, and the running of a newspaper, which fittingly was called *The Independent* (*Tongrip Shinmoon*). Several hundred Club members and spectators attended the forum each Sunday at Independence Hall to participate in fervent discussions on the aggressions of foreign countries, national sovereignty, political democracy, and citizens' rights (Lee, 1984: 303). The Club's newspaper, *The Independent*, was published in *Hangeul* (Korean alphabet) without the use of any Chinese characters in order to attract a wider readership among the general populace with a special focus on Western liberal political ideas (Lee, 1984: 303-304). Another newspaper, *Hwangseong Shinmoon*, representing Confucianist ideas of reform, was aligned with the Club as well. In 1898, the Independence Club also proposed to convert the Privy Council into a parliamentary assembly and run a *Manmingongdong-hoe* (mass meeting), where not only elites but also members of general the populace could express their political views. Traditionally, this had been a kind of mass town hall meeting put together by the political elites at the end of the Great Han Empire; it was being used to establish a modern liberal democratic political institution in Korea for the first time.

Although the Independence Club movement eventually failed to achieve its goal, it did leave significant impacts on the formation of national resistance against Japanese colonialism and on civil society in the modern sense, which continued on through the anti-military dictatorship movement in the era of Seoul. The overall impacts of the Club included the following: first, it formed a public sphere by running a newspaper and hosting mass meetings with a forum for public debate among a wider spectrum of citizens; second, it introduced Western liberal political ideas, which served later as an education base for consolidating modern citizens and heteronomical forces against Japanese colonial forces; third, it expanded the horizon of heteronomical forces in traditional Korean politics by opening up Club membership to people of all levels of society and pulling together incumbent government leaders, intelligentsia, and the masses, thereby paving the way for the upsurge in heteronomical forces. The fall of the Joseon Dynasty to Japan ignited a surge of resistance.

In this perspective, the Independence Club contributed to the consolidation of leaders in the traditional realms of hegemony and heteronomy. Interaction with the global force of Japan affected the prototype of the relations that had existed in Korea among the traditional rule of hegemony, hierarchy, and heteronomy, and the Kyeongseong era vividly exemplified this transformation. The failure of the Independence Club to carry out its goal did not kill the seeds of the modern social and political movements that were demanding the recovery of national sovereignty from Japan, the development of strong industrial economy, and the provision of opportunities for liberal education to the masses; in fact, many social and political movement organizations followed in the Independence Club's footsteps. However, Japanese colonial headquarters

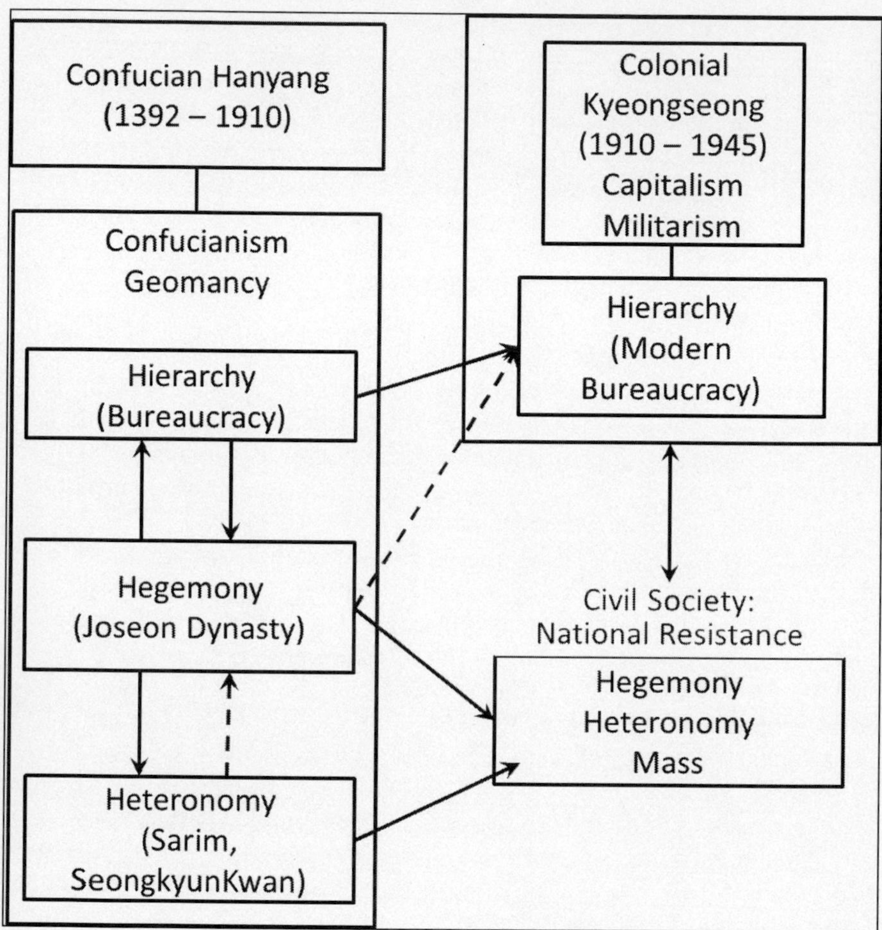

Figure 4.5 Hanyang to Kyeongseong. Created by author Han, Jangwoo.

repressed such movements by mobilizing military and police forces, and the Independence Club was dismissed.

The first to do so, the Korea Preservation Society (Boanhoe), organized in 1904 to protect the uncultivated land of Korea from Japan, and achieved some degree of success. Japan, winning recognition from other Western powers, such as Russia, England, and America in the early 20th century, moved immediately to establish a protectorate over Korea (Lee, 1984: 309). Specifically reacting to the formation and collaborating activities of Ilchinhoe, which was a front organization crafted by Japan, several indigenous political associations were formed. The first autonomous political organization to take a stand against Ilchinhoe was the Society for the Study of Constitutional Government

(Heonjeongyungoohoe). In 1904, Kongjihoe was founded by the former members of the Independence Club for the purpose of internal political reform. There were also numerous socially and politically motivated movement organizations, such as Spokesmen for the People (Inmin Taeeuihoe), Korea Self-Strengthening Society (Taehanjaganghoe) in 1906, the Korea Association (Taehanhyuphoe), Association for Redemption of the National Debt in 1907, and the New People's Association (Shinminhoe), among others.

An important element in the upsurge of heteronomical forces under the Japanese colonial control was that they were "anathema alike to both the Korean government and to Japan" (Lee, 1984: 329), which nourished the seeds of civil disobedience that would later blossom in the Seoul era in opposition to the military capitalist state dictatorship. Thus, in this era, a strong stance against preexisting power and government orientation was formed.

Liberal Educational Institutions in the Sacred Space

As illustrated in figures 4.3 and 4.4, an interesting fact is that most of these prestigious private schools were located around the so-called sacred space in the northwestern region of the capital city. Even though Confucian political power had been completely removed by Japan, the people's will to recover their state power had been greatly strengthened. In accordance with the people's belief system, they still projected their loyalty toward the lineage and legitimacy of state power that had been inherited from the Confucian Joseon era even though most of the social structure and system that had upheld the Confucian hierarchical order, such as the caste system, lay in ruin. The students, who had traditionally been given the right to speak out against power and who were now equipped with new Western liberalism, now occupied the "sacred space" that represented the lineage of the old dynasty; this suggested several important points.

First of all, students had become much stronger than in the Joseon Dynasty. During the Joseon era, students were in a more privileged position than the common people. Their privilege to criticize the ruling elites and to participate in politics was granted to them by the ruling elites, not by the people. Accordingly, students' privilege was taken for granted as part of the Confucian hierarchy. Now, though, people identified students as a social group that occupied the traditionally recognized "sacred space" where the Confucian shrines were located, as shown in figure 4.3.

Numerous private schools had been established since 1883 as patriotic responses to the challenges posed by imperial powers like Japan, China, and Russia. The first of these was Wonsan Academy, established in Northern Korea, and twenty-eight other private schools sprang up by 1909 (Lee, 1984: 331-332).

The founders of these schools, who had been active in political movements, committed to these educational establishments for the purpose of laying the foundation for an independent Korea (Lee, 1984: 331). In the northern part of the peninsula, American missionaries had been very active in the early 20th century and had a strong influence upon the emergence of these new private schools in securing funds, setting curricula, and teaching staff members. Out of twenty-nine private schools, twenty were located in the sacred space within Seoul (as shown in fig. 4.4), five in Pyeongyang (northern capital of Joseon), and one in Gaeseong (the capital of Goryeo Dynasty) with three in other provinces. Other schools founded by Koreans were also related to Christianity since their founders were Protestants. As mentioned briefly above, by the time that Korea was officially annexed in 1910, the total number of private schools had reached some 3,000 (Lee, 1984: 332). Their political intention seems to be apparent in the concentration of their schools between and around the palaces (as shown in fig. 4.5). Lee explains that "The private schools of that day served not only to disseminate the new learning but also are renowned as hotbeds of the national movement" (Lee, 1984: 332). The locations marked as black circles in figure 4.4 coincide approximately with the "Y area" in figure 5.1 in which politically preeminent Confucian architecture had been concentrated during the Hanyang era. Also, nine of these private schools were founded by US missionaries, such as Methodists (Northern and Southern) and Presbyterians (Northern and Southern). Considering the contending relationship that existed between the United States and Japan until the former yielded its interest in the Korean Peninsula to the latter through the Taft-Katsura Secret Agreement in 1905, the presence of American Christian missionaries and their efforts to found liberally oriented private schools must have been perceived as a threat to Japanese plans to annex the Joseon Dynasty.

The new liberal educational institutions founded by private citizens and American missionaries introduced Western democracy and liberal political ideas to young Koreans, motivating them to take political action against Japanese colonial rule. For example, in 1918, President Woodrow Wilson's *Fourteen Points* ignited the national resistance movement against Japanese colonial authority, which will be explained in more detail at the end of this chapter. As shown in figures 4.3 and 4.4, most of these new educational institutions were located in areas near Confucian shrines. Those places were associated with the political hegemony and legitimacy of the Joseon Dynasty and symbolized the center toward which the masses projected their loyalty. By situating the liberally oriented schools in these highly revered locations, these new liberal and modern educational institutions were able to legitimize themselves as the inheritors of the hegemony of the Joseon Dynasty and symbolize their political anti-colonial stance of resistance. Such placement also signified the synthesis of Confucianism and Western liberalism, and posed a serious challenge to Japan since the United States was behind these new liberally oriented private schools as well. It is not surprising that these new private schools and their students became heralds of the anti-Japan national movements, inherited legitimacy from the Hanyang era tradition, and went on to become the strongest dissenting voices in Korean society. That the locations of the old Confucian shrines and new private schools match almost exactly serves as evidence of how strategic was the use and occupation of the hegemonic sacred places of the Hanyang era by these new, liberally oriented private schools. Recognition by the masses empowered students to resist the illegal Japanese annexation of their country. At the same time, people's attachment to "sacred space" as a source of legitimate Korean state power was becoming more pronounced, as evidenced by the events related to King Kojong's funeral in 1919. Specifically, a group of independent leaders produced and signed the Korean Declaration of Independence to be proclaimed at "Pagoda Park, site of sacred shrines," where thousands of ordinary people congregated to pay their last respects to the late King and hear the declaration. Thus, students took to the forefront in demonstrating their resistance to Japanese imperial power.

Christianity and the Western political ideology of liberal democracy were two foreign influences that impacted the ideological nature of the heteronomical forces of Korea. The limited Confucian heteronomical forces were now armed with new Western political and religious ideology and joined by patriotic elites from the hegemonic and hierarchical realms of the Joseon Dynasty. The dissenting voice that had been built into the Confucian government of the Hanyang era transformed into a society of belligerent nationalism during the Japanese occupation and then re-emerged as democratic forces during the Seoul era (1960-1987).

In the Confucian culture, state power had unilaterally controlled society. A dissenting voice from society was generally controlled so that it would not grow into a real threat to the Confucian regime. During the Kyeongseong period, however, people believed in the students more than they believed in the former Confucian social elites, whom they blamed for letting the country be defeated by Japan. For the first time in Korean history, social forces checking and balancing the state power were recognized as fulfilling a legitimate role in society in their efforts to recover independence.[21] Now, two competing legitimate political powers—the former Confucian hegemonic elites and the heteronomical forces—took a united stance for the "recovery of national right." These two competing powers would ultimately return to their original positions and functions after liberation from Japanese colonial rule, but their tactical alliance now served the important purpose of resisting the atrocious colonial policies of the Japanese. Voices upheld by university students and intelligentsia acquired political legitimacy among the masses as such individuals established themselves as the ultimate spokespeople of the public. People generally respected the students' intelligence and courage to stand up against the repressive political regime. Thus, students were usually tolerated and granted much more leniency even when they misbehaved. Teachers in the high schools encouraged their students, for example, to go out into the streets and fight against the illegitimate regime. When occasionally they were caught in some misdeeds, they were treated with much more leniency than regular citizens because they represented the voice of justice in political settings. Students in 20th-century Korean society continued to receive such reverence and inherited the tradition of upholding the voices as the ultimate litmus test for the survival of a political regime. This is why the mass gave tacit approval to radical student demonstrations against the government during the Seoul era while also tolerating the despotic power of state; their sentiment toward the state covered a wide range of opinions. Even though both the legacies of Neo-Confucian political doctrine and Japanese colonial experience are far from the modern democratic ideals and creeds, a new heteronomical force emerged out of this antagonistic political history and later played a decisive role in achieving substantive democracy in modern Korea.

This Confucian tradition of recognizing students' privilege and duty to stand up against despotic or unrighteous political power experienced an important transition from Confucian to liberal political orientation mainly due to the founding of private schools by American missionaries or patriotic but liberal Confucian elites. For example, the very first modern hospital (*Kwanghyewon*) in the Great Han Empire, where students studied medicine, was established in 1885 in a village north of Hanyang, where a large amount of yangban elites lived. Later in 1899, when the school and hospital became independent from each other, the hospital was set up in the house of the former Prime Minister, Kim Hong-Jip. Similarly, Boseong Professional School, the predecessor of Korea University, was founded by one of the highest government officials, Lee Yong-Ik, in the former Russian Language School in order to take advantage of the Russian power to check Japanese authorities.[22]

American missionaries also founded many prestigious private schools, usually in prestigious locations such as former palaces or near tombs of the royal family. For example, in 1886, a missionary named Mrs. Scranton founded Ewha Hakdang (the predecessor of Ewha Womans University), the very first modern school for women, in Jeong-dong. In 1935, under Japanese colonial rule, Ewha built a new campus in Yonhee-dong, where a royal harem tomb had been located. In 1886, a missionary named H. G. Appenjeller founded Baejae Hakdang in Jeong-dong. In 1917, an American missionary, Mr. Underwood, founded Yonhee Professional School, the predecessor of Yonsei University, in Shinchon where Yonhee Palace had been located during the Joseon Dynasty. Most of these private schools were located in the western area and in the northern village, where yangban elites had lived, the best area for housing during the Hanyang period. During the Joseon Dynasty, the Confucian shrines, which were one of the most important Confucian institutions, were located in this northwestern area.

Thus situated, modern educational institutions inherited the legitimacy that had been acquired by the Confucian shrines; space was the medium for transferring political value from one institution to another. As expressed in figure 4.4, a confrontational composition between the Korean educational sphere of influence in the northwest region and the Japanese political and economic sphere of influence in the southeast region began to develop within Kyeongseong.

Even the Japanese Government-General decided to build Kyeongseong Imperial University, the predecessor of Seoul National University, where the National Confucian Academy (Seongkyunkwan) had been located. This clearly shows that even the Japanese wanted to uphold their authority by positioning their imperial university in the place where the highest national educational institution had traditionally been located.

Another institution that played an important role in the resistance movement against Japan was religion. The strength of its appeal was due in part to a psychological factor—the acute feeling of the Korean people that belief in Christianity would atone for their society's failings that had led to the loss of Korea's nationhood. On a lesser scale, there were other religious movements that also served to instill a deeper sense of nationalist consciousness in the Korean people. Cheondokyo too conducted an extensive cultural program that included the publication of the nationalist newspaper *Independent News* (*Mansebo*).

For example, one of the famous clandestine nationalist movement organizations was the New People's Association (*Sinminhoe*), organized in 1907 by An Chang-Ho around a core of Korean Christians who carried on the tradition of the Independence Club. There also was the Association of the Korean People (*Choson Kungminhoe*), another Christian group organized in 1917 under the leadership of Chang Il-Hwan (Lee, 1984: 339-340).

The nationalist movement was coordinated through various religious organizations—*Cheondokyo* (Religion of the Heavenly Way), Christian, Buddhist, and others—and the central figures were those thirty-three men who signed the Korean Declaration of Independence as representatives of the Korean people. Taking advantage of the fact that funeral rites scheduled for the former king, King Kojong, would bring throngs of people to Seoul from all over the country, they determined to act two days before this event. At the same time, students gathered in Seoul's Pagoda Park to hear the Declaration read aloud, after which they marched through the streets peacefully, shouting "Long Live Korean Independence" (Lee, 1984: 341). In modern Korea, the headquarters of all these religions are located in the so-called sacred space in Seoul. Such a tradition of religious institutions and leaders functioning as important sources of heteronomical forces and nationalism has been continuously reproduced in contemporary politics too. For example, in the major uprisings and demonstrations against military dictatorship in the 1960s to the 1980s, almost identical anti-government forces composed of university students (Confucian students), intelligentsia or *Jaeya* (Confucian literati in the local provinces, Sarim during the Joseon Dynasty), and religious leaders had decisively contributed to the overthrow of the dictatorship and the achievement of democracy. Two consecutive eras of authoritarian control expanded and consolidated the heteronomical force, which ultimately brought about democracy in a country where the seeds of democracy were not believed to have been planted.

Another element that factored in the development of the modern sphere of public deliberation was the widespread emergence of newspapers, which sprang up like mushrooms after rain. As an important institution empowering the dissenting voice, the media helped to establish the rule of heteronomy in Korean politics as an important power base. Korea's first newspaper was the thrice-monthly *Hanseong Sunbo*, published by the government's newly created Office of Culture and Information in 1883 through the efforts of Kim Ok-Kyun and other members of the Progressive Party (Lee, 1984: 329). Following soon after were the *Independence* in 1896, the *Capital Gazette* (*Hwangseong Shinmoon*) in 1898, *Korea Daily News* (*Taehan Maeil Shinbo*) in 1905 despite the tightened grip of Japanese censorship against Korean newspapers, and the *Mansebo* by Cheondogyo (aboriginal Religion of the Heavenly Way) in 1906. When Japanese censorship tightened and newspapers lost the freedom to openly criticize Japan's policies of aggression, the English journalist Ernest T. Bethell joined with Yang Ki-Tak to found the bilingual *Korea Daily News* (*Taehan Maeil Shinbo*) in 1905. Since it was controlled by an Englishman, and since Japan and England were allies, the *Korea Daily News* managed to evade Japanese censorship (Lee, 1984: 330).

Also, the publishing of Korean-owned newspapers that were written in Hanguel, such as the *Tonga Ilbo* and *Choson Ilbo,* helped to reach a larger readership and played a critical role in resisting Japanese colonial rule and dictatorship in modern Korea. Thus, the organs of the Korean press made a major contribution toward raising the level of the Korean people's political consciousness. These two newspaper companies also occupied one of the ideal spots within Kyeongseong, located in Taepyung-ro near the Six Ministries Street, which was the area of Japanese influence near the Confucian sacred zone. This area was a new center of economic power of the Japanese version of capitalism, which naturally formed a line of confrontation between this new economic center and old politically sacred Confucian dominance. This new economic center was located directly below the East-West axis, showing a clear contrast between traditional Joseon and new Japanese capitalism.

The March First Independence and the Role of Students in Korea's Heteronomical Force

Although the anti-imperial movement was first initiated by the Independence Club, many similar organizations followed in its path of national resistance for the recovery of independence. Such movements culminated in the March First Independence Movement on March 1, 1919, when the Korean people took to nationwide demonstrations in the streets. The most salient feature of the Korean nationalist movement during the Kyeongseong era was the outbreak of "student-led demonstrations" focusing specifically on demands for independence (Lee, 1984: 363), which is this chapter's main argument—i.e., that civil society in Korean political history originated from the Seongkyunkwan and the Confucian literati of the Sarim society in the Joseon Dynasty, and that the tradition of their loyal opposition continued through the student-led movement of resistance against Japanese colonial rule in the Kyeongseong era and later against the military dictatorship of state capitalist development in the Seoul era. The Joseon tradition of placing the highest emphasis on Confucian education for the youth was carried over to the period of Japanese imperial rule during which liberally oriented private schools blossomed in the sacred space of the Joseon Dynasty, which served as a seedbed in the national resistance movement for the recovery of independence. As the limited and co-opted heteronomical forces of the Joseon Dynasty transformed into an expanded heteronomical force due to the addition of hegemonic forces in the colonial period, students played a central role in the resistance, as demonstrated by the March First National Independence Movement in 1919, the June 10 Independence Demonstration in 1926, and the Kwangjoo Student Movement in November 1929. The student initiatives against the unjust power of Japanese imperial rule (1910-1392) and the military dictatorship (1961-1987) have always been central in major political upheavals since the Joseon Dynasty and served as a barometer of legitimacy for each of these political regimes. The general populace closely monitored the intensiveness of students' demonstrations against these regimes, and when the masses joined them at the vanguard of Korea's modern political history, the regimes came toppling down. Accordingly, the emerging power of young voters in the major elections of the 21st century is nothing new considering the historical background of how student demonstrations and their strong influence upon the Korean people have become a kind of tradition in Korea's political culture.

The two major student-led demonstrations against Japan's imperial rule occurred in the context of the last two kings' funerals in 1919 and 1926, respectively. Woodrow Wilson's doctrine of the self-determination of nations, articulated in his *Fourteen Points* in 1918, ignited a national movement in Korea against Japan. Korean leaders in exile formed two organizations: the New Korea Youth Association (*Shinhan Cheongnyundang*), which was organized in January 1919 by Korean patriots in Shanghai for diplomatic efforts to gain international recognition of Korean independence, and the Korean Young Independence Corps (*Joseon Chyungnyun Tokripdan*), organized in January 1919 by Korean students in Tokyo. The latter overtly demanded independence with a series of resolutions. Lee (1984: 341) indicates that "This event gave immense encouragement to those in Korea who had been seeking means to bring the independence movement into the open, and within a month nationwide demonstrations had erupted," which serves as evidence of this chapter's main argument. Thirty-three representatives of religions, including Cheondogyo (Religion of the Heavenly Way), Christianity, and Buddhism, and other intelligentsia initiated a historical resistance movement against Japan, which officially served as a transformation of heteronomical force from limited built-in dissenting voices to nationwide opposition forces against Japanese colonial government and then later played a pivotal role in overthrowing existing power in the Seoul era as well. These were the representatives who had formerly written a Declaration of Independence, and on March 1, they proclaimed that Korea had now become an independent nation.

As soon as they finished proclaiming the Declaration of Independence at the Taehwagwan, the thirty-three signers informed the Japanese authorities of their action—in a manner reminiscent of the Seongkyunkwan students' complaints at the King's chamber door in the Joseon Dynasty—and were immediately arrested. It was the signers' plan for the independence movement they had launched to be carried forward first of all by the students and then spread among the masses. Not only students but shopkeepers, farmers, laborers, and other citizens joined in, while Koreans employed by the Government-General also found ways of showing their sympathy (Lee, 1984: 342).

The national eruption of street demonstrations, in fact, was led by students who had gathered around the thirty-three representatives and marched through streets in peaceful procession. This is how the greatest mass movement in Korean history began and how university students later decisively contributed to democratization in 1987 through a series of aggressive demonstrations

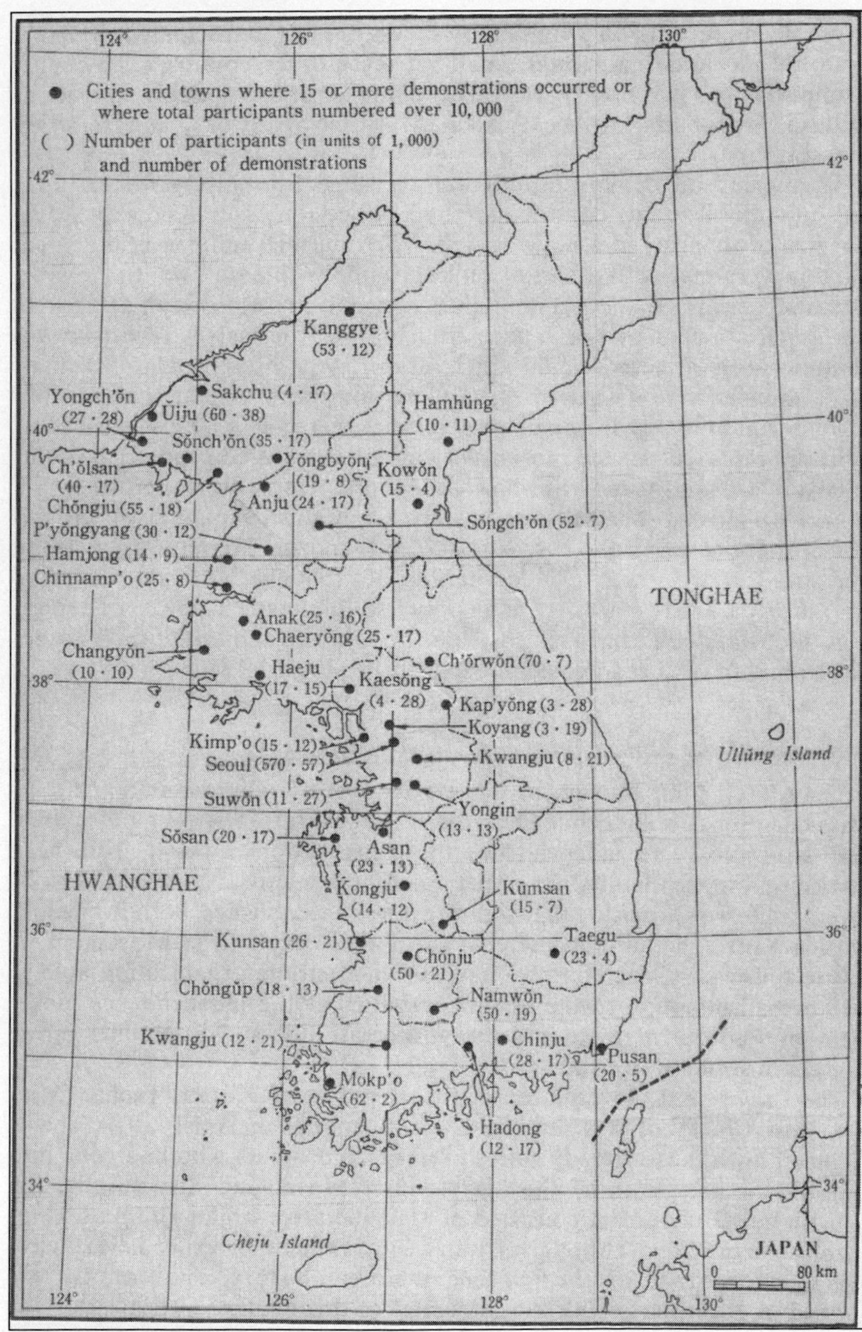

Map 4.1 The March First Movement (Lee, 1984: 343)

against the military regime. Their stance against the Chun Do-hwan regime attracted support from the general populace and sympathy in June 10 1987, which played a critical role in ending the dictatorship, as will be examined in the next chapter.

Map 4.1 (Lee, 1984: 343) clearly illustrates the scope of these nationwide demonstrations.

The enormity of the movement, which is evident in this map, can also be conveyed through statistical figures. More than two million Koreans directly participated in more than 1,500 separate gatherings, and such demonstrations quickly spread to Manchuria, the Russian Maritime Territory, and other areas overseas (Lee, 1984: 344). The Government-General of Japanese colonial authority officially reported a total of 46,948 arrests with 7,509 killed, 15,961 injured, and as many as 715 houses destroyed or burnt (Lee, 1984: 344). The liberally oriented educational institutions that started to be established in the late 1880s produced much of the student demonstrators, as discussed in the previous section. The direct outcome of this movement was the foundation of the Provisional Government of the Republic of Korea (*Daehan Minkook Imshi Jeongboo*) in April 1919 in Shanghai. Even though it was a government in exile, it played a central role in bolstering the national resistance against Japan, and shaped Korea's first government in 1948. It had both administrative and deliberative organs. The fact that it was created not to restore the old monarchy but to create a republic was a revolutionary change in Korean political history and a reflection of the demands made by the Korean people in the March First National Independence Movement.

This chapter has argued that the Confucian origin of the limited heteronomical forces (i.e., Seongkyunkwan Confucian students and the Neo-Confucian literati groups and central elites of the Joseon Dynasty) was strengthened quantitatively and qualitatively by the addition of the other two types of rule. Facing a common enemy and the demise of national independence, the former elites and leaders from the realms of hegemony and hierarchy in the Confucian Joseon Dynasty chose to join the limited and co-opted dissenting voices of the National Confucian Academy students and the Sarim, thereby magnifying the voice of nationalism and belligerent dissent. The hegemonic and hierarchical presence of the central state could have been a major stumbling block if there had been no common enemy, such as Japanese colonial rule, as Lipset pointed out: "The greater the importance of the central state as a source of prestige and advantage, the less likely it is that those in power—or the forces of opposition—will accept rules of the game that institutionalize party conflict and could result in the turnover of those in office" (1994: 4). The existence of a common enemy, however, made the above observation inapplicable in the Korean case;

these strong heteronomical forces continued to challenge the military dictatorship during the period from 1961 to 1987. While most citizens were tacit about the military dictatorship—not because they agreed with political leadership but due to the effectiveness of its economic modernization policy—consistent student demonstrations against the Park Chung-hee regime (1961-1979) and his successor General Chun (1980-1987) finally toppled the military dictatorship in 1987 when this tacit majority joined the student initiatives.

A class-based analysis of the role of the middle class and labor unions (see, e.g., Koo, 1991; Jones, 1998; Han, 1995) will be necessary to determine how the outcome of economic development and consequential changes in the class structure affected the course of democratization in Korea. Some of these approaches will be discussed in the following chapter; however, this book's main goal is to trace the three different types of rule through the three main eras in order to explain how the prototypes of state-society relations, state centrality, and heteronomical forces were established in the Hanyang era, how these prototypes were transformed through the Kyeongseong era, and how all of these changes contributed to the developmental state and simultaneous phenomena of unprecedentedly fast economic development and democratization in modern Korea. Thus, although the socioeconomic class approach merits attention in further research, it lies beyond the scope of this book.

Figure 4.5 delineates the changes that Japan's colonial rule brought to the prototype of the three different rules formulated during the Hanyang era. First, the Confucian state hegemony was supplanted by Japanese military imperial rule; however, Japan was trying to take full advantage of the loyalty projected by the masses by erecting political and economic symbols and buildings of their own in the sacred space that had been established by the Joseon Dynasty and by damaging the Confucian symbols of Joseon power. In some sense, Japan's colonial rule, with its strong state power apparatus and hierarchically organized and modernized bureaucracy, strengthened the centrality of state power in Korean political culture. Also, Japan introduced capitalism, reversing Joseon's ideology of denigrating commercial and mercantile activities, and as a result, industrial power became a new power symbol to Koreans. The most salient feature that the Kyeongseong era brought about was the occurrence of structural changes to the original, limited heteronomical forces. A number of liberal political organizations, such as the Independence Club and others that were created at the end of the 19th and the start of the 20th century, combined with newly founded private schools during Japanese protectorate and colonial control to lead the nationwide anti-Japanese demonstrations on March 1, 1919, and two other major political upheavals against Japan in 1926 and 1929. Most importantly, the tradition of student demonstrations grew stronger in the Japanese colonial period and later blossomed into the most belligerent element of the opposition against the military dictatorship during the modern era of Seoul. Thus, the loyal opposition and semi-opposition transformed into a belligerent nationalism and ultimately into a strong civil society. This is how this book explains Korea's simultaneous phenomena of rapid economic development, led mostly by strong state legitimacy to intervene in the economy, and its process of democratization that lasted from 1961 to 1987.

NOTES

1. This problem was pointed out by Dr. Moon Chung-in in a comment made during the final stages of this book's completion, and it represents an issue essential to perfecting this book's main argument; however, this book's main thesis is to suggest that such spatial arrangements in the capital city's layout and architectural monumentality serve as evidence of established state-society relations, not as a causal explanation of which spatial arrangements caused such power configurations to develop between state and society, and between state and economy. I would like to thank Dr. Moon for prompting this clarification.
2. See Figure 4.2.
3. Japan established a protectorate over Korea after it won recognition from Russia, England, and the United States of its paramount interests in the Korean Peninsula through a front organization, *Iljinhoe*, in 1905. See Lee (1984: 309-310).
4. On the Joseon Dynasty's *axis mundi*, see figure 3.7. As an aerial view, image 4.2 clearly shows that the new Government-General building was built to block the view of the main Palace office building.
5. See Lee, Sang-Hae (1991), p. 55.
6. Koreans were required to worship at Japanese Shinto shrines, and there were some Christians, such as Chu Ki-cheol, who refused and consequently lost their lives.
7. Professor Seo in Seokyung University in Korea reported 154 cases in which the Japanese intentionally destroyed the natural environment to diminish the energy and power that originated from the soil and was believed to protect the Joseon Dynasty. See Cheong (1994), pp. 245-247.
8. See Park, In-Seok and Ham, In-Seon (1991).
9. Cheong (1994), p. 58. See also Lee, (1984), p. 346.
10. See Hur (1994), pp. 100, 111, 124.
11. On the Japanese buildings on the Six Ministries Street, see Lee, Kang-Geun (1991a), pp. 273-275.
12. See Lee, (1984), pp. 346-347. In May 1910, Japan appointed General Terauchi Masatake as the new Resident-General, and explicitly entrusted to him the mission of effecting the annexation. While still in Tokyo, before taking up his new post, he had secured an agreement that yielded police power in Korea to Japan, and he had

aggrandized the Japanese gendarmerie forces by 2,000 men and given them charge of police functions (Lee, 1984: 313). In 1911, some 7,749 military police, or gendarmes, and 6,222 regular police were deployed throughout the country. In 1912, over 50,000—and in 1918 the incredible number of more than 140,000—Koreans were placed under arrest (Lee, 1984: 314). This demonstrates how the Confucian principle and Korean tradition of civilian superiority over the military was reversed.

13. The province that has embraced the capital city from the Joseon Dynasty to the present.

14. In the 1930s, important buildings on this new axis included the Headquarters of Government-General, Kyeongseong Boocheong (City Hall), Kyeongseong-bu Minkwan (City Assembly), the Supreme Court, Choson Bank (State Bank), Siksan Bank (Shokusan Ginko in Japanese), Kyeongseong Post Office, the Oriental Development Company, Kyeongseong Daily News, Kyeongseong Chamber of Commerce, Kyeongseong Electric Co., the Government-General Center for Commerce and Industry, and Choson Hotel. See Sohn (1991), p. 35.

15. For data on Japanese investment in Korea, this book cites Lee's *A New History of Korea* (1984) exclusively based on the international recognition of its reliability as the definitive, authoritative Korean history textbook. There is one more Korean history textbook that is widely read, *Korea: Old and New: A History*, published in 1990 by the Korea Institute and Harvard University. A short remark in the foreword of this book affirms the academic reliability of Lee's data. In the publication of the latter, it was "decided that it should simply condense the account in Professor Lee's time-tested book."

16. For the historical facts on this issue, Refer to Lee (1984), p. 350.

17. This literally means a "financial clique." It is a Japanese word designating a group of conglomerations, which was replaced by the *keiretsu* in the 20th century.

18. A *cheongbo* is a unit of land. One cheongbo is the equivalent if 2.45 acres.

19. It was the doctrine of the self-determination of nations that provided the impetus to transform the Korean nationalist movement. This doctrine was put forward by the American President Woodrow Wilson as an integral part of the post-WWI peace settlement. See Lee (1984), p. 340.

20. See Lee, Young-Han, 1992, p. 90.

21. The Provisional Government of the Republic of Korea (*Taehan Minkook Imsi Jeongbu*) that was established in Shanghai in April 1919 serves as a good example of how the rule of heteronomy was accepted in the Korean political system and culture at that time. The fact that the Provisional Government was created not as a restoration of the old monarchy but as a republic by the heteronomical social forces due to "Resistance Nationalism" reflects the power that the Korean people had manifested in the March First Movement (Lee, 1984: 344-345).

22. See Lee, Young-Han (1992), ibid., p. 100.

Chapter Five

The Seoul Era: The Emergence of the Developmental State and Democracy

LEGACIES OF THE HANYANG AND KYEONGSEONG ERAS

This chapter aims to provide a comprehensive explanation of how Korea simultaneously achieved rapid economic development and democratization during the period of 1962 to 1987, two phenomena customarily taken up as separate issues with no integrated framework to explain their concurrent development. While chapter 3 explored the issues of integral and hegemonic state power as well as Confucian state-society relations in the Hanyang era, chapter 4 examined how such prototypes of state-society relations, as well as the nature of Confucian integral state and the heteronomical forces, were impacted through interaction with imperial Japan and its colonial policies. Against that background, this chapter seeks to examine significant changes that were added to the prototype of the developmental regime that Korea inherited from both the Hanyang and Kyeongseong eras and explain how these two simultaneous phenomena were achieved. This understanding will be accomplished by looking into four major forces—military, bureaucracy, enterprises, and students—and assessing their influences on the city layout of Seoul. This is one way of explaining the developmental and democratization processes simultaneously from the indigenous perspective without inadvertently reifying the despotic rule of the military regime or exclusively focusing on an economically efficient bureaucracy and concentrated foreign aid mostly from the United States in the geopolitical context of the Cold War. This effort may also provide an alternative to grand theories such as modernization and dependency theory. Furthermore, if successful, it will address the question raised at the very beginning of this book—namely, why did these phenomena occur simultaneously in Korea?

As this chapter begins, let us focus on the elements that are essential to the success of a developmental state: integral power based on the consent of the masses and a developmental structure (i.e., a stable, centralized government, a cohesive bureaucracy, and effective coercive institutions) and the right to intervene in the economy. Previous chapters explained how the state's legitimacy was established and embedded in the minds of the masses and the state-society relations over more than a thousand years of Korean political culture with Confucianism and geomancy occupying a central location. In the modern era of Seoul, President Park Chung-hee engaged in a major ideological attack against the ancient regime, Confucian traditions, and Japanese colonial control, saying "First, we must reflect upon the evil legacies of our past history, slough off the factional contentiousness inherited from the [Joseon] Dynasty, and slavish mentality resulting from the Japanese colonial rule, and firmly establish a sound National Ethics. Without a human revolution, social reconstruction is impossible" (Park, 1962: 4). His sharp criticism also targeted Japanese colonial legacies, saying "Japanese colonial rule over Korea was cruel and inhuman oppression by military and civilian policemen with the brutal temper of merciless samurais," (Park, 1962: 109) and "Japanese militaristic rule further blocked the formation of Korean national capital and stunted the economic growth of farmers" (Park, 1962: 110). His critiques of the unfortunate past, however, were mostly empty rhetoric and justifications of his hard drive for modernization, although they were also genuine in some sense; what he utilized for his economic development plan was what he inherited from the Hanyang and Kyeongseong eras.

Ultimately, from these two eras, the Park regime inherited several legacies: (1) state centrality (from both), (2) political intervention in the economy (from both), (3) centralized and modernized bureaucratic control and emphasis on industry over agriculture (from Kyeongseong), and (4) heteronomical forces of militant opposition (initiated in Hanyang and expanded through Kyeongseong) as was expounded at length in chapters 3 and 4. These features can be identified in the continuities and changes of the city layout and design, the locations of major institutions within the city layout, and the architectural monumentality. Ultimately, the developmental state played a strategic role in taming domestic and international market forces and harnessing them to a national economic interest, and belligerent democratic forces arose to finally overthrow military rule at the end of a successful developmental period in 1987.

Now, we are ready to examine the process of democratization in greater depth, centering on the role of university students as a major source of heteronomical force in Korea, as explained in chapters 3 and 4; however, before delving into this matter, several brief points must be made. First of all, referring to Korea's achievement of democratization in 1987 does not mean that a democracy, in the complete sense of that term, was fully achieved at that time. What "democratization" does mean in this book is that a persistent movement led by university students toppled the military regime and critically contributed to the 1993 establishment of the first civilian regime in Korea's history. In this sense, with the June 10 Resistance of 1987, it is fair to say, substantial democratization was achieved.

Second, such democratization should generally be understood as a political movement, not as one based on class struggle. Despite a few scholarly attempts, neither labor unions nor other interest groups nor the middle class have been shown to have played a critical role in Korea's democratization. The university students were central in most of the major sociopolitical movements in Korea, and it was not until the June 10 Resistance of 1987 that the student-led street demonstrations were finally joined by the middle class to draw the final line against the military dictatorship. Previously, the middle class, despite their enhanced economic status, had comprised the majority that tacitly supported the military regime for the sake of its successful economic development policy and leadership. Labor unions were harshly suppressed by the military regime, in the context of the national confrontation against the North's communist regime, and were thus unable to exert their maximum influence until the June 10 Resistance, even though labor unions were indeed present during the rapid industrialization.

Third, it is generally agreed upon in the literature that this central role of the university students in Korea's major political transformations stemmed from that of the National Confucian Academy's various demonstrations, as explained in chapter 3, during the Joseon Dynasty and continued through the Kyeongseong era in the form of national resistance against of Japanese colonial control (Buzo, 1984; Han, 2010; Kihl, 1994; Koo, 1991; Lee, 1984; Pak, 1980; Yang & Henderson, 1958). Many scholars point out that the tacit majority was neither ready nor willing to challenge or fight the capitalist state dictatorship until the student-led demonstrations came to the fore in 1987 and galvanized their involvement (Pak, 1980; Koo, 1991; Woo-Cumings, 1991). President Park was clearly aware of the majority's tacit agreement with his economic drive for rapid modernization when he said, "Many factors contributed to the successful achievement in foreign trade, but first of all the deep understanding and cooperative efforts of the people with the government are highly appreciated. It teaches us the good lesson that lamenting over poor natural resources and technical backwardness will be of no help in solving our problems" (Ministry of Public Information, 1966: 169).

What made the role of the students more powerful was the people's acknowledgement of their function as bearers of moral witness regarding the arbitrariness of power elites and the injustice of society, which could be said to have originated from the Confucian Hanyang era (Yang & Henderson, 1958; Lee, 1984). Further studies on the role of classes may reveal the socio-economic basis for the role played by the middle and working classes in the democratization in Korea; currently, though, there are no widely accepted scholarly works that take such a class approach on the case of Korea. After the major achievement of the June 29 Declaration in 1987, many sectors of society became much more actively involved in political discourse, including the labor unions.

This case study of Seoul will look closely at the locations of the major economic and political institutions that played a vital role in the simultaneous developmental and democratization processes of modern Korea as evidence of continuities and changes made through modernization and shaped by both the Hanyang and Kyeongseong eras. In addition, this case study will illustrate how various social and political forces, grounded in the rules inherited from the Hanyang and Kyeongseong periods, operated toward the simultaneous achievement of economic and political development. Also, the heteronomical forces, which constantly challenged the hegemonic and hierarchical state during the developmental period (1960s-1980s) and finally toppled the military dictatorship in 1987, will be analyzed based on changes in power configurations among these three forces as reflected in the layout of the capital city, Seoul.

While the Hanyang era bequeathed to Seoul the principles of political superiority over the economy and the legitimacy of government to intervene in economic affairs, it was primarily the Kyeongseong era that strengthened the Korean people's belief in strong state tradition by touching off Resistance Nationalism. As explained in the previous chapter, however, the Kyeongseong period also reversed several significant legacies of Hanyang: (1) the Confucian economic conception that esteemed agriculture over commerce and industry; (2) the unilateral government control of, and superiority over, economic sectors; (3) the strict class system of the Joseon Dynasty; and (4) the traditional Confucian principle of civil superiority over the military. The Seoul period inherited the political products that had been developed through the operation of the types of rule on the state and on state-society relations over time.

The Seoul era was influenced by these legacies of the Hanyang and Kyeongseong eras. In the geographical configuration of Seoul, two dominant legacies from the Hanyang and Kyeongseong eras are still clearly visible: (1) politically important institutions still occupy the "Core of Sacredness" zone (Z in fig. 5.1), which is primarily the result of Hanyang's geographical arrangement; and (2) major economic institutions are concentrated in the "Lower Triangle Containing Comparatively Profane Economic

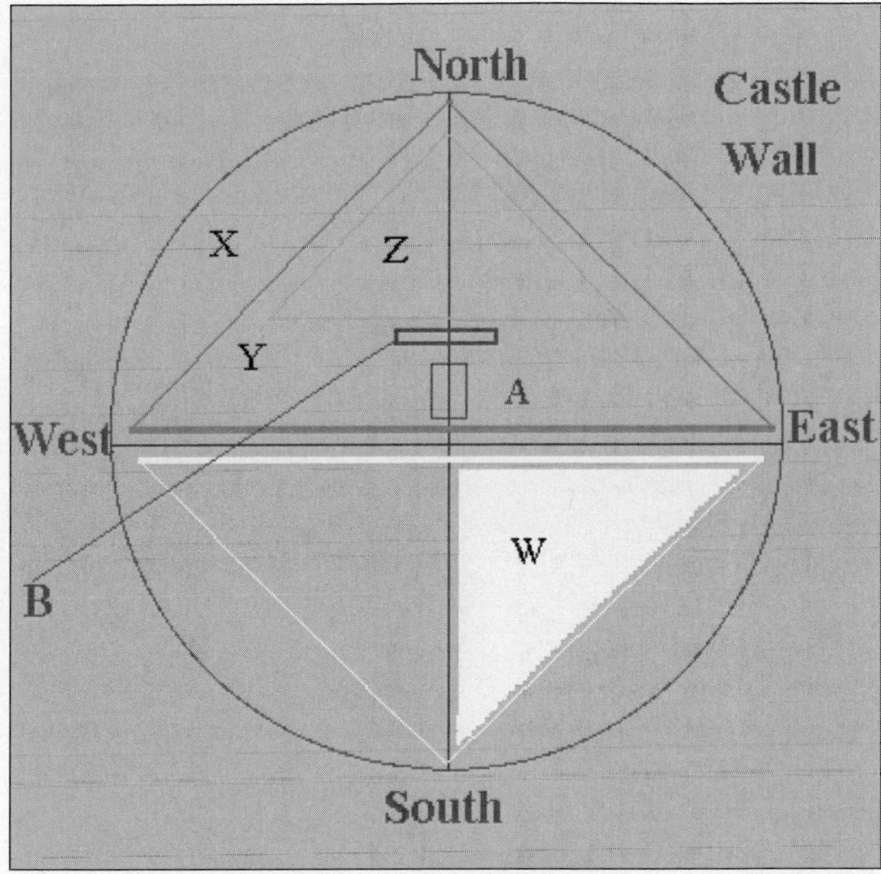

Figure 5.1 Representation of the Degrees of Sacredness within Hanyang Castle. Y: Upper triangle containing politically preeminent sacred space, Z: Core of sacredness, the royal palace itself, W: Lower triangle containing comparatively profane economic sector, A: The Six Ministries Street, B: Youngje Bridge, a symbolic line distinguishing the core of sacredness Z from Y. Created by author; Han, Jongwoo.

Sector" (W in fig. 5.1), which originated partly from Hanyang but mainly from Kyeongseong. To this day, the basic city layout places political institutions along the *axis mundi* and economic institutions in the lower profane zone. What happened during the Kyeongseong era was that Zone W of the capitalist center greatly expanded as a result of global interactions with the capitalist world economy through Japan. As we will soon see, the most prestigious political institutions during the Seoul era still concentrated in the sacred Zone X, restoring to a certain extent the contrast between political sacred space and that which is capitalist and profane.

Building upon the historical legacies of the geographical configurations of the previous two periods, the city layout and architectural monumentality in the Seoul era reflects the continuity of the principles of political hegemony over economy and the development of economic sectors. As a result of the city's legibility, geographical and architectural configurations represent changes and continuities in the political and economic power relations of the two eras. The Park regime formulated a new hegemonic rule of "supreme order of economic development," which became manifest in the physical forms of Seoul. Further, as inheritors of the legacies of the previous two eras, dissenting social forces also influenced the process of economic development in the modern city. Indeed, the relationship between hegemonic and heteronomical forces is the key to understanding the process of simultaneous economic and political developments, rather than focusing only on the powerful military regime and its efficient and forceful bureaucracy in the 1960s and '70s. An examination of the early Park era in particular, starting from his military coup in 1961 and ending in the mid-1980s, reveals the dynamic interaction of competing rules through the operation of social forces.

UNDERPINNINGS OF THE PARK REGIME

President Park was highly critical of Korea's past. For this reason, a brief overview of Korea's historical eras will provide a sense of that which Park's rhetoric criticized so strongly. The establishment of the unified political force of the Goryeo Dynasty (936-1392) had ended the tripartite division of the Korean Peninsula. Before that time, the Korean Peninsula was ruled by the Three Kingdoms—Goguryeo (37 BC-AD 660), Baekje (18 BC-AD 660), and Shilla (57 BC-AD 935)—however, the real centralization of political power as a nation was not achieved until the reign of the Joseon Dynasty (1392-1910), which was based on the foreign ideology of Confucianism. The subsequent thirty-five-year colonial control by Japanese militarism was followed by three years of US military government control (1945-1948) and then the Korean War (1950-1953).

By the end of World War II, the Korean people were keenly aware of being ravaged and exploited by outside powers (Han & Ling, 1998: 64-65). Not only had they suffered Japanese colonization for almost half a century (1910-1945), but now they were having to contend with a postwar American paternalism that exacerbated the devastation left by civil war (1950-1953) (Cumings, 1981). Hence, a dominant image of the Korean man in postwar Korean literature was that of the "walking wounded." His body and soul "deprive[d], distort[ed], destroy[ed], and . . . pulverize[d]" by the war, the walking wounded passed through life as a victim of history (Kim, 1978: 13).

With his military coup of 1961, Park Chung-hee sought to counter this national anomie by appropriating Western masculinist capitalism. Furthermore, he derided Korea's emasculated status by citing an old Korean folksong that described a cuckolded husband who, upon finding his wife with another man, simply moaned, "What am I to do? What am I to do?" If this man were a Westerner, Park retorted, he would shoot them with a pistol. Having been a graduate of Japanese Army Academy and an officer of the Japanese military in Manchuria, President Park was well aware of how the Japanese government had successfully broken away from the Japanese Ancient Regime of the feudal system and modernized the country by learning from Western developed capitalism during the Meiji Reformation around 1868. While admiring Japan's conversion into a Westernized masculine state and society, President Park aspired to follow Japan's path of success by attributing the failure of the Korean state to the ancient Confucian regime. "Alas," Park sighed, "how good and gentle [i.e., passive] are our forefathers!" (Park, 1969: 95). Park's avenging pistol came in the form of hypermasculinized economic development. In other words, he appropriated the Japanese focus on development much in the same way that the Japanese appropriated the legitimizing trappings of Joseon geomantic principles but with a twist. He rallied society to vindicate Korea's subjugation within a Hobbesian world of economic competition: "Let's Fight and Construct!" (*saumyeo geonseolhaja*), "Export Is the Only Way to Survive" (*soochoolmani salgilida*), "Exports as Total War" (*soochool chongryeokjeon*), and "Trade as War!" (*mooyeokjeonjaeng*). In a similar vein, the Park regime referred to workers as industrial or export "soldiers" (*saneob* or *suchul jeonsa*).

First, though, he asked, "How can we export and construct without political stability?" (Park, 1969: 268). Toward this end, he hailed the "manliness" of his regime: it was masculine, purposeful, and the savior of the people. Park constantly emphasized "the strength of the state" (*kukryeok*) and its need to "regenerate the nation" (*minjok jungheung*). In contrast, all previous regimes were considered to be ineffective and shameful. Note, for example, this untitled poem by Park (1969 [2]: 326) written in the 1960s:

> Work hard and sweat!
> The whirring of the machines reverberates like music.
> Young girl
> in a second-class carriage
> reading French poems,
> to me, your

tender hands
are undesirable.
We have to work.
Beautiful hands, through you
we have become poor and exploited.
Although the young girl's beautiful hands
aren't ugly,
beautiful hands are our enemy.[1]

Park's exhortation to "work hard and sweat" contrasts with his veiled reference to previous leaders as being like a "young girl" with "tender [i.e., spoiled] hands." This includes the king and aristocracy of the Joseon Dynasty (1392-1910) as well as the leaders of the Syngman Rhee regime (First Republic, 1948-60) and the short-lived Chang Myon (Second Republic, 1960-61) government. The former Park blamed for Japan's colonization of Korea and the latter two for the country's chronic poverty and destruction after World War II. Allusions to a young girl "reading French poems" conveys Park's disdain for these former leaders whom he accused of being more interested in a decadent, foreign-worshipping lifestyle than in relieving the people's hardships. Not only do these spoiled hands impoverish the nation, this poem suggests, but they also exploit the Korean people. In stating that "tender hands / are undesirable," the poem implicitly justifies Park's purge of all former officials.

As elaborated above, President Park's speech in 1962 aptly describes the situation of Korea at the time: "In the dawn of our modern history, when modernization and the advance of the Western European great powers in the Orient began, Korea, known as the 'Hermit Kingdom' and the 'Land of the Morning Calm,' disappeared from the world into its dark history of subjugation" (Park, 1962: 107). In this view, the history of premodern Korea represented the dark days of the agriculture-oriented economy of poverty and the occupancy of Japanese militarism.

In 1945, when Korea was liberated from Japanese colonial rule at the end of World War II, political activities that had been suppressed now came to the fore and Koreans who had lost their country for thirty-six years suddenly found themselves united by the goal of purging Japanese colonial remnants and recovering their statehood. Koreans from all different levels of social status passionately participated in the first modern election in 1948; in fact, the voter turnout in the General Election, the first-ever modern vote, was 95.5 percent. From the First Republic to the Second (1948-1960), the average turnout in five National Assembly elections was 90.7 percent.[2] Clearly, the heteronomical social forces that had been massively galvanized by the atrocity of Japanese colonial rule were now transformed into a power base for nation building.

As an external force, a Western political and economic system was introduced into traditional Korean society through the stationing of an American Military Government from 1945 to 1948 when Park successfully seized political power through a military coup in 1961. In particular, the new political system of democracy—based on the three separate powers of administration, legislation, and judiciary—was adopted. Economically, Korea was now incorporated into the world capitalist system. Koreans witnessed extensive changes in the fundamental framework of their political and economic systems, and the new name "Seoul"[3] was given to the capital city.

Historically, the Park regime was in a politically vulnerable position due to the illegitimacy of its seizure of power through military coup. At the heart of this threat was the fact that the Park regime now had to deal with the massive heteronomical forces that had accumulated during the Kyeongseong era. Among them, university students in modern Korean society were the legitimate and most aggressive heirs of the heteronomical forces. The resistance movement against colonial Japan was, in fact, building the nation as a modern political society after their liberation from Japan. Indeed, the heteronomical force played the most central role in this process; however, the civil dictatorship of President Rhee (1948-1960) compelled the nation-building forces to revert to their original mission, i.e., that of the opposition forces.

The April 19 Revolution of 1960 served as a watershed in the revival of the tradition of student demonstrations, and the Park regime then had to face these aggressive dissenting voices and forces of opposition when it seized power from the Second Republic in 1961. The most imminent task for Park's regime was to find a way to overcome its political illegitimacy. Economic modernization, the catchphrase of the military coup, became the best way to pacify the dissenting voices and fortify its political legitimacy by embracing the less demanding majority. Park's idea was most clearly expressed in his first major speech on the status of the Korean economy on January 5, 1962, when he pledged to "carry out our economic policy on a step-by-step basis toward industrialization. His pledge was a direct expression of our effort to depart from physiocracy, namely, from the belief 'that farming is the foundation of national wealth,' which we have held for a long time" (Lee, 1978: 452-453).

To achieve this goal, the Park regime desperately needed foreign assistance, especially Japanese financial aid. Thus, in 1965, the Korean and Japanese governments signed a normalization treaty. Interestingly, the United States had been trying to mediate between the Korean and Japanese governments since 1951 to help them achieve such normalization (Kim, 1988: 139); however, President Rhee had lacked a strong motive to normalize relations with Japan due to the Korean people's extremely high animosity toward their former colonizers. President Rhee did not want to risk re-opening relations with Japan at the expense of his political reputation. Rather, he clung to strong anti-Japanese policies in response to national sentiment.[4] As could have been predicted, during the Park regime, students railed against the government's efforts to normalize relations with the Japanese. In 1964, in "Conducting a Funeral for National Democracy," the United Front of Students deplored the talks with Japan as humiliating to the nation (*Choson Daily News*, 1985: 108).

The dilemma facing Park's regime was "whether to carry on its [Korea's] fruitless and often wasteful confrontation [with Japan] or, in recognition of the new balance of power in Asia, take advantage of its [Korea's] former foe to seek its own economic takeoff" (Shim, 1985: 26). In other words, to Park, obtaining Japanese economic aid was essential in order to develop the economy and thereby maintain Korea's political power and secure international recognition for his regime. In his speech, Park explained "Unfortunately, we are presently confronted with vital tasks to compete with other advanced countries, in exploring new export markets for increased export potential, and maintaining international confidence and reputation" (Ministry of Public Information, 1966: 140). Thus, despite severe anti-government demonstrations, the Park regime was able to obtain financial aid as a form of reparation for colonial rule and attract Japanese capital investment. As Shim (1985: 26) notes, "funds from this source laid the skeletal structure for South Korea's subsequent industrialization." At the same time, Park's success in normalizing Korea's relationship with Japan and securing funds for modernization ignited massive anti-Japan and anti-Park regime demonstrations that created a confrontational relationship between the military dictatorship and its opposition until the end of his regime in 1979. The legacy of Korea's heteronomical forces of national resistance were completely revived and transformed into modern democratic forces through this occasion.

Interestingly, there was another reason that the Park regime normalized relations with Japan. Korea's basic industrial structure had been framed by the Japanese colonial Government-General and Japanese entrepreneurs during their thirty-five-year rule. For the sake of further economic development, it was essential to have cooperative relations with Japan as the economic structure of these two countries was highly compatible. Such was the legacy left by Kyeongseong.[5] Even the American Military Government reassigned many important missions to those who had been collaborators with colonial Japanese authority.[6] Those who had run businesses or companies during the Kyeongseong era were able to initiate economic activities in Korea after the National Liberation. Park's regime recognized that Korea had to take advantage of what Korea had gained from Japanese rule in terms of its economic system. Therefore, his regime's economic policy was nothing but pragmatic toward Japan, a bitter colonial foe but a fateful neighbor with growing economic power in the region.

In his book, President Park (1969[2]: 29) says that "in life, the economy precedes politics or culture," and he argues that "the fundamental role of the state is to guarantee people's life legally, politically, and economically. In a developing country like Korea, priorities should be on economic guarantees rather than political or cultural ones" (1969[1]: 277). Such emphasis on economic development stems partly from Park's judgment, which attributes the chronic poverty and national hardship to an unproductive, abnormally developed political structure. He personally saw the post-liberation period (from National Liberation from Japan to his rise to power in 1961) as a continuity of such a wastefully oriented political structure as that of the Joseon Dynasty (Park, 1969[1]: 850).

The Park regime's modernization policy divided the heteronomical forces that had formed during Japanese colonial rule into a tacit majority and radical dissident groups. The majority of people had experienced repressive states and economic hardship during both the Hanyang and Kyeongseong eras; however, in the choice between political dictatorship and poverty, economic survival took precedence over political freedom for the tacit majority. In other words, the majority was willing to tolerate political dictatorship as long as their quality of life was improved.

Statistics on the increase in income seem to show that most Koreans had good reason to tolerate the authoritarian government. First of all, Korea experienced a rapid increase of income unrivaled by other countries. Amsden (1989: 197) finds that "While it took English workers seventy years to raise their real earnings by roughly 150%, Korean manufacturing workers achieved a comparable gain in about 20 years from 1955 to 1976." Some may attribute the perception of rapidity to the fact that wages in Korea rose from a very low base; however, because wages rose from such a low level, the relative satisfaction of the beneficiary was that much stronger. In terms of income equality, too, there seems to be good reason for the majority of Koreans to tacitly assent to the severe oppression of the dissent movement. By comparison with Brazil, the wage gap between managers and production workers in Korea is relatively narrow.[7] By the 1980s, in Brazil, the pay of a general manager in the manufacturing industry had reached an amount 162 times more than that of an unskilled laborer (Amsden, 1989: 231).

This context provided a good reason to oppress radical dissident groups, i.e., legitimate oppression for an economic policy on behalf of the majority. This is the legacy that the Hanyang period of Confucian hegemony left to modern Korea. The Park regime was able to apply political leverage between the two different heteronomical forces: the radical student activists and the tacit majority. The Park regime's pragmatic policy for economic development, based on the legacies of the Kyeongseong period, fit well with the people's submissiveness to authoritarian political structure and with the ideological roots of government intervention in the economy, both of which the Hanyang period bequeathed.

HEGEMONIC SEOUL

For a variety of reasons, the legibility of modern Seoul is less than that of its previous incarnations. Shapiro (1992: 86) indicates that "In the present condition, the economic, social, political, and administrative practices of space that constitute the modern city are not represented in the form of visible structures, and, more generally, the connections between policy discourse and spatial strategies are less clear." In modern times, as figure 5.2 clearly shows, the city boundaries have greatly expanded. Furthermore, in the process of the city's growth, the narrow sense of the hegemonic architectural monumentality of the Confucian state centrality has mostly been lost. The decentralization of the institutions, functions, and population, as they spread beyond the traditional boundaries of the capital city by relocating into the outskirts of the city and other areas, diluted the centrality of traditional power symbols as well as the dichotomous contrast between sacred and profane that had been articulated so clearly during the Hanyang era. A quick glance at the population during the Hanyang period will demonstrate just how much the capital city has expanded. According to Won (1990: 77), the population during the Hanyang era ranged from 80,572 to 238,119 compared to Seoul's current population of more than 10.46 million as of 2013. Now, Seoul has become a metropolitan city of great renown throughout the world, and the price of land is skyrocketing. Accordingly, the potential for projecting political value onto space is becoming weaker and weaker. Also, due to technological developments in architecture, an ideal location can be shared by many entities through the construction of skyscrapers. At the same time, technological developments can be used to help overcome the disadvantages of an unpopular location. Shapiro (1992: 87) holds that "Insofar as work relations depend on speed and the timing of communications, geographic space dissolves in favor of what Paul Virilio has called chronospace." All of these facts encourage the decentralization of power related to spatial configurations.

The basic structure of the new capital city, however, owes much to the Hanyang and Kyeongseong eras. Although the Joseon Dynasty's dichotomy of sacred and profane in the spatial organization has diminished over time, it would be inaccurate to say that modern social space has been wholly

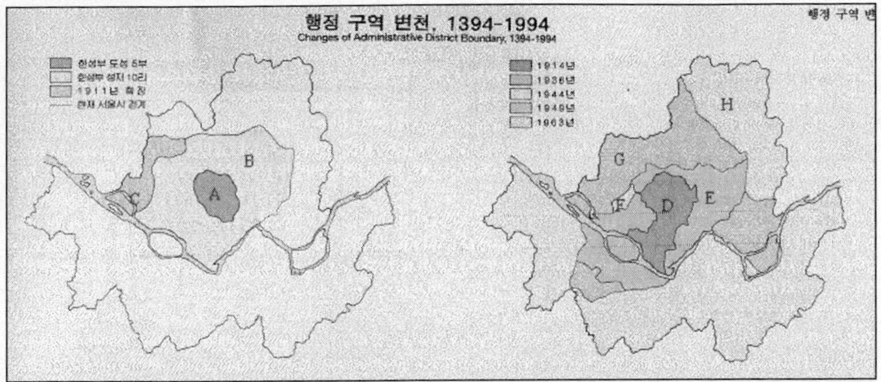

Figure 5.2 Expansion of Administrative District Boundaries, 1394-1994. A. Hanyang Castle (1392-1910), B. Hanyang (1392-1910), C. 1911, D. 1914, E. 1936, F. 1944, G. 1949, H. 1963. Lee, Ki-Seok & Noh, Hee-Bang (1994), p. 16.

desacralized. Rather, the continuity of both Z and Y in figure 5.1, representing state hegemony and political superiority over economy, respectively, runs counter to the modern tendency of diluting the attachment of power to place.

It would be insufficient, however, to simply note that the dominant spatial practice in modernity is horizontal, for within the horizontal orientation there is considerable contention over space as well. For example, as various municipal authorities and distant economic forms of power vie to control urban space, struggles are arising between proximate and distant centers of power. Even within locales, spatial practices are intricately articulated with other forces.

In today's Seoul, important political institutions seek to maintain their occupancy of the so-called sacred space that has been associated with state authority since Hanyang. Likewise major economic institutions, such as corporate headquarters and banks, strive to maintain physical proximity to state institutions in order to maximize support from government as was done in both the Hanyang and Kyeongseong eras.

Political and Military Institutions

The legacies of the Confucian Hanyang era—the relative strength and centrality of state over society and the loyalty of the masses to the integral power of state—in fact, worked as favorable bases for the political and military power of the Park regime. The Park regime sought to restore the state hegemony by restoring the tradition of state hegemony and propagating the pragmatic idea of maximizing economic efficiency. The sacred space created by the *axis mundi* and Confucian and geomantic principles was fully utilized by the Park regime to strengthen its prestige and authority and overcome its vulnerability; this took the form of locating major political and military institutions around the Core of Sacredness (Zone Z in fig. 5.1).

Architectural support for Park's strategy appears in the layout of Seoul. First of all, the Blue House (Presidential office and mansion, *Cheongwadae*) symbolizes the peak of power in Korean society. It is located within the main palace district, Kyeongbok, which is considered the most sacred prestigious

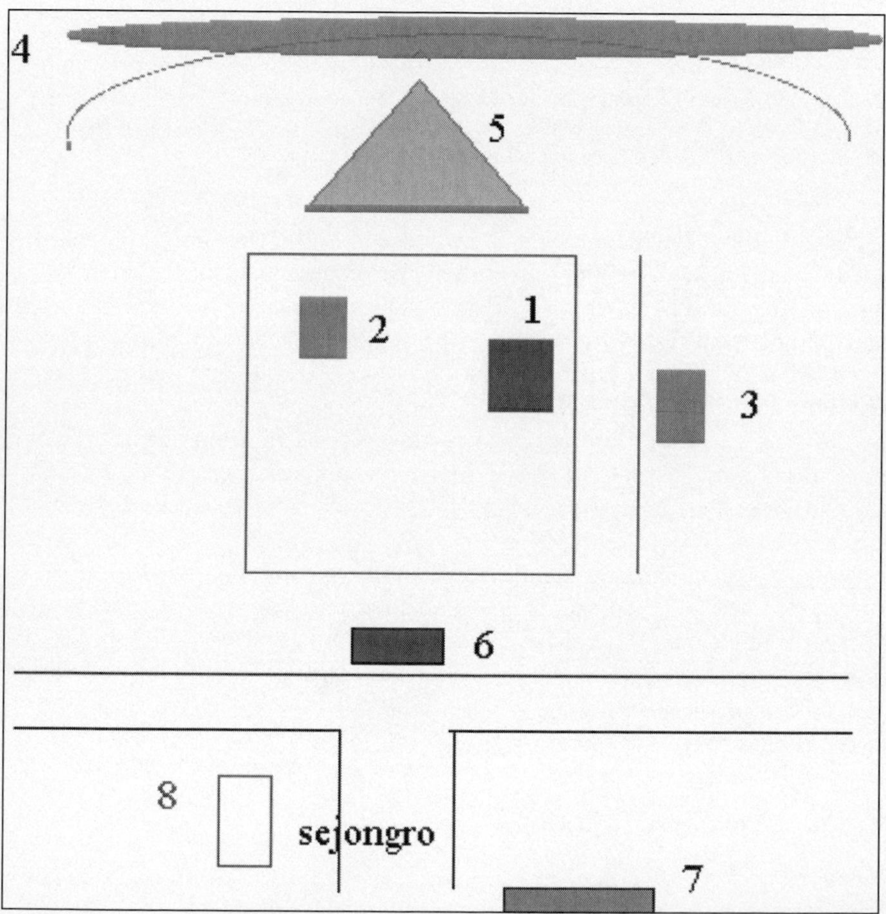

Figure 5.3 Locations of Major Military Institutions around the Cheongwadae (The Blue House, Presidential Mansion). 1. Cheongwadae , 2. 30th Division, 3. Defence Security Command , 4. 33rd Division, 5. Mt. Baekak, 6. Kwanghwamoon, 7. Army Capital Garrison Command (located far south of this map), 8. United Government Office Building. Created by author; Han, Jongwoo.

space in Korea's political history. Next, the Park regime reopened the Headquarters building of the Japanese Government-General (Chungangcheong, called "Central Hall" under the American Military Government) as the administration building of the Third Republic of Korea (Cheong, 1994: 68). The First and Second Republics had not used this former Japanese Headquarters building because it symbolized Japanese oppression and exploitation of the Korean people. In general, the public opinion supported the idea of destroying the former Japanese colonial headquarters building and constructing a new administrative building; however, the Park regime decided not to do so for economical and pragmatic reasons.[8]

Another salient architectural phenomenon in the late 1960s and early '70s was the tendency to restore stately symbols of the Joseon era, such as the main gate of Kyeongbok Palace, the Kwanghwamoon (#6 in fig. 5.3). The Kwanghwamoon had been moved to the east side of the palace by the Japanese authorities as a means of destroying Joseon's Confucian hegemonic order, and had also been heavily damaged during the Korean War. In 1968, however, the Park regime restored this gate to its original site. As this instance shows, though President Park severely criticized the unproductive and politically oriented Confucian Joseon Dynasty, he also sought to strengthen his political legitimacy by restoring the old dynasty's politically symbolic architecture. In 1978, in the middle of the Six Ministries Street, a statue was erected of Admiral Lee, a national hero from the Joseon Dynasty who had defeated the Japanese navy. In a similar vein, the Sejong Cultural Center was constructed from 1974 to 1978 to show off the government's success in economic development. The Center symbolized the state's restoration of power through its economic development plan and improvement of economic conditions for the masses at that time. In all of these architectural designs and buildings, President Park's attempts to reconnect to the heyday of Joseon's Confucian hegemonic state tradition are apparent.

Since the Park regime had seized power through military coup, it had to legitimize the basis of its power. The Kyeongseong era had reversed the Confucian principle of civil superiority over the military, and the military was the most advanced sector of Korean society in the 1960s. As a reflection of the importance of this military power to the Park regime, core military institutions began to concentrate around this core sacred space (fig. 5.3).

After National Liberation, American rational bureaucratic systems (e.g., professional national service system, position classification) and a performance rating system were introduced; however, in terms of bureaucratic practices, Japanese bureaucratic customs and administrative rules remained in effect because most of the positions in the public administration of the American Military Government were still filled by bureaucrats who had been recruited during the Japanese colonial period. Thus, a bureaucratic system was formed with a double structure—American rational in shape and Japanese in practice (Kim & Kim, 1995: 301). The Korean War lent momentum to the establishment of a modern bureaucratic system in Korea. During the Korean War (1950-1953), the Korean military was introduced to a modern American military and scientific bureaucratic system of management. Thus, the Korean military became the first beneficiary of modernized managerial and organizational techniques of the American bureaucracy, especially of military logistics. In 1953, the Korean Army created the Office of Personnel Management within the Bureau of Personnel Staff. Through this office, the US military introduced a modern managerial bureaucratic technology and management system that included an archival system, a secret document system, basic planning procedures, the decimal management system for documents, and even the use of typewriters.

After the Armistice in 1953, the Army authorities sent approximately 1,000 officers and 2,000-3,000 soldiers to US military institutions mainly for military operations (Kim & Kim, 1995: 302). Through them, management techniques of organization were also transferred. In addition, there were two important military academic institutions that contributed to the consolidation of these leading-edge techniques: the ROK Army Logistics School and the National Defense College. ROK Army Logistics School (1956-present) offered a special course in planning and management techniques, attended exclusively by general and field-grade officers of the ROK Army, in addition to some officers from the other services. Chronologically, this was the first institution in Korea where a full-fledged advanced management course was conducted using the case method. The student body of the National Defense College (1956-present) included officers of the general and field grades from all of the services, as well as selected senior civil servants from civilian ministries. Most of the visiting lecturers for the non-military courses, of which there were many, were university professors, high government and bank officials, and noted journalists.[9] Thus, the Korean military was the first organization to become fully modernized, even before government or entrepreneurial organizations. In fact, the military coup in May 1961 provided momentum for spreading these modern American managerial techniques into government organizations and later into economic institutions such as the chaebols. In other words, the military was able to lead the other social institutions not only by the means of its physical power but also by its general management capabilities. Thus, it was not only physical force but also the management skills of the military regime that overwhelmed economic actors in the 1960s and '70s; and it was not until later in the '80s that the power of the economic sector eventually outstripped this military lead.

Since military officers could be appointed as civil government officials, the military's superior managerial capacity gradually challenged the Confucian tradition of civil superiority over the military and began challenging the historical dominance of the bureaucracy in the Korean political system as well. Confucianism has always held that the military should obey civil leadership. Despite the impact of the Japanese emphasis on military power during the Kyeongseong era, this Confucian principle had persisted throughout Korean history; however, the American Military Government introduction of this advanced scientific management system enabled the Korean military to become the most advanced sector in Korean society, starting in the late 1940s and continuing until the collapse of the military regime in 1987.

The military's rising power and influence began to be reflected in their policy of moving into governmental buildings and more prestigious sections of the capital city, such as the Six Ministries Street (fig. 5.3). Even during the Hanyang era, the Byeongjo (Defense Department) was located in the Six Ministries Street; however, the relative power of the military in modern Korea is not comparable to that of Byeongjo during the Confucian Hanyang era. When the power of the Park regime reached its peak, the government devised a special system to recruit military officers, especially Army officers who had served more than three years as captains, to serve as government officers with a ranking equivalent to that of the fifth level, which is the rank given to those who have passed an official recruiting examination (*Haengjeongkosi*) for national civil service. This system was suggested to the President in 1976 by Army Headquarters through the Department of National Defense. That same year, around 100 military captains were given the rank of fifth level officer. Even though there was still a recruiting examination for national civil service, this special system of recruiting military officers into government posts utilized a special exam devised only for them. A general exam required candidates to pass five subjects in the first round and seven in the second; however, only two subjects were given in each round to those who had served as military captains. While the regular exam was based on unlimited competition, the special system was based on none.

For example, in 1985, 100 out of a total 12,908 applicants passed the national civil service exam and became government officials[10]—a 1:129 ratio. For the special examination, however, 52 captains applied, and all became government officers. Between 1976 and 1990, a total of 784 captains were recruited as government officers.[11] Clearly, this special system of recruiting military captains as government officials was specially designed to exercise military influence on the civil service, which shows the extent of the military's dominance in the bureaucracy. In particular, the Ministry of Home Affairs was one of the most powerful ministries for maintaining social order under the military regime, as it physically supported the regime's power. By arranging for the second largest amount of cadet-bureaucrats to be in the Seoul Metropolitan Government, military groups tried to exert great influence upon the most developed city in Korea. The National Tax Administration, with sixty-five cadet-bureaucrats, was the most effective means for increasing the power of the military regime and controlling civil economic organizations. Lastly, the Board of Audits and Inspection was the best means for controlling the bureaucracy. By establishing the dominance of the military in these two powerful monitoring organizations, the Park regime built a power base for complete control over corporations and other social organizations. Therefore, the recruitment of military officers into the powerful ministries and other government organizations meant more military influence in the former sacred zone of the capital city.

This military influence in Korean society is vividly reflected in the location of the Army Capital Garrison Command (fig. 5.3), which functions as a kind of royal guard for the president within the capital and which has played a critical role in protecting the military regime since the Third Republic. This Army Capital Garrison Command[12] is composed of six major divisions: the 30th, the 33rd, Anti-Aircraft Defense, Military Police, Field Artillery, and Special Attack Corps. The 30th Division is the most important unit, the so-called Royal Guards, who protect the Blue House, Kyeongbok Palace, and major state institutions within it.[13] As shown in figure 5.3, it is located in the most sacred space in Seoul.

The 33rd Division protected the outer area of the Blue House, major state institutions, and Kyeongbok Palace. In 1968, North Korean guerillas successfully penetrated into the region very close to the Blue House and shocked the nation—they had come to kill President Park. They were never stopped or questioned until they reached this most sacred space. That is why this 33rd (#4 in fig. 5.3) Division keeps watch over Baekak Mountain. That is also why the Head of the Army Capital Garrison Command was appointed by the President, so that the President could absolutely count on his allegiance. The Anti-aircraft Defense division was located in Yongsan, where Japanese Army Headquarters had been located, and it dispatched its sub-units all over Seoul. The Military Police were located within the Headquarters but controlled checkpoints on all bridges of the Han River. Finally, the Field Artillery unit was located to the Northeast of the Blue House, protecting it from unexpected attacks from North Korea.

Another important military institution that played a key role in supporting the military regime was the Defense Security Command (#3 in fig. 5.3). Its main functions were to watch over internal-military movements, to collect information on domestic political movements, and to report directly to the President. While the Army Capital Garrison Command (#7 in fig. 5.3) was devised to protect the President and most state institutions around the sacred space from possible North Korean attacks or military coup, this Defense Security Command gained political power and extended its function to include political affairs as well. One of its main political missions was to detect and prevent any military insurgence and to deal with civil opposition. For this reason, it was located just west of the outer wall of the Kyeongbok Palace within walking distance of the Blue House. These two military units were critical to the safety of the president and power structure and to the consolidation of political power in Korea as well.

This influence of the military on government organization resulted in actual reformation and changes in the government's administrative system as well.[14] In the late 1960s and early '70s, these modern managerial bureaucratic techniques were further transplanted from military to economic sectors. Public enterprises played a catalytic role in transplanting these managerial techniques from military to civil economic sectors.[15] The high managerial positions of major public enterprises were mostly recruited by the military cadre. The Korea National Housing Corporation created a new operational rule for its organization by establishing regulations for personnel management, office code, and job analysis, as well as a performance rating system in 1962.[16]

Until the early 1960s, no enterprises had conducted job analysis. In 1965, Gold Star, one of Korea's most successful enterprises, began to institutionalize a modern managerial technique by composing a Personnel Committee.[17] Another good example can be found in Jeiljedang Co. It was the first enterprise to recruit workers through a competitive open examination; however, it was not until the late '60s that it adopted a performance rating system and established a promotion provision, and it was not until the early '70s that it adopted job analysis techniques as well.[18] Another kind of momentum that catalyzed the dissemination of modern bureaucratic managerial techniques from the military to enterprise was the privatization of public enterprises in 1968.[19]

The main point that this section aims to make clear is that the military force during Korea's period of rapid industrialization focused on cultivating not only physical power but also the most advanced management and leadership skills, thereby reversing the Confucian principle of civil superiority over the military, and exerted its advanced position among various societal sectors. This military influence was clearly reflected in the geographical form of modern Seoul's city layout.

Economic Reflection of Hegemonic Seoul

Shim (1985: 27) properly describes modern Korea's urgent pursuit of economic development as the "evil effects of the so-called economism—a euphemism for the idea that South Korea must pursue economic development by whatever means available, irrespective of ethical or moral dictates. What was good for Daewoo or Hyundai was good for the country, and vice versa." The ultimate goal of catching up economically with advanced countries and rising out of the chronic poverty that had persisted since the Joseon era dictated every aspect of modern society, including architectural designs that featured state agencies and private business enterprises as symbols of national priority.

Against this backdrop, the predominant trend in the designs of the buildings constructed around the late 1960s and early '70s was a reflection of the hegemonic idea of the Seoul era—that is, maximizing economic efficiency and recourse to the state hegemony. The predominant concepts of bigness, highness, and pragmatism were embodied in the building designs and construction (Lee & Kim, 1994: 40), thereby emphasizing the values of state authority and economic efficiency through modernized architectural technology. The general feature represented most in the building designs of the 1960s and '70s was the lofty "slip" form, which emphasized verticality and showed off the grandiosity of both government and corporation buildings—the two main driving forces of Korea's economic development. The government and political leadership, as well as both public and private economic institutions, were respected even in their building designs not because of their physical power but due to their national task of bringing the country out of poverty and into a competitive economic catch-up race against economically advanced countries throughout the world. The government administration and business conglomeration buildings demonstrate this well.

The United Government Office Building (Jeongbu Jonghap Cheongsa) was built in 1969 in Chongro-gu Sejong-ro, adjacent to the Chungangcheong (former Japanese Colonial Headquarters, later used as Central Hall by the US Military Government), and was used as the core of the administrative department until the Second United Government Office building was constructed in 1982. This building was designed by the US architectural firm PA&E, utilizing the slip form, which was being applied for the first time in Korea to emphasize the verticality of official buildings centered on business functions. Upholding the two main ideologies of modern Korea—government leadership in economic development and economic pragmatism—the lofty slip form lends an air of grandiosity, authority, and respect, differing from the architectural monumentality of Confucian political institutions which reflected the geomantic principles of the Joseon Dynasty. These two characteristics shaped the nature of the developmental state in Korea. Also, this was the heyday of the influence of America in both geopolitical and economic context, a country admired by Koreans at that time for its political and educational liberalism and technology as well as economic and political hegemony in world politics. Fittingly, the influence of American architecture and technology was reflected in the design and function of these buildings as well.

Architectural reflections of the era's ideologies abound in the economic sector as well. The Samil Building (meaning the "First of March," representing the Day of Independence), located along the Cheonggyecheon roadside, symbolized the developed aspect of Seoul as the city's highest building in the late 1960s; it was constructed out of simple cubic forms in a typical international style.[20] The Tower Hotel, which was originally designed for guests of the Liberty Center (i.e., the government's anti-communism education center), was renovated during this era to feature 245 rooms for commercial use. This building emphasized the concept of monumental architecture in a different way than the horizontality of the Liberty Center. Rather than utilizing the logic of a planar frame basically composed of four pillars, the Tower Hotel represented rising power through its extreme verticality.[21]

All of these buildings built during the 1960s emphasized a vertical, megastructure monumentality, representing the power of the state and economic development. The size and height of these buildings reflected the intention of government and entrepreneurs to strengthen their power, authority, and economical pragmatism in terms of office space and function. In these designs, international and American influences were especially apparent; however, the prime goal of this book in general, and of this section in particular, is not to discuss architectural or urban designs in and of themselves but rather to examine how major ideological, socioeconomic and sociopolitical powers are reflected in those forms as evidence.

Since the Third Republic of Korea, buildings with hegemonic associations have occupied the Six Ministries Street (fig. 5.4). As mentioned above, the United Government Office Building was located on the site where the Ministry of Rite of the Joseon Dynasty and the Japanese Gendarmerie Headquarters had once stood. Figure 5.4 shows the locations of major government and private institutions around the sacred space, especially on the Six Ministries Street.

The Sejong Cultural Center (#6 in fig. 5.4), the largest cultural facility newly built, was erected from 1974 to 1978 at the site where the Civil Assembly Hall had burned down. This architecture decorates Sejong Street (A in fig. 5.4) alongside the *axis mundi* of Seoul by means of its roof and edifice, which arouses strong emotions for Koreans by harkening back to the heyday of the Joseon Dynasty.[22] At the top left side of the Six Ministries Street (present Sejong-ro) was the Japanese Police Headquarters, built during the Kyeongseong period, which had been used as the National Police Headquarters before being destroyed by the Korean government. In 1987, a new National Police Headquarters was built. Now, this space on the Six Ministries Street is temporarily being used as a parking lot. The power embedded in

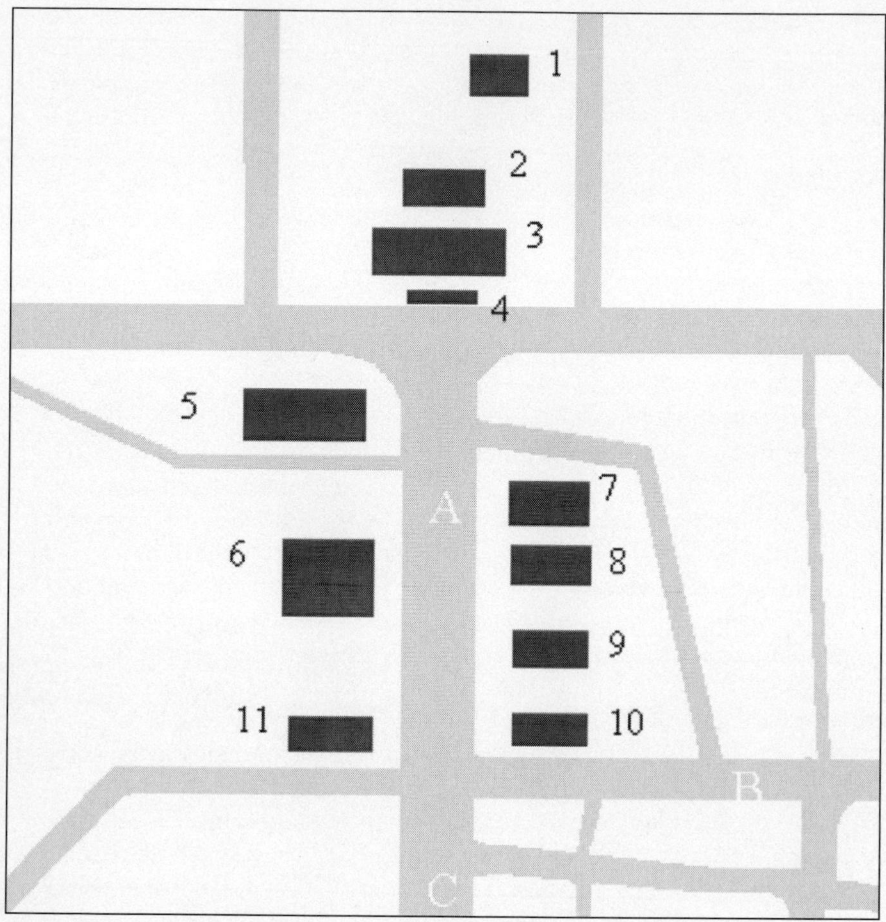

Figure 5.4 Major Government and Business Institutions in the Sacred Space in the Seoul Era. A. Sejongro (Former Six Ministries Street), B. Chongro, C. Taepyungro, 1. The Blue House, 2. Keunjeongjeon, 3. National Museum (Former Governor-General Headquarters, now destroyed in 1995), 4. Kwanghwamoon, 5. United Government Office Building, 6. Sejong Cultural Center, 7. Ministry of Culture & Sports, 8. American Embassy, 9. Korea Telecom, 10. Kyobo Building, 11. Hyundai Building. Created by author; Han, Jongwoo.

those specific zones was constructed in the minds of the people in the Joseon Dynasty. Analyzing what institutions occupy that region is another way to illustrate the power relations among those institutions during a particular era, to decode how three different types of rule of political community have evolved, and to reveal the nature of a political community within a particular time frame.

The office building for the Ministry of Culture and Sports (#7 in fig. 5.4) and the US Embassy building (#8 in fig. 5.4) are located side by side on the Six Ministries Street. These twin buildings were built by the US architectural company Binel from 1960 to 1962. The US government intended to use the former for the US Operations Mission (USOM) building.[23] The USOM, an agency that implemented US-aid policy in Korea in the early 1960s, distributed US aid and implemented major industrial reconstruction projects coordinating between the Korean and American government. Accordingly, it exerted a great influence upon the Korean government. The fact that the USOM Korea was located on the Six Ministries Street reflects the political symbol and centrality of the sacred space of the Six Ministries Street (Sejong-ro) in Korean politics. In 1968, it was renamed the "US Agency for International Development" (USAID). After the USOM's mission had been completed, this building was used for the Economic Planning Board, which played a highly significant role in the rapid economic development in Korea. Now, this building has become the office building for the Ministry of Culture and Sports, and the other building is still being used as the US Embassy. The presence of two American buildings on Six Ministries Street serves as an indication of how influential the United States has been in Korean politics and economy. At the same time, this also demonstrates that even a country as powerful as America needed to occupy a prestigious, so-called sacred, spot in order to convince Koreans of its power in their country.

Korea Telecom (#9 in fig. 5.4) is a new addition to the sacred zone, located next to the US Embassy building. During the Hanyang era, economic institutions, especially commercial ones, were set apart from the area of state centrality because they were considered as profane and detrimental to Confucian governance. The changed nature of the Seoul era, however, is demonstrated by this policy of allowing industrial and commercial institutions to share the sacred space with political intuitions. During the Kyeongseong period, economic power expanded, which in turn altered the space allocation framework of the capital city; however, economic institutions were still mostly concentrated in the profane space south of the main axis,[24] as shown in figure 5.1, with the exception of the telecommunication industry. During the Kyeongseong period, the Japanese Telecommunication Agency was located on the Six Ministries Street. This shows continuity with the basic structure that was established during Japanese colonial rule.

The Kyobo building (#10 in fig. 5.4), which was built from 1978 to 1983, is located at the east end of the Six Ministries Street (present-day Sejong-ro). This building was built mainly for business purposes, including twenty-one foreign bank branches and agencies (fig. 5.4). The existence of twenty-one foreign bank branches on this street serves as another indicator of the growing influence of capitalist development, explaining why these institutions are concentrated in the area marked "A" in figure 5.5. Across the street is a building that belongs to Hyundai (#11 in fig. 5.4), Korea's leading chaebol. It displays no outstanding architectural features, but its location reflects the rising influence of business in Korean society since all of the other buildings on this street are political, administrative, or public. As the Korean economy developed, this growing economic power came to be reflected in the buildings that occupied the so-called sacred space. Among the buildings on the Six Ministries Street, buildings such as the United Government Office Building, the Sejong Cultural Center, the twin buildings, and the Kyobo building reflected the hegemonic ideas of bigness, highness, and pragmatism, with the exception of the Japanese Police Headquarters.

In addition to our analysis of individual buildings, a broader look at the regions where major chaebols and corporations concentrated will reveal the continuity of the area that was maintained from the Kyeongseong era (fig. 5.6). The capital city still bears traces of the two major forces that shaped it during the process of modernization—political and economic institutions. The latter were mostly rooted in the area where Japan had brought modern capital institutions to challenge Joseon's traditional political symbols on the northern end of *axis mundi.* As figure 5.6 shows, the economic center of the

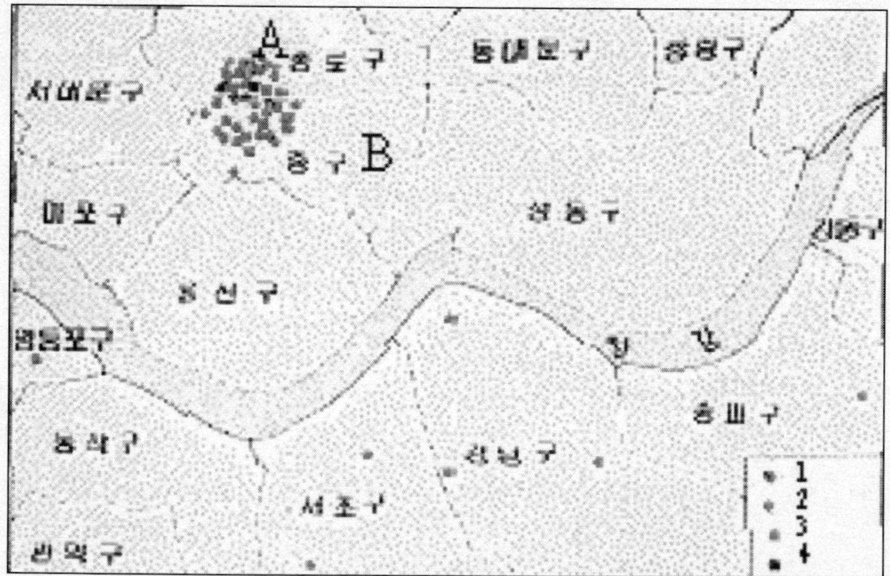

Figure 5.5 Locations of Foreign Branch Banks, 1993. A. Chongro-gu, B. Choong-gu, 1. North America, 2. Asia, 3. Europe, 4. Others. Source: Lee & Noh (1994), p. 37.

colonial era (i.e., Zone W in fig. 5.1) continued to serve as the economic center for modern Korea. In the Seoul era, Chung-gu and Chongro-gu became the area of greatest prestige; the core of Seoul's political and economic affairs is now focused in the Joseon Dynasty's sacred space centering on the main Palace, the Six Ministries Street, the center of economic activities in Chong-ro, and the triangle zone of the Kyeongseong period. An investigation of the content of the buildings around these two administrative districts will show how important these two districts, which have functioned as the center

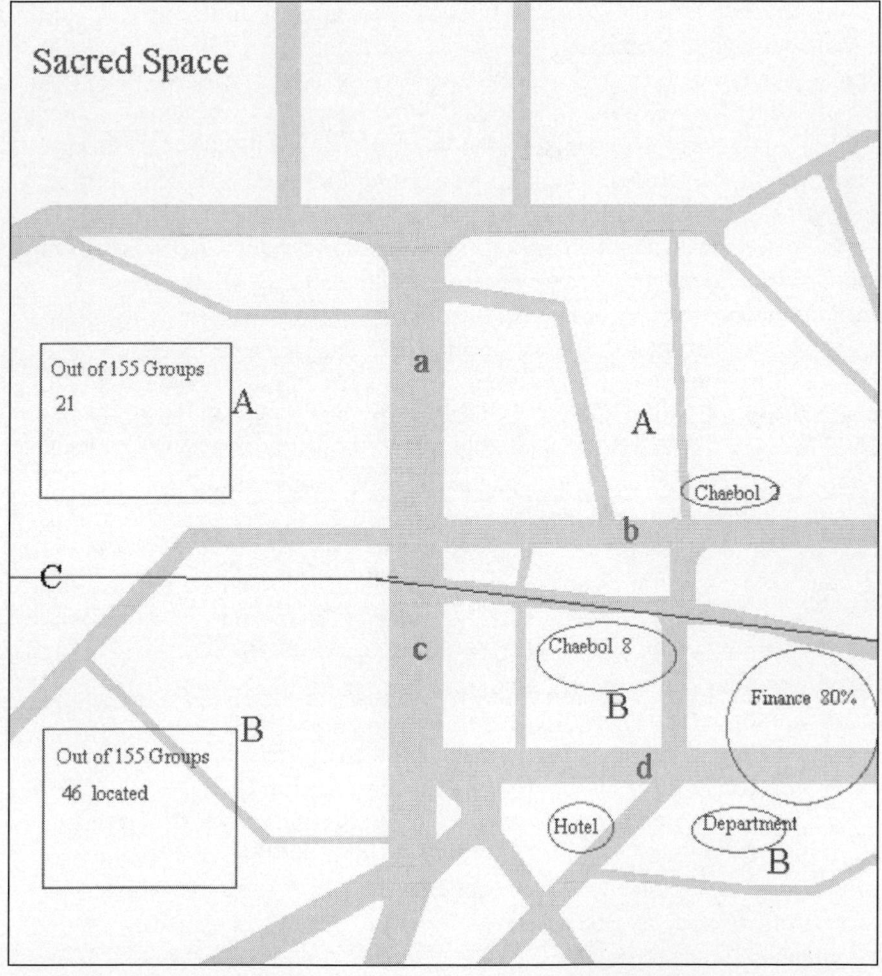

Figure 5.6 Economic Functions Concentrated in Two Districts of Seoul. A. Chongro-gu, B. Choong-gu, C. Borderline between Chongro-gu and Choong-gu, a. Sejongro, b. Chongro, c. Taepyungro, d. Euljiro. Created by author; Han, Jongwoo.

of political and economic activities through the Hanyang and Kyeongseong eras, still continue to be in Korean society. figures 5.5 and 5.6 show how densely economic functions in Seoul are concentrated in the two traditionally recognized districts of Chung-gu and Chongro-gu.

Taepyung-ro and Eulji-ro in particular, which served as the center of Japanese economic affairs, still continue to be the center of Korean finance and big business headquarters. According to the 1993 Yearbook of *Maeil Economic Newspaper*, there was a total of 155 groups[25] in Korea in 1992: 46 were located in Chung-gu; 26 in the Kangnam and Seocho-gu, the newly developed districts south of the Han River; 21 in Chongro-gu; and 18 in Yeouido and Youngdeungpo. Strikingly, almost half of these groups were located in the most prestigious area in Seoul. Seventy-two percent of all groups are located in Seoul. Only two major chaebols—Hyundai and Gold Star—are not located in this district. Nevertheless, the biggest chaebol, Hyundai, is located in Chongro-gu. Therefore, it would be no exaggeration to say that this district, Chung-gu, has taken charge of the Korean economy.[26]

Furthermore, according to Cho (1990), eight of the ten chaebols[27] have headquarters located in the Chung-gu. Cooperative relations between government and chaebols played a key role in the miraculous economic development of Korea. The fact that most chaebol headquarters are located in this district clearly supports that claim. The formation of a political and economic center in this prestigious zone was positively affected by state hegemony and the legitimacy of government intervention in the economy, both of which penetrated into the belief system of the Korean people simultaneously, as well as the cooperative relations between government and business during the Kyeongseong period. These headquarters had to occupy this zone in order to have close relations with the government officials who controlled the economy as a whole. The extent to which foreign banks and their branches were concentrated in Seoul is evident in figure 5.5.

Other statistics show the hegemonic position of these two districts in terms of economic activity. According to Chung-gu Borough Office (1994: 423),[28] there were 2,083 finance, trade, and state enterprises in Seoul in 1994. Among them, 35 percent (731) were in Chung-gu, and 12.7 percent (267) in Chongro-gu. The total of these two districts accounted for 47.7 percent (988) of total enterprises. Significantly, 80 percent of all financial institutions and the headquarters of banks were concentrated in Chung-gu, which was the center of Japanese financial institutions during the Kyeongseong period. Thirty-eight foreign banks were also located in this district (Chung-gu Borough Office, 1994: 436) in 1994. Furthermore, if insurance companies and stockbrokerages are included, this district accounted for the core of the financial institutions (Chung-gu Borough Office, 1994: 438). This fact reflects the inertia of the Kyeongseong era. Ten out of 24 of the most luxurious hotels were located in this district too, which implies that it was also a center for international cooperation (Chung-gu Borough Office, 1994: 441). Most of the best department stores were also concentrated in this district, which means that it functioned also as the center of commercial activities.

Not only business buildings but also politically important institutions were located in this district. Of all the government buildings in Seoul, 52.6 percent were concentrated in the districts of Chung-gu and Chongro-gu. Of all foreign institutions, which were mainly embassy buildings, in terms of their space, 97 percent were also located in these regions (Chung-gu Borough Office, 1994: 423).

From the information above, several points can be distilled. First, the origins of Confucian political authority stemmed from geomancy, and Confucian political hegemony was reflected in the city design, architecture, and relative arrangements of political and economic institutions in the Hanyang era. In this way, space and architecture were used as a medium for containing Confucian hegemonic ideas. Through the penetration of these two major ideologies—*pungsujiri sasang* and Confucianism—into the everyday lives of the people, the Joseon Dynasty's power structure maintained strong state hegemony. The spatial factor functioned as a core medium to convey political ideas and symbols of power. During the Kyeongseong period, despite some changes, the idea of space as a symbol of power continued. Then, through centralized bureaucratic organization and institutions, the government's legitimacy to intervene in the economy was further strengthened in the Seoul era. The historical origins of these prestigious regions explain their continuity through the eras of Korea's history. Even during modern Korea's era of Seoul, this arrangement endured, despite the fact that correlative relations between space and power became somewhat less evident as Korean society continued to modernize and its economy to develop.

Second, even though the hierarchical subordination of economic institutions to political institutions was largely leveled during the Kyeongseong period, state hegemony over economic activity in general was maintained. This explains why economic institutions such as chaebols, financial institutions, and commercial complexes are concentrated in Chung-gu.[29] The closeness of enterprise to the major powerful political institutions means a guarantee of government support on a large scale. Even the US Embassy once asked the Korean government for a new space within ten minutes' walking distance from the Blue House (Cheongwadae). In addition, this center of political and economic activity has become an international center. Here, it is necessary to have a "forward-genealogical understanding" (Cho, 1993: 28) of the past as reflected in the space and architecture.

As mentioned in chapter 4, for both the Japanese colonial authorities and the Park regime, the best way to compensate for their weak political legitimacy and cripple the dissenting and opposition forces was to exploit existing political symbols and create a culture that encouraged the masses' loyalty to the centrality of the state by capitalizing on belief systems that had already been embedded into the minds of the Korean nation over the long history of Korean state-society relations. To achieve this, Japanese colonial authority had exploited generic sources of Korea's political symbols, thereby rationalizing and strengthening its own political authority. Japan had also adopted various policies to distort people's sense of loyalty to Korea's state by damaging natural sacred landscapes or destroying the architectural and city layout of state hegemony and centrality, including symbolically meaningful topological configurations, or manipulating Confucian architectural monumentality, which has been discussed in detail in chapter 4.

Japan attempted to gain political authority by appropriating the Confucian and geomantic hegemony of state and bureaucracy; similarly, the Park regime capitalized on state hegemony and the hierarchical relationship between government, business, and society by pointing to economic progress as proof of the success of state leadership over economic sectors and society, thereby strengthening the state's legitimacy to intervene in economic affairs. Furthermore, the strength of the heteronomical forces stemmed in part from the length of their roots, as they had been centrally co-opted during the Hanyang era and subsequently expanded and reinforced during the Kyeongseong era. This tradition is what the Park regime sought to weaken, which again serves as evidence of this book's argument about the prototype of state hegemony and the origins of heteronomical forces and civil society in Korea.

As Japanese colonial authority intended to oust the old Confucian hegemony from the "sacred space" of Joseon's political legitimacy and to substitute Japanese influence in its stead, thereby transforming Hanyang into Kyeongseong, the Park regime took advantage of old Confucian hegemony and its hierarchical system, and took specific steps to weaken the heteronomical factors of Seoul's city layout.

HIERARCHICAL SEOUL

Both the Hanyang and Kyeongseong eras left deep imprints on the capital city's hegemonic layout that lasted well into the Seoul era. The factors that have been pointed out by most development theorists as social forces contributing toward the accomplishment of Korea's rapid economic development are the military, bureaucracy, and entrepreneurs. As mentioned earlier, development theorists inadvertently reify despotic rule by the military and its attendant economically efficient bureaucracy in developing economies; however, focusing overly on the military dictatorship's dependence on physical power neglects the fact that the military organization after National Liberation became the most modernized social organization in Korean society and served to lead the other two social groups—i.e., the bureaucracy and entrepreneurs (especially chaebols)—that played a motivating role in Korea's economic development. It was not only the military's dictatorship and physical power but also its advancement of the most modernized managerial bureaucratic system that put the military at the top of the hierarchical pyramid of Korean society, enabling it to lead other social groups in economic development. With new prominence, the major military institutions came to occupy positions within the "Core of Sacredness" Zone flanking the Presidential Mansion (Cheongwadae) (figs. 5.3 and 5.4).

Other important factors that were believed to have greatly contributed to Korea's economic development are the Economic Planning Board (EPB), the famous Five-Year Economic Development Plan, and the cronyism of politicians and businessmen. A close look at these factors provides better explanations of the actual aspects of the developmental state.

The EPB was created to produce and implement industrial policy. As the most powerful bureaucracy for economic development, it was heavily utilized by President Park, who made it accountable directly to him in the implementation of efficient economic incentives for corporations and chaebols as well as the planning of strategic national industries. This government agency had exclusive rights to budget planning and allocations as well as personnel appointments. All other government agencies had to follow the EPB. The EPB describes its own roles as follows: "The government will set policies and establish rules and regulations to protect the public interest, including the nation's deep interest in economic growth, and it will adapt and adjust its policies and regulations to changing circumstances, but in making policy changes, the impact on the private sector will be given serious consideration" (EPB, 1962: 175). Other industry-related government ministries, such as the Ministry of Commerce and Industry (MCI), closely coordinated government policy on commodity export and import plans with the EPB. Almost every economic policy and plan was reviewed by an import/export sub-committee consisting of representatives from EPB, MCI, Korea Trade Promotion Corporation (KOTRA), USOM/K, and Nathan and German Advisory Group, taking into account overseas market demand and expected import substitution (EPB, 1962: 178). President Park's emphasis on export was reiterated frequently in his major speeches and policy guidelines: an emphasis on export was derived from President Park's thinking that "the factor for attaining self-reliant economy is exactly export," and this development strategy was most suitable, he believed, to developing the economy of a nation like Korea with a dearth of natural resources (Lee, 1978: 451).

President Park consistently followed up on the Five-Year Economic Development Plan, which had been set by the EPB and other ministries, by asking college professors to assess their outcome. The TPB tightly monitored and planned economic policy and coordination among government agencies, as demonstrated in their statement: "By faithfully adhering to the principles of a competitive market economy during the Second Plan and by exploiting the advantages which accrue from such an economy, the overall objective of an efficient and active national economy can be achieved along with the following major targets: (1) The emphasis will be placed on attainment of food self-sufficiency, reforestation and development of marine resources" (EPB, 1962: 33). Industrial policy in the Second Plan was directed toward the attainment of self-sustaining growth and the establishment of a broad industrial base to support higher levels of living standards in the future (EPB, 1962: 79-80).

Even though it was a military organization that had transmitted the gospel of modern bureaucratic techniques to private enterprise, as the economy grew in the 1970s, it was the conglomerates, and especially the chaebols, that became some of the most powerful social groups in Korean society. Kim and Kim (1995) point out that the fastest-growing gigantic organization since the National Liberation was civil enterprise. According to their study, enterprises with more than 300 employees numbered 100 in Korea at that time. These 100 enterprises accounted for 0.1 percent of total enterprises with more than one employee; however, they accounted for more than 20 percent of all employees and more than 30 percent of total salary.[30] Among big enterprises, the position of chaebols in the Korean economy was salient. The added value produced by twenty chaebols accounted for 7.1 percent in 1973 and maintained a level over 25 percent in the 1980s.[31]

In addition to manufacturing, the position of chaebols in the Korean economy cannot be overemphasized if we count their position in finance, construction, and social services. Compared to the Hanyang era, the social position of commercial and industrial activity rose dramatically. Kim and Kim (1995: 317) contend that conglomerates in the 1980s were partially able to overcome their status in regards to their relations with government by means of their capabilities in concentrated capital accumulation and their increased organizational power. Even though conglomerates' power did not reach a level equivalent to that of state power, they were able to establish themselves as a collective bargaining power at a certain level such that they were able to start seeing their interests reflected in the power structure. As evidence of chaebols' rising economic power, Kim and Kim (1995: 317) point out that the new military power in 1980 did not purge them. In fact, when former president Chun and new military leaders seized power in 1980, it was the politicians, bureaucrats, and members of the mass media whom they purged in order to secure their political legitimacy.

There is, however, still a lingering belief in the Confucian legacy which does not view running a business as being on par with political activity. For example, in the 1992 presidential election, when the president of Hyundai, Chung Joo-young, ran for president, his candidacy was regarded as both a reflection of the upgraded social position of entrepreneurship in Korean society and a challenge to those who believed in the superiority of political over economic power. Even columns and editorials in major daily newspapers pointed out that, due to people's tendency to consider businessmen as being of low status, he should not run for president. Claiming that people did not want a businessman to ever run for president, they described Chung's candidacy as a great mistake (Chang, 1992; Lee, Soo-keun, 1992; Oh, 1992). Compared to both the Hanyang and Kyeongseong eras, the government of the Seoul era was intensively involved in the economy, not for the government's use as in the case of the Joseon Dynasty but for the sake of economic development itself. Also important to note is the fact that government intervention in the economy is not a contemporary phenomenon created by the Park regime—the ideological origins legitimizing government intervention in the economy date back to the Confucian hegemonic era as analyzed in chapter 3.

Even though it was during the Park regime that chaebols grew intensively,[32] the origins of collusive relations between state and enterprise date back to the First (1948-1960) and Second Republics (1960-1961). Kim and Kim (1995) highlight some factors that made the birth of chaebols possible: power elites selling the enemy's (Japanese) property to their clients,[33] monopolistic supply of US aid dollars, and foreign loans for a few enterprises in the 1950s.[34] Even though the chaebols were small in terms of scale and number, it was in the 1950s that they first emerged under the First and Second Republics; these were chaebols based on cronyism between state and economy.

After the May 16 military coup, the Park regime enacted a law purging those who had made their fortunes illicitly; however, the original plan to purge thirty businessmen and bureaucrats by imposing heavy fines had to be withdrawn because the goal of economic development could not be achieved without those businessmen. Thus, rather than purging them, the Park regime simply coerced them into participating in the economic development plan of the military government, letting them donate their property to the government and forming the Association for Promoting Economic Reconstruction, which later became the Federation of Korean Industries. Thus, a compromise was reached between the military government and the economy by enacting another special law that gave an indulgence to these transgressors. This served as a moment of establishing cronyism in politics and the economy (*Jeongkyung yoochak*); however, this tradition of adherent relations between state and economy had been established long before the Park era—it was not a military legacy. The adherent relations between state and economy stemmed from the First (1948-1960) and Second (1960-1961) Civil Republics. Under the Second Republic in particular, the same law to purge the makers of illicit fortunes had been enacted (Lee, Man-hee, 1993: 57). All of these factors have generally been considered creatures of the Park regime; however, the historical background and origins of those institutional arrangements, including the establishment of the EPB and the Five-Year Economic Development Plan, must be considered.

Another unsubstantiated belief is that relations between state and economy were based on the state's strong unilateral control. Detailed study of this issue leads us to a slightly different understanding. The Park regime had the burden of compensating for its lack of political legitimacy through an extreme focus on economic development. Meanwhile, the regime was constantly being met with fierce anti-military demonstrations from politicians, students, and the people in general. Thus, the military regime could not purge the makers of illicit fortunes. As mentioned briefly above, the Park regime needed these illicit fortune makers for economic development so that the regime could prove its capabilities and thereby ensure their own political legitimacy in the eyes of the masses while oppressing the strong movement of dissent. Thus, it would be more accurate to say that relations between the military government and the economy were based on mutual compromise and cooperation rather than on the military government's dictatorial control.

It wasn't until the early 1970s that a coercive government policy on chaebols first appeared. Through the first and second Five-Year Economic Development Plans, the economy greatly improved, and the regime thereby became able to ensure mass support for its capabilities in economic policy. Also, changes in the international environment served as an impetus to consolidate Park's dictatorship. East-West Detente drove the Korean Peninsula into an emergency situation fearing North Korean attack. Eventually, the Park regime declared the October Reformation (*Shiwolyoushin*), thereby strengthening the President's power. Such a change was also reflected in economic policy. In 1972, the Park regime froze enterprises' debt, the so-called 8.3 Jochi (August 3rd Decree). The government's power to influence and the reliance of enterprises on government began to reach its peak. Around this time, economic affairs were tightly controlled by political logic, and the so-called Heavy and Chemical Industry Policy was announced in January 1973 (Lee, 1993: 190), a very anti-economic policy assigning a heavy and chemical industry to each chaebol. They were given no freedom to choose their industry; however, the chaebols were heavily subsidized by government in their new assignments. Such lopsided government control of the economic sector changed in the 1980s. As the economy grew and became more technology-oriented, the government's coercive policy eventually became a burden to the economy.

Another important social group is the bureaucracy; in fact, it is the most organized and powerful group in Korea today. The total number of national civil servants, which was 25,000 in the early 1960s, increased to 90,000 by the mid-1990s; the rate of increase of national civil servants surpassed that of the population.[35] The core agent leading Korea's economic success was the EPB, which designed and implemented the so-called miracle formula—i.e., the Five-Year Economic Development Plan for the take-off and drive to maturity of the Korean economy. After the Korean War, there were some reconstruction plans, such as TASCA (1954-1956) and NATHAN (1954-1959); however, these ended without achieving any clear gains. The idea of devising the Five-Year Economic Development Plan originated from India's five-year economic plan.[36] However, President Rhee, who was a strong anti-communist, objected to this planning model due to its Stalinist Communist economic influences.[37] Under the Second Republic (1960-1961), discussions continued on the making of an economic plan. Lee Hahn-been addressed the problems of the Indian plan by bringing together the functions of budgeting and implementing[38] and later, in July 1961, created a super-Ministry—the EPB. Again, it is important to note here that the EPB was not a totally new creation of the Park regime but had been founded by bureaucrats at the start of the Republic of Korea. Bureaucrats' involvement in Korea's economic development has always been direct and central. This hegemonic position in Korean society was clearly reflected in the site of the United Government Office building and the EPB on the former Six Ministries Street (now Sejong-ro).

Table 1.1 shows an interesting fact: throughout the three eras of Hanyang, Kyeongseong, and Seoul, the bureaucracy maintained its influence as a national basis of hierarchical organizing principle. The Hanyang era was characterized by several types of controls: (1) the centralized Confucian bureaucratic system (i.e., recruiting through national civil service entrance examinations) and multitiered hierarchies of officials with distributed responsibilities and powers; (2) central controls over craftsmen and other industrial activities; (3) a national identification system for the gentry, masses, and slave classes; and (4) regulations on every aspect of people's lives. During this era, government controls and regulations over economic activities were strongly established, and, as a result, state intervention in the economy was taken for granted in the minds of the masses. The military force was not the only variable involved in the strong implementation of industrial policy; such policy was deeply embedded in Korea's state-society relations. Then, the Kyeongseong era added modern systems to the Confucian bureaucracy. The claim that Korea's efficient bureaucracy was the main force for rapid industrialization, taming domestic economic actors, and effectively adapting to international environments for competition, is not completely wrong, but the origins of such efficient bureaucracy were neither military dictatorship nor exclusively American influence. The indigenous historical perspective and approach that we have taken in our exploration of this issue has brought us to the point where we can now appreciate how the uninterrupted presence of a strongly centralized bureaucratic tradition of control over economic activities from the Hanyang era, strengthened through Japanese colonial control and inherited by the Park regime, may be one of the most fundamental sources of Korea's developmental phenomenon.

An interesting phenomenon in the composition of Korea's government positions in the era of modern Seoul was that university professors took most ministerial positions in the Korean bureaucracy. According to Yang (1996), in the Kim Young-sam government, from February 25, 1993, to November 4, 1994, professors accounted for 30.9 percent of all ministerial positions, while politicians accounted for 23.5 percent, and bureaucrats 22.2 percent. In the sixth Republic (President Rho from 1987-1992), bureaucrats accounted for 35.8 percent, professors 20.8 percent, and military 15.1 percent.[39] Yet, this phenomenon dates back to the Third Republic. In 1965, President Park Chung-hee appointed seventy professors to evaluate the results of the First Five-Year Economic Development Plan. This continued until 1981. The evaluative role of these professors during the military regime seems to have shifted such that, in more recent years, professors have begun taking most of the ministerial positions in the bureaucracy. Kuroda Kasuhiro, head of the Korean branch of the Sankei Newspaper, points out that, in Japan, there is not even one case of a professor being appointed as minister or staff member for a Prime Minister. Thus, the Korean phenomenon truly is exceptional.[40] It is exceptional because the professors have no experience related to administrative tasks and become obstacles to the promotion of orthodox bureaucrats.

There are several possible explanations for this interesting phenomenon. First, professors play a leading role as a constant source of original, though often idealistic, thinking about socioeconomic development, as Lee (1968) suggests. Thus, each regime appointed professors based on the expectation that they would play a creative role in socioeconomic development; however, there seems to be a more important reason for this interesting phenomenon—namely, the legacy of the Hanyang period and the fragile legitimacy of the military regime. In the Joseon Dynasty, every bureaucrat had a Confucian academic background. This tradition, in large part, gave rise to the strong tendency of professors to occupy ministerial positions in the Seoul era. In Japan, where the Confucian virtue of "courage" in the *samurai* class was emphasized, there was no tradition of scholarly hegemony, or of scholars in prominent social positions. The Park regime in Korea, to compensate for its weak legitimacy, took advantage of this tradition. While borrowing professional ideas and knowledge from professors, the military regime incorporated professors, who were at the top level of the Korean social hierarchy and heteronomical forces of university students, into the regime's political structure. In other words, recruiting professors as the heads of military government was a tactic aimed to debilitate the main antagonistic force against military regime—university students.

HETERONOMICAL SEOUL

Chapters 3 and 4 featured some discussion of the heteronomical forces involved in Korea's politics. Among these forces were student activists, church leaders, intelligentsia, and journalists. Later in the 1980s, workers and unions were added as another important component of the opposition forces and civil society in Korea; however, the unions were not fully developed until June 29, 1987, when the ruling party presidential candidate declared the *Eight Points of Democratization*. More quantitative studies may be able to shed some light on the role of the middle class in the democratization process and their impact upon it. As described at the start of this chapter, from Hanyang to Kyeongseong, Korea's most enduring source of heteronomical force was consistently the university students. Chapter 3 specifically explained how students of the National Confucian Academy were recognized by Confucian royal authority, central Confucian elites, and the masses. There were quite a few ways available to them for raising their voice and exerting their influence over the central government because, first of all, they were the offspring of central high-level elites and the future leaders who would be maintaining the Joseon political system; in fact, they were the future power elites. Joseon's Confucian ideology valued students as the nation's future literati, and this view has roots reaching back as far as the Goryeo Dynasty. Only graduates of Kukjakam, the national university during the Goryeo Dynasty, and Seongkyunkwan (during the Joseon Dynasty) were eligible to apply for the national civil service examination. This tradition continues today with the recruitment of government officials from Korea's elite universities. Accordingly, students in Korea's hierarchical society have been regarded as an incipiently powerful group.

Legacies of the Hanyang and Kyeongseong Eras

The essence of the heteronomical forces in the Joseon Dynasty, including the Neo-Confucian literati (sadaebu) in the local provinces, was their role as a built-in or co-opted force of loyal opposition. The limited and moderate nature of the heteronomical forces during the Hanyang era was dramatically transformed when the nation faced Japanese colonial control in 1910. After the March First National Movement, national resistance movements against Japanese colonial authority spread throughout the nation and forged an extensive alliance among all classes—including the former Confucian hegemonic elites, students, sadaebu, and religious leaders—as a united national force of opposition. This movement was severely suppressed by the Japanese military; however, the effect of this movement was serious enough to threaten the Japanese authorities and ignite active resistance nationwide. Many scholars agree that among these expanded dissenting voices, students from institutions of higher education were central in Korea's major political revolutions and uprisings, and that opposition movements led by university students during the Seoul era can be traced back to their Hanyang and Kyeongseong predecessors (Dong, 1988; Kang et al., 1993; Han & Ling, 1998; Lee, 1984; Han, 2012).

As pointed out earlier, the whole spectrum of Korea's democratization movements can be characterized as political rather than as stemming from class struggle (Cho, 2000: 37-38). Over the three eras of Korea's political history, what these students accomplished was to raise voices of dissent against existing power regarding the immorality and injustice of the leadership and its policies. Thus, Korea's democratization was initiated by students playing the vanguard role of tilting political challenges against the ruling political regimes. Approaches from the perspectives of modernization theory, which is a linear paradigm of economic precedence over political development, and dependency theory, which explains consistent underdevelopment, fail to accurately depict Korea's concurrent economic development and democratization. In this perspective, this book confirms the importance of an indigenous historical analysis of the way in which non-Western, Confucian state-society relations resulted in a developmental state and strong civil society. Clearly, the Western explanation of the origins of democracy is not the only one; there can be various forms of democratization as long as they meet certain universal qualifications (Sen, 1999). One of the most critical qualifications in the Western notion of the development of democracy is that the public sphere emerge as the power basis of the bourgeoisie and begin to seize power, as occurred in the transitions from feudal to modern Europe. The public sphere that functioned during Confucian Joseon was not motivated economically but rather by a Neo-Confucian moralistic and political perspective. Moreover, it was built into the central power structure and expanded during the Joseon Dynasty's first encounter with global forces. The nature, origins, and evolution of democracy can vary from state to state; the Korean version is one of many.

A brief investigation of Korea's history reveals the critical role played by student activism in the achievement of democracy. During much of the 1950s, Korean students were politicized largely in reaction to the Rhee administration's attempts to counterbalance and neutralize the challenges of increasingly vocal opposition in post-Armistice Korea. At the peak of this student activism, many believed that "[student demonstrations] can be a major catalyst of political change" (Dong, 1987: 234). This was the case in April 1960 when demonstrations contributed to the ousting of then-President Syngman Rhee (Buzo, 1984: 61). After the collapse of Rhee's dictatorial government, chronic unrest swept the nation for nine months (Shim, 1985: 26). What helped to consolidate the power of Park's coup was its shrewd timing. Here, the social unrest that had resulted from the April 19 Revolution, which brought Rhee's dictatorship down, functioned as a negative factor providing a credible justification for military intervention.

Until recently, other social forces such as labor unions and civil organizations were insufficiently strong to withstand the despotic power of the state, so students were the only resort for voicing popular justice. In fact, student movements against despotic state power both directly and indirectly contributed to the establishment of labor unions in Korea especially during the 1970s and '80s. Considering labor-student solidarity to be a cornerstone of effective political struggle, students infiltrated factories, hiding their status as students, and secretly educated workers on how to organize labor unions. The underlying theme of student protest from 1960s to the present has been that students function as seekers of justice in society and thus must speak out against immorality, evil, and corruption wherever it exists—especially in the state. Such was the case in May 1980, when student protests precipitated the complete takeover of the government by Chun Do-hwan (Buzo, 1984: 61). Students decried the older generation and its evil state as "the nation's enemy," which, consequently, had to be destroyed. Accordingly, student statements often left little room for compromise or negotiation. Descriptions of "the enemy" in the students' statements—whether the state or the older generation—were typically dramatic, extreme, and florid. For example, "vicious arbitrariness" and "perpetrator of state" became the most popular catchphrases during the 1980s.

From the onset of the Fifth Republic, which followed the bloody Kwangju Massacre of 1980, campus activists became the single most cohesive, persistent, and effective force of opposition in South Korea (Dong, 1988: 170).

Students successfully incorporated many disparate groups into an organized force of opposition. In the mid-1980s, student activists launched special programs to incorporate other social groups, such as labor workers, farmers, and even high school students. According to Dong (1987: 249), the number of former student activists obtaining employment in factories was estimated to be about 1,500 in 1986. Also, through the "farm village activity movement" (*Nonghwalundong*), students sought to raise the political consciousness of farmers and organize them into a force of opposition as well.

University students truly believed themselves to be an intellectual vanguard whose societal and moral duty was to fight social injustice, especially arbitrary state power. Ultimately, it took twenty-six years (1961-1987) for South Korea's student activists to successfully coalesce with the alienated citizens—mainly members of the middle class in their twenties and thirties—and force the military-controlled government of the Fifth Republic to surrender to the popular demand for democratic reforms (Dong, 1988: 185).

The "ideological coherence, organizational resilience and political autonomy" (Dong, 1987: 254) of the student activists in Korea was quite an exceptional phenomenon. Moreover, Korean students' active involvement in politics has significant implications for those seeking insight into the dynamics of political opposition and economic development in other countries, especially countries experiencing both concurrent economic development and authoritarian political rule. The presence of such militant opposition forces in Korea had a significant impact upon economic development by driving the illegitimate military regime to a stance of fanatical economic development (Dong, 1987: 233). To the Park regime, whose political legitimacy was seriously challenged by militant heteronomical forces, the accomplishment of economic development was the best way to counter oppositional accusations and acquire political support from the conservative majority, thereby making up for its lack of political legitimacy. For the Park regime, as briefly mentioned before, the majority's desire for economic development provided a pretext for oppressing the militant heteronomical forces. In these class dynamics lies a key to understanding the role of the developmental state within a sociopolitical context rather than in terms of technical industrial policy, which many developmentalists focus on instead.

While it is true that the upsurge of the heteronomical forces in Korea directly originated from the legacy of the Kyeongseong period, the fundamental origin of students' role in Korean politics is traceable to the cultural-legitimacy factor—i.e., the Confucian tradition of student demonstration during the Hanyang period (cf., Wilson, 1988; Henderson, 1968; Dong, 1987, 1988; Buruma, 1987; Buzo, 1984). Both the Hanyang and Kyeongseong eras exerted significant influence upon the formation of the heteronomical forces of the Seoul era. The root from which all of these heteronomical forces in Korean society arose, though, was student power. During the Hanyang period, the official heteronomical force was the students in the National Confucian Academy located in the upper triangle, which contained politically preeminent sacred space (Y in fig. 5.1). In the early 20th century, institutions of liberal educational, which became a significant source for the upsurge of heteronomical forces against Japanese colonial rule, also concentrated in this location, as shown in figure 4.4. The fact that President Park tried to move Seoul National University in the early 1970s from one of the most sacred spaces to the outer ring of the city demonstrates the regime's need to marginalize students' power by expropriating the university's traditional location within the sacred space. Regardless of such manipulation, the fact that "Seoul has more universities, on more lavish campuses, than any capital city in the world" (Buruma, 1987: 37) serves as an indication of the vigor and continuity of the heteronomical forces that concentrated in the sacred zone over these eras.

The legacy of the Hanyang era can be found in the people's view that students' involvement in politics is culturally legitimate. Thus, student activists in Seoul have inherited an old Confucian mandate to bear moral witness to the world regarding the deficiencies of rulers and the ills of society (Wilson, 1988: 1067-1068). The Confucian origins of the activism of students and professors in modern Korea are well documented.

> The remonstrations of scholars at the royal court were an established government mechanism for the 500-year span of the Joseon Dynasty. Remonstrations were very frequent, petty to all but the zealot, uncompromising, and strongly moral in substance. Often, scholars and students of the National Confucian Academy—the Seongkyunkwan—would assemble, debate an issue and then march through the streets of Seoul to the palace to present the resultant demands. From such models, the belief—that scholarly institutions had a moral obligation to check the perceived immoralities of government—became enshrined in national history and embedded in popular consciousness in a manner that finds no parallel either in China or Japan. (Buzo, 1984: 62-63)

In fact, students have long viewed themselves as the "only and last citadel for maintaining the justice" in Korean history, an expression frequently included in students' statements over the years. One of the main themes of students' statements from the 1960s to the present is that "because we are the incarnation of the justice in our society, we have to stand up against current immoral, evil, vicious, and corrupt despotic power." This duty is one that students have taken as a given. Also, professors who belonged to the highly recognized group of intelligentsia in Korea acknowledged the legitimacy of students' role in politics. In a statement made on April 25, 1960, supporting student demonstrations against Rhee's regime, they proclaimed that the "student demonstration is the manifestation of a genuine sense of justice and the expression of national spirit against unrighteousness."[41] Dong (1987: 251) points out that this general sentiment toward student radicalism is shared by most Korean intellectuals and a great many of the South Korean people.

The students' statement quoted above vividly shows the continuity of the tradition of student demonstration from the Kyeongseong period. In the April 19 Revolution Statement delivered by the students of Seoul National University (April 19, 1960), students contended that the "present situation is caused by a ferocious arbitrariness of despotism disguised outwardly as democracy and freedom. . . . Now, we [students] carry a torch of freedom with our father and brother who shouted for freedom under Japanese atrocities."[42] As discussed in chapter 4, before Japanese colonial rule began, the major high-level educational institutions were established based on Western liberalism. All of these institutions became major universities in the Seoul era and played a vanguard role in student activism against the military regime. From the 1960s to the 1980s student activists were effectively controlling most of the important study circles in major universities, including Seoul National, Korea, Yonsei, Seongkyunkwan, and Ewha in Seoul as well as Chonnam University in Kwangju.[43]

Moreover, it was students from these universities, with the exception of those from Sogang University, which was founded by the Catholic Church, who invaded the US Information Service building in May 1985 in response to the US government's tacit approval of the brutal oppression of demonstrators in the Kwangju Uprising of 1980. All of these universities still remain at the original sites where they were founded; in other words, the locational archetype of major universities has been maintained from the Kyeongseong period. Accordingly, Seoul became the mecca for student activism with dozens of institutions and more than 500,000 students. As Buzo (1984: 65) aptly points out, "people are predisposed to allow the students to assume the role of conscience of the nation, and this is done with relish."

The attitude of the most people toward student demonstrations and authoritarian state policy was ironic—while South Korea's majority agreed with the students' heteronomical position in society, they also signaled tacit submissiveness toward the authoritarian state; authoritarianism on the part of the rulers was matched by submissiveness on the part of the ruled.[44] There is another reason that people showed a kind of tacit complicity with the authoritarian state, aside from the comprehensive influence of the Confucian state hegemony established in the Joseon Dynasty—namely, there had been an improvement in the quality of life, which was the tangible and direct result of the absolute order of the economism proclaimed by the authoritarian government. "People's per capita gross national product rose to some US$2,000 a year—a figure much higher than in some countries which retain the system of direct elections" (Shim, 1985: 27).

In the Korean developmental state, the hyperfeminized society performs all duties by nurturing the growth of its socioeconomic "first sons"—i.e., the corporations or chaebols. Throughout the intensive developmental period of the 1960s and '70s, the state subsidized Korea's conglomerates at the expense of the people: low wages, restrictive labor policies, low-interest loans, tax incentives and breaks, administrative incentives for risky investment, favorable exchange rates, access to foreign borrowing and exclusive access to foreign natural resources, and the creation of special economic zones to entice foreign investment (Han & Ling, 1998: 67-68). Also, 43 percent of total circulating capital in Korea's economy and almost 15 percent of its foreign loans were specially allocated to chaebols by government in 1964 (Cho, 1994: 176, 187). Examples of special arrangements abound. In 1973, the state established a special government fund for chaebols, allocating to them 59 percent of the total loan capital available that year (Cho, 1994: 187). Similarly, in the 1970s and '80s, the state helped chaebols win lucrative contracts overseas, especially in the Middle East (Ling, 1984).

In modern Korea, university students as the traditional first sons were replaced by the chaebols. Han and Ling (1998: 68) argue that as heirs to the family estate, so to speak, the chaebols basked in the protection of both state and society. A survey conducted in 1987 to assess Korean's perception on chaebols found that 68 percent of Koreans criticized them for covertly making special arrangements with government, including unfair state subsidies and bank loans, curbs on wages, tax breaks, unfair provision of monopoly status, and inflationary profits. Nevertheless, the majority of interviewees, 84 percent of the sample, also indicated that the chaebols had substantially contributed to the national economy (Cho, 1994: 305, 309). At the same time, government continued to discipline the chaebols whenever they acted impertinently.

Han and Ling argue that such advancement of the chaebol displaced Korean society's traditional first sons, students of the Seongkyunkwan and their successors in modern Korea. They were the legitimate heirs of governing structures and elites and the future of patriarchal Joseon. Historically regarded as society's future leaders and visionaries, modern Korea's university students felt obligated to protest social injustices but found themselves increasingly marginalized in Korea's political landscape (Han & Ling, 1998: 68). For example, such displaced students harshly attacked the chaebols: "Let's dismantle the comprador chaebols that fill their bellies by selling the nation!"; "Tear down the swindling, thieving, monopolistic chaebol!" (Kang, 1993:

381, 386). A student flyer from 1986 declared: "Our target is the comprador chaebol that exploits the masses' labor while remaining blind to their own avariciousness." Upon graduation, though, these students invariably joined ranks with the chaebols as executives, bankers, researchers, bureaucrats, and the like, which led to an escalating sense of cynicism, alienation, and anomie among Korea's young professionals (Han & Ling, 1998: 68).

President Park Chung-hee, in his speech in Seoul for the presidential election campaign of April 27, 1971, attributed rapid economic development to the sweat and hardship of the citizens, sharing statistics on Korea's unprecedented economic development as proof: "According to the statistics of the World Bank and the UN, the Republic of Korea was ranked third out of 120 countries for its development speed during the last ten years. At the same time, we were ranked the first in the development speed of export in the world" (*Choson Daily News*, 1985: 144). Then, he warned that "social unrest would invite North Korea's attack," and make the nation no longer "able to work, to construct, and to send our children to schools. And people would lose their will to invest and run a business. Also, foreigners would not try to invest or co-invest, and cooperate with us," concluding that "anti-government demonstrations would be a serious obstacle to further economic development, and would invite North Korean attack" (*Choson Daily News*, 1985: 157).

Most student statements underscored a confrontation between a despotic power (the state or a particular politician) and the masses (*minjung*), which resembles a phenomenon from feudal times, namely, the exploitative relationship between a king and his people. Such a dual structure in people's minds—i.e., agreeing with students' demands while signaling their tacit approval for authoritarian government leadership—could be found even within the universities; the faculty, while maintaining their own authoritarian structure, shared the same righteous ethos as the students. This double structure can also be found in the community as a whole, where restraints of law and order still sometimes run a poor second to declarations of sincerity (Buzo, 1984: 63).

Just as the main principle contributing to the establishment of the heteronomical forces in the Hanyang period was foreign, the major sources of ideology and methodology for the dissent movement in the Seoul era were foreign as well, i.e., Western liberal and democratic ideology and Marxism that came primarily from Japanese sources. Buruma (1987: 36) keenly points out that "It is the height of historical irony that many of the Marxist texts read by South Korean students are Japanese. Radicals also use handbooks compiled by the Japanese student movement in the 1960s." He further argues that the dissent movement in Korea tends to borrow major ideology from foreign sources. According to him (1987: 36-37):

> . . . the apparent contradiction between the often extreme nationalism of South Korean student radicals and their constant use of foreign ideas is in fact not a contradiction at all. One key to understanding the dilemma of the Korean intelligentsia is precisely this conflict between dependency on outside powers and a cultural sense of self. The more South Koreans borrow from abroad, the harder they must kick, the more they must proclaim South Korean superiority and uniqueness—especially, one must add, if the borrowing is from Japan.

Needless to say, the anti-American South Korean nationalists drew many of their ideas from the United States itself, often disseminated by academics returning from US universities (Buruma, 1987: 37).

In the Seoul era, other major heteronomical forces, such as religious groups (especially Christian and Catholic) and mass media, also played a significant role in standing up against the major hegemonic forces of the military elites and business leaders. All of these heteronomical forces maintained the legacy from the Hanyang and Kyeongseong eras in terms of their headquarters' locations and the continuity of their function as major voices of dissent.

In conclusion, the heteronomical forces of the Seoul era stemmed from seeds that had been planted and nourished in the Hanyang and Kyeongseong eras, and sought to restore the tradition of the Joseon Dynasty's civilian superiority over the military. Professors, in their statement in June 1986, proclaimed: "Since we believe that the present political crisis derives primarily from the fact that the current regime rose to power illegitimately, we feel that the only way to overcome the crisis is to recover the legitimacy of the government by establishing a truly 'civilian government'" (Dong, 1987: 250). Also, the heteronomical forces targeted illicit activities of rising economic powers such as chaebols, in an effort that was described as "a more protracted and focused opposition against business elite that, rightly or wrongly, is seen as immoral" (Wilson, 1988: 1080).

Naehun, the Korean Confucian manual mentioned earlier regarding the position and role of women in society, clearly conveys the extent to which the patriarchal family structure pervaded Confucian society. A Korean proverb says "civilization would collapse if society allowed 'a hen to crow.' As clearly reflected in this heavily gendered view of the divided role between men and women, the husband was the head of the family and the wife was an assistant to the husband, helping him to manage family matters. Such gendered structure also shaped the different roles and positions between sons and daughters. The first son was the sole inheritor of the entire family estate, while daughters did not count in the family's business since they eventually would belong to their husband's families once married. Subsequent sons supported the family and its future patriarch—i.e., the first son. Until their marriage, daughters provided free labor for the family (Han & Ling, 1998: 67).

The *Naehun* specifies three duties for the proper Confucian daughter-wife: (1) to serve her parents-in-law, (2) to obey her husband, and (3) to care for and advise her children. Even with her children, the proper Confucian wife-mother must maintain a hierarchy of care.

First Phase of the Student Movement for Democratization: Within the Campuses, 1980-1981

Table 5.1 summarizes the major phases of democratic movements that occurred between the 1970s and the '90s when two major political developments were achieved: the collapse of the military dictatorship in 1987 and the establishment of the first civilian government in 1993. After the *Eight Points Declaration for Democratization* on June 29, 1987, labor unions blossomed; and after the establishment of the 1993 civil democratic government, civic organizations prospered in various social, economic, and environmental sectors. These two achievements marked the fundamental watersheds of democracy in Korean political history.

In the 1970s, demonstrations against the Park regime were mostly confined to campuses. The specific goal of protestors was to repeal the Yushin Constitution, which had been passed in 1972 to extend Park's power and control anti-military democratic forces as well as deal with dramatic changes that were occurring in international politics after the 1969 Nixon Doctrine and normalization between the United States and China. The Yushin Constitution was heavily criticized as a scheme to allow President Park and the military regime absolute power, including the possibility of no term limits for Park himself. Although university students (as the traditional "first sons") had a clear sense of continuing the tradition of Confucian and anti-Japanese national movements by manning the front lines against unlawful and immoral political regimes, there was no organized alliance to connect campuses and organizations, nor was there any strategy for drawing support from the masses at that time. The movements were confined by the military regime to campuses mostly in Seoul and remained limited to only a few groups of participants among the intelligentsia, such as university professors and non-elected democratic groups of leaders called *Jaeya*. Yet, persistent opposition movements finally brought the Park regime to an end in 1979 when student demonstrations in Busan and Masan in Kyeongnam Province ignited anti-regime movements across the nation. Then, on October 26, President Park was assassinated by his closest aid. In the aftermath, the strife between pro- and anti-Park forces ended with a military coup led by General Chun on December 12, 1979.

The popular demand for democratization, however, was suppressed by General Chun Doo-hwan and his military junta. In Kwangju, the capital city

Table 5.1 Characteristics of Political Regimes and Democratic Movement Politics in Each Period

Periods		1970s	1980-1987	1988-1992	1993-2002
Regimes		Military developmental dictatorship (Park Chung-hee Regime)	Military developmental dictatorship (Chun Doo-hwan Regime)	Transition from military to civilian government (Roh Tae-woo Regime)	First civilian government (Kim Young-sam & Kim Dae-jung)
Types of Democratic Movements, Politics	Issues	Anti-Yushin democratic movements	End of military rule, movements based on 3 M's: *minjung* (masses), *minjok* (nation), *minju* (democracy)	Democratization of sectors	Environmental, welfare, women's rights, citizens' rights, health, transportation
	Organizations	Non-elected democratic leaders group, churches	Nationwide alliance of democratic organizations	Social movement organizations by sector (labor, farmers, education, women)	Civic organizations, special interest groups
	Agents	Students, intelligentsia	Students, intelligentsia, workers, farmers, the poor	Workers, farmers, teachers, and representatives of each sector	Urban middle class
	Mode of demonstration	Direct actions (demonstrations, gatherings, stay-in strikes)	Direct actions (demonstrations, gatherings, occupation, suicide)	Direct actions (demonstrations, gatherings, stay-in strikes, occupation, strikes)	Institutional action, indirect participation

Source: (Cho, 2000: 115)

of South Cheolla Province, Chun's military junta massacred around 2,000 people in May 1980, and Chun's method of restoring order, i.e., unprecedented massive killings of citizens by military, left a permanent taint on his rule. Since every military operation at that time was under US military authority, protesters believed that the US government was somehow involved in these military operations or responsible for this massacre. Accordingly, students seized and occupied the American Cultural Institute on March 18, 1982, demanding to know the true state of US involvement in the massacre and an apology from the US government.

Despite the enormity of the violence in Kwangju, which left a still-uncounted number of deaths and thousands of wounded, the student organizations failed to make any progress toward democratization at that time, mainly due to the lack of organization in their movement, their lack of a strategy to reach the masses, and brutal repression from the military regime.

Second Phase of the Student Movement, Targeting the Masses, 1982

As student organizations began evaluating the causes of their failure to topple the military regime, they soon reached two different conclusions. The first group, the Murim School, concluded that the movement had failed because it had not drawn support from the masses, who were neither ready nor willing to challenge the military dictatorship. As mentioned above, the majority tacitly agreed to developmental dictatorship because the regime's industrialization policy seemed to be achieving tangible gains in the form of enhanced quality of living and higher economic status. Thus, the Murim students changed their movement's strategy from ineffective demonstration to one of educating the masses in each channel of socialization. Moreover, as part of this effort, they led labor workers to unionize (Kang, 1988: 24; Cho, 2000: 130-131). During the Park and Chun regimes, unionization was heavily oppressed. The 1987 June Resistance was the watershed in labor movements with the passing of a new labor law and the blossoming of unions and movements. Their strategy was similar to Gramsci's notion of "war of position," which represents a long-term strategy for acquiring ideological and moral leadership from the masses.

The other group of students, the *Hakrim*, challenged this strategy, arguing that organized and committed student organizations should continue to take a central role independent of the masses; they argued that the masses were not trained to achieve the goal of bringing down the military regime and that it was the students' role to focus on political direction. Gramsci's notion of a "war of maneuver" that specifically targeted the core power structure of the regime seems to perfectly describe the argument of the Hakrim group.

Third Phase of the Student Movement: Nationwide Organization and Quantitative Expansion, 1983-1986

What this historical debate among the student organizations recognized was the lack of consciousness and willingness to bring the military dictatorship down among the masses. At last, the Murim group won the debate against Hakrim group. Appreciating the need to educate the masses about the current political situation, students gradually decided to demonstrate before and with the masses. Accordingly, they shifted the location of their demonstrations from the campuses to the streets. In November 1982, demonstrations by the students of Seongkyunkwan University signaled this tactical shift, reaching the masses by filling the streets; this was followed by a series of demonstrations in major political and highly visible institutions and locations. In 1983, for example, they occupied the building of the ruling Minjeong Party building, police stations, and newspaper agencies. Also, starting in 1984, students began working with workers and unions. In 1984, 2,000 students from forty-two universities organized the Alliance of Students for Democratic Struggle and issued a statement demanding the end of labor union oppression on November 3. Kang (1998) also documented increased numbers and intensified degrees of student demonstrations: 191 students on November 1985 were arrested for occupying the ruling party educational center; 159 students were arrested at the May 3, 1986, Incheon demonstration; and 1,525 students were arrested for the October demonstration in Keonkuk University in 1986.

The occupation of the Catholic Church of Myeongdong in Seoul shows that these students had learned from the first phase of their movement. This protest arose in response to Chun's refusal to accept the people's demands for a constitutional amendment to the presidential elections. The background is as follows: In June 1985, there had been a mass uprising against Chun's military regime. Then, in April 1986, there arose a strong popular demand for amending the constitution; the main theme of this demand was to change the presidential election from an indirect election by the puppet organization of the electoral college to one of direct representation. Initially, Chun's regime seemed to compromise with the people on this amendment, but then in June 1985 the regime decided to keep the old constitution unchanged.

Churches also played a role as the supervisors of student demonstrations and the ultimate umpires on the moral status of the regime. Catholic priests not only appealed to students not to resort to violence but also actively mediated between students and police to achieve peaceful resolutions. Often, the priests persuaded police to guarantee that there would be no arrests or violence toward students and that the students would be allowed to return home safely. They sought to ensure that the honor of all involved—i.e., students, priests, and police—was respected. In conclusion, these student movements began to attract attention from the tacit majority of the masses and gained political legitimacy among students and anti-military social forces as well.

Fourth Phase of the Student Movement, Ending the Military Dictatorship, 1987

The end of the military dictatorship was precipitated by the death of two students in a series of anti-dictatorship demonstrations in 1987. On January 14, Seoul National University student Park Jong-cheol was tortured and killed, attracting national attention to the brutal repression of the anti-military regime forces. The regime's desperate efforts to cover up this brutality ignited the people's anger toward the dictatorship. Immediately, a series of aggressive student demonstrations broke out, and the masses began showing greater willingness to engage in these student-led movements of opposition against military dictatorship. On June 10, 1987, the head of the ruling party, Roh Tae-woo, was about to be nominated as presidential candidate while students were organizing one of the most massive demonstrations ever mobilized in downtown Seoul, reminiscent of the March First National Resistance Movement against Japanese colonial authority. As the police began to disperse the crowds, another student, Lee Han-yul of Yonsei University, was hit by a tear gas bullet and died later that same day as the ruling party candidate was nominated. The death of Lee marked a turning point against the ruling party and military regime; in fact, the nationwide street demonstrations mobilized 4 to 5 million citizens each day in the period following Lee's death (Cho, 2000: 124). Finally, the masses joined the students, and their involvement tipped the scales—suddenly, the military regime volunteered to return to direct presidential elections with a five-year term.

Thus, the anti-military dictatorship movements led by university students from 1970 to 1987 underwent a series of dramatic shifts from their disorganized reactions to the Park regime's attempt to extend its power to the more strategic and organized demonstrations by student, religious, and labor groups working together. This book confirmed important facts about the origins of heteronomical forces, the role of students in democratization, and the political nature of Korea's democratic movements. Throughout the political history of 20th-century Korea, university students have been principal actors in major social and political transformations; and students in the 1980s clearly identified themselves as successors of their Hanyang and Kyeongseong predecessors (Cho, 2000: 129). Although some student demonstrations may seem like the work of amateurs, students have become the most organized political and social force in Korea. Though they were keenly aware of the labor problems in Korea, it was not an economic motive that led them to participate in the opposition movement—their actions have always been politically motivated.

It is interesting to hear the perspectives of older generations and the ruling elites on these student demonstrations. Judges' admonitions of those students who had been arrested for anti-government actions seem clearly linked to the Confucian paradigm of regarding students as immature actors in society or the "first sons" of the family. For the most part, older generations tend to make the criticism that students should be aware of their status as students and behave accordingly. A common criticism of student actions is based on the belief that students are too young to make sound judgments and thus should remain within the boundaries of their academic lives as defined by society. Students were also warned that their involvement in violent political movements would be taken to mean that they had surrendered their "politically immune" student status. Interestingly, students who blame the ruling elites for engaging in political actions that extend beyond the boundaries of their role and the ruling elites who blame the students for the same transgression both fit within the dominant mode of Confucian thinking.

In November 1985, another example of students and government leaders holding each other to the Confucian code of conduct arose when a Special Statement was issued by the Interior Minister, Chung Seok-mo, on students' occupation of the Democratic Justice Party (*Minjeong Dang*) Headquarters. Parents of students, senior citizens, and neighbors were encouraged to dissuade problematic students from violent political activity by showing deep concern and warm affection. In the past, despite damage to state property and the loss of public personnel, the government/state tended to show an attitude of leniency and tolerance toward the illegal and violent political activities of students simply because they were students; however, intrusion into the Headquarters of the Democratic Justice Party posed a fundamental challenge and serious threat to the authority of the state and Parliamentary democracy. These students even tore down the national flag. This admonition from the top elites of the ruling party also confirms the political nature of student demonstrations and the democratization process in Korea, further evidence that the domestic political discourse was still strongly rooted in Confucian perceptions.

NOTES

1. This poem in Korean was translated by Dr. Choi Joo-ri, professor in the Department of English, Ewha Womans University. I want to extend my sincere thanks for her meticulous work on this poem.

2. See, Kim Kwang-woong (1990), pp. 37 and 283. The average turnout in elections for members of the National Assembly was 92.3 percent.

3. The name "Seoul" originated from that of the capital city of the Shilla Dynasty, *Seorabeol*, which was transmuted to *Sheobeul* and then finally to *Seoul*. In the early Three Kingdom era, the Seoul area belonged to Baekje Dynasty and was called *Wiryeseong*. After the peninsula was unified by the Shilla Dynasty, it began

to be called *Hansanju* and later *Hanyang-gun*. During the Goryeo Dynasty, it was changed to *Yang-ju* and then *Hanyang-bu* in the reign of King Chungryeol in 1308. The founder of the Joseon Dynasty, Yi Seong-gye, finally called it *Hanseong-bu*; however, the general public had called it "Seoul" since it had been transmuted from *Seorabeol* in the early Three Kingdom era.

4. For example, President Rhee declared the so-called Rhee Syngman Line, an Exclusive Marine Sovereignty, against Japan in 1953, expelling Japanese fisherman.

5. Japanese withdrawal from the Korean Peninsula accompanied the withdrawal of Japanese technology and capital that had been invested in Korea. Thus, the Korean economy, especially the industrial sector, shrunk significantly. For example, before Japanese withdrawal, there were 14,856 companies in the industrial sector; after National Liberation, this number decreased to 5,249, a decrease of 64 percent. Also, there was a 77 percent decrease in the number of employees from 549,751 to 122,159. See Kim and Kim (1995), p. 275. "In 1945 through 1965, technology transfer came mainly from the United States. After 1965, however, Korea relied primarily on technology transfer from Japan." On Japanese technological influence on Korea's economy, see Amsden (1989), pp. 231-233.

6. Kim and Kim (1995), *op.cit.*, p. 301.

7. In 1980, managers were paid almost 4 times as much as production workers in Korea. While this is far greater than the wage difference between managers and production workers in United States (1.79 times greater in 1977), the rate of wage increase for Korean production workers was greater than that for managerial workers from 1965 to 1984. See Amsden (1989), p. 231 on the comparison of relative occupational wage structure, and p. 199 on the rate of relative occupational wage increase in Korea.

8. It will cost an estimated $6M just to dismantle it. The Korean government estimates another $426M will be required to build a new national museum, which will replace the former Japanese Headquarters building. See *Choongang Daily News*, August 7, 1995. The decision to dismantle this building that was built by Japanese colonial headquarters was made by President Kim Young-sam when he was inaugurated in 1993, and dismantlement began on August 15 (i.e., the Day of National Liberation from Japanese colonial control) in 1995 and was completed in November 1996.

9. See Lee (1968), p. 88.

10. Henceforth "cadet-bureaucrats."

11. Among them, 55 have retired and 729 are still in government positions: 131 in the Ministry of Home Affairs, 83 in the Seoul Metropolitan Government, 65 in the National Tax Administration, 38 in the Board of Audit and Inspection, 34 in the Ministry of Education, 29 in the Customs Administration, 27 in the Ministry of Construction, 24 in the Ministry of Commerce and Industry, 24 in the National Railroad Administration, 23 in the Ministry of Foreign Affairs, 21 in the Ministry of Labor, 20 in the Ministry of Transportation, 16 in the Ministry of National Defense, 16 in the Ministry of Government Administration, 12 in the Economic Planning Board, and 8 in the Supply Administration.

12. Its name was changed to "Capital Defense Headquarters" in the early 1980s. It was located in Pildong in Chung-gu, one of the most developed and prestigious areas in Seoul. Then, it moved south of the Han River in the early 1990s.

13. The location of these core units of the Army Capital Garrison Command and the Defense Security Command are secret. See Lee (1996), p. 468.

14. Six major changes occurred: (1) the creation of a new office only for the general administrative agency in July 1961; (2) government re-organization in October 1961; (3) the introduction of the system of personnel management in October 1961; (4) the adoption of a new office management system in March 1962; (5) the revision of the National Public Servants Law for a new personnel management system in April 1963; and (6) the adoption of a position classification system from 1963 to 1966. See Kim and Kim (1995), p. 303.

15. Perkins (1994: 658) argues that the success of strong interventionist industrial policy in Northeast Asian Highly Performing Asian Economies can be explained by the superiority of the government's managerial capacity over that of entrepreneurs. Analysis of the military leadership of managerial capacity toward bureaucracy and entrepreneurs aptly provides a background explanation for Perkins' argument.

16. Kim and Kim (1995), *op.cit.*, p. 304.

17. *Ibid.*, p. 305.

18. *Ibid.*, p. 306.

19. Major public enterprises that were privatized in 1968 include Korea Shipbuilding and Engineering Corporation, Korea Marine Transport, Inchon Heavy Industry Corporation, Korea Transport Corporation, Korea Machinery Industry, Korean Airline, and Korea Steel. See, *ibid.*

20. Korean Institute of Architects, *op.cit.*, p. 152.

21. *Ibid.*, p. 250.

22. *Ibid.*, p. 157.

23. *Ibid.*, p. 150.

24. The point here is not to draw an unrealistic comparison between early 1900 economic scale with that of the 20th-century advanced Korean economy. Rather, it is important to note that the dichotomous framework of sacred and profane spaces and places was consciously maintained in the Kyeongseong era, whereas the Seoul era took selective steps to continue to capitalize on the sacred hegemony of state and purge the traces of heteronomical forces from both the sacred and profane districts.

25. "Group" in Korea means a big enterprise that has many subsidiary companies. A chaebol can be called a "group"; however, the term "group" includes enterprises smaller than chaebols as well.

26. Seoul City Hall (1994), *op.cit.*, pp. 367-368.

27. These are Samsung, Hyundai, Gold Star, Daewoo, Sunkyung, Ssangyong, Hanjin, Kia, Lotte, and Hankook Hwayak.

28. This was the *History of the Central District*, which was commissioned to be written and published by Seoul City Hall.

29. Of course, the whole sphere of Seoul has been expanded, mainly to the south of the Han River. According to recent Seoul city planning, there are three centers in Seoul: Chung-gu and Chongro-gu, Youngdeungpo, and Jamsil. The first center is planned for major management functions, the second for industry, and the third as a commercial center. See Chu (1983), p. 31.

30. *Ibid.*, p. 308.

31. *Ibid.*, p. 310.

32. Specific policies that contributed to the consolidation of chaebols include the following: export-driven policy since the 1960s, the 8.3 Loan Freeze in 1972, Heavy and Chemical Industry Policy since 1973, the General Trading Company in 1975, the Adjustment Policy on Heavy and Chemical Industries in 1980, the Rationalization Policy of Foreign Construction in 1985, and the Industry Development Law in 1986. See, *ibid.*, p. 312.

33. After National Liberation, the capital value of Japanese property accounted for 91 percent of total domestic capital. It was disposed of by the American Military Government and the First Republic with incomparably favorable conditions to enterprises. For example, purchasers were supposed to pay 10 percent of the current price on a fifteen-year hire-purchase plan. The government arranged bank loans for those who wanted to buy but had no money since prices kept soaring and the value of currency had dropped to 1/300 of what it had been for the fifteen years prior to the time of borrowing. Thus, the borrowers were able to pay back a loan of "expensive" money with "cheaper" money. See Lee (1990), pp. 24-25.

34. Kim and Kim (1995), *op.cit.*, p. 312.

35. *Ibid.*, p. 289. In 2008, the total number of civil servants in Korea reached about a million.

36. The Director of the Finance Bureau, Lee Ki-Hong, studied India's plan as a model for Korea when he was dispatched to the ECAFE in 1958. Later, other bureaucrats also took the Indian plan as a model for Korea. Together, they created the Five-Year Economic Development Plan based on the Indian plan. See Lee, Man-Hee (1993), p. 79.

37. *Ibid.*, p. 54.

38. *Ibid.*, p. 76.

39. See Yang (1996), p. 320.

40. *Ibid.*, p. 333.

41. *Choson Daily News* (1985), pp. 79-80. The translation was done by the author directly from the original statement.

42. *Ibid.*, pp. 77-79. In the April 19 Statement, made by students of Korea University, students saw their school as the "headquarters of Resistance Nationalism against Japanese colonial rule." See, *ibid.*, p. 75.

43. Dong (1987), *op.cit.*, p. 239. Chonnam University is an exceptional case, playing a vanguard role in student activism after the Kwangju Massacre in 1980. It is exceptional in that Chonnam University is not located in the capital city.

44. See Wilson (1988), p. 1070.

Chapter Six

Korea's Simultaneous Achievements Reconsidered

By utilizing a constructivist approach and evidence drawn from spatial arrangements and architectural artifacts, as well as classical literature and texts, we have traced the complex and unique interactions that occurred among the hegemony, hierarchy, and heteronomy of each era in the history of Korea's capital city.[1] Our indigenous approach yielded authentic findings by unearthing the roots of Korea's state-society relations and applying the insights thus gained to the analysis of the unique political and economic challenges that Korea faced. This book's central aim has been to draw from Korea's own history and indigenous sources an explanation of how an economically underdeveloped Joseon Dynasty and the traditionally authoritarian political system of Confucianism could end up achieving globally recognized rapid and sustainable economic development and vibrant democracy in Asia. Ultimately, this is the question of how to explain the simultaneous phenomena of economic and political advancement in Korea's late developmental period from the 1960s to the '80s. In the literature, the state was singled out as the most important factor in Korea's late development without providing any relative perspectives on the state's counterpart—namely, society. Finally, the lens of state-society relations led us to examine the relative roles of the developmental state and aggressive civil society in Korea's economic and political development as well as the consequent changes during the three main eras of Korea's capital city.

MAIN QUESTIONS

As a whole, in our discussion, we have aimed to identify and explain the unsubstantiated factors that have contributed to Korea's rapid and sustainable economic development, most of which occurred during the Park regime from the 1960s to the 1980s. We have also sought to elucidate how Korean society was able to achieve democratization during this same period despite many unfavorable conditions, including the strong legacy of military dictatorship, the presumably anti-democratic ideology of Confucianism, and the repressive and militaristic colonial control of Japan. The most important angle of attack adopted in this analysis was the question of how these two simultaneous phenomena can be analyzed through the use of a single integrated paradigm.

By far, the most essential point in this effort is to locate the power of state and identify its relations to society. More specifically, it is necessary to focus on what factors made possible the phenomenon of the developmental state and the emergence of an exuberant civil society out of nowhere. Was it facilitated by the fact that the Park regime relied upon its military power to do all that a typical developmental state must do? If so, then how can underdevelopment be understood in Third World countries that operate under similar military regimes? Did democracy fall from the sky? Was it due to the American introduction of liberalism after national liberation in 1945? Setting aside the military power of a developmental regime, it is important to ask what other variables have been involved in a successful developmental regime and particularly in Korean society. This book has considered American economic aid and Cold War international politics as factors that helped the Korean economy to gain access to the biggest market and most advanced technology possible. Other major theories of social science, such as modernization and dependency, were examined in terms of their limited applicability to the Korean case due to their characteristics as grand theories. Along these lines, we adopted an indigenous source of political and social ideologies that have critically affected the thinking, political culture, and political systems of Korea over the course of the nation's history since the Three Kingdom period. Although Confucianism and geomantic principles have been the *modus operandi* in Korean political culture for over a thousand years, they have been ignored due to their authoritarian and unscientific nature; yet, they have consistently impacted the consolidation and transformation of political power throughout Korean history. These two sources composed the changing soil in which every political regime in Korean political history was grounded; furthermore, these were two of the main components of existing power in Korea, according to Foucault's conceptualization of dispersed power of knowledge. Thus, it might be an oversimplification to say that the legitimacy of the developmental state's intervention in the economy and its power to force industrial policy and mobilization on societal actors and institutions were produced by the physical aspect of the Park military regime. On this topic, Foucault was correct to point out that power is not constructed by the wills of individuals or collectives; rather, "power is constructed and functions on the basis of particular powers, myriad issues, myriad effects of power"—e.g., Confucian and geomantic political cultures intermingled with Taoistic understanding of the nature and human affairs in Korean history. Thus, we have sought to understand the historical origins of the developmental state in Korea and the establishment of heteronomical forces in a Confucian-oriented society.

To address the questions raised above, Korean and foreign scholars have commonly applied two grand theories to Korea. The first was modernization, which argues primarily that economic modernization is a prerequisite for democratization in Third World countries. Seymour Martin Lipset, who was one of the founders of modernization theory and a supporter of the belief that economic modernization has a positive impact on consequent democratization, eventually reconsidered his argument on the prerequisites of democratization in his famous 1993 Presidential Address to the American Sociological Association. After re-evaluating the widely accepted notion of a causal nexus between capitalistic economic development and democracy, he concluded that such a nexus remains "merely associational," not causal. Any generalization reached by means of a formula tends to be misguided as is often found in grand theories that generalize a causal relationship between independent and dependent variables. In fact, the level of analysis in grand theory is so general that its theorists are often unable to make logical connections between theory and well-grounded observation: "They never get down from the higher generalities to problems in their historical and structural contexts. This absence of a firm sense of genuine problems, in turn, makes for the unreality so noticeable in their pages" (Wright, 1959: 33). The major flaw of modernization theory's explanation of Korea's economic and political development is that these two phenomena occurred simultaneously and not as consecutive links in a chain of causation. If we follow the path taken by Western countries according to modernization theory, Korea in the 1960s was unprepared for democratization because it was still traditional and not economically ready.

Rather than rehashing such arguments about which came first—economic or political development—Lipset (1994: 5-17) emphasizes cultural factors. Indeed, he views cultural factors as being more important than economic ones, as well as the particular contexts of each country where the nature of strategic interactions among groups of various strengths (i.e., minority political groups and major actors) is multivariate in their power struggle toward democratization. Remaining somewhat hazy on the impacts of Confucianism upon democracy, however, Lipset merely introduces opposing arguments on this issue. Karl's point (1990: 19), quoted by Lipset (1994: 16), suggests a new research direction to "clarify how the mode of regime transition (itself conditioned by the breakdown of authoritarian rule) sets the context within which strategic interactions can take place because these interactions, in turn, help to determine whether political democracy will emerge and survive." This point provides insight into how we can understand Korea's democratization process since this book argues that the democratization was achieved concurrently with, and not as a by-product of, economic modernization. In addition, by the time that the military dictatorship was toppled and democracy was ready to enter full swing around the 1980s, the effect of economic development was not yet strong enough to produce a politically motivated and capable middle class, working class, and labor unions, as discussed in chapter 5. Though both the middle class and labor unions were present during the massive opposition movement against Park's military regime, they were incapable of leading or playing a critical role in the democratic movement. Instead, the middle class remained a politically tacit majority for economic reasons, and the labor union, which had not reached its full power, remained helpless against the repressive labor policy of the military regime.

Few studies have been conducted on the formation of socioeconomic forces in Korea with regards to their roles in Korea's democratization. Even though Lipset concludes that the link between economic development indicators and democracy is not causal but merely associational, there is a strong consensus that a transformation of class structure in Western democracy has always strengthened pro-democratic socioeconomic forces such as the middle and working class. In this perspective, Koo's 1991 study on the formation of the middle class and its influence upon Korea's democratization set the standard for this field. After investigating changes in occupational structure from 1955 to 1985, Koo (1991: 486) points to the explosive increase in the middle class, including the increase in professional, managerial, and clerical workers from 6.7 percent to 16.6 percent in the two decades from 1963 to 1983, and finds that the middle class played a deterministic role in the outcomes and the concrete forms of democratization and the formation of the working class. Koo's analysis, however, remains equivocal and sometimes contradictory in regards to the question of what factor played the most decisive role in contributing to the demise of the military dictatorship and the emergence of a democratic political system in Korea. Most scholars, including Koo (1991: 494), agree that it was the Resistance of June 10 in 1987, led by university students and radical intelligentsia, that marked the watershed of such democratic revolution in Korea. Koo's research on the rise and influence of the middle class, however, also acknowledges that within three months of that "vanguard role" (Koo, 1991: 496) being played by the students in June 10 Resistance of 1987, three thousand labor disputes arose, "more than the total number of labor conflicts that occurred during the entire period of the Park and Chun regimes (1961-1979)." In conclusion, no major socioeconomic studies have examined the issue of how the economic development during the developmental process affected the formation of the middle class or how the emergence of this middle class, in turn, contributed to political development in Korea.

Pak (1998: 66) also finds that there were approximately 2,800 strikes at that time, as compared to the yearly average of around 200, which had remained steady until 1986. In other words, despite their support for democracy, the role of the middle and working classes in the democratization process remained more supportive than deterministic (Koo, 1991; Pak, 1998: 60, 65). Pak (1998: 65) specifically claims that "the role of the middle class was crucial in influencing the response of the military regime, but not that it was the central actor," and adds that the working class participated in the democracy movement "in a limited way." Also, until the June Resistance in 1987, the working class lacked the right to collectively bargain because the military regime had blocked legislation for the collective bargaining rights of unions (Pak, 1998: 58). For this reason, university students stopped attending school and instead began working in the factories, hiding their student status, surreptitiously helping workers to organize more labor unions for better protection of their rights. Pak (1998: 60) argues that it is essential "to examine the internal development of the democracy movement itself, and how it interacted with various class forces," focusing on the critical role played by students and the sources from which such legitimacy may have derived. Korean nationalism against Japanese colonial control contributed to the consolidation of dissenting voices, Pak (1998: 61) finds, and then Korea's democratization was complicated by Cold War confrontation with the communist North.

In discussing what factors led to Korea's democracy, Lipset considers education as more important than either income or occupation. In his own words (1960: 40), Lipset argues that "If we cannot say that a 'high' level of education is a sufficient condition for democracy, the available evidence suggests that it comes close to being a necessary one." Ironically, though, Korea has long maintained a high level of education, an indicator in Lipset's economic development variable, yet economic underdevelopment continued till the late 1980s. Lipset (1960: 40) argues that no higher correlation should be anticipated with economic development "even on theoretical grounds because, to the extent that the political subsystem of the society operates autonomously, a political form may persist under conditions normally adverse to the emergence of that form. Or a political form may develop because of a syndrome of unique historical factors even though the society's major characteristics favor another form." As Lipset argues, a generalization between economic indicators and democracy is not applicable to the Korean context for two reasons: (1) democratization was achieved through a long series of political movements led mostly by highly educated university students, intelligentsia, and other social opposition forces before the middle and working classes began to play a decisive role in the democratic movement; and (2) democratization was achieved under the four democracy-adverse historical legacies of the Confucian Joseon Dynasty, Japanese colonial occupancy, American Military Government, and the subsequent Cold War bi-polar confrontation with communist North Korea.

More importantly, Lipset (1960: 29) states, "I am primarily concerned with the social conditions like education which serve to support democratic political systems, and I will not deal in detail with the internal mechanisms like the specific rules of the political game which serve to main them. A comparative study of complex social systems must necessarily deal rather summarily with the particular historical features of any one society." What this book has attempted to accomplish is to answer Lipset's call for comparativist research: to thoroughly explain the internal historical power dynamics (i.e., Korea's particular historical and cultural features) among the three types of rule over the history of a particular nation. Long embedded in Confucian political history was the legitimacy of university students and formerly co-opted Confucian civil society (Sarim) in their role as voices of dissent against the hegemonic political order and power. The internal mechanisms and dynamics that existed between the hegemonic Confucian political order, which was shared and maintained by the royal family and scholarly bureaucrats, and the voices of dissent within this hegemonic framework (i.e., Sarim, Daegan, and Seongkyunkwan) provide a key to understanding the vanguard role played by university students in the democratization of modern Korea. This book's focus has been very close to Pak's view (1998) that the internal development of the democracy movement and its methods of interacting with various class forces can best be understood if reconstructed in the context of the competition for legitimacy among Confucian forces and their successors. The interplay between Korea's Confucian legacy and democratization process is explained well by Kihl: "Confucian cultural legacies such as respect for education and hierarchy have impacted the ways in which the confrontation between regime and opposition was carried out and managed" (1994: 48).

Similarly, Woo-Cumings (1999: 20) states, "The power of the developmental state grows both out of the barrel of the gun and through its ability to convince the population of its political, economic, and moral mandate." While it is obvious that the power of both Japanese militarism and Park's military dictatorship in modern Korea can be attributed to "the barrel of the gun," Woo-Cumings remains unclear about their source of legitimacy and actual capacity to make political, economic, and moral mobilizations. In her search for the answer, Woo-Cumings (1999: 20) claims "Western observers have had a hard time understanding the legitimacy of the developmental regime in East Asia, often confusing it with a cultural (or 'Confucian') penchant for political acquiescence. 'Asian values' account for East Asia's weak civil societies, if not developmental state legitimacy (which remains a puzzle)." This penchant has kept scholars from looking more deeply into the factors at work in the case of Korea.

To examine Korea's democratization, several distinctive features of the Korean political system must be considered. First of all, it is essential to note that the political ideologies which served as the major state ideologies during the main eras of Korean history—the Joseon Dynasty, Japanese colonial control, and American Military Government—were not native but came from foreign countries. The Confucianism that was upheld by the Joseon Dynasty as a supreme state ideology for more than 500 years, and which served as a key to the establishment of centralized bureaucracy, was of Chinese—not Korean—origin. Confucian political culture thoroughly penetrated into every realm of Korean society. Similarly, the Japanese governance system which adopted British (e.g., Parliamentary and political party systems) and Prussian (e.g., constitution) models of government was also implanted from outside during Japan's unprecedented control of thirty-five years. And lastly, the American liberal political system was introduced through the influence of American protestant missionaries starting in the late 19th century and continuing throughout the American Military Government from 1945 to 1948. At the same time, ironically, those foreign political ideologies equipped the dissenting voices with justifications to stand up against power that was based on other foreign ideologies (Buruma, 1987): overthrow of Buddhist Goryeo by Neo-Confucian Joseon and resistance against Japan by liberalism and Christianity. Such a phenomenon may sound contradictory but has been a pattern inherent to major changes of political system throughout Korea's political history. In short, Korea has been the place of conflicts among major powers. And whenever these superpowers—i.e., China, Japan, Russia, England, and the United States—collided with each other, their ideologies and culture became involved as well. New external power and its ideology had always formed the basis of resistance nationalism in Korea and played the catalytic role of reforming old domestic institutions and systems as and refreshed the nature of heteronomical forces.

Second, hybridity arose as a by-product of the existence of three different political eras with different foreign ideologies. Indeed, in contemporary modern Korean society, these three ideologies have become three sources of political legitimacy, each competing for different constituencies. The Confucian legacy still lingers in Korea's political culture, upholding strong state and government as a virtue and maintaining hierarchical and authoritarian mores. Japanese occupation strengthened the rigidity and hierarchy of the strong state tradition, and the American Military Government introduced liberal political ideology and economic modernization policy, which seem antithetical to Confucian political ideology. Because these three different sources of political ideology each appealed to different political constituencies, they complicated the political dynamics involved in the process of democratization. For example, Confucian and Japanese militarism were supported by a right-wing conservative constituency that desired a stronger role for central state after both national liberation in 1945 and the Korean War in 1953, whereas liberalism was responsible for bringing forth the anti-military dictatorship movement throughout the post-colonial period. The anti-government demonstrations were set off in part by the introduction of liberal democracy; however, the major heteronomical forces involved in this series of demonstrations, as well as their legitimacy, can be traced back to the earlier periods of Korea's political history as examined in previous chapters. The power of student elites to serve as checks and balances in Korean politics stemmed from their role in Confucian court politics, and thus was embedded in Korean politics long before the introduction of American liberalism in the mid-20th century.

That the political ideology originated from foreign sources has very important implications for the domestic power structure and mechanism by which power is balanced between the rulers (hegemony and hierarchy) and the ruled (heteronomy). The degree to which the hegemony is vulnerable depends greatly upon whether the political ideology is aboriginal or foreign in the context of competition for political legitimacy between hegemony and heteronomy. Ruling power groups that are based on an aboriginal political ideology tend to be less vulnerable than those that are based on a foreign political ideology. In other words, when a heteronomical force claims that the hegemony has violated the ruling ideology, for example, the hegemonic group becomes much more fragile if their ruling ideology is foreign, especially when that heteronomical force has been given the responsibility to uphold the foreign state ideology. This book views such situations as competition for legitimacy between hegemonic and heteronomical forces centered around a state ideology of foreign origin.

In the literature, current analyses tend to look to military despotic rule as an explanation for rapid economic development. Such reification, however, connotes a distorted view of the economic development of NICs in general and of Korea in particular as being negative or atypical. This book finds that the need to account for Korea's developmental phenomenon as an exceptional case stems from the lack of systematic theoretical bases for such state-society relations. By focusing solely on either state or society, current literature often fails to address the nature of state hegemony, which is mutually (re)constructed and (re)produced over time by both state and society.

Often embedded in Western culture is the tendency to separate politics from the economy. In other words, dichotomous and confrontational relations between the state and economy are deeply rooted in belief systems of the West. Accordingly, the literature on the East Asian developmental state has focused disproportionately on either coercive state power or the private market principle; however, a different type of relationship between state and economy was established in Korea under the Confucian influence. State and economy were seen as mutually inclusive and cooperative; in fact, politics and the economy were inseparable. The norm in Confucian Asian culture has been not to separate these two domains, not even in official settings. In this non-liberal form of state-society relations, politics took a position of precedence over economy, and an essential feature of the developmental state was its capacity to intervene in economic matters. Such a tendency of intervention in the economy by public institutions, including direct government subsidies for growing industries for the purpose of competing with already established economies in the global market, is also found in the relationship between state and economy in the United States; however, it is uncommon to officially declare such a direct mutual relationship in the American *laissez-faire* context, whereas governments in Europe with more traditional relationships between government and economy take direct government subsidies toward their own industry more for granted. The Korean case is more like the European cases. In this perspective, it is important to ask, "From what source did the state obtain this legitimacy to intervene in the economy?" In other words, to understand the role of the developmental state in Korea, we must consider not only the current situation but how it came about as well.

To gain new insights into the workings of the developmental state in Korea, we have applied Onuf's paradigm of three different types of rule to the Korean context. This framework provides criteria to operationalize the rule and rules in a given society into the relations of state and society. Our investigation of how the current situation came about included four states of inquiry: (1) the historical origins of state hegemony during the Joseon Dynasty; (2) state-society relations in a non-Western, non-liberal context; (3) local-global interaction and its impact on state hegemony; and (4) changes in state hegemony over time. In addition to textual sources, non-textual research material has enabled us to reconstruct the rules as manifested in the above-mentioned four categories. For example, to articulate relations between state (politics) and society (economy), we examined geographical and spatial arrangements, such as city layout, city monumentality, and building structures. Such areas of research provide reliable, consistent, and predictive evidence that reflects hegemonic political and economic ideals as manifested in concrete forms, supporting Gramsci's and Mann's conceptualization of state hegemony as well as the appropriateness of Onuf's methodological paradigm. To illuminate how the rules embedded in this evidence actually operated in the power relations among major social forces, this book delineated the power configurations that existed among those major social forces over three major eras in the political history of Korea.

SUMMARY OF FINDINGS

What has our investigation found? Principally, this book provides a generative explanation of the process by which the state achieved legitimacy to intervene in the economy. This explanation recognizes that the rules of state-society relations are embedded in Korean political culture and adapt to new phenomena. Through the lens of Onuf's paradigm, this book also demonstrates Gramsci's conception of the integral state, which features both political and ideological domination. The articulation of Confucian state-society relations incorporates the spontaneous consent given by the ruled (i.e., Gramsci's notion of ideological domination). Whereas claims about military despotic rule and the apparent submissiveness of the people are merely descriptive, this generative account explains how the strong state and the people's consent each came about. Tracing the rule-governed workings of state-society relations over time in Korea disputes the reification of despotic rule along with its concomitant negative connotations.

Table 6.1 summarizes the major rules established during the Joseon Dynasty in Onuf's formulation of three distinctive types of rule.

Upon examining the foundation of the developmental state's strong state leadership, which made Korea's unprecedented economic growth possible, we find that the major principles that gave rise to Korea's developmental state were formed over several eras of Korea's history. A major principle in the making of the developmental state is the establishment of Confucian state hegemony over all aspects of society, including the economic sector. The Confucian state hegemony is constituted of three sub-rules. First, by defining the role of politics as one of statecraft providing people with economic well-being, Confucianism takes a position of political precedence over the economy, thereby providing the bureaucracy with an ideological legitimization of tight control over the economic sector. Second, civil superiority over the military was established as a major political rule of Confucian state hegemony. And as a last sub-rule related to economic sector, in Confucian Joseon society, industrial and commercial activities were highly limited and controlled due to the Confucian elites' fear that these economic sectors would corrupt the people and potentially challenge Confucian political authority;

Table 6.1 Major Rules of the Hanyang Period

Rule	Major Rules (H: Hanyang)	Forces
Hegemony	H-A. Confucian State Hegemony H-a. Political precedence over economy H-b. Civil superiority over military H-c. Commerce/Industry given low status	King, Confucian scholars and bureaucrats
Hierarchy	H-B. State's Legitimacy to Intervene in Society H-d. Law for hierarchical political & social structure H-e. Tight control of economic activities for government's needs and political purposes	Confucian scholars and bureaucrats (CSB)
Heteronomy	H-C. Confucianism – Foreign (Extraterritoriality) H-f. Co-opted, embraced, limited, dissenting voice (loyal opposition or semi-opposition)	Confucian students (CS), Sarim, and bureaucrats (Daegan)

thus, industrial and commercial activities were allowed only to the extent that they satisfied the needs of the Confucian bureaucracy.

The legitimacy of state intervention in the economy established during the Joseon Dynasty was quite political. The case of Hanyang substantiates the claim that the Confucian state's hegemony and political legitimacy to intervene in the economy were firmly manifested in spatial form in the choice of its capital city, the city's Confucian monumentality, and its administrative codes; conversely, these physical manifestations sustained the centrality of the state hegemony and supported its legitimacy to intervene in the economy.

The two most important elements in the legibility of Hanyang are the intentions of Confucian political ideology and the city's integration into nature by geomancy. This demonstrates Harvey and Agnew's claims[2] in that the capital city of the Joseon Dynasty functioned as a place where the state hegemony was propagated and the people's recognition of that legitimacy was incorporated as their recognition of the state's direct link with Heaven, the ultimate source of the mandate to govern. The site of Hanyang was chosen for its resemblance to the ideal celestial archetype in which Polaris represented the source of the Will of Heaven. From this extended the North-South *axis mundi*, representing the line connecting the macrocosmos (Heaven or Celestial Archetype) to the microcosmos (Hanyang, Kyeongbok Palace, and the King).

In relation to this *axis mundi*, the cardinal orientation, including the East-West axis, branched out in all directions. Within this ideal place, a dichotomous concept of sacred and profane clearly and hierarchically divided the space into various places. Such divisions are evident within the capital's walls (fig. 5-1). The outer circle in this figure, marked by X, represents an overall "sacred place X" compared to the regions outside of Hanyang castle. Its topological configurations (fig. 3-2) clearly resemble the Celestial Chart of Jamiwon (astronomical quadrants centered on Polaris) shown in figure 3.1. The upper triangle is the "sacred place Y," representing political dominion over economic activity, which is limited to the East-West axis. All of the important Confucian political, bureaucratic, and educational institutions were located within this "sacred place Y," making Confucian political monumentality and its superiority over the economy fully evident (map 2.2). Hierarchically partitioned space was utilized as a means to enhance Confucian state hegemony. The Confucian government's tight control over economic activity was reflected in the detailed regulations of the Administrative Code of Joseon, the *Kyeongguk daejeon*. As examined earlier, all government officials in central and provincial offices were rigidly limited in number and assigned to one of 18 ranks. The central government enlisted 2,841 craftsmen for approximately 129 different kinds of work in 30 government offices. Such strict control was also applied to slaves and students. In this way, the Confucian government tightly controlled personnel and material resources.

A good example of that control can be found in figure 3.9, "Market Plan with Prescribed Sections for Trading in Each Commodity" for *Yukuijeon*. Such strict regulation of economic activities can be interpreted as a close tie between state and economy, a relationship that can still be found in the modern developmental period of Seoul. According to the rationale of this book's findings, it seems likely that the chaebols of Korea's modern economy originated from Yukuijeon; however, the chaebols differ in that the tight control of economic activities during the Hanyang period existed not for the purpose of developing the economy itself but to satisfy government demands. Indeed, government controls in the Hanyang era aimed to suppress the rise of commercial and industrial social forces, which were regarded as a threat to the Confucian political ideal. Also, accommodation for the dissenting voice, though co-opted and relatively weak, during the Hanyang period is evidenced in the location of the National Confucian Academy and several government institutions within the sacred grounds as government-embraced forces of heteronomy.

The legacy of the Hanyang era experienced both continuities and changes during the Kyeongseong era. The main category of continuation involved the appropriation of the value reflected in various forms of special arrangements. The changes included the massive destruction and degradation of major Confucian political institutions as well as the implanting of Japanese imperial authority in their stead and the introduction of a capitalistic economic system. Even though "Confucian" state hegemony was replaced by Japanese imperial authority, due to the strength of the state under Japanese imperialism, the tradition of strong state continued. Table 6.2 summarizes these continuities and changes.

As table 6.2 shows, the principle of political precedence over the economy remained in place, despite the replacement of Confucian state hegemony by Japanese imperial authority, so state intervention in the economy continued, with even more strength than before. Compared to the Confucian tradition of political precedence over economic power, Japanese colonial authority added to this tradition the military superiority over the civil superiority of Confucian Joseon. Also, in terms of bureaucratic control of society, the tradition from the Hanyang period was generally maintained; in fact, it was strengthened through the introduction of a more centralized, modern administrative legal system first from Japan and then from the US military. In that way, the rigidity of the military management system was added to the traditional Confucian civil bureaucracy.

On the other hand, the Kyeongseong period reversed some old principles and introduced new ones. "Local-global interaction" refers here to interaction between the traditional Confucian order and Japanese modernized imperial capitalism, which had a significant impact on the political and economic system in Korea. Politically, as a result of Japanese imperial militarism, the Confucian principle of civil superiority over the military was reversed. Economically,

Table 6.2 Continuities and Changes during the Kyeongseong Era

Rule	Hanyang	New Rules (K: Kyeongseong, N: New Rules)	Forces
Hegemony	H-A H-a H-b	K-A. Japan's Imperial Authority (Supplants Confucian Political Institutions) K-a. Political precedence over economy (continued) K-b. Military superiority over civil power (a reversal) K-c. Commerce/Industry given high status (a reversal) KN-1. Introduction of Japanese capitalism	Japanese bureaucrats (JB), collaborators, Japanese military (JM), Capitalists
Hierarchy	H-B H-d H-e	K-B. State's Legitimacy to Intervene in Society (continued) K-d. Law for political & social control (strengthened) K-e. Cooperative relationship between state & economy for development of economy itself (modified)	Same as above
Heteronomy	H-C H-f	K-C. Western Liberalism + Christianity + Traditional Religion à Mainly Foreign K-f. Upsurge of heteronomical forces based on united stance (drastic transformation)	Former CSB, students, religion, mass media, missionaries, the people

** "H" stands for Hanyang and "K" for Kyeongseong. "KN-1" means the first new rules added during the Kyeongseong period.

the Confucian agricultural industry was forced by Japan to adopt the new power and system of capitalism, thereby reversing the Confucian tradition of treating commercial and industrial activities as lowly. Consequently, the lopsided governmental control was transformed into more cooperative relations between state and economy for the development of the economy itself. Also, for the purpose of expanding the Japanese sphere of influence into the Asian continent, the Japanese government promoted capitalistic development with the intention of using the Korean Peninsula as a springboard. Interestingly, such a move contrasts the way in which Confucian political authority suppressed commercial and industrial activities in order to protect itself from potential threats. Thus, a collusive relationship between state (government) and economy was established. Though both cases were based on political motives, they harbored very different purposes. While seemingly opposite, both suppression and encouragement of the economic sector served political ends. This illustrates the continuing rule of Confucian political precedence over the economy.

All of these continuities and changes were clearly reflected in Kyeongseong's spatial arrangements. The "sacred place Y" in figure 5.1 remained a site where political institutions were highly concentrated, as it had been during the Hanyang era. The locations of major political institutions, such as the Governors-General Headquarters directly in front of the main office of the King, or the Japanese Infantry Corps and Gendarmerie Commander in the former Six Ministries Street, clearly substantiate the claim that political values were embodied in the space, a claim which is further evidenced by the Japanese appropriation thereof. There was no better space than "sacred place Y" for legitimizing Japanese colonial rule, appropriating the people's strong attachment to that space; however, the presence of both military and police institutions in the former "sacred place Y" shows the reversal of the Confucian principle of civil superiority over the military. Also, the systematic occupation and appropriation of the former Confucian sacred zone was the best means to frustrate the national identity and debilitate the nationalism of the defeated Confucian Koreans.

Another important change resulting from Japan's introduction of capitalism can be found in the development of the former "profane place W" of the Hanyang era into a more substantial commercial, industrial, and financial center. Such a development of the former profane area reflects a dramatic shift in the belief system from the Confucian notion of commercial/industrial activities as lowly. This reversal also reflects a change in the relationship between state and economy from unilateral control of the economy by government to more cooperative relations between the two.

Among the changes made in this period, there are two highly salient features: the strengthening of state hegemony and the upsurge of heteronomical forces. Ironically, the fall of Joseon to imperial Japan, in fact, made the people's attachment to hegemonic Confucian state and their aspirations for the recovery of their own state even stronger. The atrocities of Japanese oppression effectively reinvigorated the tradition of powerful and legitimate dissent in Korean society, which later played a vital role in confronting the military dictatorship and accelerating the democratization process in modern Korea. In particular, the students who were equipped with the resources of Western liberalism and Christianity inherited the legacy of state hegemony and were granted the legitimacy to stand up against injustice. New educational institutions founded mostly by American missionaries and old Korean elites became concentrated within the "sacred place Y," which illustrates the continuity of the heteronomical forces appropriating the political legitimacy of this former Confucian zone. This serves as evidence that the power of the students was concomitant with the Korean people's traditional belief of the legitimacy invested in this geographical location, as shown in figures 4.3 and 4.4.

This shows how Korea's interaction with Japan actually contributed toward the consolidation of state hegemony in Korea over the long term and increased the presence of heteronomical forces in Korean society. In effect, Japan's occupation made the masses more sympathetic and patriotic toward the Confucian hegemony and its hierarchical governance system, which in fact had exploited them under a strong caste system for over a half-century. It was the confrontation between Korea's Confucian political order and modernized Japan during this Kyeongseong period that fully harnessed the essential conditions for the developmental state: (1) legitimate state intervention in the economy based on Confucian tradition of political precedence over the economy and (2) a collusive and mutually enforcing relationship between the state and a capitalistic economy. In addition, the strong hierarchical forces, represented by the bureaucracy and originating from the Hanyang era, were continued and inadvertently strengthened by the Japanese modernized centralized bureaucratic system.[3] The continuation of these strong hierarchical forces was a result of this local-global (i.e., Korean-Japanese) interaction that the Park regime inherited when it came to power in 1961. This substantiates the argument that despotic rule based on military power and economically efficient bureaucracy is not the sole explanation for the developmental phenomenon of the 1960s and '70s in Korea. Also, by indicating the role played by heteronomical forces, this book showed how state power is mutually (re)constructed and (re)produced over time in both state and society using Onuf's reconstitutive rules of hegemony, hierarchy, and heternomy.

Tracing this line through to modern times, we can view Seoul as containing all of these major rules that characterize a developmental state or developmental phenomenon as well as vibrant civil society and democracy. Of course, correlative relationships between space and power are currently not as legible as they were in Hanyang and Kyeongseong; however, the old spatial paradigm is still clearly at work. This contention is supported by two important facts: the most important political institutions still occupy the former Six Ministries Street; and the economic sector, which developed during the Kyeongseong period, still functions as a core of economic activity in Korea. In short, the spatially embedded legacies of Hanyang and Kyeongseong are still in effect, mainly within the castle walls. Those legacies continue to function through the social forces manifest in the power configurations that led to the developmental phenomenon of the 1960s and '70s. Looking at this spatial evidence may be the simplest way to understand the power configurations among major players and political culture even in Korean society today. Once the existence of the rules and the operation of social forces in history has been established through geographic, textual, and architectural evidence, the three preeminent rules of hegemony, hierarchy, and heteronomy can be applied to modern Seoul, showing the operation of social forces under the influence of those types of rule. These are summarized in table 6.3 below.

Table 6.3 synthesizes historical continuities and changes in terms of developmental features and new rules added during the Seoul period. The new rules of "supreme order of economic development" and "economic pragmatism" are reflected in Seoul's modern skyscrapers. Based on these continuities and changes, this book sought to answer two questions: (1) how hierarchically hegemonic forces actually contributed to economic development, and (2) what role was played by heteronomical forces in the economic development of the 1960s and '70s in Korean society.

Furthermore, this book makes the criticism that current analyses tend to limit their treatment of Confucianism to the psychological, sociological, and journalistic levels of analysis; it is reductive to treat Confucianism as either the deterministic variable explaining authoritarian political culture or a source of the national character traits of diligence, high aspiration for education, and submissiveness. Such attitudes toward Confucianism often end up making culturally deterministic interpretations, such as "X is unique because of Confucianism," or "Confucianism invariably entails X." On the contrary, Confucianism is a dynamic and evolving entity that can function as a fundamental source of explanations accounting for East Asian political culture. Indeed, the most crucial sources for explaining the centrality of state power and non-Western, non-liberal state-society relations in Korean society are Confucianism, geomancy, and the mixture of Taoism and aboriginal beliefs, which have adapted repeatedly in response to internal and external challenges affecting state hegemony over time. Furthermore, this book explored the possibility of building "a theory of Confucian civil society" by

Table 6.3 Types of Developmental Rule in the Seoul Era

Rule	Old Legacies	Rules of the Seoul Era (1960s-70s)	Forces
Hege-mony	H-A H-a, K-a K-b K-c	Recourse to state hegemony Developmental legitimacy SN-1. Supreme order of economic development SN-2. Economic pragmatism	Park regime, tacit majority
Hierar-chy	H-B, K-B H-d, K-d K-e	State legitimacy to intervene in economy + Managerial capability	Military, bureaucracy, entrepreneurs
Heteronomy	H-C K-C	American liberalism + Socialism SN-3. Breakup of former united stance of dissenting voices à Militant minority + tacit majority	Students, middle class, church, labor, mass media, intelligentsia

** "S" stands for Seoul. "SN-1" stands for the first new rule added during the Seoul period, "SN-2" for the second new rule, and so on.

illuminating the role of the heteronomical forces involved in the process of economic development as well as the formation of resistant nationalism. In short, Confucianism is an indispensable source for building a formal theory that enhances our understanding of East Asia's political economy and of a non-Western developmental model.

IMPLICATIONS OF THE METHOD AND CONVENTIONAL THEORIES

The constructivist approach provides theoretical insight into the reconstruction of the social norms and types of rule of state-society relations that are historically and culturally embedded in Confucian societies. Especially useful in this regard is Onuf's framework, which operationalizes state-society relations by formulating three different concepts of rule and rules: hegemony as instruction, hierarchy as direction, and heteronomy as commitment. His paradigm consistently re-articulates and illuminates the nature and interdynamics of state-society relations as they adapt in each of the three periods of Korea's capital. Applying his framework also renders a sociopolitical analysis of the dynamics among the social forces involved in Korea's process of economic development. For example, to a regime that was born lacking political legitimacy, the existence of militant heteronomical forces becomes a serious political threat, driving it to adopt a fanatical economic development plan in order to co-opt the consent of the majority. Indeed, the substantial growth of the economy allayed the masses' demands for political freedom and allowed for the suppression of the heteronomical resistance. Thus, the domestic political confrontation between the military regime and resistant heteronomical forces could actually be said to have contributed to the developmental phenomenon in modern Korea.

The application of Onuf's paradigm over a series of historical eras traces dynamic relations among the major stakeholders that contributed toward the emergence of the developmental state and democratization in Korea. Ahistorical approaches, which are incapable of pointing out such continuities, tend instead to emphasize either contemporary domains such as East Asia's geopolitical and strategic context, which brought about US military protection and enormous economic aid to East Asia, or effective bureaucratic measures for export-drive economic policy. Thus, it is essential to look into the historical context of developmental phenomena.

Spatial arrangements within the city corroborate the applicability of Onuf's theoretical framework to the Korean context, for the social forces associated with each of the three types of rule have their own location within the layout. From the local-global perspective, incoming forces found their respective locations within the areas already designated for the operation of each rule. For example, Japanese colonial authority, wishing not to destroy the hegemonic authority of the state and planning instead to claim it for itself, chose not to destroy the Royal Palace and constructed its own headquarters athwart the line of sight between the Palace and the Six Ministries Street. As for the hierarchy, the Japanese bureaucracy replaced the Confucian bureaucracy. Also, by the time of Korea's colonization, Christian missionary influence, which later became the foundation of most modern educational institutions, had already gravitated toward the area of the Confucian students. From that position, they formed part of the future heteronomical resistance to Japanese occupation.

As this evidence demonstrates, Onuf's rules are predictive of the unfolding city layout and the power configurations among social forces within the unique political culture of the country under investigation. In the city layout of Korea's capital, geomantic principles and Confucian political ideology motivated the spatial disposition of social forces. Clearly, another country with a different political culture would have laid out the capital city and positioned its social forces differently, i.e., according to a framework and rules of its own, which further validates the need for an indigenous approach.

Without understanding such non-Western and non-liberal state-society relations, there are few options but to attribute the success of the developmental state either to military dictatorship or the free market principle. Neoclassical theorists, by overemphasizing and limiting their analyses to the free market principle, fail to illuminate dynamic relations between state and society (economy) in Korea's economic development. More importantly, in all three case studies starting from the Joseon Dynasty, there is overwhelming evidence of preeminent state hegemony. The Hanyang case examines how not only Confucian ideology but also traditional geomancy and Taoistic influence in daily life contributed toward the establishment of Confucian state hegemony during the Joseon Dynasty. This combination of geomancy and Taoism together formed a dominant political way of thinking that penetrated people's perception of power and their notion of hegemonic state and its relationship with society long before the Joseon Dynasty even began. By incorporating these widely held belief systems into the construction of the capital city, ruling elites legitimized their Confucian political hegemony and integral or infrastructural state power.

On the other side, developmentalists also fall short of providing a comprehensive understanding of Korea's developmental phenomenon by confining their analyses to the state's superficial capabilities. Such analyses neglect to incorporate relative aspects of the state's integral power and society's role in contributing toward the process that led to the emergence of the developmental state. In the Joseon era, society recognized Confucian political power and ideology. Through the consent of the tacit majority, state hegemony and political legitimacy to intervene in the economy were strengthened. From this perspective, state power is relative, for it is the people and society that grant legitimacy to its use. Moreover, as Gramsci and Mann emphasize, when society consents to the ideological domination of the state, the state's power and political legitimacy grow stronger. Since Confucian moral and ideological domination were already embedded and internalized in the people's way of thinking and everyday life, the state could utilize the people's acceptance of Confucian, geomantic, and Taoist principles to enhance its own legitimacy.

During the Hanyang era, agriculture was viewed as the backbone of the country's economy, and the government's tight control of commercial and industrial sectors was believed to serve the Confucian ideology. Accordingly, society took state intervention in the economy for granted. Thus, the real strength of the Joseon Dynasty lay not only in the arbitrary power of the King and Confucian scholarly bureaucrats or the coercive power of their state apparatus but also in the people's acceptance of the worldviews and interests of the Neo-Confucian ideals, which had undergone a lengthy process of socialization and ultimately emerged as common sense. The assertive Confucian ideology of highly valuing agriculture and scorning commerce/industry appealed as a worldview to the majority (most of whom were involved in agriculture) and resulted in the expression of deferential, aspirational, and accommodative sets of values (Parkin, 1971). Correspondingly, Confucian ruling elites managed to establish their conception of the world as moral, inclusive, and universal, and shaped the interests and needs of the dominated class during the Joseon era, thereby reinforcing state hegemony over society in general and over the economy in particular. In this process, geomantic and Taoistic belief systems played a significant role in softening and internalizing the regulatory and exploitative Neo-Confucian governing system.

Though institutionalists avoid the dichotomous defects of neoclassical and developmentalist approaches, they believe that the developmental state has two essential characteristics: an autonomous bureaucracy and cooperation between state and economy. They are right in pointing out these two elements as key components of the developmental state's success; yet, they neglect to consider the theoretical basis from which their conception arose. The lens of local-global interaction traces both the continuity in the position of the bureaucracy and changes in the nature of the cooperation between state and economy through the three manifestations of the city.

The Japanese occupation of Korea accelerated the reversal of the traditional Confucian attitude of scorn toward commercial and industrial economic activities. The fundamental duty of commerce and industry in Confucian Joseon society was to procure the goods needed for government to function. Such a dependent position of commerce and industry was reflected in the spatial arrangement of the market in Hanyang and in the codes of administrative law regulating those activities. In the Kyeongseong era, the lowly position of commerce and industry was reversed. Furthermore, active government support for the economy was added to the traditional Confucian principle of legitimate government intervention. This meets Castell's criterion for a developmental state: "a state is developmental when it establishes as its principle of legitimacy its ability to promote and sustain development."

The developmental phenomenon, as discussed earlier, was not created by contemporary forces alone. The only social force that maintained its hegemonic position and contributed to the economic development in the Korean context was the bureaucracy. Throughout the three eras of Hanyang, Kyeongseong, and Seoul, the bureaucracy was the only social force that maintained its influence over society, especially over the economy. So, it was nothing new when the bureaucracy during the Park regime began to play a significant role in economic development. Negative points also have their roots in the past. For example, all of the institutional arrangements for economic development and collusive relations between state and business were not forged by the Park regime but arose during the First and Second Republics as well as the Hanyang and Kyeongseong eras.

This book finds it useful to look at long-term development. The work of reconstructing the rules that were embedded in the culture of each era of Korean society yields the realization that the conditions required for the emergence of a developmental state were historically formed and transformed continually over a long period of time. Ultimately, it was interaction with the global forces of capitalism represented by Japanese imperialism that furnished an occasion for the birth of the developmental state in Korea. The Park regime inherited those historical legacies with a favorable geopolitical environment and world capitalist system that has been established after World War II under American hegemony. In fact, bi-polar rivalry between the United States and the former Soviet Union intensified America's close relationship with the Republic of Korea, which allowed the transfer of technology, access to the American market, and protection under the US nuclear umbrella. The latter has drastically reduced the defense budget, in fact, which was another factor for Korea's concentrated efforts toward exports and industrialization. In the process of interaction with global forces, traditional Confucianism met with challenges from outside and adapted itself to new environments. Similarly, a theory of the developmental state should account for significant data from the past and present. Furthermore, it should provide a principled way to predict future configurations of state-society relations.

By focusing on non-Western and non-liberal types of state-society relations, this book finds that the legitimacy of state intervention in the economy does not come solely from a contemporary regime of military dictatorship but rather from historically formulated Confucian relations of state and society (economy). The source of the legitimacy of the state's capacity to intervene in the economy lies in these state-society relations as well.

STATE-SOCIETY RELATIONS IN THE DEVELOPMENTAL STATE

To understand the developmental state from the perspective of state-society relations, a contextualized approach is necessary. The application of Onuf's paradigm to the substance of a particular region (i.e., its history, geography, political culture) will yield a principled account of that region. In the case of the Korean developmental state, Onuf's paradigm is a useful tool to re-articulate the origins of the state's legitimacy and power, the relations between social forces and state, the Joseon Dynasty's response to the introduction of external forces, and the reconfiguration and adaptation of state power and legitimacy.

An important question in understanding the role of the developmental state is not what happened but what factors made it possible. The conventional definition of "developmental state" emphasizes only the power of the state to bring about the desired outcome—i.e., economic development; however, it is more fruitful to examine the dynamic interaction among competing rules through the operation of distinct social forces. As has been empirically shown, Park's military regime was a politically illegitimate fragile state; if not for the existence of militant dissenting voices, Park's fragile regime might not have become one of fanatical economic development.

To be exact, the Park regime had little strength of its own—it inherited the rules of a strong state hegemony that had historically been internalized in the political culture. The existence of militant heteronomical forces actually facilitated developmental processes by driving the Park regime into its plan of economic modernization, which satisfied the tacit majority economically and provided a political rationale for suppressing militant voices of dissent. The role of the state and state power can only be accurately examined when relative relations between state and society are considered. Based on this premise, this book substantiated Clark and Lemco's (1988: 5) claims that a "strong state in promoting development must go beyond the simplistic equation of strong states = development."

In order to discover the context within which this process occurred, our investigation proceeded through nonconventional realms of research, such as the analysis of geomantic spatial arrangements and city monumentality in terms of city legibility, city layout, and the architectural designs of public and private institutions—all of which serve as helpful resources for illuminating political and cultural phenomena, especially the establishment of the state hegemony and state-society relations in Korea. Here, the capital city is the main unit of analysis. It is especially useful to employ geographical analysis in the study of political culture because an object with a spatial boundary preserves records of the continuities and changes imprinted upon it by each period of society, thereby enabling researchers to retrace these continuities and transformations. Power relations in particular are well reflected in the spatial arrangement, architecture, city layout, and maps of each era. The practice of locating evidence of power relations and state-society relations in artifacts that reflect everyday life helps researchers to avoid reductionist tendencies in analyzing phenomena of political culture. By gathering hard evidence of state hegemony from each era's maps, topological configurations, legal documents, Confucian architectural monumentality, and city layout, this book sought to overcome the common practice of relying solely upon Confucian classical texts for evidence of political culture and power relations. It is necessary to make every effort to bring an adequately broad research realm to this inquiry because such approaches either corroborate or provide counter-evidence to conventional textual sources, thereby leading to more reliable analysis.

Whereas conventional theories leave gaps in their understanding of the developmental state in East Asian economic development, this book advances the theory that state power and its legitimacy to intervene in the economy stem from rule-governed interrelations between state and society. Therefore, the source of state power and its legitimacy is not arbitrary but rather can be reconstructed according to the rules embedded within society's own substantial context.

IMPLICATIONS

If this theory adequately explains Korea's developmental state and path toward democratic society, then the negative impression associated with reifying despotic rule and authoritarianism as a source of economic growth must be abandoned. As pointed out in the introduction, two radically different tendencies divide the current literature on the rapid economic development in East Asian NICs—overemphasis on either the role of the state seized by military power or the free market principle as the determining factor. Interestingly, these radically different perspectives on this phenomenon both stem from the Western paradigm of state-society relations. In Western countries, there is a long history of capitalist struggle against political power to secure the freedom of economic activities from the arbitrary intervention of the state. Accordingly, modern political theorists also tout the ideologies of *laissez-faire* and political liberalism as fundamental to the economic well-being of society as well as for political development, i.e., democracy. In this school of thought, both state and society (economy) believe that non-interference is in the best interest of both.

Such a perspective sees the context of East Asian economic development, and especially Korean development, as either an exception to the Western model or proof of the power of the free market principle. Proponents of this view regard the Korean case as exceptional because they believe that the state's strong interventionist policy is what made such rapid development possible. The implication of this perspective is that economic accomplishment in this region is closely associated with undemocratic political power, which implies that East Asia's experience of development offers an inappropriate model for developing countries. As a result, this perspective tends to suggest that Asian countries are incarcerated by a non-democratic authoritarian political atmosphere.[4] Another implication of such a perspective is that the free market principle made such successful economic development possible despite such an "unfavorable" political environment. To single out the virtue of Western economic mechanisms would seem to suggest that Asian countries need to convert to the Western liberal political and economic system.

This book, however, views this as a false dilemma[5] because it was neither the military dictatorship nor the free market principle that was responsible for the unprecedented economic development achieved in Korea. Rather, it was non-Western, non-liberal types of state-society relations, historically molded through local interactions with global forces over a 600-year period, that brought about Korea's developmental state and concomitant economic development, not to mention its political development. In this model, it is recognized by both state and society that the state can and should intervene in the economy for the betterment of the nation. Moreover, constant power re-configurations among hegemonic and heteronomical forces can bring forth democratic forces and systems even in an authoritarian and non-democratic political culture.

Here, it seems appropriate to ask another important question: Could the military dictatorship have accomplished rapid development without such state-society relations? The short answer to this question is no. Furthermore, Asian, non-dichotomous relations of state and society should be evaluated not as a matter of right and wrong but as a matter of difference between Western and Asian culture in terms of their ways of prescribing the normative rule for state-society relations. Thus, there is no need to convert to Western liberalism. Rather, the analysis of the Korean model from the perspective of its own history can serve as a good example for other countries seeking to understand their experience of either development or underdevelopment from the indigenous perspective of their own historical background. Moreover, the Korean experience can serve as a model of development for countries where similar relations of state and society are functioning, and can prescribe proper and effective government support for those economies. Most importantly, this book's findings support the view that there can indeed be different paths, in terms of state-society relations, for economic and political development depending upon the specific historical and cultural contexts of each country.

What this book does not claim, however, is that a certain type of state-society relations will guarantee certain economic development outcomes because the whole context of history and culture in each country must be fully accounted for. In other words, a sweeping generalization of a grand theory based on the political cultural analysis of the East Asian development experience would also be inadequate. In summary, in analyzing the economic successes of catch-up states, the main focus of research should be directed toward the rule-governed relations of state and society and how these types of rule operate within the unique context of each region.

APPLICABILITY OF THE KOREAN EXPERIENCE

In light of the economic progress being made in parts of Asia, such as Indonesia, Malaysia, the Philippines, and Thailand, it is tempting to apply the same analytical perspective on developmentalism as those which held true in the case of Korea; however, it is very difficult to establish statistical links between growth and specific forms of state intervention, and it is even harder to establish causality in Southeast Asian countries. Many scholars on the second wave of Southeast Asian NICs (Robinson et al., 1987; Yoshihara, 1988; Doner, 1991; MacIntyre & Jayasuria, 1992; McVey, 1992; Hawes & Liu, 1993) generally agree that these NICs were replicating what might be thought of as a Northeast Asian model; however, recent further development in comparative studies of Northeast and Southeast Asian NICs seems to divide this general consensus into two different positions. The first position is that a strong state capable of withstanding rent-seeking and intervention in the economy may not be a prerequisite for economic development because Southeast Asian NICs such as Malaysia, Thailand, and Indonesia have also managed to achieve recent impressive economic growth. In fact, other economies such as Malaysia attempted similar interventions but failed because the state-society relations in these countries were not the same as in Northeast Asian countries (Perkins, 1994: 660). The Malaysian government has utilized a strategy of building up state-owned enterprise, adopting the Korean model of state-led industrial policy; yet, despite the Malaysian government's efforts to emulate South Korea, it was only able to achieve very modest success in its attempts at selective industrial targeting—the state did not enjoy effective insulation from business and other societal pressures, and there was extensive reliance on foreign investment.

An opposing perspective is presented by MacIntyre (1994: 16), who questions whether the progress achieved thus far in Southeast Asia is sustainable with the existing political and institutional arrangement. In general, these Southeast Asian states have all been recognized as being relatively uninsulated from business interests.[6] The major cause of their economic success is attributed to the export-led economic system, which deepens the foreign dependency of their economic performance. In terms of domestic politics, cronyism is prevalent. In these situations, MacIntyre (1994: 16) argues, "it is not obvious that the economic policy environment which has underpinned rapid export-led industrialization can be maintained." He concludes that "political economy developments in these Southeast Asian countries during the 1990s may well come to be seen as affirming rather than challenging the statist literature pertaining to the Northeast Asian NICs" (1994: 16).

This fact seems to serve as counter-evidence to this book's main argument. In other words, the state's capability and legitimacy to intervene in the market stems not only from state power but from complex interactions between state and society as well. In a society where the rules of state hegemony and the legitimacy of state intervention in the economy have not been embedded into the political culture over a long period of history, the government's mere adoption of interventionist industrial policy would not guarantee economic accomplishment. This book does not hold that every Asian country should adopt a Northeast Asian model in general or Korea's relations of state and business in particular. What this book does claim, however, is that when evaluating a country's strategy of political economic development, one should draw criteria from the dynamic relations of state and society and not from a static model (MacIntyre, 1994: 19-20).

In order to predict a potential future path for any region, several questions must be answered. What is the region's dominant ideology? How does it promote the hegemony of the state? What is the nature and effectiveness of the hierarchical component of the society, i.e., the bureaucracy? And finally, to what extent are heteronomous forces embraced or marginalized? To yield productive answers, the answers to these questions must be understood in relation to the history, geography, and political culture of the region from an indigenous perspective. Misunderstandings such as the reification of authoritarianism in Korea, which taint the perceptions that countries have of each other, may be avoided in the future through adherence to a contextualized rule-governed approach toward understanding state-society relations. Thus, we may be relieved of the burden of judgmentalism and be freed to advance more well-founded insights in international affairs.

NOTES

1. Seoul's explosive expansion has produced many mega-city problems, such as traffic congestion, pollution, high population density, and over-concentration of national functions such as education, economy, and culture. President Park Chung-hee was the first president to plan to move the capital to the southern city of Sejongsi, but he could not execute the plan due to his assassination in 1979. President Roh Moo-hyun wanted to resolve the serious problems mentioned above but most importantly wanted to relieve the over-concentration of political power and the hegemony of the ruling class in Seoul and the metropolitan area. Thus, he proposed to move the capital to Sejongsi and passed the legislation with agreement from both the ruling and opposition parties. In 2004, the Constitutional Court ruled that a constitutional amendment was required to legalize the relocation plan since the capital city had been there for three major eras and had attained a constitutional status. This was the reaction of the conservative forces whose interests were vested in this place, which serves as evidence of how important the capital city has been in Korea's political culture, power dynamics and struggles, and political systems. Finally, the Roh administration decided to execute a partial move to this new location in December 2004. In late 2012, most government ministries and offices had moved to Sejongsi except for the Ministries of Unifications, Foreign Affairs, and a few other offices that remained in Seoul.

2. Harvey (1989: 247) argues that "spatial and temporal experiences are primary vehicles for the coding and reproduction of social relations." Also, Agnew (1993:

252) views "space either as a board or backdrop across which social processes move and are imprinted or as a set of fixed containers at particular scales for cultures and social processes." Both are re-quoted from chapter 3 on Hanyang.

3. The details of the colonial Japanese bureaucracy are beyond the scope of this book.

4. One of the frequently heard Western criticisms (Jones, 1994) of contemporary East Asian states is their alleged authoritarianism and lack of democracy. Relatedly, the typical question arises, "Is democracy achievable there?" Asian leaders (Lee, Kuan Yew, 1994; Singapore School) have rebutted such criticism with a reference to some absolute cultural difference: "Western-style democracy is not applicable to East Asia" (Kim, 1994: 189). Such a Western question is generally based on the concept of strong state and weak society in East Asia. The result is a deadlock in discussion. Moreover, such a way of thinking often used to be extended to embellish despotic rule for economic development. Refer to Zakaria (1994) on Lee Kuan Yew's idea of the Asian type of democracy. On Western scholars' response to the Singapore School, see Jones (1994), "Asia's Fate: A Response to the Singapore School."

5. Simons and Billig (1994: 15) confirms such a claim, holding that "The goals and values that have been central to Western civilization can no longer be considered universal, and the associated project of modernity is unfinished because its completion would be disastrous, even if possible, particularly on the current Euro-American model." Further, they posit the advent of the postmodern era as "a code word for the emergence of a post-Western era," and understand postmodernism as "a response to the entropy of Eurocentric discourse."

6. These economies' capacity to administer and implement specific interventions may have been less than that of Northeast Asia. Their rapid growth, moreover, has occurred in a very different international economic environment from that which Japan, Korea, Taiwan, and China encountered during their periods of most rapid growth. Thus, the problem is not only to understand which specific policies may have contributed to growth but also to understand the institutional and economic circumstances that made them viable (World Bank, 1993: 7).

Appendix 1: Gugong (or Kao-kung chi)[1]

"Thus, in 136 B.C., the I-Ching or Book of Changes, originally a manual for the interpretations of milfoil auguries, was made a 'Confucian' classic because its images could be used to explain the interrelations among many phenomena. Ideas from the school of Tao, from the school of yin-yang, and from the school of the Five Elements were drawn into the synthesis for the same purpose." (Wright, 1977: 45)

"Let us turn now to consider the characteristic features of the cosmology of the city that emerged in Han times. . . . [T]he classical source for city theory is the *Chou li* [周禮] or *Chou kuan*—particularly the last section, known as the Kao-kung chi [考工記]. . . . as Karlgren says, these texts 'represent the endeavors of the Confucian school to determine what the beliefs and rites should properly be.' In other words, they are normative and prescriptive, not historical." (Wright, 1977: 46)

"The planning of the *Gugong* is based on the precepts of feng shui, the art of placement with reference to a sense of balance, the theory of yin and yang, the orientation of the sun, the direction of wind and the flow of water courses. To the north of the *Gugong* is the Tai Hengshan and to the east is the Bohai. The water stream from the man-made Beihai comes from the *qian* (northwest) direction and flows out to the *sun* (southeast) direction according to the theory of feng shui. The stream that comes from the west is named the *Jin Shuihe* (Golden Water Stream—gold is associated with the west). The entire city is planned on an axial line to achieve balance and symmetry as a symbol of balance and harmony which are Confucian ideals and Taoist. The hierarchy, order and formality of spaces within the palatial complex were based on the order and system stated in the *Liji* (예기) and *Kao Gongji* (고공기). The palace is sited to face south which was considered as auspicious direction coinciding with the direction associated with the emperor. The city is symbolically divided into four parts—the east, south, west, and north." (Lip, 1995: 67)

"The structures in the Gugong are classified as either *yang* or *yin*. For example, the buildings used as public administration areas are *yang*, while the private or residential quarters are *yin*. The front facades are *yang* while the rear are *yin*. The rooftops are *yang*, and the roof eaves are *yin*. The sunlit courts are *yang*, and the shaded corridors *yin*. The tiers of steps with odd number are *yang*, and those with even numbers *yin*. Three (an odd number) main public palaces must be contrasted with two (an even number) residential palaces. Thus, the palace complex is divided into *waichao* (外朝 *yang*) and *neiting* (内亭, *Joseon*). *Waichao* consists of palaces for public administration and *neiting* for private residence." (Lip, 1995: 69)

Choice of Site. Each of the four main sections of the *Chou li*—corresponding to the four seasons—opens with the following passage: "It is the sovereign alone who establishes the states of the empire, gives to the four quarters their proper positions, gives to the capital its form and to the fields their proper divisions. He creates the offices and apportions their functions in order to form a center to which the people may look." This clearly expresses "the centralism so characteristic of Han ideology and makes the capital the epicenter of an orderly spatial grid extending to the far reaches of civilization. Elsewhere, the *Chou li* goes into great detail on the taking of auguries by the tortoise" (46) shell and by the milfoil, and then specifies that a major shift in the site of the capital is an occasion for consulting the tortoise. Again, the *Chou li* prescribes that in the event of a major shift of capital, the official known as the *ta-shih* shall take the plan and study it in advance." (Wright, 1977: 47)

Preparation of Site. "The *Chou li* says that when construction workers start to build a capital, they calculate the contours of the site by the use of plumb lines and water levels." (Wright, 1977: 47)

Orientation. "The *Chou li* describes the method of determining the four directions on the site by taking at various times the shadow of the sun as cast by a pole whose verticality has been assured by the use of multiple plumb lines. This method is supplemented by night observations of the polestar. . . . But elsewhere the *Chou li* prescribes a far more elaborate procedure for establishing a capital at the very center of the earth's surface by the use of five gnomons. 'Here, where Heaven and Earth are in perfect accord, where the four seasons come together, where the winds and the rains gather, where the forces of yin and yang are harmonized, one builds a royal capital.' In this passage, the siting of a capital is seen in relation to the forces of nature and to the hypostasized powers that govern all phenomena. This, I believe is an expression of the systematized organicism characteristic of Han Confucian ideology; further, it makes of a capital city a cosmic focal point—a center from which the forces of nature may be adapted to or controlled in the interests of the whole realm." (Wright, 1977: 47)

City Layout. "After the proper location is identified, the *Chou li* then directs the construction workers to lay out the city in the form of a square. As nearly as we know, a square or a rectangle was the traditional form of a Chinese city [Hanyang was exceptional in that it was circular]. But the *Chou li*'s presentation of a square form has symbolic significance as well. For the men of Han, the earth was a perfect square; thus, it was fitting that the rule of all under heaven should take place in a structure that served as a replica and symbol of the earth. The *Chou li* continues, the wall 'shall measure nine *li* on each side [Hanyang was smaller in this measure], and in each side there shall be three gates. Within the capital, there shall be nine north-south streets and nine east-west streets. The north-south streets shall accommodate nine chariot-ways.' Here, we encounter the theory of emblematic numbers that had developed before the Han but that was then incorporated into official Confucianism. As Granet put it in his brilliant essay on the subject, 'It is by means of numbers that one finds a suitable way to represent the logical sectors and the concrete categories that make up the universe. . . . In choosing for them one or another disposition which permits them to demonstrate their interplay, one believes he has succeeded in rendering the universe at once intelligible and manageable.' Three, nine, and twelve are, within this mode of thinking, particularly significant numbers: three because it represents the three sectors of the intelligible universe (heaven, earth, and man); nine because it represents three times three and is also the number that represents the ancient Chinese world (the nine provinces as established by the Emperor Yu); twelve because it is the sum of three and nine and the number of months in a year. Thus it follows that the ruler, which is seen by the Han theories as uniting in his person the three sectors of the universe and presiding over the nine provinces during the sequence of twelve months in each year, should have the numbers three, nine, and twelve in the symbolism of this capital. This systematizing element in the cosmology of city planning is, in my view, a product of the second half of the Western Han. There are further points in these prescriptions: the greater width of the north-south streets emphasizes the orientation of the city toward the south; and the fact that the streets are nine in number by implication gives importance to the central avenue approaching from the south (an importance that we find in all later capital buildings). Moreover, the prescription of a grid plan as a norm for capital cities is but one example of the ordering of space by the use of grid schemes. It belongs to the same group as the *Ching-t'ien* or well-field system, which was believed by Mencius and later Confucians to have been the land system of the early Chou;

the basic pattern is, of course, nine equal squares arranged in a larger square. It also recalls the mythological division of the empire into nine provinces by the Emperor Yu." (Wright, 1977: 48)

Disposition of the Principal Structures. "The *Chou li* sates that the ancestral hall of the prince shall be on the left (i.e., east), and the altar of the god of the soil on the right (i.e., west), . . . The palace of the prince occupies the very center of the city; to the south of his residence is his audience hall, and to the north, the market. This prescription reflects to a degree the value system of the Han Confucians. The center of mercantile activity is given the place of least honor and the minimum yang influence by being located in the northern extremity of the city [Hanyang was an exception from this Chinese idea in that the market was located in front of the Six Ministries Street, along the East-West axis]. Under the rubric 'Market Supervisor', the *Chou li* provides a circumstantial picture of a highly supervised and controlled market that may well be close to the way capital markets were managed in the latter half of Western Han. In this passage, the hierarchy of officials and the detailed duties prescribed for each reflect the legalist ideas that were incorporated into Han Confucianism as they were into the machinery of the Han state. In another passage, under the duties of the *nei-tsai*, the *Chou li* tells us that this official is to assist the empress in establishing a market, to attend to its layout and regulations, and then to dedicate it by the *yin-li* or female ritual. The commentary of *Cheng Hsuan* (2nd century AD) explains that, in establishing the capital of a state, the emperor builds the palaces whereas the empress establishes the market, which is intended to represent the harmonious and complementary nature of the interaction between male and female principles (*yang* and *yin*). That this ever happened is doubtful, to say the least, but the additional theorizing tends to underscore the *yin* character of the market location in the classical plan." (Wright, 1977: 49)

"Let us consider how much of the classical cosmology and the feng shui tradition was included in the plan of the new city. The founding emperor, Wen-ti, conducted divinations regarding the site and may have been the last Chinese ruler to do so. The outer walls formed a rectangle (not a square, as the *Chou li* prescribes), and excavations have shown the north-south walls to be only sixteen minutes west of true north. Thus, the orientation of the city was established according to the ancient cannons; it literally 'faced south,' and the central and widest north-south street served—according to *Chou li* prescriptions—as the principal axis of the city. In its siting, we find no influence of *feng shui* principles. . . . The city did have, as the *Chou li* prescribed, three gates in the south, east, and west walls, but there were more than the prescribed nine east-west and nine north-south streets. The great north-south street was wider than the others, as the Chou li prescribed." (Wright, 1977: 56-57)

"The *Chou li* had said, cryptically, 'hall of audience in front, markets behind.' Yet, in *Sui* and *T'ang Ch'ang-an*, the palace was not in the middle of the city but centered against the north wall, with only the imperial Forbidden Park (*Chin-yuan*) behind. . . . When it came to markets, there was no question of locating them behind or north of the place since the palace backed to the north wall. Rather, the two official markets were located, quite pragmatically, where they were convenient both for suppliers from outside the city and for consumers within, namely in the central east and central west parts of the city." (Wright, 1977: 57)

"Perhaps enough has been said to show that the imperial cosmology had discernible but limited authority over the planners of *Ch'ang-an*. Pragmatic considerations—convenience, functional zoning, ease of policing—outweighed the canonical prescriptions whenever a choice had to be made." (Wright, 1977: 60)

"There is no evidence that the Yung-lo emperor tried to locate the 'market behind' the palace enclosure, as enjoined by the *Chou li*. But at least in his time there were no markets in front, and the parts of Peking to the east and west of the imperial city were given over, as the *Chou li* prescribed, to the residences of the people." (Wright, 1977: 71)

NOTES

1. This excerpt of Gugong is from Wright, Arthur F. 1997. *The Cosmology of the Chinese City*, in Shinner, G. W. ed. 1977. The City in Late Imperial China, Stanford University Press. Printed with permission of Stanford University Press.

Appendix 2: Central Government Officials in the Gyeongguk daejeon

Appendix 2 Central Government Official Ranking System (*Gyeongguk daejeon*)*

	Pumgye** / Government Offices****	Jeong 1	Jong 1	Jeong 2	Jong 2	Jeong 3 Sang*** 3	Jeong 3 Ha*** 3	Jong 3	Jeong 4	Jong 4	Jeong 5	Jong 5	Jeong 6	Jong 6	Jeong 7	Jong 7	Jeong 8	Jong 8	Jeong 9	Jong 9	Note	Total
BASIC	Uijeongbu	3	2	2					2		1						2					12
	Yukjo			6	6	7					20		20	6		2		4	2	4		77
SPECIAL	Jongchinbu								1		1											2
	Chunghunbu									1		1										2
	Uibinbu									1		1										2
	Hanseongbu			1	2					1		2			3							9
	Saheonbu				1			1	2		2		24									30
	Gaeseongbu				2					1		1		1								5
	Chung-ikbu											2										2
	Seungjeong-won					6									2							8
	Jang-yewon					1					3		4									8
	Saganwon					1		1			1		2									5
	Sangseowon						1					1				1	2					5
	Tongnyewon						2	1	1		1			8								13
	Sejasigang-won	2	1	2	2			1	1		1		1		1							12
	Jong-hak								1		1		2									4
	Pungjeochang								1					1		1		1	1			5
	Gwang-heung-chang								1					1				1	1			4
	Naesusa										1			1		1		1		2	2	8
	Saonseo											1		1		1		1				4

Ui-yeong-go											1		1		1		1				4
Jang-heunggo											1		1		1		1				4
Yang-hyeongo													1		1		1				3
4 hak													8					8			16
5 bu													5						10		15
(Gak) reungjeon																			20		20
5 wi dochongbu									4		4									10	18
5 wi				12		9	14	12	54	14	123	15	201	5	309	16	483	42	1939		3248
Gyeomsabok				3																	3
Naegeumwi				3																	3
Sejagwisa										2	2	2	2	2		2		2			14
.	.	.	.	.	.	.	.	.	.	.	.	.	.	.	.	.	.	.	.	.	.
.	.	.	.	.	.	.	.	.	.	.	.	.	.	.	.	.	.	.	.	.	.
.	.	.	.	.	.	.	.	.	.	.	.	.	.	.	.	.	.	.	.	.	.
53 more government offices are assigned to officials under the same hierarchical rank system, i.e., *pumgye*																					
Total	16	6	27	48	35	38	40	28	92	54	175	91	304	25	352	32	525	98	2028	76	4090

Source: (Yun, 1986: 552-56)

* The *Gyeongguk daejeon* is the Joseon Dynasty's national code of law.

** *Pumgye*: a hierarchical rank system of government officials in the Joseon Dynasty. It is divided into *jeong* and *jong*, each of which has nine ranks (called *pum*) from 1 to 9. The highest is *jeong 1 pum* and the lowest is *jong 9 um*. There are eighteen ranks (*pum*) in total. The *pum* at the level of *jong 6 pum* and higher are divided into *sang* (high) and *ha* (low). *Dangsanggwan* refers to the officials whose *pumgye* is not lower than *jeong 3 pum sang*, and who are deemed as higher-level officials who can participate in the process of decision-making and take responsibility for it. The highest *pumgye*—namely, *jeong 1 pum*—is called *yeong-uijeong* and is the chief state councilor. Also, wives of the King and the government officials are assigned *pumgye* according to their husbands' *pumgye*.

*** *Sang*: high
Ha: low

**** Refer to the list of the government offices in Appendix 5

Appendix 3: Local Civil Officials Table

Appendix 3 Ranking System for Local Civil Officials (*Gyeongguk daejeon*)*

Pum-gye**	Provinces *** / Civil Officials ****	Gyeonggi	Chung-cheong-do	Gyeong-sang-do	Jeolla-do	Hwang-hae-do	Gang-won-do	Yeong-an-do	Pyeon-gan-do	Total
Jong 2 pum	Gwanchalsa	1	1	1	1	1	1	1	1	8
	Buyun			1	1			1	1	4
Jong 3 pum	Daedoho busa			1			1	1	1	4
	Moksa	4	4	3	3	2	1		3	20
Jong 3 pum	Sa	1								1
	Doho busa	7		7	4	4	5	11	6	44
Jong 4 pum	Su	1								1
	Seoyun								1	1
	Gunsu	7	12	14	12	7	7	5	18	32
Jong 5 pum	Yeong	1								1
	Dosa	1	1	1	1	1	1	1	1	8
	Pan-gwan	5	4	5	5	2	2	7	6	36
	Hyeolly-eong	5	1	7	6	4	3		8	34

Jong 6 pum	Gam	1								1
	Chalbang	3	3	5	3	2	2	3	2	23
	Hyeongam	14	37	34	31	7	9	4	5	141
	Gyosu	11	4	12	8	6	7	13	11	73
Jong 9 pum	Chambong		2					12		14
	Hundo	26	50	57	49	19	19	9	33	262
	Simnyak	1	2	3	3	1	1	3	2	16
	Geomnyul	1	1	1	2	1	1	1	1	9
	Yeokseung	3	3	6	3	1	2			18
	Doseung	7								7
Total		100	125	158	132	58	62	72	100	807

Source: (Yun, 1986: 560-561)
* The *Gyeongguk daejeon* is the Joseon Dynasty's national code of law.
** Refer to the note on *pumgye* in Appendix 2
*** Refer to the note on provinces in Appendix 3
**** Refer to Appendix 5

List of local civil officials: following the order of the table above

Gwanchalsa: A governor of a province

Buyun: A magistrate of a *bu* (the second largest local administrative unit next to a province)

Daedoho busa: A magistrate of *daedohobu* (a local administrative district set up for some big towns) Moksa, Sa: Country magistrates ruling *mok* (a local administrative unit, usually the second largest after *bu* or *daedohobu*)

Dohobusa: A local magistrate ruling *dohobu*, a local administrative unit, usually the second largest after *mok*

Su: A local magistrate of a *gun*, which is the largest after *mok*

Seoyun: An official praising and censuring according to local officers' work

Gunsu: A local magistrate of a *gun*, which is the largest after *mok*

Dosa: An official assisting a *gwanchalsa* (a provincial governor) by inspecting local magistrates

Pan-gwan: An administrative assistant of *gwanchalsa* or in charge of transportation

Hyeollyeong: A local magistrate of a big *hyeon* (*hyeon* is the local administrative unit after *gun*)

Gam: An official in *jongchinbu* (Office of Royal Genealogy)

Chalbang: An official in charge of *yeokcham*, a transportation and communication system for connecting the capital with local areas

Hyeon-gam: A country magistrate for a small *hyeon*

Gyosu: An official in charge of education

Chambong: An assistant caretaker working for government offices

Hundo: An official in charge of education in *4 hak* (four public schools in the capital) and in the local education institutions

Simnyak: An examiner of the medicinal material to be used in the palace

Geomnyul: A law clerk

Yeokseung: An official in charge of a transportation station

Doseung: An official who manages ferries

Appendix 4: List of Craftsmen in Central and Local Government Offices

List of Craftsmen (in an alphabetical order) by function or product:

Agyojang: Glue
Allongjang: A kind of a raincoat for a cart or palanquin
Anjajang: Saddles

Baecheopjang: Mounting pictures
Bajajang: Bamboo, reeds, or stalks linked to make a fence
Bangjikjang: Weaving of textiles
Bunjang: Powder
Byeonbijang: Dishes and containers for ritual purposes

Chajang: Carts
Cheomborojang: A flap that protects a horse rider from being splashed with mud (the exact meaning of the word is unknown)
Cheong-yeomjang: Blue dye
Cheopseonjang: Folding fans
Chiljang: Varnishing with lacquer
Chimjang: Making needles
Chimseonjang: Sewing
Chingjajang: Scales
Chokjang: Candles
Choripjang: Straw hats
Choyeomjang: Dyeing of straw hats
Chugoljang: Bells for horses or cows

Dahoejang: Belts for military uniforms
Dobaejang: Wallpaper
Dochaejang: Coloring
Dochimjang: Smoothing starched cloth by beating it with wooden sticks
Doda-ikjang: Hair ribbons worn by little girls
Dogyeorajang: Part of a horse saddle (exact meaning unknown)
Dojajang: Pocketknives or knives for self-defense
Doljang: Underfloor heating systems
Domokgaejang: Part of a horse saddle (exact meaning unknown)
Dongjang: Copperware
Doryeonjang: Cutting the edges of paper evenly
Duseokjang: Brass articles, such as a doorknobs and locks

Eochijang: Saddlecloth or saddle blankets
Eonchijang: Saddle flaps
Eunjang: Silver foundry

Gaejang: Roofing houses with tiles
Gakjajang: Carving letters in wooden blocks
Gakjang: Carving
Gandagaejang: Making headstalls for bridles
Gapjang: Armor
Geumbakjang: Gold leaf
Gojang: Drums
Gunghyeonjang: Bowstrings
Gung-in: Bows
Gungsijang: Bowstrings
Gyeongjang: Mirrors
Gyunjajang: Fixing typeset

Hanchijang: Making sweat clothes for saddles
Hapsajang: Weaving textiles by plaiting threads
Hayeomnokjang: Green paint for the purpose of protection or decoration
Hong-yeomjang: Red dye
Hwa-ajang: Embroidering shoes with flowers
Hwabinjang: Tempering iron
Hwajang (1): Long-necked shoes
Hwajang (2): Artificial flowers
Hwandojang: Traditional swords used as weapons
Hwangdanjang: Plumbic oxide for medical use
Hwang-ongjang: Earthen vessels of red clay

Hwang-yeopjang: Reeds for woodwind instruments
Hyangjang: Incense, perfume, and aromas

Ijang: Plastering
Inchuljang: Printing books
Injang (1): Seals and stamps
Injang (2): Mats
Ipijang: Leather coverings
Ipsajang: Silver thread decoration

Jaegeumjang: Embroidering clothes with gold thread
Jaejakjang: Cutting out clothes
Jaengjang: Making brass percussion instruments called *jing*
Jagyeokjang: Water clocks
Japsangjang: Roofing tiles for decoration, in the shape of animals
Jeomjang: Bamboo mats
Jeonjang(1): Blankets
Jeonjang (2): Baking bricks
Jeonpijang: Working with goat or lamb leather
Jeopyejang: Paper money
Jijang: Paper
Jogakjang: Sculpting
Jongmoajang: Hats made of horsehair
Jujang (1): Beads
Jujang (2): Casting for weapons, typeset, etc.
Jukjang: Bamboo products
Juksojang: Bamboo combs
Jupijang: Leather shoes

Maejeupjang: Knots used for buttons
Majojang: Millstones
Mamisajang: Sieves made of horsehair
Mang-geonjang: Horsehair-woven headbands
Mogwanjang: Fur hats
Mogyeongjang: Strings of wooden beads, used for a *gat* (traditional hat of bamboo and horsehair)
Mojajang: Hats
Mokjang: Making and repairing wooden objects and structures
Moksojang: Wooden combs
Mo-uijang: Fur clothes and decorations
Mukjang: Ink sticks

Najeonjang: Decorating objects by inlaying or attaching mother of pearl
Neungnajang: Silk

Okjang: Jade crafts, such as cutting, grinding, and polishing
Ongjang: Jars

Pijang: Making things out of leather
Piljang: Brushes
Pungmuljang: Instruments for Korean traditional percussion music
Pyotongjang: Containers for diplomatic documents

Saengpijang: Treating rawhide
Sageumjang: Golden thread
Sagijang: Porcelain dishes
Samojang: Hats for civil and military officials
Sang-hwarongjang: Decorating tables with (artificial) flowers
Sangjajang: Making covered bamboo baskets
Sapijang: Treating fur
Sapyejang: Shoes worn by a king or crown prince
Sedapjang: Laundry
Seokhoejang: Baking quicklime
Seokjang: Making things with stone
Seongjang: Looms
Seonjajang: Fans
Seonjang: Ships
Seopjang: Decorating objects by inlaying gold and silver into carved reliefs
Si-in: Arrows
Sojang: Combs
Soseongjang: Brushes for cleaning combs
Sucheoljang: Making cast iron cauldrons or utensils for rituals
Sukpijang: Tanning hides

Tong-gaejang: Quivers
Tongjang: Containers

Ungpijang: Treating bearskin
Usanjang: Umbrellas

Wajang: Baking tiles
Wonseonjang: Round fans made of paper or silk

Yajang: Blacksmithing
Yangtaejang: Brims of *gat* (traditional hat of bamboo and horsehair)
Yeomjang: Bamboo blinds, reed screens, and shades
Yeoncheoljang: Lead casting
Yeonjang: Tempering iron
Yeonsajang: Bleaching thread
Yuchiljang: Oil varnish
Yugujang: Making things by oiling
Yujang: Brassware
Yuripjang: Wrapping a *gat* with thin hemp cloth (traditional hat of bamboo and horsehair)

Appendix 4 List of Craftsmen in Central and Local Government Offices (*Gyeongguk dae-jeon*)* (Yun, 1986: 498-514)

Government Offices** Craftsmen ***	Gongjo	Bongsangsi	Nae-uiwon	Sang-uiwon	Gun-gisi
Neungnajang				105	
Choripjang	8			6	
Yuripjang				2	
Samojang	2			4	
Yangtaejang				2	
Doda-ikjang	2			2	
Dahoejang	2			4	
Mang-geonjang	2			4	
Mojajang	6			2	
Doryeonjang				2	
Seongjang				10	
Okjang				10	
Ongjang	13	10		10	
Seopjang	4			8	
Eunjang	8			8	
Geumbakjang	2			4	
Ipijang	2			4	
Hwajang (1)	6			10	
Sapyejang	6			8	
Sukpijang	10			8	
Hwa-ajang	2			4	
Sapijang	4			4	
Mo-uijang				8	
Hwajang (2)		6			
Jeonjang (1)	4			8	
Ipsajang	2			4	
Mogwanjang				2	
Sageumjang				4	
Chiljang	10			8	12

Duseokjang	4	4	
Majojang		4	12
Gungsijang		4	6
Yuchiljang		2	2
Jujang (2)	20	4	20
Najeonjang	2	2	
Hayeomnokjang		2	
Saengpijang		2	4
Yujang	8	4	
Baecheopjang	2	4	
Chimjang	2	2	
Gyeongjang	2	2	
Gapjang			35
Pungmuljang		8	
Jogakjang	2	4	
Mukjang		4	
Dongjang	4	4	
Gung-in		18	90
Si-in		21	150
Dojajang		6	
Jaengjang			11
Jupijang	6		
Hanchijang	2		
Allongjang	2		
Gandagaejang	2		
Piljang	8		
Jukjang	2		
Chugoljang	2		
Injang (1)	2		
Mokjang			4
Sucheoljang	30		
Yajang	4	8	130
Yeonjang		10	160

Jujang	2				
Cheomborojang	2				
Maejeupjang	2			4	
Bunjang			2		
Hyangjang			4		
Anjajang	10				
Eochijang	4				
Eonchijang	2				
Moksojang	2			2	
Soseongjang	2				
Tonggaejang	2				
Cheopseonjang	4				
Pyotongjang	2				
Agyojang					2
Chingjajang	2				
Gojang					4
Wonseonjang	2				
Byeonbijang		4			
Jaegeumjang				2	
Domokgaejang				2	
Dogyeorajang				2	
Ungpijang				2	
Jeonpijang				2	
Hwabinjang				2	
Juksojang	2			2	
Hwandojang				12	
Chimseonjang	10			40	
Hapsajang				10	
Cheong-yeomjang				10	
Hong-yeomjang				10	
Sedapjang				8	
Dochimjang				14	
Yeonsajang				75	2

Bangjikjang				20	
Choyeomjang	6			4	
Mogyeongjang	4				

Government Offices** Craftsmen***	Gyoseo-gwan	Saong-won	Naejasi	Naeseomsi	Sadosi
Yajang	6				
Gyunjajang	40				
Inchuljang	20				
Gakjajang	14				
Jujang (2)	8				
Jogakjang	8				
Mokjang	2				
Ongjang			8	8	8
Jijang	4				
Hwajang (2)			2		
Bangjikjang			30	30	
Seongjang			2	2	
Sagijang		380			

Government Offices** Craftsmen***	Yebinsi	Saseomsi	Seongong-gam	Jeyong-gam	Jang-agwon	Gwansang-gam
Ongjang	8					
Hwajang (2)	6					
Jagyeokjang						10
Majojang			8			
Jogakjang			10			
Jukjang			20			
Mokjang			60			
Seokjang			40			
Yajang			40			
Gaejang			20			
Ijang			20			

Jeonjang (2)		20		
Dochaejang		20		
Doljang		8		
Chajang		10		
Usanjang		10		
Jeomjang		10		
Yeomjang		14		
Bajajang		10		
Sang-hwarong-jang		4		
Seokhoejang		6		
Mamisajang		4		
Tongjang		10		
Agyojang		2		
Inchuljang	2			
Jeopyejang	2			
Sukpijang			2	
Mogwanjang			2	
Pungmuljang				4
Hwang-yeopjang				2
Hayeomnokjang			2	
Bunjang			2	
Hwangdanjang			2	
Jaejakjang			2	
Hong-yeomjang			10	
Dochimjang			6	
Sedapjang			4	
Chimseonjang			24	
Bangjikjang			30	
Seongjang			2	
Cheongyeomjang			20	

Government Offices** Craftsmen***	Jeonseolsa	Jeonhamsa	Naesusa	Sogyeokseo	Saonseo
Chimjang	2				
Dahoejang	6				
Seonjang		10			
Ongjang			7	4	4
Yajang			2		
Jujang (2)			10		
Yujang			5		
Sucheoljang			6		
Sagijang			6		
Mokjang			2		

Government Offices** Craftsmen***	Ui-yeong-go	Jang-heung-go	Jang-wonseo	Saposeo	Yang-hyeongo
Ongjang	4		8	10	2
Injang (2)		8			
Dobaejang		8			
ChokJang	4				

Government Offices** Craftsmen***	Jojiseo	Do-hwaseo	Waseo	Gwi-huseo
Wajang			40	
Mokjang	2			4
Yeomjang	8			
Jijang	81			
Japsangjang			4	
Baecheopjang		2		
Yajang				2
Chiljang				2

[Table 2] List of Craftsmen in Central and Local Government Offices (*Gyeongguk daejeon*)* (Yun, 1986: 579)

Provinces**** / Crafts-men***	Gyeonggi	Chungcheong-do	Gyeong-sang-do	Jeolla-do	Gang-won-do	Hwanghae-do	Yeon-gan-do	Pyeon-gan-do	Total
Gapjang	3	6	11	10	3	3	5	9	50
Yajang	40	71	121	70	36	34	36	48	456
Gung-in	18	31	59	40	17	19	26	45	255
Si-in	37	55	73	61	30	28	22	44	350
Mokjang	37	56	69	59	28	26	22	43	340
Pijang	5	56	66	61	31	28	21	45	313
Yujang	3	4	7	6	2	2	4	8	36
Chiljang	3	56	73	61	28	26	20	44	311
Sagijang	7	23	32	39					101
Gunghyeon-Jang		2	3	2	2	2	22	43	76
Jijang		130	265	237	33	39			704
Seokjang		58	272	58					388
Jogakjang		1					1		2
Majojang		2	4	5	6	7			24
Mukjang		6	8	6					20
Soseong-jang		1	3	1	1			1	7
Yugujang		64	58	55	1	1			179
Hwang-ongjang		1							1
Sojang			2	1	1				4
Seonjajang			6	2					8
Sangjajang			6	4	2				12
Seokjang					1	1	1		3
Yeoncheol-jang					2	1			3
Gakjang					1			1	2
Sucheol-jang						3			3
Jeomjang						3			3

Jongmoa -jang								1	1
Total	153	623	1,138	778	225	223	180	332	3,652

* The *Gyeongguk daejeon* is the Joseon Dynasty's national code of law.
** Refer to the list of government offices in Appendix 4.5
*** Refer to the list of craftsmen
**** The Joseon Dynasty divided its land into eight administrative districts called *paldo* (provinces): Gyeonggi, Chungcheong-do, Gyeongsang-do, Jeolla-do, Gangwon-do, Hwanghae-do, Yeongan-do, and Pyeongan-do.

Appendix 5: Students in Capital Table

Appendix 5 List of Students by Academic Department (Studying in the Capital, *Gyeongguk daejeon*)*

Academic Department / Government Offices **	Confucianism	Chinese classics	Mongolian studies	Yeojin studies***	Japanese studies	Medical school	Astronomy	Geography	Myeong-Gwahak****	Arithmetic	Law	Chemistry	Dohak*****	Total
Seonggyun-gwan	200													200
4 hak	400													400
Sayeogwon		35	10	20	15									80
Jeonui-gam						50								50
Hyeminseo						30								30
Gwansang-gam							20	15	10					45
Hojo										15				15
Hyeongjo											40			40
Dohwaseo												15		15
Sogyeokseo													10	10
Total	600	35	10	20	15	80	20	15	10	15	40	15	10	885

Source: (Yun, 1986: 570)
* *Gyeongguk daejeon* is the Joseon Dynasty's national code of law.
** Refer to the list of government offices in Appendix 4.5
*** Studies of Jurchen
**** Studies of yin and yang dealing with astrology, calendrical astronomy, geomantic philosophy, etc.
*****Taoist studies

Appendix 6: List of Government Offices

4 hak: Four public schools in the capital
5 bu: Five administrative districts into which Hanyang, the capital, is divided
5 wi: Five military commands, the central command of the Joseon Dynasty
5 wi dochongbu: Headquarters of the five military commands
5 wijang: Commanders of the 5 wi (see above)

Binggo: Ice storehouse for the palace
Bongsangsi: Managing ritual affairs and conferring posthumous epithets
Byeongjo: Ministry of Military Affairs (one of the Six Ministries)

Chunchugwan: Office for compilation of annals
Chunghunbu: Office for giving honors and benefits to meritorious retainers and their descendants
Chung-ikbu: Office established for giving honors and benefits to the founding contributors of the Joseon Dynasty and their descendants

Dochongbu: 5 wi dochongbu (see above)
Dohwaseo: Royal bureau of painting
Donnyeongbu: Office of royal relatives

Gaeseongbu: Ministry of Gaeseong, capital of Goryeo Dynasty (918-1392)
Gongjo: Ministry of Public Works (one of the Six Ministries)
Gun-gisi: Government arsenal
Gunjagam: Military provisions agency
Gwangheung-chang: Office in charge of emoluments for government officials

Gwansanggam: Office for observance of natural phenomena
Gwi-huseo: Office for making coffins and administering funerals
Gyeomsabok: Royal guard
Gyeong-yeon: System of education or a seminar in which the king learns and discusses Confucian teachings and important political issues with the court
Gyoseogwan: Office of government publication

Hanseongbu: capital city hall
Hojo: Fiscal Administration (one of the Six Ministries)
Hongmun-gwan: Office of special advisers for the king
Hullyeonwon: Bureau of military training
Hwarinseo: Public clinic
Hyeminseo: Office of medical service for commoners
Hyeongjo: Ministry of Punishments (one of the Six Ministries)

Igwisa: Seja-igwisa (see below)
Ijo: Board of Personnel (one of the Six Ministries)

Jang-agwon: Bureau of music
Jang-heung-go: Supply of items (e.g., mats, paper, oiled paper) for the palace
Jang-wonseo: Management of flowers and fruit trees in the palace
Jang-yewon: Registry where slave rosters are kept
Jeonhamsa: Management of ships and warships
Jeonokseo: Bureau of prisoners
Jeonsaengseo: Office in charge of breeding and providing animals used for national rituals
Jeonseolsa: Office in charge of tents used for rituals
Jeonuigam: Palace medical office
Jeonyeonsa: Office in charge of cleaning and repairing the palace
Jeyonggam: Office in charge of presenting goods to the king or rewarding the officials, as well as coloring, dyeing, and weaving
Jojiseo: Office in charge of manufacturing paper
Jongbusi: Office in charge of compiling and recording the genealogy of the royal family and inspecting the royal family
Jongchinbu: Office of the royal genealogy
Jong-hak: Special royal academies (education of the royal family)
Jongmyoseo: Custodians of the royal ancestral shrine
Jungchubu: Office of ministers-without-portfolio

Munsojeon: A shrine to the queen of King Taejo (progenitor of the Joseon Dynasty)

Naegeumwi: Palace guard headquarters
Naejasi: Management of certain kinds of food, clothes, and parties for the palace
Naeseomsi: Management of local items offered to the queens' palaces, and liquor and appetizers given to officers
Naesibu: Office of eunuch attendants
Naesusa: Royal estate bureau
Nae-uiwon: Royal pharmacy

Pungjeochang: Office in charge of the accounts of grain, mats, and paper
Pyeongsiseo: Office in charge of weights, measures, and prices

Saboksi: Office in charge of horses, wagons, harnesses, and livestock for the king's use
Sachukseo: Office in charge of livestock farming
Sadosi: Management of food used in the palace, especially rice, grain, and sauce
Saganwon: Office in charge of special counselors for the king
Saheonbu: Office of the inspector general
Sajaegam: Office in charge of the food items offered to the palace, such as fishes, meat, and salt
Sajikseo: Cleaning the *sajikdan* (i.e., altar for Confucian rites to the land and grain) and its walls
Sangseowon: Office in charge of seals and insignias
Sang-uiwon: Bureau of royal attire
Sa-ong-won: Palace kitchen management
Sa-onseo: Office in charge of making and supplying liquor and rice punch for the palace
Saposeo: Office in charge of managing vegetable gardens of the palace
Saseomsi: Office in charge of cotton cloth and paper money
Sayeogwon: Bureau of translation
Seja-igwisa: Guard of the crown prince
Sejasigang-won: Office of crown prince tutor
Seonggyun-gwan: National Confucian Academy
Seongonggam: Office in charge of building and repairs
Seungjeong-won: Royal secretariat
Seungmunwon: Office of diplomatic correspondence
Sogyeokseo: National Taoist temple
Suseonggeumhwasa: Office in charge of repairing, rebuilding, and firefighting for the palace, capital city, and government offices

Tongnyewon: Office of ritual affairs

Uibinbu: Office of princesses' consorts
Uigeumbu: State tribunal
Uijeongbu: State council
Ui-yeonggo: Office in charge of managing and supplying oil, honey, vegetables, and seasoning, etc., for the palace

Waseo: Office in charge of roofing tile production

Yang-hyeongo: Fund for scholarship
Yebinsi: Office for serving national guests
Yejo: Ministry of Rites (one of the Six Ministries)
Yemun-gwan: Office of royal decrees
Yeoneunjeon: A shrine to King Deokjong (a temple title of a crown prince Uigyeong [1438-1457])
Yukjo: The main administrative body of the Joseon Dynasty, comprised of the Six Ministries: Personnel (*ijo*), Taxation (*hojo*), Rites (*yejo*), Military Affairs (*byeongjo*), Justice (*hyeongjo*), and Public Works (*gongjo)*

Appendix 7: Slaves of Central Government

Appendix 7 List of Slaves of Central Government Offices (*Gyeongguk daejeon*)*

Types Govern-ment Offices**	Chabino ***	Geunsuno****	Total	Types Govern-ment Offices**	Chabino ***	Geunsuno ****	Total
Jongchinbu	10	552	562	Nae-uiwon	7	7	14
Uijeongbu	24	36	60	Sang-uiwon	65	7	72
Chunghunbu	17	130	147	Saboksi	14	8	22
Uibinbu	8	14	22	Gun-gisi	200	12	212
Donnyeongbu	8	31	39	Naejasi	79	7	86
Jungchubu	12	93	105	Naeseomsi	63	7	70
Uigeumbu	11	10	21	Sadosi	17	6	23
Ijo	12	17	29	Yebinsi	100	13	113
Hojo	17	20	37	Saseomsi	17	6	23
Yejo	15	17	32	Gunjagam	31	12	43
Byeongjo	69	22	91	Jeyonggam	35	7	42
Hyeongjo	15	22	37	Seongonggam	53	7	60
Gongjo	14	17	31	Sajaegam	30	6	36
Hanseongbu	11	15	26	Jang-agwon	7	5	12
Saheonbu	12	34	46	Gwansanggam	13	11	24
Dochongbu	26	12	38	Jeonuigam	13	9	22
Chung-ikbu	7	2	9	Sayeogwon	9	10	19

5 wijang	20		20	Sejasigang-won	6	5	11
Naesibu	21	37	58	Jong-hak	6	4	10
Seungjeong-won	9	18	27	Suseong-geumhwasa	10	5	15
Jang-yewon	269	10	279	Jeonseolsa	6	6	12
Saganwon	7	8	15	Pungjeochang	19	2	21
Gyeong-yeon	6		6	Gwangheung-chang	9	2	11
Hongmun-gwan	11	21	32	Jeonhamsa	16	2	22
Yemun-gwan	5		5	Jeon-yeonsa	48	5	53
Seonggyun-gwan	38	15	53	Naesusa		4	4
Hullyeonwon	12	15	27	Igwisa	4	8	12
Sangseowon	4	1	5	Sogyeokseo	44	3	47
Chunchugwan	3		3	Jongmyoseo	14	2	16
Seungmunwon	12	9	21	Sajikseo	9	1	10
Tongnyewon	9	22	31	Pyeongsiseo	4	1	5
Bongsangsi	151	10	161	Sa-onseo	10	2	12
Jongbusi	10	4	14	Ui-yeong-go	15	2	17
Gyoseogwan	12	5	17	Jang-heung-go	14	2	16
Sa-ong-won	11	5	16	Binggo	6	4	10

Types Government Offices**	Chabino ***	Geunsuno ****	Total
Jang-wonseo	22	4	26
Saposeo	120	8	128
Jeonsaengseo	29	1	30
Sachukseo	36	3	39
Jojiseo	90	5	95
Hyeminseo	12	2	14
Dohwaseo	5	2	7
Jeonokseo	4	1	5
Hwarinseo	14	4	18
Waseo	97	3	100
Gwi-huseo	29	6	35

4 hak	40	8	48
5 bu	20	5	25
Munsojeon	7		7
Total	2416	1480	3896

Source: Yun (1986: 580)
* The *Gyeongguk daejeon* is the Joseon Dynasty's national code of law.
** Refer to the list of government offices in Appendix 4.5
*** *Chabino*: Slaves who work in the palace or central government offices
**** *Geunsuno*: Slaves who work for the royal family and government officials

References (Materials in English)

Abrams, Philip. 1982. *The Problem of Design: The Formation of State*, New York, Ithaca: Cornell University Press.

Adelman, Irma, ed. 1969. *Development Planning: Korea's Second Five Year Plan*, Baltimore: Johns Hopkins University Press.

Agnew, John A. 1982. Technological Transfer and Theories of Development: Conceptual Issues in the South Asian Context. *Journal of Asian and African Studies* 17(1).

Agnew, John. 1993. Representing Space: Space, Scale and Culture in Social Science. In Duncan and Ley, eds. *Place/Culture/ Representation*. London and New York: Routledge.

Ahmed, A.I. Mahbub Uddin. 2004. Weber's Perspective on the City and Culture, Contemporary Urbanization and Bangladesh. *Bangladesh e-Journal of Sociology* 1(1): 1-13.

Ahn, Hae-Kyun. 1972. *Administrative Changes and Elite Dynamics*, Pittsburgh, PA: University Center for International Studies.

Ake, Claude. 1979. Social Science as Imperialism: The Theory of Political Development, Ibadan: University of Ibadan Press.

Akiwowo, Akinsola. 1988. Universalism and Indigenisation in Sociological Theory: Introduction, *International Sociology* 3(2) pp155-160.

Almond, G. 1990. *A Discipline Divided*, Newbury Park, London, New Delhi: Sage Publications.

Almond, G. and Verba, S. 1963. *The Civic Culture*, Princeton: Princeton University Press.

Amsden, A. 1985. The State and Taiwan's Economic Development. In *Bringing the State Back In*, edited by P.B. Evans, D. Rueschemeyer, and T. Skocpol, pp. 78–106. London: Cambridge University Press.

Amsden, Alice H. 1979. Taiwan's Economic History: A Case of Etatisme and Challenge to Dependency Theory, *Modern China*, 5(3).

Amsden, Alice H. 1989. *Asia's Next Giant,* New York: Oxford University Press.
Amsden, Alice H. 1990. Third World Industrialization: Global Fordism or a New Model?", *New Left Review*, 18(2):5-31.
Amsden, Alice H. 1991. Diffusion of Development: The Late-Industrializing Model and Greater East Asia, *The American Economic Review*, 81(2).
Amsden, Alice H. 1993. Asia's Industrial Revolution. *Dissent*, Summer.
Anderson, Perry. 1974. *Lineages of the Absolutist State*, London: New Left Books.
Anthias, F. 1989. Women and Nationalism in Cyprus. In *Woman-Nation-State*, edited by N. Yuval-Davis and F. Anthias, 150–169. New York: St. Martin's Press.
Appadurai, A. 1990. Disjuncture and Difference in the Global Cultural Economy. *Public Culture,* 2(2):1–24.
Appelbaum, R. and Henderson, J. eds. 1992. *States and Development in the Asian Pacific Rim*, Newbury, California, London, and New Delhi: Sage Publications.
Apter, D. 1965. *The Politics of Modernization*. Chicago and London: The University of Chicago Press.
Arbos, Xavier. 1990. Nation-state: The range and future of a concept. *Canadian Review of Studies in Nationalism*, 17: 1-2.
Armstrong, C.K., ed. 2002. *Korean society: civil society, democracy, and the state*. London and New York: Routledge.
Ashcroft, B., G. Griffiths, and H. Tiffin. 1995. *The Post-Colonial Studies Reader*. London: Routledge.
Ashley, R.K. 1988. Geopolitics, Supplementary, Criticism: A Reply to Professor Roy and Walker. *Alternatives*, 13:88-102.
Atkinson, M. and Coleman, W. 1989. Strong state and weak state. *British Journal of Political Science*, 19: 47-67.
Badie, B. and Birnbaum, P. 1983. *The Sociology of the State*, Chicago and London: The University of Chicago Press.
Balassa, Bela. 1981. *Newly Industrializing Countries in the World Economy*, Elmsford, New York: Pergamon.
Balassa, Bela. 1988. The lessons of East Asian development: An overview. *Economic Development & Cultural Change*, 36, April: 273-290.
Balassa, Bela. 1990. Korea's Development Strategy. In *Korean Economic Development*, ed. by Kwon, New York; Westport, CT; London: Greenwood Press.
Bank of Chosen. 1920. *Economic History of Chosen*, Seoul, Chosen.
Barnes, T.J. and Duncan, J.S., eds. 1992. *Writing Worlds: Discourse, Text, and Metaphor in the Representation of Landscape*, London and New York: Routledge.
Barnet, M. 1990. High politics is low politics, 1967-77. *World Politics*, 42(4):529-562.
Barthes, R. 1982. *Empire of Signs*. New York: Hill and Wang.
Bartz, Patricia M. 1972. *South Korea*, Oxford: Clarendon Press.
Bauer, P.T. and Yamey, B.S. 1957. *The Economics of Under-developed Countries*, Chicago: Chicago University Press.
Beard, Charles. 1966. *The Idea of National Interest*, Chicago: Quadrangle.
Bedeski, Robert. *South Korea's Modernization: Confucian and Conservative Characteristics*, Working Paper #21, University of Toronto-York University Joint Center on Modern East Asia, York University.

Belenky, M.F., Clinchy, B.M., Goldberger, N.R., and Tarule, J.M. 1986. *Women's Ways of Knowing*, New York: Basic Books.

Bellah, R. 1957. *Tokugawa Religion: The Values of Pre-industrial Japan*, Glencoe, IL.: Free Press.

Bendix, P.J. et al. 1978. *Development and Perspectives of the Korean Machine Industry*. Berlin: German Development Institute.

Berger, M. 1996. Yellow Mythologies: The East Asian Miracle and Post–Cold War Capitalism. *Positions* 4(1):90–126.

Berger, P. and Hsiao, H. ed. 1988. *In Search of An East Asian Developmental Model*, New Brunswick and Oxford, UK: Transaction Books.

Berger, Peter L. 1988. An East Asian Development Model? In *In Search of An East Asian Developmental Model*, ed. by Berger, P. and Hsiao, H., New Brunswick and Oxford, UK: Transaction Books.

Berger, S. 1981. *Organizing Interests in Western Europe*. Cambridge: Cambridge University Press.

Bernard, M., and J. Ravenhill. 1995. Beyond Product Cycles and Flying Geese: Regionalization, Hierarchy, and the Industrialization of East Asia. *World Politics* 47:171–209.

Berry, S., and R. Kiely. 1993. Is There a Future for Korean Democracy?, *Parliamentary Affairs* 46:594–604.

Bhabha, H. 1987. What Does the Black Man Want?, *New Formations* (1):118–123.

Bhabha. H. 1995. Cultural Diversity and Cultural Differences. In *The Post-Colonial Studies Reader*, edited by B. Ashcroft, G. Griffiths, and H. Tiffin, 206–209. London: Routledge.

Bienefeld, M. and Godfrey, M. eds. *The Struggle for Development*, Chicester: John Wiley and Sons.

Billet, B. L. 1990. South Korea at the Crossroads: An Evolving Democracy or Authoritarianism Revisited?, *Asian Survey* 30:300–311.

Bird., J. 1977. *The City: Centrality and Cities*. London and New York: Routledge.

Black, Antony. 1988. *State, Community and Human Desire*, New York: St. Martin's Press.

Blackadar, Andy and Sarah Kreckel. 2005. *Dilemmas of Foreign Aid: Debating U.S. Priorities, Policies, and Practices. The Choices for the 21st Century Education Program*. Providence, RI: Watson Institute for International Studies, Brown University.

Bollen, K. 1983. World System Position, Dependency, and Democracy: The Cross-National Evidence. *American Sociological Review* 48:468–479.

Boose, L. E. 1993. Techno-Muscularity and the Boy-Eternal: From the Quagmire to the Gulf. In *Gendering War Talk*, edited by M. Cooke and A. Woollacott, 67–106. Princeton, NJ: Princeton University Press.

Bowie, A. 1991. *Crossing the Industrial Debate: State, Society, and the Politics of Economic Transformation in Malaysia*, New York: Columbia University Press.

Boyd, R. N. 1984. The Current Status of Scientific Realism. In *Scientific Realism*, edited by Leplin, J., Berkeley and Los Angeles: University of California Press.

Bradford, C. 1987. *Trade and Structural Change in Pacific Asia*. Chicago: Chicago University Press.

Brandt, V. 1987. Korea. In *Ideology and National Competitiveness*, edited by Lodge and Vogel, Cambridge: Harvard Business School Press.

Bratton, Michael. 1989. Beyond the State: Civil society and Associational Life in Africa. *World Politics*, XLI(3), April.

Brinton, M. C. 1993. *Women and the Economic Miracle.* Berkeley: University of California Press.

Brown, D., and. D.M., Jones. 1995. Democratization and the Myth of the Liberalizing Middle Classes. In *Towards Illiberal Democracy in Pacific Asia*, edited by D. A. Bell, D. Brown, K. Jayasuriya, and D.M. Jones, 78–106. New York: St. Martin's Press.

Bruce, J. 1923. *Chu His and His Masters: An Introduction to Chu His and the Sung School of Chinese Philosophy*, London: Probsthain & Co.

Bruner, J. 1986. *Actual Minds, Possible Worlds*, Cambridge, MA: Harvard University Press.

Bruun, O. 2003. Fengshui in China: Geomantic Divination between State Orthodoxy and Popular Religion, Honolulu: University of Hawaii Press.

Buchanan, J.M. and Tollison, R.D., and Tullock, G. eds. 1980. *Towards a Theory of the Rent-Seeking Society*, College Station, TX: Texas A. & M. University Press.

Buci-Glucksmann, C. 1980. *Gramsci and the State* (translated by David Fernbach), London, Lawrence and Wishart.

Buruma, Ian. 1987. Right This Way for the Demonstration of the Day. *Far Eastern Economic Review*, 15 January.

Buzo, Adrian. 1984. Student Activism—in South Korea It's an Age-Old College Tradition. *Far Eastern Economic Review*, 17 May.

Callow, T. 1995. Nationbuilding in Korea, A Research Report submitted to the Faculty in Fulfillment of the Curriculum Requirement of Air War College, U.S. A.

Cammack, Paul. 1989. Review article: Bringing the state back in?, *British Journal of Political Science*, 19:261-290.

Caporaso, James A. 1978. Dependence, dependency, and power in the global system: A structural and behavioral analysis, *International Organization*, 32(1): 13-43.

Caporaso, James A. 1989. Introduction: The state in comparative and international perspective. In *The Elusive State*, edited by Caporaso, CA: Sage Publication.

Carnoy, M. 1984. *The State and Political Theory*, Princeton, NJ: Princeton University Press.

Casanova, P. G. 1965. *Internal Colonialism and National Development*, Washington University: Social Science Institute.

Castells, Manuel. 1992. Four Asian Tigers With a Dragon Head. In *States and Development in the Asian Pacific Rim*, edited by Appelbaum and Henderson, Newbury Park, London, and New Delhi: Sage Publications.

Cawson, A. 1986. *Corporatism and Political Theory*. New York: Basil Blackwell.

Cawson, A., Holmes, P., and Stevens, A. 1987. The Interaction between Firms and the State in France. In *Comparative Government-Industry Relations*, edited by Wright and Wilks.

Chakravarty, Sukhamoy. 1987. Marxist economics and contemporary developing economies. *Cambridge Journal of Economics*, 11:3-22.

Chamberlain, Heath B. 1993. On the Search for Civil Society in China. *Modern China*, 19(2), April:199-215.

Chang, H.Y. and Myers, R. 1963. Japanese Colonial Development Policy. *Journal of Asian Studies*, 22.

Chang, Ha-Joon. 1993. The Political Economy of Industrial Policy in Korea. *Cambridge Journal of Economics*, 17.

Chang, Ha-Joon., and Kozul-Wright, Richard. 1994. Organizing Development: Comparing the National Systems of Entrepreneurship in Sweden and South Korea. *The Journal of Development Studies*, 30(3).

Chang, Kwang-Chih. 1964. Some Dualistic Phenomena in Shang Society. *The Journal of Asian Studies* 51(1): 23-45.

Chang, Sen-Dou. 1963. Some Aspects of the Urban Geography of the Chinese Hsien Capital. *Annals of the Association of American Geographers* 53(2):109-143.

Chang, Sen-Dou. 1963. The Historical Trend of Chinese Urbanization. *Annals of the Association of American Geographers* 53(2):109-143.

Chatterjee, Partha. 1990. A Response to Taylor's "Modes of Civil Society. *Public Culture*, 3(1), Fall:119-132.

Cheek, T. 1992. From Priests to Professionals. in *Popular Protest and Political Culture in Modern China*, Wasserstrom and Perry, CO: Westview.

Chen, E.K.Y. 1979. *Hyper-growth in Asian Economics: A Comparative Study of Hong Kong, Japan, Korea, Singapore and Taiwan*, London: Macmillan.

Chenery, H.B. 1975. The Structuralist Approach to Development Policy. *American Economic Review Papers and Proceedings*, 65(2).

Chenery, H.B. 1979. *Structural Change and Development Policy,* London: Oxford University Press.

Cheng, L., and P. C. Hsiung. 1992. Women, Export-Oriented Growth, and the State: The Case of Taiwan. In *States and Development in the Asian Pacific Rim*, edited by R. P. Appelbaum and J. Henderson, 233–266, New York: Sage.

Cheng, T. 1989. Democratizing the Quasi-Leninist Regime in Taiwan. *World Politics* 41:471–499.

Cheng, Tun-Jen. 1990. Political Regimes annd Developmental Strategies: South Korea and Taiwan. In *Manufacturing Miracles*, edited by Gereffi and Wyman, Princeton, NJ: Princeton University Press.

Chilcote, R. 1981. *Theories of Comparative Politics: The Search for a Paradigm Reconsidered*. Boulder: Westview Press.

Chirot, Daniel. 1985. The Rise of the West. *American Sociological Review*, 50: 181-195.

Cho, Byung-Koo. 1992. Economic Customary Practice and Ethics of Koreans. *The Academy Review of Korean Studies*, 15(4), December: 84-85.

Cho, D. S. 1994. *A Study of Korea's Chaebol*. Seoul: Economic Daily.

Chodak, Szymon. 1989. *The New State: Etatization of Western Societies*, Boulder and London: Lynne Rienner Publisher.

Choi, Hochin. 1971. *The Economic History of Korea: From the Earliest Times to 1945*, Seoul: Samsung Printing Co., Ltd.

Choi, Jang Jip. 1989. *Labor and the Authoritarian State*, Seoul: Korea University Press.

Chosun Ilbo. 1989. Dongeui daesaeng semyung sanyung goohung (Three Students of Dongeui University Sentenced to Death). September 29, p. 1.

Chosun Ilbo. 1996. Chunssi sahyung—Rhossi moogi (Mr. Chun Sentenced to Death, Mr. Rho Sentenced to Life in Prison). August 6, p. 1.

Chosun Ilbo. 1953. (August 8).

Chu, Y. 1989. State Structure and Economic Adjustment of the East Asian Newly Industrializing Countries. *International Organization* 43(4):646–672.

Clark, Cal and Lemco, Jonathan. 1988. The Strong State and Development. *Journal of Developing Societies*, 4.

Clark, Cal., and Chan, Steve. 1992. *The Evolving Pacific Basin in the Global Political Economy*, Boulder and London: Lynne Rienner Publishers.

Cleveland, H. 1949. *Next Step in Asia.* Cambridge, MA: Harvard University Press.

Clifford, Mark L. 1994. *Troubled Tiger: Businessmen, Bureaucrats, and Generals in South Korea*, Armonk, NY, and London: M.E. Sharpe.

Clower, R. et al. 1966. *Growth Without Development: An Economic Survey of Liberia*, Evanston, IL: Northwestern University Press.

Cohen, P.A. 1984. *Discovering History in China.* New York: Columbia University Press.

Colclough, Christopher. 1991. Structuralism versus Neo-liberalism. in *States or Markets?*, edited by Colclough and Manor, Oxford, UK: Clarendon Press and Oxford University Press.

Cole, D. 1979. Free Enterprise vs Government Regulation. *Asian Affairs*, 7(2), Nov/Dec.

Cole, D. and Lyman, P. 1971. *Korean Development: The Interplay of Politics and Economics*, Cambridge: Harvard University Press.

Cook, A. H., and H. Hayashi. 1980. *Working Women in Japan*. Ithaca, NY: Cornell University Press.

Corbo, V. and Suh, Sang-Mok. 1992. *Structural Adjustment in a Newly Industrialized Country: The Korean Experience*, Baltimore and London: Johns Hopkins University Press.

Corbridge, S. 1986. *Capitalist World Development: A Critique of Radical Development Geography*. Hong Kong: Rowman & Littlefield.

Corlett, William. 1989. *Community without Unity*, Durham and London: Duke University Press.

Cotterell, Arthur. 1993. *East Asia: From Chinese Predominance to the Rise of the Pacific Rim*, New York and London: Oxford University Press.

Cotton, James. 1989. From Authoritarianism to Democracy in South Korea. *Political Studies*, 37(2): 244-259.

Cox, R. 1987. *Production, Power, and World Order*. New York: Columbia University Press.

Cox, R. 1995. Civilizations: Encounters and Transformations. *Studies in Political Economy* (47):7–31.

Cox, W.R. 1983. Gramsci, hegemony, and international relations: An essay in method. *Millennium*, 12(2): 162-175.

Creel, H.G. 1995. Confucius and the Struggle for Human Happiness. *Global Community in the Western-Pacific Rim*, edited by Murray, G.

Crowe, N. 1995. *Nature and the Idea of a Man-Made World*, Cambridge, MA, and London: The MIT Press.

Cumings, B. 1981. *The Origins of the Korean War.* Princeton, NJ: Princeton University Press.

Cumings, B. 1984. The Origins and Development of the Northeast Asian Political Economy: Industrial Sectors, Product Cycles, and Political Consequences. *International Organization* 38(1):1–40.

Cumings, B. 1988. "World System and Authoritarian Regimes in Korea, 1948–1984." In *Contending Approaches to the Political Economy of Taiwan*, edited by E.A. Winckler and S. Greenhalgh. Armonk: M.E. Sharpe.

Cumings, B. 2005. *Korea's Place in the Sun*, New York and London: W.W. Norton & Company, Inc.

Cumings, Bruce. 1984. The Legacy of Japanese Colonialism in Korea. In *The Japanese Colonial Empire*, edited by R.H. Myers and M.R. Peattie, Princeton: Princeton University Press.

Cumings, Bruce. 1987. The origins and development of the Northeast Asian political economy. In *The Political Economy of the New Asian Industrialism*, edited by F. Deyo, Ithaca: Cornell University Press.

Dahrendorf, Ralf. 1990. Has the East joined the West? *New Perspective Quarterly*, 7(2), Spring.

Dalhman, C. 1989. Structural Trade and Change in the East Asia Newly Industrial Economies and Emerging Industrial Economies. In *The Newly Industrializing Countries in the World Economy*, edited by R. Purcell, Boulder and London: Lynne Rienner.

Davidheiser, Evenly B. 1992. Strong states, Weak states: The role of the state in revolution, *Comparative Politics*, 24(4), July.

D'Costa, Anthony P. 1994. State, Steel and Strength: Structural Competitiveness and Development in South Korea, *The Journal of Development Studies*, 31(1).

de Franco, Silvio. 1988. Korea's Experience with the Development of Trade and Industry: Lessons for Latin America, Economic Development Institute Policy Seminar Report, No. 14.

de Kadt, E. 1985. Of Markets, Might and Mullahs: A Case for Equity, Pluralism and Tolerance in Development, *World Development*, 13(4), April.

Deans, P. 1996. The Capitalist Developmental State in East Asia. In *State Strategies in the Global Economy*, edited by R. Palan and J. Abbott with P. Deans, 78–102, London: Pinter.

Denny, R. 1994. Singapore, China, and the Soft Authoritarian Challenge. *Asian Survey* 34:231–242.

Deuchler, Martina. 1992. *The Confucian Transformation of Korea*, Cambridge, MA: Council on East Asian Studies, Harvard University.

Development. In *Bringing the State Back In*, edited by Evans and Rueschmeyer and Skocpol, New York: Cambridge University Press.

Deyo, F.C. 1987a. State and Labor: Modes of Political Exclusion in East Asian Development. In *The Political Economy of the New Asian Industrialism*, edited by F.C. Deyo, Ithaca, NY: Cornell University Press.

Deyo, Frederic C. 1987b. *The Political Economy of the New Asian Industrialism*, Ithaca: Cornell University Press.

Deyo, Frederic C. 1992. The Political Economy of Social Policy Formation. In *States and Development in the Asian Pacific Rim*, edited by Appelbaum and Henderson, Newbury, California, London, and New Delhi: Sage Publications.

Diamond, L. 1992. Economic Development and Democracy Reconsidered, *American Behavioral Scientist*, 35: 450-499.

Dietz, James L. 1992. Overcoming underdevelopment: What has been learned from the East and Latin American experiences? *Journal of Economic Issue*, 26(2), June.

Dirlik, A. 1994. The Postcolonial Aura: Third World Criticism in the Global Capitalism. *Critical Inquiry* 20:328-356.

Dogan and Pelassy. 1984. How to Compare Nations, NJ:Chatham House, 11.

Donaldson, L.E. 1992. *Decolonizing Feminism: Race, Gender, and Empire Building.* Chapel Hill: University of North Carolina Press.

Doner, Richard. 1991. Driving a Bargain: Automobile Industrialization and Japanese Firms in Southeast Asia, Berkeley: University of California Press.

Doner, Richard F. 1992. Limits of State Strength: Toward an Institutionalist View of Economic Development, *World Politics*, 44, April:398-431.

Dong, Wonmo. 1987. University Students in South Korean Politics, *Journal of International Affairs*, 40, Winter/Spring.

Dong, Wonmo. 1988. Student Activism and the Presidential Politics of 1987 in South Korea. In *Political Change in South Korea*, edited by Ilpyong Kim and Young Whan Kihl, New York: Korean PWPA, Inc., distributed by Paragon House.

Dore, R. P. 1965. *Education in Tokugawa, Japan.* London: Routledge and Kegan Paul.

Douglass, M. 1994. The Developmental State and the Newly Industrializing Economies of Asia. *Environment and Planning* (26):543–566.

Drakakis-Smith, David and Bale, John. eds. 1992. *Pacific Asia*, London and New York: Routledge.

Dryzek, John S. 1992. The good society versus the state, *Journal of Politics*, 54(2), May.

Duncan, J. 1990. *The City as Text*, Cambridge: Cambridge University Press.

Duncan, J. and Duncan, N. 1988. (Re)reading the Landscape, *Society and Space*, 6: 117-126.

Duncan, J. and Ley, D. eds. 1993. *Place/Culture/Representation*, London and New York: Routledge.

Duvall, R. 1978. Dependence and Dependencia Theory: Notes toward Precision of Concept and Argument, *International Organization*, 32(1): 51-78.

Dyson, Kenneth H.F. 1980. *The State Tradition in Western Europe*, New York: Oxford University Press.

Dyson, Kenneth., and Wilks, S. eds. 1983. *Industrial Crisis*, Oxford: Basil Blackwell.

Easterly, W. 2003. Can Foreign Aid Buy Growth? *Journal of Economic Perspectives*, 17(3): 23-48.

Easthope, A. and McGowan, K. eds. 1992. *A Critical and Cultural Theory Reader*, Toronto and Buffalo: University of Toronto Press.

Eckert, Carter J. 1991. *Offspring of Empire: The Koch'ang Kims and the Colonial Origins of Korean Capitalism*, 1876-1945, Seattle: University of Washington Press.

Eckert, Carter J., Ki-baik Lee, Young Ick Lew, Michael Robinson, and Edward W. Wagner. 1990. *Korea Old and New History*. Seoul: Ilchokak Publishers.

Eisenstein, Z.R. 1994. *The Color of Gender*. Berkeley: University of California Press.

Eitel, E.J. 1984. *Feng-Shui*, Singapore: Graham Brash.

Eliade, M. 1954. *Cosmos and History: The Myth of the Eternal Return*. New York: Harper Torchbooks.

Eliade, M. 1957. *The Sacred and the Profane: The Nature of Religion*. Orlando, Austin, New York, San Diego, Toronto, London: A Harvest Book Harcourt, Inc.

Elshtain, J.B. 1992. Sovereignty, Identity, Sacrifice. In *Gendered States*, edited by S. Peterson, 141-154. Boulder, CO: Lynne Rienner.

Enloe, C. 1989. *Bananas, Beaches, and Bases*. Berkeley: University of California Press.

Evans, Peter. 1979. *Dependent Development*, NJ: Princeton University Press.

Evans, Peter. 1987. Class, state and dependence in East Asia: Lessons for Latin Americanists. In *The Political Economy of the New Asian Industrialism*, edited by F. Deyo, Ithaca: Cornell University Press.

Evans, Peter. 1989. Predatory, developmental and other apparatuses: A comparative analysis of the Third World State, *Sociological Forum*, 4.

Fanon, F. 1963. *The Wretched of the Earth*. New York: Grove Press.

Feith, H. 1981. Repressive-Developmentalist Regimes in Asia. *Alternatives* (VII):491–605.

Femia, V.J. 1981. *Gramsci's Political Thought*. Oxford: Clarendon Press.

Feng, Yi. 1997. Democracy, Political Stability and Economic Growth, *British Journal of Political Science*, 27:391-418.

Ferguson, A. 1991. *Sexual Democracy*. Boulder, CO: Westview Press.

Fernandes, T. 2006. Authoritarian Regimes and Democratic Semioppositions: The end of the Portuguese dictatorship (1968-1974) in comparative perspective, Working Paper, WP5-06, Instituto de Ciências Sociais Universidade de Lisboa.

Feuchtwang, S. 1987. Fanonian Spaces. *New Formations* (Spring):124-130.

Fiori, G. 1970. *Antonio Gramsci, Life of a Revolutionary*, London: New Left Books.

Fish, S. 1989. *Doing What Comes Naturally*, Durham, NC: Duke University Press.

Fisher, J. 1989. *Mothers of the Disappeared*. Boston: South End Press.

Flanagan, S.C. and Aie-Rie Lee. 2000. Value Change and Democratic Reform in Japan and Korea, Comparative Political Studies, 33(5): 626-659.

Forgacs, D. and Nowell-Smith, G. eds. (translated by Boelhower, W.). 1985. *Antonio Gramsci: Selections from Cultural Writings*, Cambridge: Harvard University Press.

Foster-Carter, Aiden. 1987. Korea: From Dependency to Democracy?, *Capital & Class*, 33.

Fowler, James. 1999. The United States and South Korean Democratization, Political Science Quarterly, 114(2): 265-288.

Freedman, Amy L. 2004. Economic Crises and Political Change Indonesia, South Korea, Malaysia, *World Affairs*, 166(4): 185-196.

Friedman, D. 1988. *The Misunderstood Miracle: Industrial Development and Political Change in Japan,* Ithaca, NY: Cornell University Press.

Friedman, M. 1980. *Free to Choose*, New York: Harcourt Brace Jovanovich.

Friman, Richard H. 1993. Neither compromise nor compliance. In *The Limit of State Autonomy*, edited by Skidmore and Hudson, Boulder: Westview Press.

Fu, Zhengyuan. 1993. *Autocratic Tradition and Chinese Politics*, Cambridge: Cambridge University Press.

Fujita, K. 1987. Gender, State, and Industrial Policy in Japan. *Women's Studies International Forum.* 10(6):589–667.

Fukui, H. 1992. The Japanese State and Economic Development: A Profile of a Nationalist-Paternalist Capitalist State. In *States and Development in the Asian Pacific Rim*, edited by R.P. Appelbaum and J. Henderson, 199–226. New York: Sage.

Fukui, Haruhiro. 1992. The Japanese State and Economic Development. In *States and Development in the Asian Pacific Rim*, edited by Appelbaum and Henderson, Newbury, California, London, and New Delhi: Sage Publications.

Fukuyama, F. 1992. Capitalism & Democracy: The Missing Link, *Journal of Democracy*, 3(3): 100-110.

Fukuyama, F. 1995. Confucianism and Democracy, *Journal of Democracy*, 6(2):20-33.

Fukuyama, F. 2000. *The Great Disruption: Human Nature and Reconstruction of Social Order*, New York, London, Toronto, Sydney, and Singapore: Simon and Schuster.

Furtado, C.M. 1963. *The Economic Growth of Brazil: A Survey from Colonial to Modern Times* (1963), Los Angeles: University of California Press.

Galenson, Walter, ed. 1985. *Foreign Trade and Investment: Development in the Newly Industrializing Asian Economics*, Madison: University of Wisconsin Press.

Garnier, M., Hage, J., and Fuller, B. 1989. The strong state, social class, and controlled school expansion in France, 1881-1975, *American Journal of Sociology*, 95(2), September:279-306.

Gereffi, G. and Wyman, D. 1989. Determinants of Development Strategies in Latin America and East Asia. In *Pacific Dynamics*, edited by Haggard and Moon, Korea: CIS-Inha University Press; and Boulder, CO: Westview Press.

Gereffi, Gary. 1990. Big Business and the State. In *Manufacturing Miracles*, edited by Gereffi and Wyman, Princeton, NJ: Princeton University Press.

Gereffi, Gary. 1992. New Realities of Industrial Development in East Asia and Latin America. In *States and Development in the Asian Pacific Rim*, edited by Appelbaum and Henderson, Newbury, California, London, and New Delhi: Sage Publications.

Geremek, B., Varga, G., Milosz, C., O'Brien, C., and Rabossi, E. 1992. *The Idea of a Civil Society*, National Humanities Center.

Gergen, K.J. 1986. Correspondence versus Autonomy in the Language of Understanding Human Action. In *Metatheory in Social Science*, edited by D.W. Fiske and R.A. Shweder, Chicago: University of Chicago Press.

Gergen, K.J. and Gergen, M.M. 1991. Toward Reflexive Methodologies. In *Research and Reflexivity*, edited by F. Steier, Newbury Park, CA: Sage.

Gerschenkron, A. 1962. *Economic Backwardness in Historical Perspective*, Cambridge, MA: Belknap Press of Harvard University Press.

Giddens, A. 1982. *Profiles and Critique in Social Theory*, Berkeley and Los Angeles: University of California Press.

Giddens, Anthony. 1984. *The Constitution of Society*, Berkeley and Los Angeles: University of California Press.

Gilligan, C. 1982. *In a Different Voice: Psychological Theory and Women's Development*, Cambridge: Harvard University Press.

Gills, B. 1993. The Hegemonic Transition in East Asia: A Historical Perspective. In *Gramsci, Historical Materialism and International Relations*, edited by S. Gill, 186–212. Cambridge: Cambridge University Press.

Gleysteen, Jr. W.H. and Romberg A. 1987. Korea: Asian Paradox, *Foreign Affairs*, 65(5), Summer.

Gold, T.B. 1986. *State and Society in the Taiwan Miracle*. White Plains, NY: M.E. Sharpe.

Gold, Thomas B. 1986. *State and Society in the Taiwan Miracle*, Armonk, NY: Sharpe.

Goodman, N. 1978. *Ways of Worldmaking*, Indianapolis: Hackett.

Goodman, N. 1984. *Of Mind and Other Matters*, Cambridge: Harvard University Press.

Goodman, N. and Eligin, C. 1988. *Reconceptions in Philosophy and Other Arts and Science*, Indianapolis: Hackett.

Gordon, Alec. 1993. Imaginary Histories and the Real Thing: A Critique of Anderson and Benda on the "Autonomous State" in Indonesia. *Journal of Contemporary Asia*, 23(4).

Gordon, C. ed. (translated by Gordon, C., Marshall, L., Mepham, J., and Soper, K.). 1972. *Power/Knowledge: Selected Interviews & Other Writings, 1972-1977, by Michel Foucault*. New York: Pantheon Books.

Gough, Ian. 1975. State Expenditure in Advanced Capitalism, *New Left Reivew*, 92, July/August.

Gourevitch, Peter A. 1977. International trade, domestic coalition, and liberty, *Journal of Interdisciplinary History*, 8, Autumn.

Gourevitch, Peter A. 1984. Breaking with orthodoxy, *International Organization*, 38, Winter.

Gourevitch, Peter. 1986. The Social Bases of the Autonomous State, in *Politics in Hard Times*, Ithaca and London: Cornell University Press.

Grabowski, Richard. 1994. The Successful Developmental State: Where Does It Come From? *World Development*, 22(3).

Graham, Norman A. 1991. The Role of the Military in the Political and Economic Development of the Republic of Korea, *Journal of Asian and African Studies*, 26: 1-2.

Gramsci, A. 1971. *Selections from the Prison Notebooks*, New York: International Publisher.

Gramsci, A. 1990. *Selections from political writings, 1910-1920*, (with additional texts by Bordiga and Tasca; selected and edited by Quintin Hoare; translated by John Mathews), Minneapolis: University of Minnesota Press.

Granato, Jim, Ronald Inglehart and David Leblang. 1996. Cultural Values, Stable Democracy, and Economic Development: A Reply, *American Journal of Political Science*, 40(3): 680-696.

Granovetter, Mark. 1985. Economic Action and Social Structure: The Problem of Embeddedness, *American Journal of Sociology*, 91(3): 481-510.

Grant, W. 1985. *The Political Economy of Corporatism.* London: Macmillan.

Grazia, S. D. 1973. *Masters of Chinese Political Thought*. New York: Viking Press.

Green, R.H. 1974. The Role of the State as an Agent of Economic and Social Development in the Least Developed Countries, *Journal of Developing Planning*, 6: 1-40.

Greenberg, E. and Mayer T., eds. 1990. *Changes in the State*, Newbury Park and London and New Delhi: Sage Publications.

Greenhalgh, S. 1994. De-Orientalizing the Chinese Family Firm. *American Ethnologist* 21(4):746–775.

Greenspan, A. 2007. *The Age of Turbulence: Adventure in a New World*, New York: Penguin Press.

Grossberg, L., Nelson, C., and Treichler, P. eds. *Cultural Studies*. New York and London: Routledge, 295-337.

Gulati, Umesh C. 1992. The foundations of rapid economic growth: The case of the Four Tigers, *American Journal of Economics and Sociology*, 51(2), April.

Habermas, Jurgen. 1989. The Public Sphere. In *Rethinking Popular Culture*, edited by Mukerji and Schudson, Berkeley: University of California Press.

Habermas, Jurgen. 1991. *The Structural Transformation of the Public Sphere*, Cambridge: The MIT Press.

Haboush, JaHyun Kim. 1988. *A Heritage of Kings: One Man's Monarchy in the Confucian World*, New York: Columbia University Press.

Haggard, Stephan. 1986. The newly industrializing countries in the international system, *World Politics*, 38: 343-370.

Haggard, Stephan. 1990. *Pathways from the Periphery*, Ithaca, NY: Cornell University Press.

Haggard, S. and T. Cheng. 1987. State and Foreign Capital in East Asian NICs. In *The Political Economy of the New Asian Industrialism*, edited by F. Deyo, Ithaca, NY: Cornell University Press.

Haggard, S., and T. Cheng. 1987a. State Strategies, Local and Foreign Capital in the "Gang of Four." In *The Political Economy of the New Asian Industrialism*, edited by F. Deyo, 84–135. Ithaca, NY: Cornell University Press.

Haggard, S., and Moon, Chung-In. 1983. Liberal, Dependent or Mercantile? The South Korean State in the International System. In *The Antinomies of Interdependence*, edited by J. Ruggie, 131–190. New York: Columbia University Press.

Haggard, Stephan and Moon, Chung-In., eds. 1989. *Pacific Dynamics*, Boulder: Westview Press.

Haggard, Stephan., and Moon, Chung-In. 1990. Institutions and Economic Policy, *World Politics*, 12: 210-37.

Hahm, Chai Bong. 2004. Ironies of Confucianism, *Journal of Democracy*, 15(3): 93-107.

Hahm, Pyong-Choon. 1967. The Korean Political Tradition and Law: Essays in Korean Law and Legal History, Royal Artistic Society Korea Branch, *Monograph Series*, no. 1, Seoul: Computer Press.

Hall, J. and Ikenberry, J. 1989. *The State: Concepts in Social Theory*, Minneapolis: University of Minnesota Press.

Hall, John A. ed. 1986. *States in History*, United Kingdom: Basil Blackwell Ltd.

Hall, Peter A. 1986. *Governing the Economy*, New York: Oxford University Press.

Hamilton, Clive. 1983. Capitalist Industrialization in East Asia's Four Little Tigers, *Journal of Contemporary Asia*, 13(1).

Hamilton, Clive. 1984. Class, State, and Industrialization in Korea, *Institute of Development Studies Bulletin*, 15(2): 38-43.

Han, J. and Ling, L.H.M. 1998. Authoritarianism in the Hypermasculinized State: Hybridity, Patriarchy, and Capitalism in Korea. *International Studies Quarterly*, 42: 53-78.

Han, J. 2007. From Indifference to Making the Difference: NNIs and Patterns of Political Participation Among Korea's Younger Generations. *Journal of Information Technology and Politics*, 4(1).

Han, J. 2009. Korea's beef crisis: the Internet and Democracy. *Australian Journal of International Affairs*, 63(4), December: 505-528.

Han, J. 2012. *Networked Information Technologies, Elections, and Politics: Korea and the United States*, Lanham, Boulder, New York, Toronto, Plymouth, UK: Lexington Books.

Han, Sang-jin. 1995. Economic Development and Democracy: Korea as a New Model?, *Korea Journal*, 35(2): 5-17.

Han, Seung Soo. 1984. Of Economic Success and Confucianism, *Far Eastern Economic Review*, 20, December.

Han, Young Woo (trans. By Chaibong Hahm). 2010. *A Review of Korean History*: Vol. 2: Joseon Era. Seoul, Gyeonggido: Kyongsaewon.

Haraway, D. 1992. The promises of monsters: a regenerative politics for inappropriate/d others. Lawreace Grossberg, Cary Nelson, Paula A. Treicher, eds. In *Cultural Studies*, New York: Routledge.

Harp, J. 1991. Political Economy/ Cultural Studies: Exploring Points of Convergence, *Canadian Review of Sociology & Anthropology*, 28(2).

Harris, Nigel. 1989. Review Article: The Pacific Rim, *The Journal of Development Studies*, 25, April.

Harris, Nigel. 1992. States, Economic Development, and the Asian Pacific Rim. In *States and Development in the Asian Pacific Rim*, edited by Appelbaum and Henderson, Newbury, London, New Delhi: Sage Publications.

Hartz, Louis. 1955. *The Liberal Tradition in America*, New York: Harcourt, Brace.

Harvey, David. 1989. *The Condition of Postmodernity*, Cambridge, MA, and Oxford, UK:Blackwell.

Hawes, G. and Liu, H. 1993. Explaining the Dynamics of the Southeast Asian Political Economy: State, Society, and the Search for Economic Growth, *World Politics*, 45(4), July.

Hayden, E.W. 1982. Internationalizing Japan's Financial System. In *Japan's Economy: Coping with Change in the International Environment*, edited by D. Okimoto, 89-122. Boulder, CO: Westview Press.

Hein, Simeon. 1992. Trade Strategy and the Dependency Hypothesis, *Economic Development & Cultural Change*, 40(3), April.

Helgesen, Geir. 1998. *Democracy and Authority in Korea: The Cultural Dimension in Korean Politics*, New York: St. Martin's Press.

Henderson, Gregory. 1968. *Korea: The Politics of the Vortex*, Cambridge, MA:Harvard University Press.

Henderson, J. and Appelbaum, R.P. 1992. Situating the State in the East Asian Development Process. In *States and Development in the Asian Pacific Rim*, edited by Appelbaum and Henderson, Newbury, London, New Delhi: Sage Publications.

Henderson, J. 1993. Against the Economic Orthodoxy: On the Making of the East Asian Miracle. *Economy and Society*. 22(2):200-217.

Heo, Uk., And Tan, A.C. 2001. Democracy and Economic Growth: A Causal Analysis, *Comparative Politics*, 33(4): 463-473.

Heper, Metin. 1992. The strong state as a problem for the consolidation of democracy: Turkey and Germany compared, *Comparative Political Studies*, 25(2), July:169-194.

Hinnebusch, Raymond A. 1993. State and Civil Society in Syria, *Middle East Journal*, 47(2), Spring.

Hintze, Otto. 1975. The preconditions of representative government in the context of world history. In *The Historical Essays of Otto Hintze*, edited by F. Gilbert, New York: Oxford University Press.

Hirschman, Albert. 1945. *National Power and the Structure of International Trade*, Berkeley: University of California Press.

Hirschmeier, J. and Yui, T. 1981. *The Development of Japanese Business 1600-1980*, London: George Allen.

Hofheinze, R. and Calder, K.E. 1982. *The Eastasia Edge*, New York: Basic Books.

Holbrooke, Richard. 1986. East Asia: The Next Challenge, *Foreign Affairs*, 64(4), Spring.

Holsti, Kal J. 1986. Politics in command: Foreign trade as national security policy, *International Organization*, 40(3): 643-671.

Hsiao, H.M. 1988. An East Asian Development Model. In *In Search of An East Asian Developmental Model*, edited by Berger and Hsiao, New Brunswick and Oxford, UK: Transaction Books.

Huang, P.C. 1993. "Public Sphere"/"Civil Society" in China?: The Third Realm Between State and Society. *Modern China*, 19(2): 216-240.

Hungtington, S. 1968. *Political Order in Changing Societies*, New Haven: Yale University Press.

Hunt, M. 1987. *Ideology and U.S. Foreign Policy.* New Haven, CT: Yale University Press.

Huntington, S.P. 1996. Democracy for the Long Haul, *Journal of Democracy*, 7(2): 3-13.

Huntington, S.P. 1991. The Third Wave: Democratization in the Late Twentieth Century, University of Oklahoma Press.

Huntington, Samuel P. and Lawrence E. Harrison. 2000. Culture Matters

Hwang, Byung Tai. 1979. Confucianism in Modernization: Comparative Study of China, Japan, and Korea, Ph.D. Dissertation in the University of California, Berkeley.

Hyam, R. 1992. *Empire and Sexuality.* New York: St. Martin's Press.

Ikenberry, J. and Lake, D. 1988. Introduction: Approaches to Explaining American Foreign Economic Policy, *International Organization*, 42(1).

Ikenberry, John G. 1986. The irony of state strength: Comparative responses to the oil shocks in the 1970s, *International Organization*, Vol. 40, No. (Winter, 1986), pp. 105–137.

Im, H.B. 1987. The Rise of Bureaucratic Authoritarianism in South Korea. *World Politics* 39(2):231–257.

Irwan, Alexander. 1987. Real Wages and Class Struggle in South Korea, *Journal of Contemporary Asia*, 17(4).

Iwao, S. 1993. *The Japanese Woman.* New York: Free Press.

Jackson, Robert H. 1990. Quasi-State: Sovereignty, International Relations, and the Third World, Cambridge: Cambridge University Press.

Jacobs, Norman. 1985. *The Korean Road to Modernization and Development*, Urbana and Chicago: University of Illinois Press.

Jeffords, S. 1989. *The Remasculinization of America: Gender and the Vietnam War.* Bloomington: Indiana University Press.

Jencks, C. 1980. The Architectural Sign. In Broadbent, G., Bunt, R., and Jencks, C. 1980. *Signs, Symbols, and Architecture*, Chichester, New York, Brisbane, Toronto: John Wiley & Sons.

Jessop, Bob. 1990. *Putting the Capitalist State in its Place*, Pennsylvania: Pennsylvania State University Press.

John, Michael. 1988. The Peculiarities of the German State, *Past & Present*, 119, May.

Johnson, C. 1987. Political Institutions and Economic Performance. In F. Deyo, ed. *The Political Economy of the New Asian Industrialism*, Ithaca, NY: Cornell University Press.

Johnson, C. 1989. South Korean democratization: The role of economic development, *The Pacific Review*, 2(1):1-10.

Johnson, Chalmers. 1982. *MITI and the Japanese Miracle*, Stanford: Stanford University Press.

Johnson, J. 1980. *Latin America in Caricature.* Austin: University of Texas Press.

Jones, David Martin. 1998. Democratization, Civil Society, and Illiberal Middle Class Culture in Pacific Asia. *Comparative Politics*, 30(2): 147-169.

Jones, E. 1994. Asia's Fate: A Response to the Singapore School. *National Interest* 35:18-28.

Jones, K. 1993. *Compassionate Authority.* New York: Routledge.

Jones, L.P., and I. Sakong. 1980. *Government, Business, and Entrepreneurship in Economic Development: The Korean Case.* Cambridge, MA: Harvard University Press.

Jones, M. 1998. Democratization, Civil Society, and Illiberal Middle Class Culture in Pacific Asia. *Comparative Politics*, 30(2): 147-169.

Joongang Ilbo. 1995. Kyungje baljachui (A Trace of Economy). August 15, pp. 30–31.

Joongang Ilbo. 1995. Shinsedae jeongchieuishik: Saejeongchijilseo yulmang (New Generation's View on Politics: Aspiration for a New Political Order). August 31, p. 12.

Kahn, H. 1979. *World Economic Development: 1979 and Beyond.* London: Croom Helm.

Kahn, Herman. 1984. The Confucian Ethic and Economic Growth. In *The Gap Between Rich and Poor: Contending Perspectives on the Political Economy of Development*, edited by Mitchell A. Seligson, Boulder: West View Press.

Kalton, M. 1979. Korean Ideas and Value, *Philip Jaisohn Memorial Paper*, no. 7, Philip Jaisohn Memorial Foundation, Pennsylvania.

Kang, Kyung-Sik and Whang, In-Joung. 1982. The Role of Government in Korea's Industrial Development, Paper presented at the *International Forum on Industrial Planning and Trade Policies, KDI*, Seoul, June.

Kang, S., et al. 1993. *A History of Student Movements in the 1980s*. Seoul: Hungsungsa.

Kang, Won-Taek and Hoon Jaung. 1999. The 1997 presidential election in South Korea, *Electoral Studies*, 18(4):599-608.

Karl, L. 1990. Dilemmas of Democratization in Latin America. *Comparative Politics*, 23: 1-21.

Katzenstein, P. ed. 1978. *Between Power and Plenty: Foreign Economic Policies of Advanced Industrial Countries*, Madison, WI: University of Wisconsin Press.

Katzenstein, Peter J. 1976. International Relations and Domestic Structures, *International Organization*, 30, Winter.

Katzenstein, Peter. 1985. *Small States in the World Market*, Ithaca, NY: Cornell University Press.

Kawashima, Y. 1987. The Place and Role of Female Workers in the Japanese Labor Market. *Women's Studies International Forum* 10(6):599-611.

Keightley, David N. 1973. Religion and the Rise of Urbanism (Review article of The Pivot of the Four Quarters by Paul Wheatley. *Journal of the American Oriental Society* 93(4): 527-538.

Ketcham, Ralph. 1987. *Individualism and Public Life*, New York: Basil Blackwell.

Kiely, Ray. 1994. Development Theory and Industrialization: Beyond the Impasse, *Journal of Contemporary Asia*, 24(2).

Kihl, YW. 1994. The legacy of Confucian Culture and South Korean Politics and Economics: An Interpretation, *Korea Journal*, 37, Autumn.

Kim, Bun Woong and Rho, Wha Joon, eds. 1982. *Korean Public Bureaucracy*, Perspectives in Korean Social Science I, Seoul: Kyobo Publishing Inc.

Kim, C. 1978. Images of Man in Postwar Korean Fiction. *Korean Studies*, 2:1-27.

Kim, D. J. 1994. Is Culture Destiny? The Myth of Asia's Anti-Democratic Values. *Foreign Affairs*: 180-194.

Kim, Dae Jung. 1994. Is Culture Destiny?: The Myth of Asia's Anti-Democratic Values (A Response to Lee Kuan Yew), *Foreign Affairs*, Nov./Dec.

Kim, E.M. 1993. Contradictions and Limits of a Developmental State: With Illustrations from the South Korean Case. *Social Problems* 40(2):228-249.

Kim, Eugene, Kihl, Y.W., And Chung, D.K. 1973. Voter Turnout and the Meaning of Elections in South Korea, *Asian Survey*, 13(11): 1062-1074.

Kim, H. 1993. A Theory of Government-Driven Democratization: The Case of Korea. *World Affairs* 156(2):130-140.

Kim, Han-Kyo. 1970. Review: Problems of Political Development in Korea, *Comparative Politics*, 3(1): 127-139.

Kim, J. 1985. *Studies on Gender Roles in Elementary School Texts.* Research report no. 200-4. Seoul: Women's Development Institute.

Kim, Kwan Bong. 1971. *The Korea-Japan Treaty Crisis and the Instability of the Korean Political System*, New York: Praeger.

Kim, Kwang Suk and Roemer, M. 1979. *Growth and Structural Transformation*, Cambridge: Harvard University Press.

Kim, Kyong-Dong. 1988. The Distinctive Features of South Korea's Development. In *In Search of An East Asian Developmental Model*, edited by Berger and Hsiao, New Brunswick and Oxford, UK: Transaction Books.

Kim, Y. 1986. The Position of Women Workers in Manufacturing Industries in South Korea: A Marxist-Feminist Analysis. Working Paper No. 6, sub-series on Women's History and Development. The Hague: Institute of Social Studies.

Kim, Yung-Myung. 1997. Asian-Style Democracy: A Critique from East Asia, *Asian Survey*, 37(12): 1119-1134.

King, Anthony D. 1995. Re-presenting World Cities: Cultural Theory/Social Practice. In *World Cities in a World-System*, edited by P.L. Knox and P.J. Taylor, Cambridge: Cambridge University Press.

King, Roger. 1986. *The State in Modern Society*, NJ: Catcham House.

King, Ross. 1996. Emancipating Space: Geography, Architecture, and Urban Design, New York and London: Guilford Press.

Kirk, D. 1973. The Bold Words of Kim. *New York Times*, January 7.

Knack, S. 2004. Does Foreign Aid Promote Democracy? *International Studies Quarterly*, 48: 251-266.

Koester, D. 1995. Gender Ideology and Nationalism in the Culture and Politics of Iceland. *American Ethnologist* 22(3):572-588.

Kohli, Atul. 1994. Where Do High Growth Political Economies Come From? The Japanese Lineage of Korea's Developmental State, *World Development*, 22(9).

Koo, Bon Ho. 1992. *Sociocultural Factors in the Industrialization of Korea*, San Francisco, CA: ICS Press.

Koo, H. 1987. The Interplay of State, Social Class, and World System in East Asian Development: The Cases of South Korea and Taiwan. In *The Political Economy of the New Asian Industrialism*, edited by F.C. Deyo, 165-181. Ithaca, NY: Cornell University Press.

Koo, H., and E.M. Kim. 1992. The Developmental State and Capital Accumulation in South Korea. In *States and Development in the Asian Pacific Rim*, edited by R.P. Appelbaum and J. Henderson, 121-149. New York: Sage.

Koo, Hagen. 1991. Middle Class, Democratization, and Class Formation: The Case of South Korea. *Theory and Society*, 20:485-509.

Korean Development Institute. 1978. Long-Term Prospect for Economic and Social Development, 1977-91, Seoul, Korea.

Kosaka, M. 1985. The International Economic Policy of Japan. In *The Challenge of China and Japan: Politics and Development in East Asia*, edited by S.L. Shirk, 282-289. New York: Praeger.

Krasner, S. 1978. *Defending the National Interest: Raw Materials Investments and U.S. Foreign Policy*, Princeton, NJ: Princeton University Press.

Krasner, Stephen D. 1984. Approach to the State, *Comparative Politics*, 16(2), 223-246.

Kratochiwil, Friedrich. 1989. *Rules, Norms, and Decisions*, New York: Cambridge University Press.

Krishna, S. 1993. The Importance of Being Ironic: A Postcolonial View on Critical International Relations Theory. *Alternatives* 18(3):385-417.

Krueger, A.O. 1979. *Studies in the Modernization of the Republic of Korea: 1945-1975*, Cambridge, MA: Council on East Asian Studies, Harvard University Press.

Krugman, Paul. 1994. The Myth of Asia's Miracle, *Foreign Affairs*, Nov./Dec.

Kuah, Khun-Eng. 1990. Confucian Ideology and Social Engineering in Singapore, *Journal of Contemporary Asia*, 20(3).

Kugler, Jacek., and Domke, William. 1986. Comparing the Strength of Nations, *Comparative Political Studies*, 19, April.

Kuznets, Paul W. 1977. *Economic Growth and Structure in the Republic of Korea*, New Haven and London: Yale University Press.

Kuznets. 1982. *Brazil and Mexico: Patterns in Late Development*, Philadelphia: Institute for the Study of Human Issue.

Kwon, Jene K. 1990. The Uncommon Characteristics of Korea's Economic Development. In *Korean Economic Development*, New York; Westport, CT: London: Greenwood Press.

Lal, D. 1983. *The Poverty of Developmental Economics*, Hobart Paperback 16, London: Institute of Economic Affairs.

Lal, Deepak. 1984. The Political Economy of the Predatory State, *World Bank Discussion Paper*, Washington DC: The World Bank, June.

Lal, S. 1981. Developing Countries in the International Economy: Selected Papers, London: Macmillan.

Lamming, G. 1995. The Occasion for Speaking. In *The Post-Colonial Studies Reader,* edited by B. Ashcroft, G. Griffiths, and H. Tiffin, 12-17. London: Routledge.

Landes, D.S. 1965. Japan and Europe: Contrasts in Industrialization. In *The State and Economic Enterprise in Japan*, edited by W.W. Lockwood, 93-182. Princeton, NJ: Princeton University Press.

Landes, D.S. 1969. The Unbounded Prometheus, Technological Change and Industrial Development in Western Europe from 1750 to the Present, Cambridge, UK: Cambridge University Press.

Late-Industrializing Model and Greater East Asia, *American Economic Review*, 81(2), May.

Lau, Lawrence. ed. 1990. *Models of Development: A Comparative Study of Economic Growth in South Korea and Taiwan*, San Francisco: An International Center for Economic Growth Publication, ICS Press.

Lee, Ki-baik. 1984. *A New History of Korea*. Seoul: Ilchokak.

Lee, Ki-baik. 1984. Trans. by Wagner, E.W. and Shultz, E.J. *A New History of Korea*, Cambridge, MA and London: Harvard University Press.

Lee, Kuan Yew. 1994. A Conversation with Lee Kuan Yew. Interviewd by Fareed Zakaria in *Foreign Affairs*, 73(2), March/April.

Lee, Man-Ki. 1978. Ideology and Practice in Korea's Economic Development, *Korea Observer*, 9(4), Seoul: The Academy of Korean Studies.

Lee, S. 1982. *Korean Filial Piety.* Seoul: Jimoon.

Lee, Y.H. 1969. *The Political Culture of Modernizing Society Political Attitudes and Democracy in Korea.* Yale University Press.

Lee., Hahn-Been. 1968. *Korea: Time, Change, and Administration*, Honolulu: East-West Center.

Leeson, P.F. and Nixon, F.I. 1988. Development Economics and the State. In *Perspectives on Development,* edited by Leeson and Minogue, Manchester and New York: Manchester University Press.

Leeson, P.F. and Minogue, M.M. eds. 1988. *Perspectives on Development*, Manchester and New York: Manchester University Press.

Lefebvre, Henri. 1976. Reflections on the Politics of Space. Trans, Enders, M. *Antipode*, 8, May.

Levy, Jack S. and Vakili, Lily. 1989. External scapegoating by authoritarian regime. Paper presented at the annual meeting of the APSA, Atlanta, 31 Aug.-3 Sep.

Levy, Jr., Marion J. 1992. Confucianism and modernization. *Society*, May/June.

Lewis, Bernard. 1990. State and civil society under Islam. *New Perspective Quarterly*, 7(2), Spring.

Lewis, John P. 1955. *Reconstruction and Development in South Korea*, Planning Pamphlet No. 94.,Washington, DC: National Planning Association.

Lijphart, A. 1975. *The Politics of Accommodation: Pluralism and Democracy in the Netherlands.* Berkeley: California University Press.

Lim, Hyun-Chin. 1982. *Dependent Development in Korea: 1963-79*, Seoul: Seoul National University Press.

Lim, Youngil. 1981. Government Policy and Free Enterprise. *Korea Research Monograph*, no. 6, Berkeley: Institute of East Asian Studies, University of California, Berkeley.

Ling, L.H.M. 1984. East Asian Migration to the Middle East: Causes, Consequences, and Considerations. *International Migration Review* 18(1):19-36.

Ling, L.H.M. 1988. Asian Corporatism: Post-Mao China's Developmental Model. Paper presented at the Annual Meeting of the International Studies Association, March 30-April 2, St. Louis.

Ling, L.H.M. 1994. Rationalizations for State Violence in Chinese Politics: The Hegemony of Parental Governance. *Journal of Peace Research* 31(4):393-405.

Ling, L.H.M. 1996. Hegemony and the Internationalizing State: A Post-colonial Critique. *Review of International Political Economy* 3(1):1-26.

Ling, Lily. 1994. Hegemony and the Internationalizing State: A Postcolonial Critique. Paper presented at the International Studies Association, 28 March-1 April, Washington, DC.

Ling, Lily. 1994. Rationalizations for State Violence in Chinese Politics: The Hegemony of Parental Governance. Unpublished manuscript, January 13.

Linz, J., and Stepan, A. 1978. *The Breakdown of Democratic Regimes*. Baltimore and London: The Johns Hopkins University Press.

Linz, J., and Stepan, A. 1996. Toward Consolidated Democracies. *Journal of Democracy*, 7(2): 14-33.

Lip, Evelyn. 1995. *Feng Shui: Environments of Power*. London: Academy Editions.

Lipset, S. 1960. *Political Man: The Social Bases of Politics*. New York: Doubleday & Company, Inc.

Lipset, S. 1994. The Social Requisites of Democracy Revisited: 1993 Presidential Address. *American Sociological Review*, 59: 1-22.

List, F. 1966. *The National System of Political Economy*, New York: Augustus Kelley.

Little, I.M.D. 1970. *Industry and Trade in Some Developing Countries,* London: Oxford University Press.

Little, I.M.D. 1982. *Economic Development: Theory, Policy, and International Relations*, New York: Basic Books.

Lodge, George C. 1987. Introduction: Ideology and Country Analysis. In *Ideology and National Competitiveness*, edited by Lodge and Vogel, Cambridge: Harvard Business School Press.

Loubser, J. 1988. The Need for the Indigenisation of the Social Science, *International Sociology*, 3(2): 179-187.

Luedde-Neurath, R. 1986. "Import Controls and Export-oriented Development," Westview Special Studies on East Asia.

Luedde-Neurath, Richard. 1988. State Intervention and Export-oriented Development in South Korea. In *Developmental States in East Asia*, edited by White and Wade, London: Macmillan.

Lyotard, Jean-Francois. 1984. *The Postmodern Condition* (1979), trans., Bennington, G. and Massumi, B. Manchester University Press.

Macdonald, D.S. 1990. *The Koreans: Contemporary Politics and Society*, Boulder: Westview Press.

MacFarquhar, R. 1980. The Post-Confucian Challenge. *The Economist*, 67, February 9.

MacIntyre, A. and Jayasuriya, K. eds. 1992. *The Dynamics of Economic Policy Reform in South-east Asia and the South-west Pacific*, Singapore: Oxford University Press.

MacIntyre, Andrew. 1994. Business, Government and Development: Northeast and Southeast Asian Comparisons. In *Business and Government in Industrialising Asia*, edited by MacIntyre, Ithaca, NY: Cornell University Press.

Madsen, R. 1993. The Public Sphere, Civil Society and Moral Community: A Research Agenda for Contemporary China Studies. *Modern China*, 19(2): 183-198.

Mahon, Jr., James E. 1992. Was Latin America too rich to prosper? Structural and political obstacles to export-led industrial growth. *Journal of Development Studies*, 28(2): 241-263.

Mahon, Rianne. 1991. From bringing to putting: The state in late twentieth-century social theory. *Canadian Journal of Sociology*, 16(2).

Mann, Michael. 1986. The autonomous power of the state: Its origins, mechanisms and results. In *States in History*, edited by J. Hall, Oxford: Basil Blackwell.

Mansbach, R.W. and Vasquez, J.A. 1981. *In Search of Theory*, New York: Columbia University Press.

Mansbridge, Jane. 1992. A deliberative perspective on Neocorporatism. *Politics and Society*, 20(4), December: 493-505.

Manzo, K. 1991. Modernist Discourse and the Crisis of Development Theory. *Studies in Comparative International Development*. 26(2-3):3-36.

Mardon, R. 1990a. The State and Industrial Transformation in the Republic of Korea, *Journal of Social, Political and Economic Studies*, 15: 457-482.

Mardon, R. 1990b. The State and the Effective Control of Foreign Capital: The Case of South Korea, *World Politics*, 43: 111-137.

Markovic, Mihailo. 1988. Strengths and stresses of socialist states, *Society*, May/June.

Mason, E. and Kim, Mahn Je. eds. 1980. *The Economic and Social Modernization of the Republic of Korea*, Cambridge: Harvard University Press.

Mason, ES. et al. 1980. The economic and social modernization of the Republic of Korea, Cambridge, MA: Harvard University Press.

Mastanduno, Michael, Lake, and Ikenberry. 1989. Toward a realist theory of state action, *International Studies Quarterly*, 33: 457-474.

Mbembe, A. 1992. The Banality of Power and the Aesthetics of Vulgarity in the Postcolony. *Public Culture* 4(2):1-30.

Mcclintock, A. 1993. Family Feuds: Gender, Nationalism and the Family. *Feminist Review* 44:61-80.

McLennan, G., Held, D., and Hall, S., eds. *The Idea of the Modern State*, Milton Keynes: Open University Press.

McNamara, Dennis L. 1992. State and Concentration in Korea's First Republic, 1948-60, *Modern Asian Studies*, 26(4).

McVey, R. 1992. The Marginalization of the Southeast Asian Entrepreneur. In *Southeast Asian Capitalists, Southeast Asia Program*, Ithaca: Cornell University Press.

Memmi, A. 1965. *The Colonizer and the Colonized*. New York: Orion.

Mies, M., V. Bennholdt-Thomsen, and C. Von Werlhof. 1988. *Women: The Last Colony*. New Delhi: Kali for Women.

Migdal, Joel S. 1988. *Strong Societies and Weak States: State-Society Relations and State Capabilities in the Third World*, Princeton: Princeton University Press.

Mikanagi, Y. 1995. Understanding Japan's "Undemocracy": A Study on Equal Employment Opportunity Law. Paper presented at the conference on Gender and Global Restructuring: Shifting Sites and Sightings, May 12–13, University of Amsterdam, Netherlands.

Mills, C.W. 1959. *Sociological Imagination*, New York: Oxford University Press.

Ministry of Public Information. 1966. The Road Toward Economic Self-Sufficiency and Property, ROK.

Mitchell, T. 1984. Administrative Tradition and Economic Decision Making in Korea, *IDS Bulletin*, 15(4).

Moon, Chung-In. 1988. The Demise of a Developmentalist State? *Journal of Developing Societies*, 4.

Moon, Chung-In. 1990. Beyond Statism, *International Studies Notes*, 15, Winter.

Moon, Chung-in. 1995. Democratization, Globalization, and Changing State-Business Relations in South Korea, prepared for presentation at a conference on Democratization and Economic Performance in South Korea organized by the Center for Asian Studies, University of Texas, Austin, April 21-23, 1995, pp. 2-3.

Moon, K.H.S. 1997. Prostitute Bodies and Gendered States in U.S.-Korea Relations. In *Dangerous Women: Korean Women and Nationalism,* edited by E. Kim and C. Choi, 141-173. London: Routledge.

Moore, Barrington. 1966. *Social Origins of Dictatorship and Democracy*, Boston: Beacon Press.

Morishima, M. 1982. *Why Has Japan "Succeeded"?* Cambridge, UK: Cambridge University Press.

Muller, Edward N. 1995. Economic Determinants of Democracy, *American Sociological Review*, 60(6): 966-982.

Myrdal, G. 1957. Economic Theory and the Underdeveloped Regions, London: Duckworth.

Nam, C.H. 1995. South Korea's Big Business Clientelism in Democratic Reform. *Asian Survey* 35(4):357-366.

Nam, Chong Hyun. 1981. Trade and Industrial Policies and the Structure of Protection in Korea. In *Trade and Growth of Advanced Developing Countries in the Pacific Rim*, edited by Hong and Krause, Seoul: Korea Development Institute.

Nam, J.L. 1994. Women's Role in Export Dependence and State Control of Labor Unions in South Korea. *Women's Studies International Forum* 17(1):57-67.

Nandy, A. 1988. *The Intimate Enemy.* Delhi: Oxford University Press.

Nelson, J.A., and M.A. Ferber. 1993. *Beyond Economic Man.* Chicago: University of Chicago Press.

Nettl, J.P. 1968. The State as a Conceptual Variable, *World Politics*, 20, July.

New York Times. 1973. Foe of Korean Chief, Abducted in Tokyo, Is Released in Seoul. August 14, pp. A1, 10.

New York Times. 1973. Seoul Sets Limits on Freedom of Press. December 29, p. A2.

Newman, O. 1981. *The Challenge of Corporatism.* London: Macmillan Press.

Nolan, Peter. 1990. Assessing Economic Growth in the Asian NICs, *Journal of Contemporary Asia*, 20(1).

Nordlinger, Eric A. 1981. *On the Autonomy of the Democratic State*, MA: Harvard University Press.

North, Douglass. 1990. *Institutions, Institutional Change and Economic Performance*, Cambridge, MA: Cambridge University Press.

Nurkse, R. 1953. Problems of Capital Formation in Under-developed Countries, Oxford: Oxford Unversity Press.

Nussbaum, Bruce. 1997. Capital, Not Culture, *Foreign Affairs*, 76(2): 165.

O'Donnell, G. 1994. Delegative Democracy, *Journal of Democracy*.

Obbo, C. 1989. Sexuality and Economic Domination in Uganda. In *Woman-Nation-State*, edited by N. Yuval-Davis and F. Anthias, 79-91. New York: St. Martin's Press.

Office of Planning and Cooperation. 1973. Evaluation Report of the First Year Program: The Third Five Year Economic Development Plan, Office of the Prime Minister, ROK.

Ogle, George E. 1990. *South Korea: Dissent within the Economic Miracle*, London and New Jersey: Zed Books Ltd.

Oh, J.K. 1968. *Korea Democracy on Trial*, Cornell University Press.

Oh, Sang-Lak. 1968. The Role of Government in Korean Marketing, *Seoul National University Economic Review*, 11,(1), Seoul.

Ohkawa, K. and Rosovsky, H. 1973. *Japanese Economic Growth*, Stanford, CA: Stanford University Press.

Okin, S.M. 1987. Justice and Gender. *Philosophy and Public Affairs* 16:42-72.

Oliver, R. 1993. *A History of the Korean People in Modern Times: 1800 to the Present*. Newark: University of Delaware Press, and London and Toronto: Associated University Press.

Oliver, R.T. 1993. *A History of the Korean People in Modern Times, 1800 to the Present.* London: Associated University Presses.

Olugbade, Kola. 1992. The Nigerian state and the quest for a stable polity, *Comparative Politics*, 24(3), April.

Onis, Ziya. 1991. The logic of the developmental state, *Comparative Politics*, 24: 109-126, October.

Onuf, Nicholas. 1989. *World of Our Making*, Columbia, SC: University of South Carolina Press.

Onuf, Nicholas. 1996. Hegemony's Hegemony: International Political Economy in Constructivist Terms, Working Draft for presentation to the 37th Annual Convention, International Studies Association, San Diego, California, April 16-20, 1996.

Osawa, M. 1993. Bye-Bye Corporate Warriors: The Formation of a Corporate-Centered Society and Gender-Biased Social Policies in Japan. *Annals of the Institute of Social Science* 35:157-194.

Packenham, Robert A. 1973. *A Liberal America and the Third World*, Princeton: Princeton University Press.

Paik, H.S. 1993. Labor Market Segmentation and Male-Female Wage Differentials in Korea. Master's thesis. Seoul: Sookmyung Women's University.

Pak, C.Y. 1980. Political opposition in Korea, 1945-1960, Seoul: Seoul National University Press.

Pak, Sejin. 1998. Two forces of democratisation in Korea. *Journal of Contemporary Asia*, 28(1): 45-73.

Palais, James B. 1975. *Politics and Policy in Traditional Korea*, Cambridge, MA. and London: Harvard University Press.

Parboni, Riccardo. 1983. Capital and the nation-state: a reply to Frieden, *New Left Review*, 137.

Park, C.H. 1969. *The Collected Works of President Park Chung Hee: My Love, My Homeland.* Vols. 1-6, edited by S.B. Shik. Seoul: Jimoongak.

Park, Chong-Min and D.C. Shin. 2006. Do Asian Values Deter Popular Support for Democracy in South Korea? *Asian Survey*, 46(3): 341-361.

Park, Chung Hee. 1962. *Our Nation's Path: Ideology of Social Reconstruction*, Seoul: Dong-A Publishing Company.

Park, K.A. 1993. Women and Development: The Case of South Korea. *Comparative Politics* 25:127-145.

Park, Sangsop. 1987. The Failure of Liberal Democracy in Korea, 1945-1979. In Kim, K. ed. *Dependency Issues in Korean Development*, Seoul: Seoul National University Press.

Park, Won Kyu. 1986. Government Behavior, Market Structure and Export Performance: The Korean Case, Ph.D. Dissertation, Cornell University.

Parkin, F. 1971. *Class Inequality and Political Order*, New York: Holt, Rinehart & Winston.

Parry, B. 1987. Problems in Current Theories of Colonial Discourse. *Oxford Literary Review* (1-2):27-35.

Pateman, C. 1988. *The Sexual Contract*. Stanford, CA: Stanford University Press.

Pateman, C. 1989. *The Disorder of Women.* Stanford, CA: Stanford University Press.

Paulsson, G. 1959. *The study of cities: Notes about the hermeneutics of urban space.* KØbenhavn: Munksgaard.

Pennick, N. 1979. *The Ancient Science of Geomancy: Man in harmony with the earth*, London: Thames and Hudson Ltd.

Perkins, Dwight H. 1994. There are at Least Three Models of East Asian Development, *World Development*, 22(4), 655-661.

Perotti, Robert. 1996. Growth, income distribution, and democracy: What the data say, *Journal of Economic Growth*, 1(2): 149-187.

Peterson, Merrill D. ed. 1975. *The Portable Thomas Jefferson*, New York: Penguin Books.

Petracca, M.P., And M. Xiong. 1990. The Concept of Chinese Neo-Authoritarianism. *Asian Survey* 30(11):1099-1117.

Phillips, A. 1991. *Engendering Democracy.* University Park: Pennsylvania State University Press.

Phillips, A. 1993. *Democracy and Difference.* University Park: Pennsylvania State University Press.

Pierson, Christopher. 1984. New theories of state and civil society, *Sociology*, 18(4) November.

Pieterse, J.N. 1991. Dilemmas of Development Discourse: The Crisis of Developmentalism and the Comparative Method. *Development and Change*, 22: 5-29.

Poggi, Gianfranco. 1978. *The Development of the Modern State*, Stanford, CA: Stanford University Press.

Polanyi, K. 1957. *The Great Transformation*, Boston: Beacon Press.

Porter, M.E. 1990a. The Competitive Advantage of Nations, *Harvard Business Review*, March/April: 73-93.

Porter, M.E. 1990b. *The Competitive Advantage of Nations*, London: Macmillan.

Potter, David. 1997. Democratization at the same time in South Korea and Taiwan. In David Potter et al., eds. *Democratization*, Cambridge: Polity.

Prebisch, Raul. 1950. The Economic Development of Latin America and Its Principal Problems, New York: United Nations.

Przeworski, A. et al., eds. 1995. *Sustainable Democracy*, New York: Cambridge University Press.

Purcell, Randall P. ed. 1989. *The Newly Industrializing Countries in the World Economy*, Boulder and London: Lynne Rienner.

Pye, L. 1985. *Asian Power and Politics*, Cambridge: Belknap Press of Harvard University Press.

Ranis, Gustav. 1989. The role of institutions in transition growth, *World Development*, 17(9): 1443-1453.

Rankin, Mary Backus. 1993. Some Observations on a Chinese Public Sphere, *Modern China*, 19(2), April:158-182.

Rapkin, David P. 1983. The inadquacy of a single logic: Integrating political and material approaches to the World System. In Thompson, William R. ed. *Contending Approaches to World System Analysis*, Beverly Hills: Sage Publications.

Redding, S.G. 1990. *Capitalism in Contrasting Cultures*, Berlin and New York: W. deGruyter.

Reid, G. 1923. Revolution as Taught by Confucianism, *International Journal of Ethics* 33(2):188-201.

Riggs, F. 1970. The Comparison of Whole Political Systems. In Holt and Turner, eds. *Methodology of Comparative Research*, New York: Free Press.

Robinson et al. 1987. *Southeast Asia in the 1980s*, Sydney: Allen & Unwin.

Rohlen, T.P. 1983. *Japan's High Schools.* Berkeley: University of California Press.

Rooken-Smith, D.R. 1982. Japan Incorporated and Korean Troops, MA Thesis, Department of Asian Studies, University of Hawaii.

Rose, R. 1991. Comparing Forms of Comparative Analysis, *Political Studies*, 39.

Rosenstein-Rodan, P. 1943. Problems of Industrialzation of Eastern and South-Eastern Europe. *Economic Journal*, 53, June/Sept.: 202-211.

Rosenstein-Rodan, P. 1957. Notes on the Theory of the "Big Push." MIT Center for International Studies, Cambridge, MA.

Rostow, W.W. 1960. *The Stages of Economic Growth*, New York: Cambridge University Press.

Rozman, Gilbert, ed. 1991. *The East Asian Region: Confucian Heritage and Its Modern Adaptation*, Princeton, NJ: Princeton University Press.

Ruddick, S. 1995. *Maternal Thinking.* Boston: Beacon Press.

Ruggie, John G., ed. 1983. The Antinomies of Interdependence: National Welfare and the International Division of Labor, New York: Columbia University Press.

Rustow, Dankwart A. 1990. Democracy: A Global Revolution?, *Foreign Affairs*, Fall.

Safdie, Moshe. 1984. Collective Significance, *The Harvard Architecture Review* (Special Issue: Monumentality and the City), 4, Spring.

Said, E. 1979. *Orientalism.* New York: Vintage Books.

Said, E. 1994. *Culture and Imperialism.* New York: Knopf.

SaKong, I. and Y. Koh. 2010. *The Korean Economy: Six Decades of Growth and Development*, Seoul: Korea Development Institute.

Salaff, J.W. 1992. Women, the Family, and the State in Hong Kong, Taiwan, and Singapore. In *States and Development in the Asian Pacific Rim*, edited by R.P. Appelbaum and J. Henderson, 267-288. New York: Sage.

Samuels, Richard J. 1987. The Business of the Japanese State: Energy Markets in Comparative and Historical Perspective, Ithaca, NY: Cornell University Press.

Sanda, M. 1988. In Defense of Indigenisation in Sociological Theories. *International Sociology*, 3(2): 189-199.

Sanger, D.E. 1995. Vietnam's Budding Market: What Role for U.S.?, *New York Times*, August 9, p. A3:1.

Sangmpam, S.N. 1986. The State-Society Relationship in Peripheral Countries. *The Review of Politics*, 48(4).

Santos, T.D. 1970. The Structure of Dependence, *The American Economic Review*, 60(2), May.

Scalapino, R.A. 1962. *Which Route for Korea?*, Asian Survey, 2(7): 1-13.

Scalapino, R.A. 1993. Democratizing Dragons: South Korea and Taiwan, *Journal of Democracy*, 1993.

Schmitter, P.C. 1982. Reflections on Where the Theory of Neo-Corporatism Has Gone and Where the Praxis of Neo-Corporatism May Be Going. In *Patterns of Corporatist Policy-Making*, edited by G. Lehmbruch and P. Schmitter, 259-279. London: Sage.

Schwandt, Thomas A. 1994. Constructivist, Interpretivist Approaches to Human Inquiry. In *Handbook of Qualitative Research*, edited by N. Denzin and Y. Lincoln, Thousand Oaks, London, and New Delhi: Sage Publications.

Schwartz, Herman M. 1994. *States versus Markets*, New York: St. Martin's Press.

Scott, C.V. 1995. *Gender and Development.* Boulder, CO: Lynne Rienner.

Seers, D. 1969. The Meaning of Development, *International Development Review*, 11(4).

Sen, A. 1999. Democracy as a Universal Value, *Journal of Democracy* 10(3): 3-17.

Shapiro, M. 1992. *Reading the Postmodern Polity: Political Theory as Textual Practice*, Minneapolis and Oxford: University of Minnesota Press.

Shils, E. 1975. *Center and Periphery*, Chicago: Chicago University Press.

Shils, Edward. 1991. The virtue of civil society, *Government & Opposition*, 26(1), Winter.

Shim, Jae Hoon. 1985. Growing Rich—at the Cost of Democracy, *Far Eastern Economic Review*, 6 June.

Shin, D.C. and McDonough, Peter. 1999. The Dynamics of Popular Reactions to Democratization in Korea, *Journal of Public Policy*, 19(1): 1-32.

Shin, D.C., Myung Chey, and Kwang Woong Kim. 1989. Cultural Origins of Public Support for Democracy in Korea, *Comparative Political Studies*, 22(2).

Simons, H. and Billig, M. eds. 1994. *After Postmodernism*, London, Thousand Oaks, New Delhi: Sage Publications.

Singer, H. 1950. Distribution of Gains between Investing and Borrowing Countries, *American Economic Review*, Papers and Proceedings, 40, May: 473-485.

Skidmore, D. and Hudson, V. 1993. Establishing the Limits of State Autonomy, in *The Limits of State Autonomy*, edited by Skidmore and Hudson, Boulder: Westview Press.

Skinner, Q. 1985. *The Return of Grand Theory in the Human Sciences*, Cambridge and Melbourne: Cambridge University Press.

Skinner, G.W., ed. 1977. *The City in Late Imperial China*, Stanford, CA: Stanford University Press.

Skocpol, T. 1977. Wallerstein's World Capitalist System: A Theoretical and Historical Critique, *American Journal of Sociology*, 82(5): 1075-1090.

Skocpol, T., Evans, P., and Rueschemayer, eds. 1985. *Bringing State Back In*, Cambridge: Cambridge University Press.

Skocpol, Theda. 1980. Political Response to Capitalist Crisis, *Politics and Society*, 10:155-201.

Soguk, N. 1993. Reflections on the "Orientalized Orientals." *Alternatives* 18(3):361-384.

Solinger, Dorothy J. 1993. China's transients and the state, *Politics and Society*, 21(1), March: 91-122.

Song, Byung-Nak. 1990. *The Rise of the Korean Economy*, Hong Kong and New York: Oxford University Press.

Spengler, J.J. 1980. *Origins of Economic Thoughts and Justice*, Carbondale: Southern Illinois University Press.

Spivak, G.C. 1988. Can the Subaltern Speak? In *Marxism and the Interpretation of Culture*, edited by C. Nelson and L. Grossberg, 271-299. Chicago: University of Illinois Press.

Springborg, Robert. 1991. State-Society Relations in Egypt, *Middle East Journal*, 45(2), Spring.

Srinivasan, T.N. 1985. Neo-classical Political Economy: The State and Economic Development, *Asian Development Review*, 3(2).

Stanis, U.F. et al. 1976. The Role of the State in Socio-Economic Reforms in Developing Countries, Moscow: Progress Publishers.

Steinberg, David I. 1998. Korea: Triumph Amid Turmoil, *Journal of Democracy* 9(2): 76-90.

Stepan, Alfred. 1978. *The State and Society: Peru in Comparative Perspective*, Princeton, NJ: Princeton University Press.

Suleiman, Ezra N. 1987. State Structures and Clientilism, *British Journal of Political Science*, 17:257-279.

Suleri, S. 1992. Woman Skin Deep: Feminism and the Postcolonial Condition. *Critical Inquiry* 18(4):756-769.

Sunkel, O. 1966. The Structural Background of Development Problems in Latin America, *Weltwirtschaftliches Archiv*, 97(1).

Tai, H.C. 1989. *Confucianism and Economic Development*. Washington, DC: Washington Institute Press.

Tai, H.C. 1989. The Oriental Alternative: A Hypothesis on East Asian Culture and Autonomy, *Issues and Studies*, 25: 10-36.

Tan, C.H. 1984. Toward Better Labour-Management Relations. In *Singapore: Twenty-Five Years of Development*, edited by P.S. You and L.C. Lim, 189-205. Singapore: Nan Yang Xing Zhou Lianhe Zaobao.

Taylor, Charles. 1990. Modes of Civil Society, *Public Culture*, 3(1), Fall: 95-118.

Taylor, P.J. 1985. *Political Geography*, London and New York: Longman.

Taylor, P.J. 1995. World Cities and Territorial States: the Rise and Fall of Their Mutuality. In *World Cities in a World-System*, edited by P.L. Knox and P.J. Taylor, Cambridge: Cambridge University Press.

Teng, S., and J.K. Fairbank. 1979. *China's Response to the West: A Documentary Survey, 1839-1923.* Cambridge, MA: Harvard University Press.

The World Bank. 1984. *Korea: Development in a Global Context*, World Bank, Washington, DC.

Thomas, E.D. 1968. *Chinese Political Thought*. New York: Prentice-Hall.

Thomas, G., Meyer, J., Ramirez, F., and Boli, J. 1987. *Institutional Structure: Constituting State, Society, and the Individual*, Beverly Hills: Sage Publications.

Thrupp, Sylvia L. 1963. The City as the Idea of Social Order. In *The Historian and the City*, edited by Hamilton and Burchard, Cambridge: MIT and Harvard University Press.

Tickner, J.A. 1992. *Gender in International Relations: Feminist Perspectives on Achieving Global Security*, New York: Columbia University Press.

Tinbergen, J. 1958. *The Design of Development*, Baltimore: Johns Hopkins University Press.

Tonak, E. Ahmet. 1986. Who needs a strong state? *Monthly Review*, 37, January.

Trewartha, Glenn T. 1952. Chinese Cities: Origins and Functions. *Annals of the Association of American Geographers* 42(1): 69-93.

Tu, W. 1993. Introduction: Cultural Perspectives. *Daedalus*, 122: vii-xxii.

Tuan, Y. 1974. *Topophilia: Study of Environmental Perception, Attitudes and Values*. New York: Columbia University Press.

Tucker, R C., ed. 1972. *The Marx-Engels Reader*. New York: Norton.

Tyrwhitt, Jaqueline. 1968. The City of Ch'ang-an: Capital of the T'ang Dynasty of China. *The Town Planning Review* 39(1): 21-37.

United Nations Korean Reconstruction Agency. 1954. *An Economic Programme for Korean Reconstruction*, March.

van Fraasen, B.C. 1981. *The Scientific Image*, Oxford: Oxford University Press.

Vanhanen, Tatu. 2000. A New Dataset for Measuring Democracy, 1810-1998, *Journal of Peace Research*, 37(2): 251-265.

Viksnins, G. and Skully, M. 1987. Asian Financial Development, *Asian Survey*, 27(5), May.

Vincent, Andrew. 1987. *Theories of the State*, New York: Basil Blackwell.

Viner, J. 1953. *International Trade and Economic Development*, Oxford, UK: Clarendon Press.

Vogel, David A. 1977. Why Businessmen Distrust Their State, *British Journal of Political Science*, 7, October.

Vogel, Ezra F. 1991. *The Four Little Dragons*, Cambridge and London: Harvard University Press.

Wade, R. 1990a. *Governing the Market*. Princeton, NJ: Princeton University Press.

Wade, Robert. 1990b. Industrial Policy in East Asia: Does It Lead or Follow the Market? In *Manufacturing Miracles*, edited by Gereffi and Wyman, Princeton: Princeton University Press.

Wade, Robert. 1982. *Irrigation and Agricultural Politics in South Korea*, Boulder, CO: Westview Press.

Wade, Robert. 1988. State Intervention in "Outward-looking" Development. In *Development States in East Asia*, edited by G. White, London: Macmillan.

Wakeman, Jr., F. 1993. The Civil Society and Public Sphere Debate: Western Reflections on Chinese Political Culture. *Modern China*, 19(2): 108-138.

Walder, A. 1989. The Political Sociology of the Beijing Upheaval of 1989, *Problem of Communism*, September-October.

Wallerstein, I. 1979. *The Capitalist World-Economy*. Cambridge: Cambridge University Press.

Walzer, Michael. 1991. The Idea of Civil Society, *Dissent*, Spring: 293-304.

Watts, M. 1993. Development I: Power, Knowledge, Discursive Practice. *Progress in Human Geography*, 17(2): 257-272.

Waylen, G. 1994. Women and Democratization: Conceptualizing Gender Relations in Transition Politics. *World Politics* 46:327-354.

Weber, M. 1951. *The Religion of China.* New York: Free Press.

Weber, M. 1951. The Religion of China: Confucianism and Taoism, Glencoe, IL: Free Press.

Wendt, Alexander. 1992. Bringing the Theory/Metatheory Gap in International Relations, *Review of International Studies*, 18:181-185.

Westphal, L., Rhee, Y., and Purcell, G. 1979. Foreign Influences on Korean Industrial Development, *Oxford Bulletin of Economics and Statistics*, 41(4), November.

Westphal, L.E. and Kim, Kwang Suk. 1977. Industrial Policy and Development in Korea, *World Bank Staff Working Paper*, no. 263, IBRD, Washington.

Westphal, L.E. 1978. The Republic of Korea's Experience with Export-led Industrial Development, *World Development*, 6(3):347-382.

Whang, In-Joung, 1969. Elite Change and Program Change in the Korean Government, 1955-1967, *Korean Journal of Public Administration*, 7(1), April, Seoul.

Wheatley, Paul. 1970. Archaeology and the Chinese City. *World Archaeology* 2 (2):159-185.

Wheatley, Paul. 1971. *The Pivot of the Four Quarters: A Preliminary Enquiry into the Origins and Character of the Ancient Chinese City*. Chicago: Aldine Publishing Company.

White, G. and Wade, R. 1988. Developmental States and Markets in East Asia. In *Development States in East Asia*, edited by G. White, London: Macmillan.

White, Gordon. 1984. Developmental States and Socialist Industrialization in the Third World, *Journal of Developmental Studies*, 21(1): 97-120.

Wiarda, H., ed. 1991(a). *New Directions in Comparative Politics*, Boulder, San Francisco, Oxford: Westview Press.

Wiarda, H. 1991(b). Toward a nonethnocentric theory of development: Alternative conceptions from the Third World. In Wiarda, ed. *New Directions in Comparative Politics*, Boulder: Westview Press.

Wiarda, H. 1991(c). Toward the future: Old and new directions in comparative politics. in Wiarda, ed. *New Directions in Comparative Politics*, Boulder: Westview Press.

Wilks, Stephen, and Wright, Maurice, eds. 1987. *Comparative Government-Industry Relations*, Oxford: Clarendon Press.

Williams, R. 1958. Culture and Society. In *A Critical and Cultural Theory Reader*, edited by Easthopee and McGowan, 1992, Toronto and Buffalo: University of Toronto Press.

Willis, E. (1992). *No More Nice Girls*. Hanover, CT: Wesleyan University Press.

Wilson, Richard W. 1988. Wellsprings of Discontent, *Asian Survey*, 28(10), October.

Winckler, E.A. 1981. Roles Linking State and Society. In *The Anthropology of Taiwanese Society*, edited by E.M. Ahern and H. Gates, Stanford, CA: Stanford University Press.

Wolin, S. 1980. Paradigms and Political Theories. In *Paradigms and Revolutions*, edited by G. Gutting, Notre Dame: University of Notre Dame Press.

Wong, A. 1981. Planned Development, Social Stratification, and the Sexual Division of Labor in Singapore. *Signs*: 434-452.

Wong, J. 1986. Regional Industrial Co-operation: Experiences and Perspective of Asean and the Andean Pact, Vienna: United Nations Industrial Development Organization.

Woo-Cumings, Jung-en. 1991. *Race to the Swift: State and Finance in Korean Industrialization*, New York: Columbia University Press.

Wood, Denis. 1992. *The Power of Maps*, New York and London: Guilford Press.

Woods, Dwayne. 1992. Civil Society in Europe and Africa: Limiting State Power through a Public Sphere, *African Studies Review*, 35(2), September: 77-100.

World Bank. 1987. *Korea: Managing the Industrial Transition*, 2 vols., Washington, DC.

World Bank. 1993. The East Asian Miracle: Economic Growth and Public Policy, New York: Oxford University Press.

Woronoff, Jon. 1983. *Korea's Economy: Man-Made Miracle*, Seoul, Korea: The Si-sa-yong-o-sa Publishers and Pace International Research, Inc., U.S.A.

Wortzel, L.H. and H.V. 1981. Export Marketing Strategies for NICs and LDC-based Firms, *Columbia Journal of World Business*, Spring.

Wright, Arthur F. 1965. Symbolism and Function: Reflections on Changan and Other Great Cities. *Journal of Asian Studies* 24(4): 667-679.

Wright, Arthur F. 1977. The Cosmology of the Chinese City. In Skinner, G.W., ed. The City in Late Imperial China, Stanford, CA: Stanford University Press.

Yang, Key P., and Gregory Henderson. 1958. An Outline History of Korean Confucianism: Part I: The Early Period and Yi Factionalism. *Journal of Asian Studies* 18(1): 81-101.

Yoffie, D. 1981. The Newly Industrializing Countries and the Political Economy of Protectionism, *International Studies Quarterly*, 25(4): 569-599.

Yoo, Se-Hee. ed. 1983. *Political Leadership and Economic Development: Korea and China*, ISSS Research Series 1, Institute for Sino-Soviet Studies, Seoul: Hanyang University.

Yoshihara, K. 1988. *The Rise of Ersatz Capitalism in South-East Asia*, Singapore: Oxford University Press.

Young, I.M. 1990a. *Justice and the Politics of Difference*. Princeton, NJ: Princeton University Press.

Young, I.M. 1990b. *Throwing Like a Girl and Other Essays.* Bloomington: Indiana University Press.

Yuval-Davis, N., and F. Anthias. 1989. *Woman-Nation-State*. New York: St. Martin's Press.

Zakaria, F. 1994. Culture Is Destiny: A Conversation with Lee Kuan Yew. *Foreign Affairs* 73 (March-April):109-126.

Zakaria, Fareed. 1994. Culture Is Destiny: A Conversation with Lee Kuan Yew. *Foreign Affairs*, 73(2), March/April.

Zeigler, H. 1988. *Pluralism, Corporatism, and Confucianism: Political Association and Conflict Regulation in the United States, Europe, and Taiwan*. Philadelphia: Temple University Press.

Zeigler, H. 1988. *Pluralism, Corporatism, and Confucianism*, Philadelphia: Temple University Press.

Zhao, Ding-Xin and Hall, John A. 1994. State Power and Patterns of Late Development, *Sociology*, 28(1): 211-229.

Zysman, J. 1983. *Governments, Markets, and Growth.* Ithaca, NY: Cornell University Press.

Zysman, John. 1983. *Governments, Markets, and Growth*, Ithaca: Cornell University Press.

REFERENCES (MATERIALS IN KOREAN)

Bae, Hyun-Mi. 1995. "A Study on Rediscovering the Archetype of Seoul City through Making a Restoration Map at the Late Chosun Dynasty," *The Journal of Seoul Studies*, 5.

Cha, Mee-Hee. 1996. "The Life of those who passed the National Civil Service Examination." In *Hankook Yeoksa Yeonkoohoi* (The Institute of Korean History Studies). ed. *How did the People in the Chosun Era Live?* Vol. II, Seoul: *Cheongnyunsa*.

Chang, Myung-Soo. 1994. *Seongkwakbaldalkwa Doshikehoik Yeongoo* (A Study of the development of Castle and City Planning), Seoul: *Hakyeon Moonwhasa*.

Chang, Seong-Hyo. 1992. *Kyohoonnamgin kieobeui jeongchi oido* (The Lessons of Enterprise's Deviation from Business), *Choongang Ilbo* (*Choongang Daily News*), Dec. 28.

Cheong, Woon-Hyun. 1994. Seoulshinae Iljemoonhwayoosan Dapsaki (On-The-Spot Survey of Japanese Legacies in Seoul), Seoul: Hanwool.

Chin, Sang-Chul. 1995. "The Landscape Style of the Chosun Dynasty's palaces through the Systems of Thought," *The Journal of Seoul Studies*, 5.

Cho, Byung-Koo. 1992. "Hankookineui kyungjekwanhaengkwa yoonrimoonje (Economic Behavior of Koreans and the Issue of Ethics)," Seongnam: The Academy Review of Korean Studies, 15(4).

Cho, Dong-Sung. 1990. *Hankook Chaebol Yeongu* (Study of Korean Chaebol), Seoul: *Maeil* Economic Newspapers.

Cho, Myung-Rae. 1993. "Seouleui Jeongchikyungjehak" (The Political Economy of Seoul), Hankook Kongganhwankyung Yunkoohoi (Korea's Space and Environment Association), Seoul Yunkoo (Study of Seoul), Seoul: Hanwool Academy.

Choi, Hochin. 1971. *The Economic History of Korea*, Seoul: *Sekyung* Printing Co., Ltd.

Choson Daily News. 1985. Saryo Haebang Sasipnyun (Historical Materials: Forty Years after the National Liberation), Seoul: Choson Daily News.

Chung-gu Borough Office, 1994. *Chungguji* (1) (2), Seoul.

Chu, Chong-Won. 1983. "Seoul Doshimboo Jaegaebal Kibonkyehoikeul wihan Yunkoo," (A Study on the Master Plan of the Urban Renewal in Seoul City), Keonchook, 27, 111.

Economic Planning Board. 1961. Korea at Work: Forthcoming Five Years of Development, ROK.

EPB. 1962. Summary of the First Five-Year Economic Plan, 1962-1966, ROK.

EPB. 1975. Economic Survey of the 1974 Korean Economy, ROK.

EPB. 1976. The Fourth Five-Year Economic Development Plan, 1977-1981, ROK.

EPB. 1966. The Second Five-Year Economic Development Plan, ROK.

Han, Sang-Bok. 1991. "*Seoul kojidoyunkoo* (A Comparative Study of Old Maps of Seoul)," *Hyangto*, 50.

Han, Sang-Kwon. 1994. "The Civic Life and Social Problems in Seoul," *The Journal of Seoul Studies*, 1.

Hong, Soon-Min. 1994. *Seoul Koongkwol* (*Seoul Palaces*), Seoul: Institute of Seoul Studies.

Hur, Young-Hwan. 1994. *600 Year's Maps of Seoul*, Seoul: Bumwoo Publishing Co.

Jang, Ki-In. 1991. "The Old Governor-General Building in Seoul," *Keonchook*, 159.

Jeong, Il-Kyun. 2007. *Iljeeuimudantongchiwa kyeonghakwon* (Japan's Imperial Control and *Kyeonghakwon*), *Sahoiwa yeoksa* (Society and History), 76.

Jeong, Seung-Mo. 1992. *Sijangeui sahoisa* (The Social History of Market), Seoul: Woongjin.

Joo, Jong-Won. 1991. "Retrospect and Prospects of Seoul," *Keonchook*, 159.

Kang, Young-Hwan. 1992. *Jipeui Sahoisa* (The Social History of Houses), Seoul:Woongjin.

Kim, Bong-Ryol (Kim a). 1991. "Reconstruction of Seoul in the 17th Century," *Keonchook*, 159.

Kim, Do Hyun. 1988. Hyundai Hankookeul duiheundeun yooksipdae Sageon (The Sixty Events that Stirred Modern Korea), Seoul: Donga Daily News.

Kim, Dong-Kyu (Kim b). 1991. "*Seouleui Poongsoojiri*" (The *Poongsoo* Geography of Seoul) (The *Poong* means "Wind" and *Soo* means "Water" in Korean), *Hyangto Seoul*, 50.

Kim, Dong-Uk (Kim c). 1991. "Shrines and Palaces of Seoul in the Choson Dynasty," *Keonchook* (*Architecture*), 159.

Kim, Eui-Whan. 1996. "Salt—From Production to Tax." In *Hankook Yeoksa Yeonkoohoi* (The Institute of Korean History Studies). ed. *How did the People in the Chosun Era Live?* Vol. I, Seoul: *Cheongnyunsa.*

Kim, Hong-Joo. 1986. A Study on the Transition of the Urban District at Old Boundary (Old Inner City) in Seoul, Ph.D. Dissertation, Seoul: Dankook University.

Kim, Hyoun Wuk. 2006. A Study on the Planning and the Management of Han-Yang by Annals of the Joseon Dynasty, a Ph.D. Thesis submitted to the Seongkyunkwan University.

Kim, Kwang-Woong, ed. 1990. Hankook eui Seonkeo Jeongchihak (Politics of Election in Korea), Seoul: Nanam Publishing Ltd.

Kim, Ki-tae. 1981. *Seongkyunkwan jonkyeongkakedaehan yeongu* (Study on *Jonkyeongkakof Seongkyumkwan*) *Kyujankak*, 4:71-91.

Kim, Pil-Dong and Kim, Byung-Jo. 1995. "*Haebanghoo Hankooksahoieui Banjeonkwa Sahoijojikeeui Byunhwa*" (Development of Korean Society after the National Liberation and Changes in Social Organization), *Kwangbok Oshipjoonyun Kinyumnonmoonjip* (A Collection of Learned Papers for The 50th Anniversary of the National Liberation Day), Seoul: Shinheoung Publishing Ltd.

Kim, Young-Don. 1952. *Chejoodo minyoe bichin Seoul* (Seoul Reflected in the Folk-song of *Cheju* Island), *Hyangto*.

Kim, Young-ju. 2008. *Joseon sidae Seongkyunkwan yusaengeui kwondang, kongkwan yeongu* (Study on *Kwondang* and *Kongkwan* of *Seongkyunkwan* in Joseon) *eonronkwahakyeongu* (Media Science Study), 8(4).

Kim, Young-Sang. 1994. *Seoul Yukbaeknyun* (1), Seoul: *Daehakdang*.

Kim, Young-Heum. 1990. A Study on the Relations between Seoul Licensed-Merchants and City-Handcraftsmen in Late Choson Dynasty: Focused on the Shinhae Tongkong Policy, Master Thesis, Seoul: Inha University.

Korean Institute of Architects. *Architectural Guide to Seoul*, Seoul: *Baleon*, 1995.

Korean Astrology Association. 1995. Korea's Astrology Map. Seoul: *Cheonmunwujukihoik*.

Kurasawa, Susumu. 1995. A Comparative Study on the Urban History of Three Historical Asian Cities (Seoul, Tokyo, Peking) Before Modernization, *The Journal of Seoul Studies*, 4.

Kyunggookdaijeon. 1986. Edited by Yoon, Kookil, Seoul: Doseochoolpan Sinseowon.

Lee, Hahn-Been. 1968. *Korea: Time, Change, and Administration*, East-West Center Press, University of Hawaii.

Lee, Jin-Ho. 1991. "*Hanseong-bu jidowa yukjoeui Yeoksajiriyeongu*" (The Map of *Hanseong-bu* and the Historical Geographies of the Six Ministries), *Hyangto Seoul*, 50.

Lee, Jong-Ko. 1993. *Chosunsidaeeui kyungjesasang* (The Economic Thought of Chosun), Seoul: Minsokwon.

Lee, Jung-Duk. 1984. A Study on Architectural and Spatial Planning for an Optimum Development of the Capital City, *Keonchook*, 28, 119.

Lee, Kang-Geun. 1991a. The Reconstruction of *Kyungbok* Palace in 1865-1867. *Keonchook*, 159.

Lee, Kang-Geun. 1991b. *Hankookeui Koonggwol* (Palaces of Korea), Seoul: Daewonsa.

Lee, Ki-Suk and Noh, Hee-Bang. 1994. *Thematic Maps of Seoul*, Seoul: Seoul Development Institute and *Sung Ji Mun Hwa Sa*.

Lee, Kyu-Mok. 1988. *Dosiwa sangjing* (City and Symbol), Seoul: Iljisa.

Lee, Kyu-Mok and Kim, Han-Bae. 1994. "Seoul Doshi Kyungkwaneui Byungcheonkwajeong Yungoo" (An Analysis of the Changing Processes of Seoul City Layout), *Journal of Seoul Studies*, 1, March 1994.

Lee, Kyu Tae. 1996. "On the Names of the Four Gates," *Chosun Daily News*, 12/3/1996.

Lee, Man-Hee. 1993. Did EPB Make Miracle Possible?, Seoul: Haedoti.

Lee, Sang-Hae. 1991. "The Issues of Restoring the *Kyungbok* Palace and *Kyunghee* Palace, and Removing the Old Governor-General Building," *Keonchook*, 159.

Lee, Seong-mu. 1967. *Seonchoeui Seongkyunkwan yeongu* (Study on *Seongkyunkwan* in early Joseon) *Yeoksahalbo* (Studies of History), 35-36: 219-268.

Lee, Seong-Tai. 1990. *Dokjeomjaebeoleui yoksa* (The History of Monopolistic Chaebol).

Lee, Soo-Keun. 1992. "*Chooijae ilgi*" (News Coverage Diary), *Choongang Ilbo* (*Choongang Daily News*), Dec. 28.

Lee, Tae-Jin. 1995. *"18-19c Seouleui Keundaijeok dosibaldal yangsang*" (The Aspects of Modern Development of Seoul during 18th-19th Centuries), *The Journal of Seoul Studies*, 4.

Lee, U-Jong. "Junggukkwa urinara doseongeui Kyehoik.

Lee, Wha-Seon. 1993. *Choson Keonchooksa* (The History of Architecture in the *Yi* Dynasty), Seoul: *Baleon*.

Lee, Yae-Won. 1996. "Why did we aim at the Commander, *Jang Tae-Wan*?" *Wolganchosun (Monthly Choson),* 2, 468.

Lee, Young-Han. 1992. "*Kodeungkyoyookkikwan Ipjiyoohungeui Byuncheonkwajeong Yunkoo*" (A Study on the Changes in the Category of Location of Higher Educational Institutions in Seoul: 1876-1975), *Hyangto Seoul*, 51.

Lee, Young-Min. 1978. "Soodoipjiseonjeongkwa cheondo joongyoseong (The Choice of Capital City and the Importance of Its Transfer)," *Jijeok*, 41.

Lee, Hwa-Seon. 1993. Choson Keonchooksa II (The Architectural History of Choson Dynasty II), Seoul: Baleon.

Lim, Duk-Soon. 1994(a). 600-Year-Old Capital City of Seoul, Seoul: Jishiksaneopsa.

Lim, Duk-Soon. 1994(b). "Changes in the City Layout of Seoul," *The Journal of Seoul Studies*, 2.

Mill, C.W. 1959. *The Sociological Imagination*, Oxford and New York: Oxford University Press.

MOGA (Ministry of Government Administration). 1990. "The Law for Recruitment of Cadet-Bureaucrats."

Moon, Jeong-Chang. 1967. "*Iljeshidaeeui Dishihyungseongkwa kui Teukjing*" (The City Evolution and Characteristics during the Japanese Colonial Rule), *Doshimoonje* (*City Problems*), 2-8, August.

Noh, Bong-Ock. 1986. "A Study on the Commercial Centers of Han Sung in the Yi Dynasty (Centered on Shichun)," *Inha Daehak Nonmoonjip* (*Inha University* Collection of Learned Papers), 11.

Noh, Dae-Whan. 1996. "How did the people in the *Chosun* era perceive the Cosmos and the World?" In *Hankook Yeoksa Yeonkoohoi* (The Institute of Korean History Studies). ed. *How did the People in the Chosun Era Live?* Vol. II, Seoul: *Cheongnyunsa*.

Oh, Byung-Sang. 1992. "*Chunghoobo paebaeeui kyohoon*" (The Lesson of the Presidential Candidate Chung Joo-Young) (President of *Hyundai chaebols*), *Choongang Ilbo* (*Choongang Daily News*), Dec. 21.

Park, Chung Hee. 1969. *The Collected Works of President Park Chung Hee* (1)*: My Love, My Homeland*, edited by Shin, Bum Shik, Seoul: Jimoonkak.

Park, Chung Hee. 1969. *The Collected Works of President Park Chung Hee* (2): *My Love, My Homeland*, edited by Shin, Bum Shik, Seoul: Jimoonkak.

Park, Chung Hee. 1962. *Our Nation's Path: Ideology of Social Reconstruction*, Seoul: Dong-A Publishing Company, Ltd.

Park, In-Seok and Ham, In-Seon. 1991. "Yongsan: Military Camp and Redevelopment," *Keonchook*, 159.

Park, Kyun-seop. 2009. *Hakmunwui jayuwa tongje: Leeokeui munjewa Jeongjoeui munchebanjeong* (Freedom or Regulation of Academics), *Korean Studies*, 30: 161-188.

Park, Younh-Ho. 1977. "The Interior Space of the Royal Audience Hall on the Choson Dynasty Period," *Keonchook*, 21, 74.

Seoul City Hall. 1994. *Choong-gu Ji* (The History of Central District), Seoul: Seoul City Hall.

Seoul Yukbaeknyunsa. 1978. Nine volumes have been published so far by Seoul City Hall.

Shin, Hang-su. 2005. *Seongkyunkwan yusaengdeuleui seongrihakjeokisangkwa hyeonsilchamyeo* (Neo-Confucian Ideals and Participation of *Seongkyunkwan* Students), *Naeileul yeoneun yeoksa* (History Opening Tomorrow), 21: 200-211.

Sohn, Jung-Mok. 1991. "The City Planning and Location of Main Architecture Under the Japanese Rule in Seoul," *Keonchook*, 159.

Sohn, Jung-Mok. 1974. "*Yichoeui dosigooseong* (The City Layout of the *Yi* Dynasty)," *Dosimoonje*, 9(3).

Won, Hak-Hee. 1988. "The City Structure of Kyungseong," *Jirihakchong*, 12(16).

Won, Young-Whan. 1990. Chosunsidae Hanseongboo Yonkoo (Studies on Hanseongboo of Chosun), Kangwon-do: Kangwon University Press.

Won, Young-Whan. 1993. "*Hanseong-boo eui jikjewa kuikineung* (The Organization of Office and Function of the City Hall in *Yi* Dynasty)," The 5th Seoul City History Conference, Seoul: Seoul City College.

Yang, Keun-Man. 1996. "The Analysis of the Merits/Demerits of Former Professors Serving as Ministers and Blue House Staffs," *Wolgan Choson*, February.

Yim, Chang-Bok. 1991. "Traditional Urban Housing and Urban Housing Culture," *Keonchook*, 159.

Yoo, Kyo-Seong. 1955. "*Seoul Yukeuijeon Yonkoo* (The Study of the Seoul Licensed-Store)," *Yeoksahakbo*, 8.

Yoon, Jeong-Seop. 1976. *Seoul dosikyehoikbyunc§heonsa* (The History of Changes in Seoul City Planning).

Yuk, W. 1984 [translated]. *Naehun* [Excerpts from *Naehun*] (written by *Sohyunwanghu Han* [Queen Han] in 1475) published in 1522.

Yun, Kook-il. 1986. *Kyungkookdaejeon Yeonkoo* (Studies on National Cannon), Pyungyang: Science Encyclopeida Press.

Index

About the Author

Jongwoo Han is visiting professor at the Graduate Institute of Peace Studies of the Kyung Hee University in Seoul, Korea. His major teaching and research areas include political economy and state-society relations of Korea; North Korea and the United States relations; networked information technologies such as online social media and its impacts upon society, election, politics and democracy; and the Korean War and Korean Unification. He has published articles in *International Studies Quarterly*, *Journal of Information Technology and Politics*, and the *Australian Journal of International Affairs* and books with Lexington Books including *Networked Information Technologies, Elections, and Politics: Korea and the United States* (2012) and *Understanding North Korea* (2013).